RACE
AND
PERFORMANCE
AFTER
REPETITION

SOYICA DIGGS COLBERT,
DOUGLAS A. JONES JR.,
AND SHANE VOGEL,
EDITORS

RACE AND PERFORMANCE AFTER REPETITION

DUKE UNIVERSITY PRESS

DURHAM AND LONDON

2020

Designed by Matthew Tauch
Typeset in Minion Pro and Bell Gothic Std
by Westchester Publishing Services Pvt. Ltd.

Library of Congress Cataloging-in-Publication Data
Names: Colbert, Soyica Diggs, [date] editor. | Jones, Douglas A.,
editor. | Vogel, Shane, editor.
Title: Race and performance after repetition / edited by Soyica
Diggs Colbert, Douglas A. Jones Jr., and Shane Vogel.
Description: Durham : Duke University Press, 2020. | Includes
bibliographical references and index.
Identifiers: LCCN 2019055647 (print) | LCCN 2019055648 (ebook)
ISBN 9781478007807 (hardcover)
ISBN 9781478008293 (paperback)
ISBN 9781478009313 (ebook)
Subjects: LCSH: Performing arts—Social aspects—United States. |
Time—Social aspects—United States. | Performing arts—Political
aspects—United States. | Racism and the arts—United States. |
Racism in popular culture—United States. | Arts and society—
United States. | Theater and society—United States. | Politics
and culture—United States.
Classification: LCC PN1590.S6 R34 2020 (print) |
LCC PN1590.S6 (ebook) | DDC 791—dc23
LC record available at https://lccn.loc.gov/2019055647
LC ebook record available at https://lccn.loc.gov/2019055648

Cover art: Theaster Gates, *Ground Rules (Free throw
possibility)*, 2014. Wood flooring. 254.3 × 374.1 × 6.5 cm. ©
Theaster Gates. Photo © White Cube (Ben Westoby).

CONTENTS

ACKNOWLEDGMENTS

Race and Performance after Repetition results in part from an initiative undertaken by the American Society for Theater Research (ASTR) to support, promote, and feature the production of research by and about people of color at ASTR. The initiative, named for the late performance theorist José Esteban Muñoz, offered a three-year funding structure and infrastructural sponsorship at ASTR's annual conference for Working Groups dedicated to the project of minoritarian knowledge production. These Working Groups were an endeavor to provide space for such research within the association and redress the organization's structured deficiencies of such knowledge production in the past. This institutional failure to nurture minoritarian knowledge production is not a surprise, nor is it unique to ASTR. As Muñoz explained, "The production of minoritarian knowledge is a project set up to fail" within majoritarian institutions.[1] He continued, "Mechanisms ensure that the production of [minoritarian] knowledge 'misfires' insofar as it is misheard, misunderstood, and devalued. Politics are only possible when we acknowledge that dynamic. This particular understanding of minoritarian knowledge should enable us to perform despite and perhaps beyond these epistemological limits. The need to produce minoritarian knowledge is a mode of utopian performativity, a certain striving that is both ideality and a necessity."[2] Muñoz's work contested and continues to contest this presumptive failure—to insist, as he put it elsewhere, on "hope in the face of heartbreak."[3]

This volume, too, risks performative misfire when it proposes that we think of race and time after repetition, even as it seeks to interrupt the repetitions that would devalue minoritarian knowledge production or consign it to the margins. Given the various temporal experiences that inform the thought and lived experience of both *performance* and *race*—repetitions, doublings, durations, intervals, afterlives, rehearsals, revivals, the ephemeral, the residual, and the emergent—this collection explores how theater/performance studies accounts or fails to account for the complex relationship between race and time. Among the questions we ask are: How might specific instances of theater/

performance open up new temporal dimensions in the study of minoritarian history and experience? What are the temporal logics of identity-based fields of knowledge? How does accounting for all performance as racialized reconfigure the positions of performer and audience? What are the politics of temporality that shape race, ethnicity, sexuality, and gender, especially as they are performed at their intersection? *Race and Performance after Repetition*'s focus on temporality offers a return to central ideas and theorists in performance studies with the possibility of new ways of knowing, being, and participating in (and beyond) US culture, including colleges, universities, professional organizations, and other institutions of research and knowledge production. Muñoz's work provides a necessary point of departure to examine how race and performance allow the emergence of performance theory anew.

When we convened the inaugural José Esteban Muñoz Targeted Research Working Session at ASTR in 2016, we did not imagine that the work would result in an edited collection. After receiving several compelling applications to participate in our session, however, we quickly realized how the collective work spoke to the field of performance studies. Although all of the participants in the Working Group did not contribute to the volume, we are grateful to have had the experience to engage with original scholarship during ASTR meetings for the three years between 2016 and 2018, as well as at an interim symposium at Indiana University. We are indebted to the workshop and conference participants for their thoughtful questions, suggestions, and rich and inspiring work, including the important voices of Christine Mok, Rosa Schneider, C. Riley Snorton, and Alexandra Vazquez. Special acknowledgment goes to Daphne Lei, president of ASTR during this time and a vital member of our Working Group, for her institutional support and intellectual contributions to this project.

We have benefited from the support and assistance of many people and institutions. The Institute for Advanced Study and the College of Arts and Humanities Institute at Indiana University provided generous grants that allowed our Working Group to meet in Bloomington in the summer of 2017, where the contributors to the volume were able to share and deepen their work with each other. Many thanks to Department of English administrators Kate Elliott and Lisa LaPlante for their support in facilitating that symposium. Thank you also to Christopher Celenza, Dean of the College of Arts and Sciences at Georgetown University, and to the Georgetown University Idol Family Professorship endowment fund and the Georgetown University Healey Family Endowed Fund for Academic Excellence for their financial support, which enabled research assistance and obtaining image permissions. Courtney Berger at Duke University Press supported this project from its inception and provided exacting feedback, as did two anonymous readers for the press. We are grateful for her careful stewardship of the volume through each stage of its development. The generosity of colleagues extends well beyond institutional affiliations, and we are grateful to many friends who have read, discussed, and offered feedback on this project. We also want to thank Amadi Ozier, Taurjahi Purdie, and Skylar Luke for preparing the volume for each round of review and for publication.

This book joins a growing set of texts that honor José Esteban Muñoz's legacy. This work could not emerge at a more pressing time, but, as Muñoz's work teaches us, these times of political and institutional turmoil are repeating, recurring, and regular. So too must be our ongoing work.

NOTES

1 Muñoz, "Teaching, Minoritarian Knowledge, and Love," 120.
2 Muñoz, "Teaching, Minoritarian Knowledge, and Love," 120.
3 Muñoz, *Cruising Utopia*, 207–13.

INTRODUCTION · SOYICA DIGGS
COLBERT, DOUGLAS A. JONES JR.,
AND SHANE VOGEL

Tidying Up after Repetition

In 1838 a black stevedore named James Weeks purchased a plot of land in what is now the Bedford-Stuyvesant neighborhood of Brooklyn. From his acquisition of property, a thriving village known as Weeksville rapidly developed. Less than two decades later, Weeksville was one of the most prosperous free black communities in the United States. It boasted its own churches, schools, stores, baseball team (the Weeksville Unknowns), medical center, social clubs, and newspaper (the *Freedman's Torchlight*).[1] It quickly became a destination for African Americans from all over the eastern states and the south and offered refuge for those seeking shelter and safety in the antebellum era. As New York City grew and expanded over the last several decades of the nineteenth century, Weeksville was gradually absorbed by the churning advance of city planning. Four clapboard cottages from the community remained standing into the twentieth century, dilapidated and disrepaired remnants of Weeksville that were all but forgotten until they were "rediscovered" in 1968 by a subway engineer who identified them as crucial landmarks of the city's history.[2]

In 2014 the Weeksville Heritage Center collaborated with the arts organization Creative Time to present *Funk, God, Jazz, and Medicine: Black Radical Brooklyn*, a month-long series of events and performances that celebrated Weeksville and its legacy. The project consisted of four community-based art pieces by different artists who drew on the sociocultural history of Weeksville. As part of this event, multimedia conceptual artist Simone Leigh curated *Free People's Medical Clinic* (FPMC), a community-based wellness center that indexed the history of black health, care, and healing from the nineteenth century to the present (figure 1.1). Specifically, FPMC wove together the past and the present as it recovered the practices of "Dr. Susan Smith McKinney Steward, the first Black woman doctor in N.Y. State and a Weeksville resident; The United Order of Tents, a secret fraternal order of Black Women nurses founded during the Civil War; and Dr. Josephine English, the first African-American woman to have an OB/GYN practice in the state of New York" and founder of the former Paul Robeson Theatre in Brooklyn.[3] Leigh memorialized the labor of these black women visionaries in a community-based project that derived its name from the health clinics and campaigns the Black Panther Party launched in the 1970s, drawing a zigzagged line of black care and self-determination from the early 1800s to the present day.[4] In doing so, FPMC continued third-wave women of color feminist-scholars' and artists' signature practice of recuperation and restoration. Perhaps most widely recognizable in Alice Walker's "recovery" of Zora Neale Hurston, this practice involves excavating works then establishing them as material foundations for subsequent work. Leigh's FPMC recuperated an assemblage of past healing practices and, through the rooms and grounds of Dr. English's house at 375 Stuyvesant Avenue, spatialities of care; they materialized not only in aspects of performance (costume, dance, gesture, *gestus*, music) but also in the bodies of its participants (figure 1.2).[5]

Leigh extended her FPMC performance through an exhibition at the New Museum called *The Waiting Room* that was partially inspired by the 2008 death of Esmin Elizabeth Green. Green, a forty-nine-year-old Jamaican immigrant, died in the waiting room of Kings County hospital in Brooklyn when blood clots moved from her legs to her lungs while waiting for twenty-four hours to see a doctor.[6] Leigh categorizes Green's quiet endurance as a "survival mechanism" and strategy that black women develop to negotiate the health-care system. Similar to FPMC, *The Waiting Room* drew from reservoirs of black women's health knowledge as a grassroots source for workshops, lectures, and classes focused on holistic care. While participants paid an entrance fee to

FIGURE I.1 Simone Leigh, *Free People's Medical Clinic; Funk, God, Jazz, and Medicine: Black Radical Brooklyn*, 2014. COURTESY OF CREATIVE TIME.

FIGURE I.2 Simone Leigh, *Free People's Medical Clinic; Funk, God, Jazz, and Medicine: Black Radical Brooklyn*, 2014. COURTESY OF CREATIVE TIME.

access *The Waiting Room*, Leigh also created *Waiting Room Underground*, a private part of the installation open during the museum's off hours and barred from spectatorship. Through solely participatory engagement, *Waiting Room Underground* took Leigh's recovered healing practices outside of the economic logics that structure the art world and the workday. The project sought to remind women of the life-sustaining qualities of disobedience in times when death is black women's reward for dutifulness.

The FPMC and *The Waiting Room* contrast usefully with another historically informed, participatory performance that pulls nineteenth-century events into the twenty-first century: Civil War battle reenactments in which thousands of men gather to painstakingly re-create historic battles as a form of living history. According to performance theorist Rebecca Schneider, such reenactments are an "intense, embodied inquiry into temporal repetition" and, like all practices of representation, are "composed in reiteration, [are] engaged in citation, [are] *already* a practice of reenactment, or what Richard Schechner has termed 'restored' or 'twice-behaved' behavior."[7] Given their status as a repetition of a repetition (their "explicit twiceness" as Schneider puts it), such reenactments become a hypercharged repetition that "trips the otherwise daily condition of repetition into reflexive hyperdrive, expanding the experience into the uncanny."[8] For Schneider the Civil War reenactor aims to get everything *exactly right*, to create again rather than merely interpret what occurred, and in doing so knowingly marks the failures and errors of traditional historiography. In this argument Schneider seeks to disrupt the common sense of repetition, seeing the repetitions of Civil War reenactors push repetition "into something entirely outside of linear, narrative time."[9] Schneider propels the possibilities of repetition well beyond its rote recitation in performance studies scholarship. Nonetheless, repetition remains the primary point of reference and basic grammar for making sense of the temporality of such confounding performances as these Civil War reenactments.

We begin this introduction with Leigh's *Free People's Medical Clinic* because this project points toward our primary concern: the limits of repetition for explaining what makes (some) performance meaningful in and as time. The FPMC was not a reenactment like those of the Civil War aficionados that Schneider describes, and the grammar of repetition mistranslates its relationship to what-comes-before. Here, FPMC's toggle between past and present is governed less by repetition than it is organized by attention and care. We take this phrasing from theater phenomenologist Alice Rayner, who invites us to think of time (in relation to performance) not as "a series of points or a line or even a circle" that may repeat or recur, but as "a modality that dismantles fixed subjects and objects and turns past, present and future into ways of manners of attention."[10] In thinking of time as a manner of attention, time appears less as a shape or direction or a reference point—something to be repeated—and more as a mood and an existential-phenomenological structure. Time, she writes, "puts attention on those things that matter most to care or concern."[11] Framing Leigh's FPMC as a *modality of time* that directs our attention to those things that matter most to care suggests an approach to performance that is to the side of repetition. We, too, see a practice of "restored behavior" in her project, but it is not the restoration or transmission of behavior repeated across time and bodies to which Schechner and Schneider refer. With Leigh's work in mind—her restoration of Weeksville's community of care and elsewhere in her oeuvre—we suggest a different understanding of performance, informed by another meaning of restore: "to give back or recompense"; "to make amends for; to compensate or make good (loss or damage) now only with *loss* as object"; to repair "a damaged, worn, or faulty object or structure to good or proper condition by replacing or fixing parts; to mend."[12] That is, performance not only as restored behavior but also as behaved restoration.

This understanding of behaved restoration decenters the emphasis on repetition in a way that is particularly (but not exclusively) attuned to race and/ as performance. Leigh's performative and interactive installation, for example, restored and repaired the practices of Weeksville's Dr. Susan Smith McKinney Steward. Her work included establishing medical care specific to the needs of women and girls. In 1881 she helped to found the Brooklyn Woman's Homeopathic Hospital and Dispensary.[13] Embodying the sort of self-determination that galvanized free African Americans to establish the village of Weeksville itself, Dr. Steward's hospital served black persons, many of whom were southerners who migrated north in search of greater access to employment and the rights of their citizenship such as land ownership. For these patients, Dr. Steward's homeopathy and medicine produced mechanisms of survival, if not resistance, to nineteenth-century institutionalized racisms. For us, they installed material remains ripe for recuperation, as FPMC proved: its restorations of past caretaking practices sustained and enriched (black) life and living in the present.

The participation of community members, medical professionals, and lay people was essential to FPMC and its healing power, which emerged as a result of community engagement and not professional intervention only. In addition to homeopathic and allopathic services, FPMC included a historical overview of pioneering black women doctors and nurses; dance; yoga and

FIGURE I.3 Simone Leigh, *Free People's Medical Clinic; Funk, God, Jazz, and Medicine: Black Radical Brooklyn*, 2014. PHOTO BY SHULAMIT SEIDLER-FELLER. COURTESY OF CREATIVE TIME.

Pilates classes; acupuncture; general health screenings including blood pressure checks and HIV tests; and health-care information sessions (figure I.3).[14] Leigh explained, "I typically work in an auto-ethnographic mode. My practice has been object-based for the most part. . . . My artwork is in large part an exploration of black female subjectivity, and I also am interested primarily in a black woman audience. Issues that often come up are labor, authorship and women as the containers of community knowledge and as a source for material culture. So when I was asked to make my work live, I thought a focus on black nurses would address many of my interests and concerns."[15] With FPMC Leigh sought to animate, to make live, familiar forms (black women as the containers of community) and underappreciated content (their knowledge), not in an effort to capitalize (again) on extractions of black women's labor but, rather, to render that labor visible and valuable as a generative communal resource in an economy of sharing.

The essays collected in this volume consider how both "performance" and "race" exist in such complex temporalities that are often quickly glossed as repetition at the expense of a more nuanced temporal vocabulary. That repetition is axiomatic in performance studies has much to do with the term's centrality in the field's founding theories and documents. Among the most influential is Richard Schechner's definition of performance itself: performance is "never for the first time. It means: for the second to the nth time. Performance is 'twice-behaved behavior.'"[16] Schechner names this process the "restoration of behavior," a kind of repetition of that "shows actual behavior as it is being behaved" but is "always subject to revision."[17] The simultaneity of sameness and difference that marks repetition, that is repetition's mark, is thus constitutive of performance, making performance an esteemed domain for the entrenchment of sociocultural norms as well as the production and articulation of critique. (It is no surprise that ritual and drag, for example, have served as the objects of analysis for several of the most important theories in performance studies.) Because scholarly consensus regards it as the action that makes the conditions of performance's aesthetics and meanings possible, repetition is a God term in performance theory.

Another notable way in which performance theorists have lodged repetition at the center of the field has been through their peculiar absorption of speech act theory from ordinary language philosophy, specifically J. L. Austin's work on the performative utterance. We say *peculiar* not simply on account of the fact that performance theory's engagement with ordinary language philosophy is limited almost exclusively to readings of only a few of Austin's lectures, but also because those readings are very often shaped by Jacques Derrida's own peculiar readings of Austin in "Signature Event Context" (1972). In that essay, Derrida attempts to understand the structure of the performative utterance, that is, what the speech act as/in an event must entail if it is to act how the speaker intends it to. To function, he concludes, the performative relies on a "general iterability," which "does not simply signify . . . repeatability of the same, but rather alterability of this same idealized in the singularity of the event, for instance, in this or that speech act."[18] Derrida's notion of iterability anticipates Schechner's definition of performance in that each requires the repetition and possible transformation of recognizable behaviors, conventions, or standards in order to transmit. Thus, performance studies' incorporation of theories of performativity, especially Derridean iterability (and later gender performativity theorized by Judith Butler), has redoubled the field's axiomatic notion that repetition is constitutive of the ontology of performance. In this volume we think in terms of corollaries rather than axioms, which all too often reify "common sense" and often cannot respond to what happens when performances outstrip our repetition-based performance theories. Performative theories of identity, all of which in one way or another assume that behavior accrues meaning over time, account for the temporal drag of so-called twice-behaved behavior and its dissident, even liberatory, possibilities for the future.

Often operating under different notions of temporality, black studies and ethnic studies have shown how Western conceptions of history and time have rendered minoritarian subjects frozen in the past, lagging behind, or perpetually on the threshold, even as historical traumas erupt in the present. One effect of this work is that minoritarian categories develop substance and significance through a dizzying back-and-forth toggle in time, in which subjects experience multiple temporalities simultaneously or out of joint. Performance, everyday or otherwise, is a crucial site of analysis here because, on the one hand, it has the capacity to perpetuate the familiar and dominant through repetitions that have consolidated into a seemingly consistent state of being or state of nature; on the other hand, it also has the capacity to warp or subvert the familiar and dominant through restorations—as repair or mending—of what has been forgotten, overlooked, misremembered, suppressed, dormant, or denied. Restorative performances might disrupt exploitative systems by making material repair or amends, however fleeting, to the exploited; that is, they can challenge the historical negation of populations and offer cultural workers in the present a useful past. Framing performances such as FPMC as acts of restoration not only focalizes practices that have gone unnoticed but also prompts one to rethink truisms and conceptual priorities in performance studies. Of all the ideas that organize the field's critical protocols, repetition is almost certainly the most ubiquitous. Yet the limitations of repetition as an analytical category obscure the aesthetic entailments and social dynamism of performances like FPMC. This volume emerges from a recognition of such blind spots vis-à-vis racialized enactments and asks how we might, if at all, understand race and/in performance in ways beyond or, at least, beside repetition. The central irony of pursuing this inquiry, of course, is that it is necessary to work through notions of repetition first.

As noted, poststructuralist theories of repetition, its ontology, and its configurations have informed some of the most authoritative scholarship in race and performance over the past half century. This volume is a provisional call to sidestep some of that legacy, in part out of a sense that repetition itself (perhaps inevitably) has become repetitive in its varied deployments across performance studies and race/ethnic studies. Of course, we are not the first to put pressure on the ingrained status of repetition in critical thought. Though the essays in this volume do not draw directly on the theories of Gilles Deleuze, they share an affinity with his philosophical project to liberate repetition from Enlightenment economies of representation. In his disquisition on metaphysics, *Difference and Repetition* (1968), Deleuze writes, "To repeat is to behave in a certain manner, but in relation to something unique or singular which has no equal or equivalent."[19] Among the concepts that anchor this definition, two have been especially significant to the intellectual and ethical projects of performance studies and critical race studies: behavior and identity. Repetition names behavior that shares an isomorphic relation with an original (i.e., an affective, corporeal, conceptual, notional, or material object) that has disappeared or otherwise eludes detection or experience. Such behavior must register as such; hence repetition can only function by way of the symbolic. Deleuze understands the symbolic as repetition's "disguise" or "mask," that which conceals repetition's utter difference from the original that cannot be repeated.[20] The symbolic, then, is repetition's vehicle and its offering, the very figure(s) of behavior through which one not only confronts the reality of unrepeatable singularities (for Deleuze, these were chiefly transcendental concepts or Ideas) but also reads the aims and impulses of the repeater. In fine, the elements of differentiation that emerge from repetition disclose identity.

Performance studies has often understood this idea in terms of failures and revelations—failures of representation, revelations of psychologies. Peggy Phelan offers a concise version in a gloss on the ontology of "realistic theatre." She writes, "The real inhabits the space that representation cannot reproduce—and in this failure theatre relies on repetition and mimesis to produce substitutes for the real. Behind the effects of the real is a desire to experience a first cause, an origin, an authentic beginning which can only fail because the desire is experienced and understood from and through repetition."[21] Despite their inevitable failures, their inability to transport participants to an origin point outside the enclosure of their own symbolic grid (i.e., to "the real"), the "substitutes" that emerge from theatrical repetition are conduits of release as well as instruments of defense against the conditions that prompted the desire for an origin(al) in the first place. Deleuze also identifies repetition's salutary potentiality ("If repetition makes us ill, it also heals us; if it enchains and destroys us, it also frees us"), and hails theater as the space par excellence where one experiences "the whole apparatus of repetition as a 'terrible power.'"[22] The theater he has in mind here is not one of representation (i.e., realist) but one that "extracts real movement from all the arts it employs. . . . In the theatre of repetition, we experience pure forces, dynamic lines in space which act without intermediary upon the spirit, and link it directly with nature and history, with a language which speaks before words, with gestures which develop before organized bodies, with masks before faces, with specters and phantoms before characters."[23] In this theater of cruelty, as he calls it after Artaud, one might encounter the ungraspable yet rousing immensity that conveys the world's plentitude, however briefly.

LeRoi Jones/Amiri Baraka yearned for such sublimity in the theater he imagined in his 1965 essay "The Revolutionary Theatre." (Baraka, like Deleuze, cites Artaud's work as a model.) Even though the Revolutionary Theatre will be a "political theatre, a weapon to help in the slaughter of these dimwitted fat-bellied white guys who somehow believe that the rest of the world is here for them to slobber on," it relies on a kind of transcendentalism that flouts the confines of racialized materialisms.[24] He writes,

> [The Revolutionary Theatre] should be a theatre of World Spirit. Where the spirit can be shown to be the most competent force in the world. Force. Spirit. Feeling. The language will be anybody's, but tightened by the poet's back-bone. And even the language must show what the facts are in this consciousness epic, what's happening. We will talk about the world, and the preciseness with which we are able to summon the world, will be our art. . . . The Revolutionary Theatre is shaped by the world, and moves to reshape the world, using as its force the natural force and perpetual vibrations of the mind in the world.[25]

The configurations and phenomenology of this theater are closer to ritual than drama; as such, repetition becomes its lifeblood if not its very ontology. In Baraka's oeuvre, *Slave Ship: A Historical Pageant* (1967) is the work that best manifests the aesthetic and philosophical principles he outlines in the essay. *Slave Ship* stages a history of chattel slavery and racialization in the New World; capture, brutal subjection, the hegemony of Christianity, and rebellion are its points of emplotment. But the play's ritualistic energies emerge from its atmospherics, which Baraka seeks to achieve through dance, harrowing wails and euphoric utterances, music (especially drumming), and spectacle. The final stage directions give a clear sense of how he conceived this aesthetic machinery: "*Enter audience; get members of audience to dance. To same music Rise Up. Turns into an actual party. When the party reaches some loose improvisation, et cetera, audience relaxed, somebody throws the preacher's head into center of floor, that is, after dancing starts for real. Then black.*"[26] The objective here is not to move participants to experience some aspect of slavery *qua* slavery, for that is an impossible achievement; rather, the aim is to create an event palpably charged with the "Force," "Spirit," and "Feeling" that charged the events *Slave Ship* repeats. To cite Deleuze again, the repetitions of *Slave Ship* "do not add a second and a third time to the first, but carry the first time to the 'nth' power."[27] This is crucially different from Schechner's definition of performance as "never for the first time" but always "for the second to the *n*th time." Baraka's *Slave Ship* exceeds itself as the repetition of a form or representation and carries itself, in its first instance, to the *n*th power.

Baraka would encapsulate this principle of repetition in the title of his 1966 essay on black musical expression: "The Changing Same." Surveying an array of forms and styles, the essay sets out to posit an ontology of black music that spans genres as disparate as R&B (e.g., Sam and Dave, Dionne Warwick, and Leslie Uggams) and what Baraka calls "the New Black Music" (e.g., Sun Ra, John Coltrane, Albert Ayler). Their "form and content," he writes, "identify an entire group of people in America. However these may be transmuted and reused, reappear in other areas, in other musics for different purposes in the society, the initial energy and image [i.e., the source of that energy] are about a specific grouping of peoples, Black People."[28] Conjured by traditional worship, an originary African spirit is the energy and image of this music, its heterogeneous New World genres and sounds "are artificial, or merely indicative of the different placements of [this] spirit"[29]—that is, the same and its changes. As Baraka would have it, then, black music is a set of repetitions that are always already different in their sonic enactments of their shared origin.

Of course, theorists have recognized repetition in its more basic sense—namely, morphological equivalence—as a cardinal feature of black cultural production. Whether textual antiphony; the lyrical and melodic arrangements of genres such as gospel, jazz, and the blues; or the linguistic structures of oral and literary "signifyin,'" repetition has furnished the engine of signification, affective momentum, and rhythm of what some have come to call "black culture." James Snead made the canny observation that Hegel, in his racist derision, actually identified the centrality of repetition to African cultural praxis, and was the first European to do so in any sort of sustained way. According to Hegel, the African orients himself in the way of nature, which is to say *cyclically*. Like all figures of repetition, the cycle is antidialectical; hence in a Hegelian framework, it precludes progressions toward higher intellectual and thereby aesthetic developments. Yet for Snead cyclicality is the very ground from which progress springs, for it is the *only* ground because the finitude of the world makes it so. He adduces developments that derive from improvisation, the "cut" (i.e., "an accidental *da capo*") and call-and-response in black music and literature, as evidence of repetition's generative power, its ability to foster innovation.[30] With ever greater force that power is affecting world cultures beyond African-derived ones, as the steady instatement of aspects of black culture as the foundation of a global popular culture suggests. Writing in the 1980s Snead remarked on this phenomenon in European modernisms and postmodernisms, framing its continuing unfolding as a stunning rebuke of Hegelianism: "The outstanding fact of late-twentieth-century European culture is its ongoing reconciliation with black culture. The mystery may be that it took so long to discern the elements of black culture already there in latent form, and to realize that the separation between the cultures was perhaps all along not one of nature, but of force."[31]

Even as we begin here with examples drawn from traditions of African American performance, which has developed an especially rich critical vocabulary for thinking about the relationship between repetition and performance, the essays that follow draw upon other traditions as well, including Caribbean, Latina/o, East Asian diasporic, and South Asian performance. Collectively, we endeavor to think race as a conceptual category as well as in its particularity. If Snead and many others have claimed that the degree to which a group embraces repetition as a formal desideratum distinguishes the identity of that group, over the past thirty years there has also been an effort among theorists to understand how repetitions of embodied mundane acts and sociohistorical practices amount to sites through which race is constructed. Proceeding from decidedly antibiologistic convictions, these projects almost always owe a debt to Judith Butler's theory of performativity and gender constitution. Butler herself demurs to "the question of whether or not the theory of performativity can be transposed onto matters of race," but her model of the production of disciplinary effects, by way of routinized normativity, that cohere to produce gender is nonetheless useful as a launching point, among others, from which to start to make sense of race—that is, if we understand race as a fictive category of human difference that has achieved an irrefutable phenomenology that organizes the world's cultural flows, economic priorities, and social logics.[32] We do not have space here to rework Butler's model into one suitable for racial constitution, but we submit that a first step in that project could be to regard what she calls "performativity" in terms of what Deleuze defines as "generality," rather than in terms of repetition. Generality "expresses a point a view according to which one term may be exchanged or substituted for another. . . . By contrast, we can see that repetition is a necessary and justified conduct in relation to that which cannot be replaced."[33] In this scheme, repetition requires an immutable, metaphysical singularity as its origin point of departure; race has no such point, thus generality better describes the recursive acts and deeds that signify race in one direction or another. Indeed, theorizing racial constitution in terms of generality not only allows for a more robust appreciation of the disruptions, slippages, and remainders that instantiate evolutions of race across times and spaces, but also helps avoid a kind of essentializing that working under the paradigm of repetition often yields.

The essays herein take a similar tack: they appreciate the inestimable value that theories of repetition have contributed to the study of race and/in performance but move to center other temporal figures of identification that are related to, but diverge from, repetition. The volume's title flags such moves; it can be read as a truncation of something like "race and performance after the turn to repetition that poststructuralist thought inspired." Given that deeply generative intellectual venture, we approach the performance of race after the poststructuralist study of repetition in order to clock other ways that race and performance appear over time and in time. In this effort we do not jettison repetition out of hand but, perhaps ironically, insist that working through and alongside repetition is a necessary first step to getting beyond its dominance as an analytical category in prevailing theories of race, ethnicity, and performance.

These theories have construed repetition as a kind of time signature, that is, a necessary temporal process in the construction of identity as well as the aesthetic formations we call theater, music, dance, ritual, pageant, and so forth. Individually and collectively, the essays in this volume demonstrate the reverse: rather than understanding race and performance as constituted through repetition, they deem repetition to be constituted by race and performance (this was Hegel's accidental conclusion, as Snead's careful rereading of him suggests). Performances of race make something like repetition knowable as repetition in the first place; what is more, they insist that repetition is but one way that past/present/future can be configured in relation to each other. With this idea in mind, the contributions to this volume bracket the familiar turn to repetition to ask what other relationships between identity and difference, between *chronos* and *kairos*, between the past and the present their behaved restorations temporalize.

The chapters in Part I, "Toggling Time: Metatheaters of Race," open this inquiry by focusing on the temporality of race, history, and form in particular instances of theater. Three contemporary productions that reimagine the history of the racial melodrama (Tavia Nyong'o in chapter 1), the black musical revue (Catherine Young in chapter 2), and hip-hop theater (Patricia

Herrera in chapter 3) ask how we might explore the ongoing vitalism of the past while stepping outside of its dramatic forms. These are revivals that drop the *re-*, productions that offer an interruption into form's repetition and approach theater history anew. Part II, "Choreo-Chronographies," moves from the proscenium stage to other instances of performance in order to consider how gesture, dance, and movement can recalibrate the temporal narratives of racial subjection. Whether in sport (Tina Post in chapter 4), black ecstatic dance (Post and Jasmine Johnson in chapter 5), new circus (Katherine Zien in chapter 6), or ritual (Elizabeth Son in chapter 7), the collective analyses in this section vividly demonstrate the range of critical possibilities when we approach performance outside the frame of repetition.

While these chapters in Part II look to the circulation of movements whose meanings exceed the repetitions that they both bear and displace, the chapters in Part III, "Temporal (Im)mobilities: Dwelling Out of Time," all take up what music misleadingly names *the rest*—an interval or pause of silence. The authors in this section consider the agency, critique, and hope that percolate in such stasis. In the arrest of repetition, these contributions demonstrate, new temporalities and new ethics can emerge. The chapters appropriately locate repetition's ar/rest within and against apparatuses of state power and violence. They consider how the time-capture of incarceration might be countered by the temporality of the dream (Nicholas Fesette in chapter 8) and how blackness can interrupt the everyday passage through public space by the intrusion of nonpresence that enacts a temporal "hiccup" (Joshua Chambers-Letson in chapter 11). The still images of Haitian photographer Josué Azor, in contrast, simultaneously perform and document an ecstatic temporality, or *dedouble*, that eludes antihomosexual violence in Haiti and produces a new erotic field (Mario LaMothe in chapter 10). A similar occupation of public space and activist response to cultures of sexual violence in New Delhi offers a performance that turns away from the temporality of being-toward-death and locates political ethics instead in a temporality of natality, one that can be generative of new solidarities (Jisha Menon in chapter 9). *Race and Performance after Repetition* is a provocation and an open question, and the different chapters advance a variety of approaches in response to this call. Some of these chapters offer less familiar ways of understanding difference, power, and resistance that are not necessarily shaped by repetition; others point out the limits of repetition for grasping the insights into race-making some performances plumb; and still others demonstrate how theater and performance redefine the concept of repetition itself. All of them propose new ways of comprehending the historicity and phenomenology of race and/ in performance.

Accordingly, the preposition "after" in our title conveys two contrary senses: "after" in the sense of behind something that comes next, of the supersession of something, but also in the sense of in the style of or in admiration of (as in Van Gogh's painting, *First Steps, after Millet* [1890]). By "after repetition," we focus our collective attention on performances whose temporal logistics operate beyond or adjacent to the dominant time signature of repetition, even when they still bear its influence. Thus, the following chapters are not a rejection of repetition (as if that were possible) but ask: How do particular performances animate time differently than the pattern of repetition that has been a crucial concept for theories of both performance and race/ethnicity since the 1960s? What models of temporality emerge instead of, alongside, or within repetition? How do some performances draw from theories or experiences of repetition differently than we might expect? Or, more simply, what other time signatures organize minoritarian performance?

A musical term, the time signature is the mark at the beginning of a score that establishes the value of a note in relation to beats and the number of beats in a measure, thus signaling to the musician the rhythm of the composition. Time signatures tell us the pace and rhythm of a performance, identify stress and meter, can be simple or complex, and can shift over the course of a particular composition. One piece may have multiple time signatures. Time signatures thus always pose questions concerning value and always put value itself in question. Musically, the time signature appears as a written notation on a score, but prior to that writing it is *felt*—it orients a particular performance or lived experience within time. Among other entities repetition might be (an ontological allegory, a rhetorical operation, a signifying chain, a rhythmic pulse, a well of influence, a technology of discipline, a comfort, a nightmare), it is a temporal mode that marks a series or sequence. Put succinctly by the philosopher of repetition Søren Kierkegaard, "Repetition and recollection are the same movement, just in opposite directions, because what is recollected has already been and is thus repeated backwards, whereas genuine repetition is recollected forwards."[34] This double movement of memory forward and backward is repetition's time signature. It is the interplay between linear time—existing on a chronological line or a signifying chain where things recur again after they have previously occurred—and cyclical time—since if tomorrow is a repetition of yesterday, then yesterday is already tomorrow and tomorrow yesterday. In toggling between line and cycle, repetition gives us seriality, division, memory, and difference. But there are other ways, we conjecture here, to contemplate and inhabit difference than via repetition.

For instance, the resonant notion of *afterlife* has recently become a paradigmatic approach to the study of race and performance. Afterlife refers to an ongoingness that belies the certain ending to a period or event, and construes this persistence of the past in the present not as a repetition but as a continuation. Scholars in Asian American studies, postcolonial studies, and black studies have pioneered this way of understanding the relationship between racial life (e.g., subjection) and time. Jodi Kim, writing from Asian American studies, traces the "protracted afterlife of the Cold War," the material and ideological structures that continue to propel American empire in the twenty-first century.[35] Similarly, Jordanna Bailkin describes how imperial habits and institutions—the "afterlife of empire"—continued to shape the everyday practices of British people in the decades after South Asian and African decolonization.[36] And in black studies, Saidiya Hartman explains the "afterlife of slavery" as "a measure of man and a ranking of life and worth that has yet to be undone. If slavery persists as an issue in the political life of black America," she writes, "it is not because of an antiquarian obsession with bygone days or the burden of a too-long memory, but because black lives are still imperiled and devalued by a racial calculus and a political arithmetic that were entrenched centuries ago."[37] In all three of these examples, the past epoch is not figured as memory or artifact but as a material and affective present. And in each example, a community's relationship to time is not (only) organized by linearity, cyclicality, and repetition. Especially in black studies, afterlife has emerged as a deeply generative idiom for scholarship that has emphasized the persistence of particular forms of racial abjection and blackness as (the mark of) social death.

In *Race and Performance after Repetition*, we take inspiration from the turn to afterlife as a modality of time that puts attention on the things that matter most to care. Specifically, the study of afterlife introduces a different time signature to race and performance than that of repetition. Rather than see the past as a series of breaks or ruptures that return again in the present, the notion of afterlife traces continuities that may be obscured by the logic of progress, revolution, rupture, or reform. In afterlife methodologies, return and haunting operate by a different logic than repetition (Beloved's return to 124 in Toni Morrison's *Beloved* [1987], for instance, is decidedly not a repetition). We align this volume with various projects that take up afterlife methodologies, though our emphasis on performance necessarily draws us less toward conditions of social death than to conditions of social life (as either immanent within or transcendent of social death). The essays that follow add to the temporal lexicon of racial performances that bear time signatures other than repetition, multiplying temporal logics much as the concept of afterlife has done. While repetition may always be operative, it is not always the master code for deciphering social processes, performances, or performativity. Repetition appears throughout this collection as less useful for understanding race and performance (and the performance of race) than the performance of race is useful for understanding repetition.

We conclude this introduction by turning to another performance that, like Simone Leigh's *Free People's Medical Clinic*, instructs us in a relationship to time, history, and identity that is inadequately grasped by the grammar of repetition: the community-based work of conceptual artist Theaster Gates. Formally a student of ceramics, urban planning, and religious studies, Gates produces artworks that sometimes take the name of public art, social works, or community-based art: site-specific productions that are not located in a gallery but in a neighborhood, an abandoned building, or on a block. He himself is leery of such art world designations, however. "I have a lot of resistance when people say the work is a kind of activist practice," he explains, because too often "when black artists do things in the 'hood, it becomes 'community art,' rather than place-based work."[38] His point is not to diminish the creation of community but to query the value-structures and ways of seeing that posit minoritarian art as purely functional and local rather than beautiful and universal. Indeed, Gates's work dismantles such habits of thoughts that oppose function/beauty and local/universal. He sets things in motion: buildings and beams, food and plateware, neighbors and neighborhoods, history and memory, time itself. His work, like Leigh's FPMC, models a principle of restoration that is less about repetition than it is about mending, giving back, and recompense.

Consider his ongoing work, *Dorchester Projects*. In 2008 Gates and his team began renovations of several of dilapidated buildings on Dorchester Street in Chicago's South Side, a predominantly African American district. In a practice that combined construction, refurbishment, design, craftwork, and similar acts of making and assembly, he oversaw the transformation of the abandoned buildings into spaces of community gathering and neighborhood conviviality. Gates redesigned the interiors with salvaged wood and timber from old Chicago factories and regional barns from the city outskirts (figure 1.4). The Dorchester buildings also include the loving preservation of salvaged material deemed worthless. The Listening Room houses 8,000 albums recovered after the closing of nearby Dr. Wax Records. The Glass Lantern Slide

FIGURE I.4 Dorchester House, 2012. © THEASTER GATES. PHOTO BY SARAH POOLEY. COURTESY OF THE ARTIST.

FIGURE I.5 Archive House interior, 2012. © THEASTER GATES. PHOTO BY SARAH POOLEY. COURTESY OF THE ARTIST.

Archive holds the discarded collection of nearly sixty thousand lantern slides that the University of Chicago's Art History Department donated to Gates after it digitized its holdings. A reading library with books on art, architecture, and design adopted from the Prairie Avenue Bookstore fills an entire floor, and complements a garden, a kitchen, and other gathering spaces for performance, display, and sociality (figure 1.5). More recently, Gates added the Black Cinema House, which screens films of the black diaspora, many overlooked, and provides space for discussion, community video classes and production workshops, and other programming. These sonic, visual, and material remnants of the past activate community in the present. So, too, do the dinners and other social gatherings that the buildings house. Dorchester is known for its communal soul food dinners and tea ceremonies that are a combination of ritual, seminar, banquet, musical concert, and memory.

Taken as a whole, the *Dorchester Projects* are a lesson in how to live together, in all of our idiorhythms and tempos. As neighbors and guests visit the houses, insiders and outsiders interact in a kind of antigentrification that is not about the displacement of populations to make room for new value but about the neighborhood and its people's immanent beauty. Gates's community performance appears as the distribution of space, of social relations, of materials, and of self—that is, the mise-en-scène of social life made from the props of neglect and disenfranchisement. This is restoration as activation. Gates explains:

> There's a way in which I imagine that materials and spaces have life in them, and rather than a constant state of becoming which is also true, that they have something extremely sacred inside them that might be sleeping or may have been put into a coma, but is living, and that we have to kind of find ways to activate the living. And if we thought about then how to activate the living inside of a space or inside of an object or inside of a situation, and at the same time, protecting this very delicate, sleeping potential, that sometimes it's like you don't need to reveal the life in order to know that the life exists.[39]

In Gates's gentle formulation, this is not performance as twice-behaved behavior or performative iteration that allows for new becomings. Rather, it is about living with the material as it presents itself to us and nurturing its offering. The materials' simple existence contains a dormant life, one that has always been there, that animates the social collaborations at Dorchester. In tending to the potentiality of his object-world, Gates activates collective living in Dorchester according to its own distinct time signature that redistributes the value of its notes and sounds a neighborhood symphony.

What is often missing in descriptions of Dorchester's dinner parties and the community ethos of Gates's work is the sheer beauty of it all. Dorchester's reorganization of interior space as well as the houses' presence on the block "puts attention on those things that matter most to care or concern."[40] The selection of materials; the contrasting textures of timbers; the spacing of shelves; the play of height and depth, light and shadow, finishedness and unfinishedness; the meticulous woodwork; the purposeful display of books and slides; the sonic vibrations of records as their music travels the walls of the house; the smells of the kitchen; the laughter of the dinners—all announce a time signature of art and performance that is to the side of repetition yet nonetheless brings the past into the present as a delicate, sleeping potential. This aesthetics of Dorchester is one reason why galleries across North America and Europe have been eager to exhibit various rooms from Dorchester houses, which are sometimes packed up and reconstructed in such art world spaces.

Another of Gates's restorative performances, *See, Sit, Sup, Sip, Sing: Holding Court* (2012), draws on this ethos of beauty-in-community but marks a shift in invitation from neighborhood drop-by to a more strangely gathering of yet-unknown sensibilities. *Holding Court* was designed for the New York City's Armory Show and since re-created in various gallery spaces. The Armory Show is an art fair founded in 1994 by four elite gallerists that functions as a marketplace for art dealers and collectors to appraise, procure, and purchase new art. The place of the artist herself in this scene is an uneasy one (the *New York Times* described it as "a top draw for heavy-hitting collectors, gallerists, celebrities, and art lovers," an endorsement that the Armory Show prominently features on its own website; you would be forgiven for wondering where the artist was).[41] In this scene, Gates arranged a social space using abandoned material from the recently closed Crispus Attucks Elementary school on Chicago's South Side—including desks, chairs, furniture, chalkboards, and other classroom ephemera. For four hours each day of the art show, Gates "held court" in the makeshift classroom he activated (figures I.6 and I.7). Attendees could sit and engage with the artist, reflecting on art, value, spirituality, aesthetics, and commerce. The project, Gates explains, was to "reuse these materials in a form for education that I am really curious about: what else can we do at the Armory besides buy art? . . . The Crispus Attucks school just kind of acts as a launching pad for a conversation about, like, how does redevel-

FIGURE I.6 *See, Sit, Sup, Sit, Sing: Holding Court.* View of the exhibition *Radical Presence: Black Performance in Contemporary Art*, Walker Art Center, Minneapolis, July 24, 2014–January 4, 2015. © WALKER ART CENTER. PHOTO BY GENE PITTMAN. COURTESY OF THEASTER GATES.

FIGURE I.7 Theaster Gates, *Holding Court.* View of the exhibition *Radical Presence: Black Performance in Contemporary Art*, Walker Art Center, Minneapolis, July 24, 2014–January 4, 2015. © WALKER ART CENTER. PHOTO BY GENE PITTMAN. COURTESY OF THEASTER GATES.

opment and reinvestment happen? What's the relationship between this art market and possible urban renewal and redevelopment?"[42] Reassembling bits of the decommissioned school (of which 96.9 percent of students at closing were low income, 99 percent were black, and 48 percent were identified as homeless) in the middle of the Armory Show and filling its seats with different bodies modifies the tempo of the elite art fair with the tempo of community organization as urban renewal.[43]

In *Holding Court*, then, Gates suspended the time of the fair as a marketplace of opulent exchange in his animation of a different kind of social architecture and aesthetic value, akin to Simone Leigh's *Waiting Room Underground* and its step outside of the economic structures and value systems of the art world marketplace. The title of the performance gestures to the project's search for forms and tempos appropriate to contingent circumstances or shifting moods. Asked about the meaning of the syncopated sibilant title—*See, Sit, Sup, Sip, Sing*—Gates replied, "If I'm responding to a question, what's the best form to respond in? So some of it is just like, you know, I want to sip on my brandy, I want to sip on my tea. We could convene—this could be a dinner conversation. It might lead me to singing, and singing might be the best form to respond to a thing. I just like those words together."[44] Equal parts lecture, seminar, debate, conversation, provocation, song, and chitchat, *Holding Court* was above all a scene of pedagogy that aspired to dehierarchize the directionality of knowledge and instruction. Gates walked around the space, diagrammed his thoughts and art projects on a chalkboard or a large roll of white paper, engaged with those gathered, climbed on the table, and sometimes sang in response to questions. In this way, *Holding Court* foregrounded the interconnection between social form and aesthetic form. The refurbished materials from Crispus Attucks—the life dormant within them—imbued this gathering with a temporality that is something other than repetition. They provided a texture of education, instruction, and discipline, but also the secrets of elementary school: passed notes, initials carved into desks, looks exchanged on the way to the pencil sharpener, hallway passes, necessary free lunch, the pleasures and terrors of recess, rapt attention for a caring teacher, the peace of resting your head on your desk when you finish the assignment early. Crispus Attucks does not offer itself as a *usable past*, in that modernist sense of instrumentalizing earlier works in the service of some new aesthetic or as a means to an end, but as a *useful past*, in the sense of seeing the value of the past in terms of use rather than exchange. We think of it as the difference between consumption and collaboration.

Like the dinners at Dorchester, *Holding Court* was dedicated to the use of past objects and refused the logistics of repetition. In an interview with art historian Tom McDonough, Gates responds to—or, rather, dodges—the question of time, repetition, and recovery in his work:

TM: Is it in the nature of the [Dorchester] project, then, to recognize what lies latent in those spaces or to realize those potentials? I'm curious about what the balance is between the futures and pasts of buildings.

TG: You know, Tom, maybe I just like sweeping. It may not have anything to do with the reclamation of a past moment. Maybe sometimes it does, but it's not necessarily the creation of something new out of something old; sometimes it's just the inclination, or compulsion, to make something with what's around you, to tidy up the untidy.[45]

This tidying up is akin to what we described, in relation to Leigh's *Free People's Medical Clinic*, as behaved restoration as a form of mending or repair. It is time as a "a modality that dismantles fixed subjects and objects and turns past, present and future into ways of manners of attention," especially as Gates directs that attention to the things ready-to-hand that matter most to care: a desk, a piece of wood, a meal, a neighbor, a dwelling, a question.[46] This work is not restored behavior as Schechner defines it—"living behavior treated as a film director treats a strip of film," which "can be rearranged or reconstructed . . . independent of the causal systems (social, psychological, technological) that brought them into existence"—but behaved restoration as the making good of loss (or damage), now with *loss* as the object.[47] In Gates's tidying up, the linear or cyclical interplay of past and present is not irrelevant, it is just not necessarily the first or best way to make sense of identity, community, or performance in and as time. As Gates suggests with elegant understatement, identity, community, and performance can be a tidying up of the untidy, a local act of historical sweep and historical sweeping.

While not all of the contributors to this volume address the kind of community-activating aesthetic practices that Leigh and Gates create and curate, they all describe performances of race that move to time signatures other than repetition. They ask if there are other ways we can understand the appearance or persistence of the past in the present, taking up performances as varied as theatrical reinventions, activist interventions, durational body art, choreographies of everyday life and afterlife, queer metamorphoses, ritual stutters, circus acts, and architectural flights of fancy and freedom. Yet across this variety, these essays call forth a singular gathering of minoritarian performers within and without the United States who model other time signatures in their work. Thus, this volume itself is a kind of activation and gathering in the spirit of *Free People's Medical Clinic, Dorchester Projects*, and *Holding Court*; as such, it calls for a more nuanced lexicon for apprehending time, performance, and race. Each of the essays that follow begins to contribute to such a lexicon: not only repetition, but also restoration, activation, accumulation, stasis, concurrence, simultaneity, prolepsis, leak, anticipation, projection, dream, doubling and *dedouble*, duration, swerve, multiplication, emergence, dark reparation, natality, gestation, prognosis, hesitation, hiccup, time travel, decline, glitch, pararepetition, interval, continuation, concern, and care. Not only repetition, but also . . .

NOTES

1 See Christian, "Hidden in Brooklyn"; Ramirez, "Haven for Blacks."
2 For more on the history of Weeksville and its recovery, see the Weeksville Heritage Center; Wellman, *Brooklyn's Promised Land*.
3 "Simone Leigh."
4 See Nelson, *Body and Soul*.
5 See S. Davis, "Room for Care."
6 Sayej, "Simone Leigh's *The Waiting Room*."
7 Schneider, *Performing Remains*, 2, 10.
8 Schneider, *Performing Remains*, 14.
9 Schneider, *Performing Remains*, 26.
10 Rayner, "Keeping Time," 32.
11 Rayner, "Keeping Time," 32.
12 *Oxford English Dictionary*, s.v. "restore," http://www.oed.com; *Oxford English Dictionary*, s.v. "repair," http://www.oed.com.
13 L. Alexander, "Susan Smith McKinney," 173.
14 "Free People's Medical Clinic."
15 Bradley, "Going Underground."
16 Schechner, *Between Theater and Anthropology*, 36.
17 Schechner, *Between Theater and Anthropology*, 36, 37.
18 In Derrida, *Limited, Inc.*, 119
19 Deleuze, *Difference and Repetition*, 1.
20 Deleuze, *Difference and Repetition*, 17, 18.
21 Phelan, *Unmarked*, 126.

22 Deleuze, *Difference and Repetition*, 19, 10.

23 Deleuze, *Difference and Repetition*, 10.

24 Baraka, *Home*, 237.

25 Baraka, *Home*, 237–38.

26 Baraka, *Slave Ship*, 259.

27 Deleuze, *Difference and Repetition*, 1.

28 Baraka, "Changing Same," 123.

29 Baraka, "Changing Same," 126.

30 Snead, "On Repetition in Black Culture," 150.

31 Snead, "On Repetition in Black Culture," 153.

32 Butler, *Gender Trouble*, xvi.

33 Deleuze, *Difference and Repetition*, 1.

34 Kierkegaard, *Repetition*, 3.

35 J. Kim, *Ends of Empire*, 110.

36 Bailkin, *Afterlife of Empire*.

37 Hartman, *Lose Your Mother*, 6.

38 "Carol Becker in Conversation with Theaster Gates," 19.

39 "Public Art (Now)."

40 Rayner, "Keeping Time," 32.

41 See Armory Show.

42 "Theaster Gates AI Interview."

43 See "Attucks" (Every Chicago Public School Is My School); "Attucks" (School Cuts); "Homeless Children."

44 Quoted in "Theaster Gates: *Holding Court* (2012), part 1."

45 McDonough, "Theaster Gates."

46 Rayner, "Keeping Time," 32.

47 Schechner, *Between Theater and Anthropology*, 35.

PART I
TOGGLING TIME
METATHEATERS
OF RACE

There is a dark mass
following me.

LATASHA NEVADA S.
DIGGS, *TWERK*

So Far Down You Can't
See the Light

Afro-Fabulation in Branden Jacobs-
Jenkins's An Octoroon

In the opening scene of Branden Jacobs-Jenkins's 2014 play, *An Octoroon*, the character "BJJ" turns to the audience, to whom he has just related a series of confessional exchanges with his therapist and declares: "Just kidding. I don't have a therapist. I can't afford one. . . . You people are my therapy."[1] It's a memorable line, even if, minutes later, BJJ—a metatheatrical character representing the playwright of the play the audience is watching—goes back to relating further exchanges with his therapist.[2]

So, does he have a therapist or does he not? As a question asked of a fictional character, albeit one based on the actual playwright (and played, in the 2014 premiere at Soho Rep by actor Chris Myers, who bears a passing resemblance to the real Jacobs-Jenkins), we cannot provide a definite answer. In the productions I saw, the smart-aleck line was spoken to a New York City theater audience (an audience presumably quite familiar with therapy) by a black actor playing a black playwright who was publicly processing the "drama" stirred up during the original workshop production of the play, several years earlier at Performance Space 122 (also in New York City). In that production, several white male cast members very dramatically quit the production midway, then badmouthed both it and the playwright in the downtown press. At issue was the transtemporality of adapting racist melodramatic stock figures from the nineteenth century for the contemporary stage, and the challenge this presented to modern, ostensibly nonracist actors trained to empathize with their roles. If Freud famously distinguished between "acting out" versus "working through" psychic trauma, the ambiguous declaration of BJJ that the theater was his therapy splits the difference: it is an acting out that is a working through, and a working through that is an acting out.[3]

What does it mean, this chapter asks, when the burden of acting out historical memory falls upon black subjects in an anti-black world? Can black performance live up to the demand that it repair and make good the hard feelings that crop up for contemporary white subjects when forced to confront the traumatic origins of their own enjoyment of, and possessive investment in, whiteness?

Jacobs-Jenkins's transformation of the theater house into a stand-in for the therapist's office is but the first of a series of metamorphoses the audience collectively experiences over the course of *An Octoroon*, which is an adaptation of one of the most well-known racial melodramas of the nineteenth century, Dion Boucicault's *The Octoroon* (1859). By the end of the new play, the theater will also have been transformed into an auction house, with white men calling out their bids from seats in the audience and, almost as unsettlingly, into a giant camera, with the back wall of the set falling toward the audience (in the Soho rep production) with a giant clack that is reminiscent of nothing so much as the mechanical click of the camera's shutter. By folding the theatrical, therapeutic, commercial, and photographic into each other in this complex but convincing way, *An Octoroon* fabulates a history of racial melodrama that keeps contemporary audiences on the hook. Transforming the mise-en-scène, and indeed the entire performing environment, interrupts the confidence with which we might dismiss as static or stereotypical the stock characters of melodrama. Instead, we are obliged to consider how ostensibly anachronistic modes (such as melodrama and blackface minstrelsy) are constantly reactivated within ostensibly postmodern modes (such as reality TV and theatrical colorblind casting). Witnessing all the onstage "acting out," it is we in the audience who are obliged to do the "working through."

But can performance really be therapy? And therapy for whom? The sting of BJJ's opening joke is that he has inducted the paying audience against their expectations into a sort of "wild" analysis.[4] "Wild" analysis was Freud's derogatory term for a sudden and/or out-of-context deployment of a psychoanalytic insight (such as quacks and pop psychologists are particularly prone to). Contemporary drama often traffics in precisely this kind of quicksilver insight—particularly so when one considers the close psychic proximity of wild analysis and the joke. In what ways, then, might we be entitled to read this "wildness" of Jacobs-Jenkins's play in terms of the mercurial transformations it subjects its characters and audiences to? The immediate context of BJJ's harangue was the intense pressure placed on being a black playwright in an American theatrical tradition saturated with racial minefields that are so often left to black theater artists alone to navigate. Just as the roles and length of treatment in the clinic are disrupted in the "wild" analysis, so too the assigned roles in the theater are disrupted in *An Octoroon*, in which BJJ is at once actor, director, playwright, and patient on the couch. His "identity" as a black man hardly ensures a consistency of self across these roles (even as this is emphatically not a postracial play). To the contrary, BJJ is driven manic by the racially inconsistent application of the expectation of an identification of actor with role. "God forbid any actor of color not have to jump at the chance to play an offensive bag of garbage so far from his own life," BJJ rants, "but which some idiot's going to describe as representative of 'the Black experience in America,' but the minute you ask a white guy to play a racist whose racism isn't 'complicated' by some monologue where he's like 'I don't mean to be racist! It's just complicated!' he doesn't return your phone calls."[5]

In addition to having to deal with the ongoing inequalities and discrimination of antiblack racism, *The Octoroon* opens by noticing how the black performer-playwright is given the added burden of performing historical memory for predominantly white audiences who might prefer to continue forgetting. We might even call this expectation the racial contract of the American stage, if we borrow philosopher Charles Mills's provocative claim that the US social contract always presumes a preceding "racial contract" in which access to civil equality is made contingent upon whiteness (and proximity to whiteness).[6] Although Mills does not discuss theater or performance per se, he does outline how this racial contract norms space (in the manner referenced above wherein the theater becomes an auction house becomes a camera): "Conceptions of one's white self," Mills notes, "map a microgeography of the acceptable routes through racial space of one's own personal space."[7] The cross-racial casting of black actors in white roles in *An Octoroon* contrasts the use of this same technique in the commercial juggernaut *Hamilton* (2015), insofar as estrangement effects aim here to disrupt the white racial nomos, rather than to renew their glamour.[8]

The plot of *The Octoroon*, as readers in nineteenth-century studies well know, is based upon the workings of precisely such a contract in the antebellum United States. The melodramatic plot concerns the revelation that Zoe, a visibly white woman of "one-eighth" black ancestry, has been raised up as a free woman, but is in fact part of the chattel property of the Terrebonne plantation in Louisiana and must be sold off to pay the debts of the plantation's dying patriarch. Boucicault's play relies upon the white, nineteenth-century audience feeling torn between respect for the rule of law and the payment of debts, on the one hand, and the traumatic spectacle of a visibly near-white woman being sold into "white slavery" on the other. The frisson of "white slavery" in the original performance relied on the casting of white women to play Zoe, emphasizing the unnaturalness of her enslavement. Although Jacobs-Jenkins's adaptation (which calls for a black or mixed-race actor to play Zoe) is the product of a conditionally integrated stage, it repeatedly reinvokes that presumptive whiteness of the contemporary audience, which his play shows to be part of the afterlives of slavery. The white norms of the American theater, in other words, are shown to be consistent with the racial geography of stage masters, mistresses, slaves, overseers, and itinerants.

What the original play cannot make manifest, that is to say, is what Jacobs-Jenkins's adaptation insists upon: the assumptive logic whereby the *unnaturalness* of Zoe's enslaved status relies upon the *naturalization* of the slave status for the other black characters in the play. At a formal level, we see this evidenced in the continual resistance that *An Octoroon* pays to its generic characterization as the "contemporary American play" it undoubtedly also is. *An Octoroon* in both text and performance registers frequent and sudden tonal shifts away from theatricality: into rap, reality TV, and other anachronistic performance idioms. I would argue these shifts result from a quixotic attempt to disrupt the racial contract of theater from within the terms provided by the theater itself. What I have been calling the "wildness" of the work surfaces in its continuous metamorphoses that bring the play into contact, however briefly, with adjacent cultural spaces in popular culture in which black performance disrupts the ordered norms of civil society.[9]

If *An Octoroon* subjects the racial contract of the American stage to a kind of "wild" analysis, as I have so far argued, where does that leave us and the cast at the end of the play? Is this analysis terminable or interminable? Forgoing dreams of racial healing, transcendence, or a postracial society, I argue that *An Octoroon* settles in for something like the eternal recurrence of antiblackness. This isn't as depressing as it seems! There can be something antidepressive, Jonathan Flatley has argued, to the melancholic realization that wrong life cannot be rightly lived.[10] The title for this chapter, speaking directly to this point, is drawn from a line from the song the cast sings at the end of the play, a point in performance which is traditionally meant to distance actor from role in the standard curtain call. Here, however, the cast first performs an original song (fulfilling the archaic definition of melodrama as "drama with music") that confesses how the play is surfacing "something's wrong, we never can put right." In disavowing the obligation to bring the story to a satisfying modern resolution (and I will return to the formal ending of the play below), the play and the cast throw the "working through" of this history back out onto the audience. The song even claims (a bit surprisingly to me) that *An Octoroon* is "a gory allegory" rather than, as I would have assumed, a postmodern pastiche. But whether it is allegory, pastiche, or melodrama is hardly to the point: all fall within the racial contract of the American stage. Perhaps the version of the production that best succeeds in what I have called its attempt to disrupt theater's racial contract is the production that never actually was: the abortive original production that proved literally untenable for the white actors. If one considers how black performance originates in a freedom that prompts coercion, perhaps the only *real* disruption of the racial contract of American theater would come in the implausible (and doubtless illegal) scenario in which white actors were somehow obliged to perform against their will in a play of a black writer's devising. Short of this compulsory performance of whiteness, the play settles in for leaving us with the eternal recurrence of antiblackness ringing in our ears, a little earworm that tunnels into our memory, opening out a pathway in memory and the imagination to an impossible and unrepresentable outside.

WILD ANALYSIS AND DARK REPARATION

The Afro-fabulist, I would argue, faces a double bind whenever she or he delves into the travestied history of race. The contemporary playwright is at war with the emotional matrix of the scene they are evoking, and must betray their sources and source texts, paradoxically, if they would be true to them.[11] The work of staging blackness under the terms of the racial contract, in a play like *An Octoroon*, entails much more than simply documenting or representing black lives in a holistic or realistic fashion (such as, by contrast, one sees occurring in the well-regarded plays of August Wilson and Lorraine Hansberry). Nor is it a matter of reperforming the original racial melodrama in such a way as to do its black characters some sort of ersatz, belated justice.[12] More nearly, it is a matter of grappling with terrain that is overdetermined by the traumatic "scene of subjection," as Saidiya Hartman has influentially termed it.[13] If a first analytic pass through the text alerts us to the presence of a Freudian "acting out"/"working through" dyad, a second can bring to mind some post-Freudian work on the intergenerational transmission of trauma through coded or clouded words. This is evident in the very title of the work. In the opening monologue of *An Octoroon*, it is suggested that the idea to adapt the play comes from the playwright's therapist, when she stumbles upon the meaning of the term "octoroon." This archaic racialism here becomes, in terms spelled out in the post-Freudian writings of Maria Torok and Nicolas Abraham, a "cryptonym": a mysterious or unclear term whose reintroduction into living speech cannot be resolved simply by defining or explaining it, but that instead serves as a kind of "magic word" whose obscurity unleashes a whole complex and volatile transtemporal process.[14] What might be at stake then, in Jacobs-Jenkins's titular strategy of demoting this troublesome, magical word from the definite ("the") to the indefinite ("an") article?

One answer to this question might come from reminding ourselves that, if the racial contract of the contemporary theater commands the black body to stage the historical meanings of "race" for an ostensibly colorblind or post-racial society, then at least, *An Octoroon* suggests, this performance can be one in which the theater as an art form (if that is not too expansive a claim) can somehow be induced to do the work of reparation. The reparative position, after all, is what is sought for as a goal within an object-relations analysis. If this therapeutic aim seems eccentric to the concerns of theatrical analysis, recall that the promise of relief from depression is dangled, as the play opens, before the playwright as the reward for the work of dramatic adaptation. The white therapist voices a standard neoliberal conception of the self as "blocked" by depression and prescribes creative expression as a means of relieving that blockage. Never mind that this premise spectacularly backfires! Understanding that creativity is linked to working through of racial depression helps explicate the play's twinning of two playwrights—Branden Jacobs-Jenkins and Dion Boucicault—who stage a homosocial rivalry over the generic fate of melodrama, past and present. Boucicault—an offensive stereotype of a drunken Irishman—is restored to the stage from which his brand of once ubiquitous melodrama has been more or less banned, there to exact his revenge. Through this doubling, *An Octoroon* stages the return of the repressed as the key to a new examination of this play that, as a "mortgage melodrama," has everything to do with debt.[15] *The Octoroon*, that is to say, was an enormously influential nineteenth-century play that I have taught in the past as a period piece and unstageable in our present era. This consignment of Boucicault and his scandalous images to the "no-longer-conscious" becomes grist for Jacobs-Jenkins's creative mill.[16] But it is precisely in reviving the unrevivable that *An Octoroon* also swerves away from a more received understanding of doing reparative work. Instead of reviving *The Octoroon*, or Boucicault's literary reputation, *An Octoroon* tears both images down to their phantasmatic component parts and then patches them back to together in a highly subjective, speculative bricolage. In order to distinguish this process from reparative work writ large, perhaps it would prove heuristically useful to refer to this process as a negative or dark reparation.

One place we can see this strategy I am calling dark reparation at work is in the multiple casting of a single actor across racially discrete roles. Rather than promote a universal or humanistic conception of the theater, I argue that what this multiple casting does is foreground the incommensurability of these roles that are nonetheless poached and stolen across racial lines. Thus, the script calls for a single actor to play BJJ, the white savior George, and the white villain M'Closky; another actor is cast as the Irish playwright Boucicault, the noble savage Wahnotee, and the auctioneer; and a third actor is to play the playwright's assistant, the house slave Pete, and the pickaninny Paul. Through these directives, I would suggest, *An Octoroon* sympathetically lampoons the aspiration of both colorblind and multicultural casting in the theater. The point is neither to avoid stereotypes nor to imagine that they can be harmlessly cited as irrelevant to our present racial order. Rather, here dark reparative work takes on similar connotations to the concept of "dark play," which Brian Herrera defines as a kind of game in which some of the players are "in the dark," unaware of how those "in the know" are using and manipulating them.[17] Dark reparation (like wild analysis) mostly avoids scenarios of perfect transparency and informed consent. It instead seeks to escape the double bind of theatrical naturalism by accelerating past the sticking points upon which the original workshop production foundered. It seeks to overcome the dominant temporal frame of repetition by producing difference and diffraction between historical roles and present-day realities.

Perhaps the most memorable and controversial coup of Jacobs-Jenkins's adaptation, in this respect, appears in his reimagining of two female slaves Minnie and Dido, characters who are ostensibly insignificant to the larger plot, bystanders in their own lives, but who become central to Jacobs-Jenkins's dramatic imaginary. The characters of the two house slaves Minnie and Dido are written, shockingly, in contemporary urban black vernacular, a decision that effects a continuous estrangement effect on the viewer. Unable to project distance between stage lives under slavery and our own present day, the audience is obliged to confront our own contemporary appetite for lowbrow black comedy as a legacy of chattel slavery, and the gendered relations of domination and subjection it reproduced. What is more, it is obliged to grapple with these profane idioms as a source of resistance and subversion. When the slaves are put up for sale to repay the estate's debts in *An Octoroon*, Minnie and Dido openly scheme to be bought by a riverboat captain so as to project a fantasy of control or bargaining over a situation in which they lack agency. Desperate to avoid being worked to death under the whip, Minnie concocts an impossible fantasy of the good-enough life under slavery on the river:

MINNIE: Girl, what are we gonna do?

DIDO: I don't know. I kind of liked it here.

MINNIE: Me, too. I feel bad for da Peytons.

DIDO: Why?

MINNIE: I don't know. They were some cool ass white people. I mean, they didn't never *really* beat us, you know? It coulda been worse.

DIDO: Yeah. I heard on the M'Closky plantation they actually, like, whips the slaves. With, like, a whip.

MINNIE: Whaaat?

DIDO: I know, right?

MINNIE: I am not tryin'a get bought by Mas'r M'Closky!

DIDO: Well, I saw him in that group of white men walking around inspecting things.

MINNIE: Oh no! (*Remembers something, whispering*) Wait, girl! You know who else I saw in that group?

DIDO: Who?

MINNIE: That fine ass white man who own that steamboat. With the tan? I think his name is like Rat or sum'n. Ratts? Ratty? Rabbit? Ratface? I don't know. We gotta get bought by him, girl! Imagine if we lived on a steamboat, coasting up and down the river, looking fly, wind whipping at our hair and our slave tunics and shit as we surrounded by all these fine, muscle-y boat niggas who ain't been wit a woman in years?

DIDO: I don't know, Minnie, that sounds kinda dangerous . . . [18]

This scene Jacobs-Jenkins stages might be read through what Christina Sharpe has aptly called the "monstrous intimacies" of slavery and its afterlives. In a discussion of what she terms the "sadomasochism of everyday black life," Sharpe notes how "both the theater of s/m and the sadomasochism of everyday black life appear here as direct instances of the disavowed, the *black* unspeakable."[19] Dark reparation hints at spaces of queer black succor that fall out of representation, that "sound kinda dangerous." In the exchange, Minnie and Dido scandalously seek to libidinize their position as chattel by negotiating a choice between the violent, villainous rapist and the "fine ass" slaveholder whose purchase of them might afford the preservation of a crumbling illusion of a livable life. Minnie, the bolder one, even imagines a freaky erotic undercommons among the male and female slaves on the steamboat, an image which deconstructs the main presentation of the steamboat as a melodramatic spectacle of white commerce and border justice in *The Octoroon*.[20] In this brief exchange, the telling repetition of the word "whip" gives the game away, as the fantasy of "wind whipping at our hair" pushes away the intolerable image of being whipped on the M'Closky planation.

As remorseless as this scene is, it hardly prepares the reader or audience member for the final moments in the play, where Minnie unexpectedly turns and speaks to Dido (after the entire melodramatic plot machinery has transpired to redeem George's inheritance, doom the wicked M'Closky, and potentially even spare the life of Zoe, while ensuring the slaves stay on the plantation after all):

MINNIE: You know, I would be so pissed if something were to happen that somehow rendered these last twelve hours totally moot.

DIDO: I know right? I was thinking the same thing. Like if these white folks found out like . . . Mas'r Closky like . . . killed Paul or something to intercept the letter that was supposed to save the plantation.[21]

In this passage Jacobs-Jenkins mocks the entire melodramatic structure of the play by revealing a standpoint within it from which the restoration of the social contract merely ensures their further damnation. In doing so, Minnie and Dido almost break the fourth wall and share in the dramatic irony of the audience's awareness of them as characters in a plot. The play here drives home the degree to which the structure of melodramatic feeling will redeem the plantation by restoring the racial contract of the American stage. Minnie and Dido are trapped in the hold, as Frank Wilderson might say, despite their fantasies of escape. They occupy the position of the unthought, despite their centrality to the humor of the play, and *An Octoroon* cannot revise away the indifference *The Octoroon* pays to the ordinary enslaved life.[22]

In the Soho Rep production, Captain Ratts was one of two roles played by the playwright Jacobs-Jenkins himself (the other, in disguise, was Br'er Rabbit). Without reading too much into this artistic decision, we can infer there is some significance to this casting of the playwright himself as the failed "rescuer" of these two desperate characters, whose role is comic relief, in contrast to the melodramatic Zoe. Whereas Zoe is enslaved through a cruel sequence of events, Minnie and Dido are treated, with dismissive racism, as naturally and inevitably slaves. Rather than resist their fate, they shamelessly accommodate themselves to it. Under what circumstances can such performances of "slavish" behavior prove reparative? The very degree to which Minnie and Dido are recognizable and "relatable" is a shock to the conscience of the audience member who finds the price of their enjoyment to be collusion in the systematic degradation and dehumanization of black women. Contemporary enjoyment in the folksy wisdom and creative resilience of black people under conditions of systemic antiblack violence are presented in scenes such as the above, my reading of *An Octoroon* suggests, as cobbled together from sources of psychic reparation that, far from being utopian or hopeful, are saturated with aggression and hard feelings.

In a recent essay, David Eng revisits Melanie Klein's account of the reparative position and makes the key (re)discovery that, in Klein's understanding of colonial object relations, reparation is actually a white settler practice for making good on the boomerang impact of the violence wreaked by their dispossession and enslavement of racial and indigenous others.[23] That is to say, the aggression that is repaired is, strictly speaking, a slaveholding and genocidal aggression, which must be somehow neutralized before it consumes white settler society itself. Crucially, the community that is repaired is the white settler community itself (American democracy, in Eng's reading of Klein, emerges out of the guilt over violent dispossession that is sublimated into idealistic commitments to egalitarian fraternity among white men). *An Octoroon* is alert to this dark side of the reparative position, and its dark reparativity unfolds from its consciousness of the impossibility of an ethical position within the representational mechanics of Western drama.

If the adoption of vernacular black speech (modeled again, I suggest, on reality TV and televised black sitcoms as much as "real life") is one site of the play's dark reparativity, another appears in its relationship to photography. Here, *An Octoroon* sets itself the objective of restoring to contemporary audiences the sense of drama that photographic evidence of racist violence might once have conveyed, back in the dawn of photography. To do so in the era of Black Lives Matter, where a seemingly unending stream of photographic footage of police and vigilante violence against unarmed black men and women seems to produce no consistent justice for the victims, only underscores the timeliness of this aspect of the play. In both the original and adaptation, George is a photographer, and his apparatus becomes a plot device when M'Closky murders a black child to cover his tracks, and the camera standing by, and taking a long exposure, captures him standing over the body. The recovered negative dooms M'Closky, and thus effects an implicit promise of racial justice through technological transparency. On stage, BJJ and the Playwright appear to offer a metacommentary on how this dramatic scene should work but can't at present:

PLAYWRIGHT: You know, it's really hard to describe how this scene works—

BJJ: Because it actually would have been really exciting 150 years ago—having someone caught by a photograph.

PLAYWRIGHT: They were a very novel thing—

BJJ: Which is why this whole plot more or less centered around a camera. But photographs to us? Boring. It's a cliché, but we've gotten so used to photos and photographic images that we've basically learned how to fake them, so the kind of justice around which this whole thing hangs is actually a little dated—[24]

Jacobs-Jenkins resolves this problem by substituting the photo of murdered Pete with a projection of a photograph of a lynching (in the productions I have seen, it fills the entire stage). The shock of this image—purloined from the visual archive of white supremacy and racial terror—is intended to jolt the audience out of its overfamiliarity with melodramatic sensation and, as the Assistant says at the end of the scene, "to make you feel something."[25] But what, in this wild analysis, are you meant to feel? An image meant to circulate as a curiosity or as a token of white justice (Jacobs-Jenkins revisits the theme of lynching photographs held in white archives in his play *Appropriate*) is appropriated here to do reparative work: to restore the sense of a sensational scene that risks becoming routinized in the present. But, much as Minnie and Dido's ham-fisted humor scandalously restages the monstrous intimacy of enslaved flesh, the projection of the lynching photograph recirculates the social death of the black body as a potent emblem of slavery's afterlives. The very need for the photograph to be projected, in other words, the very necessity of resorting to it in order to get the audience to "feel something," underscores the degree to which the trauma of the racial past is perpetuated in the adaptation of *An Octoroon*. But if the slave past is in this sense incommensurable—if no photographic witness can do justice to it—does this place blackness on the outside of the representable world? Or is it possible to conceive of this photograph of blackness as always already present, always there at the heart of things? Before addressing this question, let me expand a little more on what my reading so far might suggest about the future of reparative reading.

REPARATIVE READING, SLAVE REPARATIONS, AND THE REENACTMENT OF RACIAL MELODRAMA

Reparation, in contemporary black studies and queer studies (not to mention their various intersections), holds a double significance it would be somewhat premature to collapse into one.[26] The most immediate meaning of the term refers to the ongoing quest for reparations for slavery, a cause which has most recently been championed by the writer Ta-Nehisi Coates, but which has a long political history, going back to the fabled "40 acres and a mule" promised the freedpeople by Union general William Tecumseh Sherman in 1865, at the end of the US Civil War. But reparation, as I have been discussing it here, also bears a complex lineage in the psychoanalytically inflected writings of queer of color critique, particularly in the work of theorists such as José Esteban

Muñoz, Joshua Chambers-Letson, and David Eng, who variously follow the work of Eve Kosofsky Sedgwick on "reparative reading." If the reparative position from which Sedgwick proposes her method of closely reading literary and other aesthetic forms is deeply informed by her original approach to the object relations school of psychoanalysis developed by Melanie Klein, the relational approach also offers a useful framework for approaching the restaging of historical racial trauma such as *An Octoroon* attempts.

A late essay by Muñoz encapsulates the state of critical debate around reparative reading in queer studies. "Race, Sex, and the Incommensurate: Gary Fisher with Eve Kosofsky Sedgwick" addresses itself to the editing and posthumous publication of the writings of Gary Fisher by his friend and former teacher, Eve Kosofsky Sedgwick (herself also the teacher of Muñoz).[27] Despite his self-positioning as a reparative reader of this relationship, Muñoz's approach is alert to negativity insofar as it refuses the possibility of sublating antiblack racism into a harmless, postracial fetishism. Rather, to dismiss the negative as superseded by social advances that now (allegedly) afford black and white to engage in a consequence-free race play with the dark materials of erotic dominance and submission, he develops a strand of thought that sees in the very possibility of such a socioerotic entanglement a source of the incommensurable. Implicit in his work is an artful dodge through the double bind of, on the one hand, a black subject rendered mute by the collective trauma of slavery, which no act of reparations can repair, and, on the other, a queer subject forever barred from full accession to the symbolic order and, therefore, the abject and killable obscene supplement of a *jouissance* that society denies itself. Muñoz's unwillingness to cede ground entirely to either of these positions, while refusing also to ignore the force of either, is what leads me to consider his mode of dark reparativity.

What is at stake here might go out under a simple choice between paranoid and reparative—or pessimistic and optimistic—positions. Such a choice would certainly fail to grapple with the account Muñoz provides of his reading of Fisher's intense prose, the shock of its racial abjection, and the abruptness of its awareness of being-toward-death. The sense of Fisher it ultimately conveys, Muñoz argues, is a sense understood by him as a difference held in common, a being singular plural.[28] Muñoz's turn to Jean-Luc Nancy in this essay is in the spirit of something like an affirmative negation. That is to say, he did not evoke being singular plural in order to assert a false equivalence between Sedgwick and Fisher or, for that matter, between himself and Fisher as queer of color subjects. But neither did he accept the strong paranoid reading of nonequivalence and incommensurability as equivalent to domination (in particular, he was concerned to detach BDSM erotics from a quick and dirty transcoding into the Hegelian Master–Slave dialectic). Here we might align his reading with Sharpe's reminder that "we cannot dismiss s/m as or reduce it to a 'white thing,' renounce interracial sex or desire as 'sleeping with the enemy,' nor can we reduce interracial s/m or a general desire to submit, to be the sadomasochist, to a simple repetition of the historical sadism of slavery."[29] Dark reparation unlocks other modes and durations of time and temporality than a helpless repetition of the racial contract of the American stage.

Dark reparativity, outlined in Muñoz's reading of Fisher, was never a denial of the incommensurate. When he aligned the reparative, by way of the philosophy of Nancy, with "the sharing (out) of an unshareable," this was no easy sophism.[30] If we cast our eyes to the ongoing predicament of interpretation offered up to us by the scene of racial abjection, as figured in the arresting prose and poetry of the writer Gary Fisher, we can both give greater focus to the aporetic challenge *An Octoroon* will identify and begin to test out the resources of the kind of reparative reading it will advocate. Insofar as Jacobs-Jenkins is sharing out an unshareable chattel slavery, all the furious transformations, reversals, and melodramatic stratagems of the play cannot rescue or redeem Minnie and Dido. As Saidiya Hartman argues in "Venus in Two Acts," the desire to invent a romance where none was present must give way to a "critical fabulation" that risks doing violence to the fabric of history itself. But if *An Octoroon* is such an Afro-fabulation, the question becomes to what degree does it extend the problematic of Boucicault's original drama, and what degree does it, can it, annul it?

An Octoroon is not, as is the case with Gary Fisher's writings, interested in the explicit homoerotic recounting of the BDSM dynamics of the afterlives of slavery. And yet, its contemporaneity as a (queer-authored) text can be read as attempting a parallel "therapeutic" working out of the sexual and racial traumas and terrors of slavery. When BJJ, the Playwright, and the (murdered) Pete gather on stage to show the audience the lynching photograph, they are not seeking to eroticize the awful image. But they are hoping to model a process of self-shattering akin to jouissance, which Frantz Fanon thinks of in explicitly photographic terms in *Black Skin, White Masks*. The emblem of the lynched body, I would suggest, is a fragment of "another me": a violent relatedness is posited between the contemporary living playwright, the murdered character, and the "red record" of lynching in America. If the Playwright stands in, in this equation, for the white perpetrator of antiblack violence, *An Octoroon* also implicates the audience as well, sitting uncomfortably in the dark, in the spectacular reproduction of black death.

Is there an image of Muñoz's "vaster commons" of the incommensurate in *An Octoroon*? Perhaps not in the script itself. But in performance, after the closing scene of Minnie and Dido's damnation, the cast appears on stage to sing "When You Burn It Down," a haunting little refrain (written by César Alvarez) that opens with these lines:

> *There's a monstrous story*
> *It's a gory allegory*
> *never mended*
> *Something's wrong, we never will get right*
> *Cause when you're down in the well, you can't see the light.*

As a closing apologia for "burning down" and rebuilding as monstrous a story as *The Octoroon*, "When You Burn It Down" works perfectly as a way of pointing to this incommensurability of past and present. Something is wrong that will never be gotten right by the play (a perfect picture will never do the work of photographic justice), but in precisely recognizing and endlessly reminding itself—in the play and the song that appears at the end of it—that something's wrong, something's missing, the play cannot but leave you with this sense of something more. The furious transformations of *An Octoroon* are, in the end, but another iteration of the changing same, begging the question of how to make an escape, there where there is no escape, and how to have fantasy in the hold.

Although the play opens with the figure of the "black playwright" ("Now I don't know exactly what that means, but I'm here to tell you a story") to the degree that we seek a definition of blackness or black theater in it, we would miss its point.[31] By disappearing into the costume of the (nonspeaking) Br'er Rabbit, Jacobs-Jenkins openly asserts the role of fabulist-trickster: the tall tale he tells is in order to effect his escape (from low-grade depression, from the prison-house of history, from the straitjacket of theatrical convention). He is not, as he reminds us, "deconstructing African folk tales" so much as reconstructing them. Or rather, he is improvising upon the necessity and impossibility of showing and proving theater's changing same. In the camera obscura of *The Octoroon*, the playwright stumbles. *An Octoroon* is the pieces put together "by another me."

1 Jacobs-Jenkins, *Octoroon*, 9.

2 Throughout this chapter, I observe the convention of the play itself in distinguishing between the character "BJJ" and the playwright Branden Jacobs-Jenkins.

3 I draw here on Peter Brooks's well known observation of "melodrama's constant recourse to acting out, to the body as the most important signifier of meanings." "Melodrama, Body, Revolution," 19.

4 On "wild" psychoanalysis, see Freud, *Wild Analysis*.

5 Jacobs-Jenkins, *Octoroon*, 10.

6 Charles Mills, *Racial Contract*.

7 Mills, *Racial Contract*, 52.

8 I draw here on Chinua Thelwell's excellent critique of *Hamilton* in "Who Tells Your Story?"

9 Here I risk being misunderstood as idealizing hip-hop and reality TV as more "authentically" black spaces than the contemporary theater. This is very much not the point. Rather, their anachronistic disruption of the story of the Octoroon serves a more disidentificatory purpose, to use Muñoz's crucial term. See Muñoz, *Disidentifications*.

10 Flatley, *Affective Mapping*.

11 Here I call attention to one ironic consequence of Jacobs-Jenkins's play: renewed critical attention and respect paid to the melodramatic innovations of the playwright, Dion Boucicault, that Jacobs-Jenkins travesties.

12 Compare, for instance, Alice Randall's parody of a well-known myth of the gallant south, *The Wind Done Gone*.

13 Hartman, *Scenes of Subjection*.

14 I am adapting and slightly betraying the sense of cryptonomy as developed in the work of Abraham and Torok, where it connotes less a spoken word than an unspoken word hidden by a welter of substitutes and synonyms. Indeed, the work of analysis is to "discover" the magic word and get the analysand to speak it. See *The Shell and the Kernel*, 17–18.

15 On *The Octoroon* as mortgage melodrama, see Roach, *Cities of the Dead*.

16 Here I adopt a Muñozian revival of the distinction from Ernst Bloch between the psychoanalytic "unconscious" and the more political "no-longer-conscious." See Muñoz, *Cruising Utopia*.

17 B. Herrera, "I Was a Teenaged Fabulist."

18 Jacobs-Jenkins, *Octoroon*, 49–50.

19 Sharpe, *Monstrous Intimacies*, 119.

20 By "freaky erotic undercommons" I mean to connect the work of Harney and Moten (*The Undercommons: Fugitive Planning and Black Study*) with Stallings's groundbreaking *Funk the Erotic*.

21 Jacobs-Jenkins, *Octoroon*, 69.

22 Wilderson, *Red, White and Black*.

23 Eng, "Colonial Object Relations," 1–19.

24 Jacobs-Jenkins, *Octoroon*, 59–60.

25 Jacobs-Jenkins, *Octoroon*, 64.

26 See Chambers-Letson, "Reparative Feminisms, Repairing Feminism."

27 Muñoz's essay is also a response to an essay on the same subject by Ellis Hanson, although the terms of the respectful exchange between the two queer critics has less of a bearing to my present purpose here. See Hanson, "The Future's Eve"; Muñoz, "Race, Sex, and the Incommensurate."

28 Nancy, *Being Singular Plural*.

29 Sharpe, *Monstrous Intimacies*, 119–20.

30 Muñoz, "Race, Sex, and the Incommensurate," 108.

31 Jacobs-Jenkins, *Octoroon*, 7.

Audra McDonald: Sorry, but where are we—literally? Are we ghosts?

George C. Wolfe: No, real people. We were here, and now we're back.

QUOTED IN JESSE GREEN, "THE ANXIETY AND THE ECSTASY"

The Performance and Politics of Concurrent Temporalities in George C. Wolfe's *Shuffle Along*

The above exchange took place during a rehearsal for director and librettist George C. Wolfe's 2016 backstage musical *Shuffle Along, or, The Making of the Musical Sensation of 1921 and All That Followed*. The much anticipated but surprisingly short-lived show starred a nearly all-black cast to tell the story of the landmark 1921 musical comedy *Shuffle Along*. As Langston Hughes described the Jazz Age hit, "*Shuffle Along* was a honey of a show. Swift, bright, funny, rollicking, and gay, with a dozen danceable, singable tunes."[1] The 1921 musical was created by four black vaudevillians and starred performers without major name recognition when, after an arduous road tour aimed at proving its appeal to white audiences, it arrived in a theater tangential to Times Square. Yet, it became a smash success, running for over a year, forming two touring companies, and inspiring Broadway's all-black revues of the 1920s.[2] Hughes famously credited *Shuffle Along* with kicking off the 1920s' Negro vogue, and the show fueled the careers of African American performance icons Josephine Baker, Florence Mills, and Paul Robeson.[3] Yet, mainstream Broadway performance historiography has largely forgotten *Shuffle Along*.

Through metacommentary on the original production and the biographical explication of its key players, Wolfe's *Shuffle Along . . . and All That Followed* aimed to reclaim the lost time of neglected history. It invited audiences to parse the historical record while taking in Jazz Age razzle dazzle. The production disrupted typical temporal relationships that assume a static past, educating audiences by activating the transporting energies of tap choreography, fostering intergenerational knowledge transmission among the cast, and addressing Broadway as a majoritarian institution. The show was an act of writing history in order to redress neglect, a way of celebrating and explaining the significance of the original *Shuffle Along* to the Broadway community, audiences and performers alike.

The 2016 reimagining/reinvention was propelled by the combustible energy of Savion Glover's tap choreography and featured Broadway's most lauded African American performers from three generations, including six-time Tony Award winner Audra McDonald. In the epigraph, McDonald presses Wolfe for dramaturgical spatiotemporal specificity in her effort to understand Wolfe's framing device of historical characters directly addressing the audience about their careers and, eventually, deaths. McDonald's inquiry highlights Wolfe's use of time as a dramaturgical tool. In his libretto, Wolfe's atemporal framing device contrasts with the otherwise linear narrative of *Shuffle Along* and the lives of its creators and performers. The different temporal logics of the frame and the main story create a metatemporal libretto that brings, as Brian Richardson defines dramatic metatemporality, "incompatible time schemes into collision."[4] This collision created tension for McDonald as a performer attempting to ground her process. In place of the spatiotemporal specificity McDonald sought, Wolfe's reply declared a reclamation of the Broadway stage via the return of "real people," revealing a transtemporal logic to the live performance in which the characters of the show exist across or through time by intermingling their historical moment with the immediacy of stage time.[5] This transtemporality occurs via the living presence of the actors. That is, McDonald and her fellow performers mediated temporal tension (or incompatibility, per Richardson) via their bodies as they spoke, sang, and tapped to syncopated rhythms. The "we" of Wolfe's response underscores the political imperative of reclaiming and reframing the popular commercial stage to manifest a mostly forgotten Jazz Age musical comedy created by an all-black creative team during the Jim Crow era.

The story of *Shuffle Along, or, The Making of the Musical Sensation of 1921 and All That Followed* is the story of time reclaimed and snatched back. Just as time was Wolfe and Glover's foundational dramaturgical and choreographic tool in the tap metamusical, timing was the over-determining factor in *Shuffle Along . . . and All That Followed* becoming a Broadway flop. Megaproducer Scott Rudin, who is white, closed the show three months after its official opening. Rather than acknowledging that *Shuffle Along . . . and All That Followed* won none of the ten Tony Awards for which it was nominated, Rudin blamed his decision on McDonald's perimenopausal pregnancy and her resultant leave of absence.[6] In doing so, Rudin situated McDonald's gestational temporality as binary to Broadway's capitalist temporal demands. While pregnancy requires waiting, Broadway requires the immediacy of strong weekly grosses and securing advance sales. While the show was about looking back in time and seeing unexamined value, Rudin's decision was about looking to the future and not seeing secure profit. The compressed calendar time of the pre– and post–Tony Awards season ultimately determined the musical's longevity. These gestational and capitalist calendar temporalities, which were external to the show itself, existed concurrently with the show's transtemporal performance mode, and compounded the complexities of *Shuffle Along . . . and All That Followed*'s relationship with time.

The conflict between the external and internal concurrent temporalities exhibited a power imbalance between black artists and white producers that negatively connected *Shuffle Along . . . and All That Followed* to the 1921 *Shuffle Along*. Despite the professional stature and Broadway celebrity status of Wolfe, Glover, McDonald, and many of her fellow cast members, the show's abrupt closing can be read as an example of Broadway's "racial time." Political theorist Michael Hanchard characterizes racial time as "the inequalities of temporality that result from power relations between racially dominant and subordinate groups. Unequal relationships . . . produce unequal temporal access to institutions, goods, services, resources, power, and knowledge, which members of both groups recognize."[7] Hanchard's formula invites scrutiny of how Broadway's temporal politics are shaped by economic power and race. One could argue that, in the commercial context of Broadway, the power of producers over the creative team, cast, and crew is consistent across races because it is always up to the producers to fund and continue a show, no matter the show. However, Broadway has a history of usurping control over the means of production for black musicals so that, for many American musicals that tell black stories, including *Show Boat*, *Porgy and Bess*, and *Dreamgirls*, the creative team behind the story was white. This dynamic put black performers in the position of *waiting for the time* when white creative teams were interested in producing a show with black characters. By resuscitating a musical by an all-black creative team, Wolfe, Glover, and the cast were actively dismantling Broadway's history of racial time, only to have it reassert itself.

Wolfe and Glover's 2016 metatheatrical musical became an inversion of the original by starting with star power but ending so much earlier than expected. Yet, as its external temporal pressures evince, it was susceptible to the same dominant power structures of the Jazz Age/Jim Crow era. During the summer of 2016, there was yet another concurrent temporality that connected *Shuffle Along . . . and All That Followed* to the original show's historical time period. The Tulsa Race Massacre and burning of "Black Wall Street" took place in Tulsa, Oklahoma, one week after *Shuffle Along* opened in 1921. The days of violence left three hundred black people dead and ten thousand homeless.[8] In the twenty-first century, vigilante and state violence against black Americans has not ended, only transformed into a post–civil rights era of digital documentation. With the July 2016 murders of Alton Sterling and Philando Castile, state and vigilante violence against black Americans dominated headlines and displayed the apparent intractability of local police acting as agents of state racism without consequences. The murders inspired several young *Shuffle Along . . . and All That Followed* cast and crew members to organize "Broadway for Black Lives Matter" (#BWAY4BLM). Emerging as an afterlife of the Broadway show, the event connected the triumphs of the original 1921 production to the 2016 show's active reclamation of history as politically salient performance.[9] The vulnerability of the cast to the decisions of white producers, and the continued vulnerability of black Americans to state violence, instigated a temporally recursive logic of capitalism and white supremacy. The transtemporal performance mode of the show itself, the compressed temporality of the Tony Awards season, and the #BWAY4BLM effort to disrupt the seemingly cyclical temporality of extrajudicial violence against black Americans represent three concurrent temporalities of performance and politics associated with *Shuffle Along . . . and All That Followed*. Delineating these concurrent temporalities reveals the cultural significance of the short-lived show, emphatically distinguishing it from the many other "failed" shows of Broadway and allowing us to see how time marks power on and beyond the Broadway stage.

George C. Wolfe's theatrical practice is often transtemporal; the then and the now sway, tap, and collapse into each other. His prominence in US theater has spanned decades, including writing and directing the play *The Colored Museum* (1986), serving as artistic director of the Public Theater, and directing works by Tony Kushner, Suzan-Lori Parks, and Anna Deavere Smith. Among his accomplishments are Wolfe's book and direction of *Jelly's Last Jam* (1992), in which tap virtuoso Gregory Hines starred as ragtime piano player Jelly Roll Morton facing death, and a very young Savion Glover played Morton's younger self. Wolfe and Glover again collaborated on *Bring in 'da Noise, Bring in 'da Funk* (1996). Billed as "a dance musical telling the story, through tap, of black history from slavery to the present,"[10] *Noise/Funk* was extremely successful and ran for nearly three years and over a thousand performances on Broadway. These collaborations uniquely anchor Wolfe and Glover's artistic vision in informing (Broadway) theater audiences about black American (performance) history via tap. Indeed, *Shuffle Along . . . and All That Followed* can be considered the third installment in their trilogy of tap pedagogy Broadway musicals.

For a reimagining of the original *Shuffle Along*, emphasizing tap was essential. As dance scholar Constance Valis Hill writes, "Jazz tap dancing was the driving engine of *Shuffle Along*, the source of its visual, visceral, and aural excitement that propelled the musical forward."[11] Wolfe and Savion Glover used tap's "propulsive" energies to interrogate power imbalances and teach the audience.[12] Describing the intense and intentional pedagogy of *Shuffle Along . . . and All That Followed*, Glover explains, "I don't think anyone has a choice to walk out of that theatre . . . not knowing something that they didn't come in with. There's so much information in the show, something we call 'edutainment.' It's not just about putting on a show."[13] This information was largely transmitted to the audience via direct address and dialogue. However, Act 2 of *Shuffle Along . . . and All That Followed* began with a music and dance lesson, informing the audience that the jazz score of the original *Shuffle Along* introduced syncopation to Broadway and that, with syncopation, "You dance *around the one!*" The tuxedo-clad chorus repeated the phrase "Around the one!" several times while demonstrating the vitality of syncopated tap as they incorporated maxifords, perididdles, draw backs, bombershays, and variations on the Charleston into the act's opening number.[14] This scene allowed the 2016 audience to appreciate how *Shuffle Along* changed Broadway dancing and influenced the Jazz Age with its syncopated rhythms. Crucially, tap marks time with aural theatricality unmatched in other dance forms, activating the inner ear as a center of both balance and sound.[15] Thus, the song mobilized the rhythmic sound vibrations of tap to reverberate knowledge.

SHUFFLE ALONG, 1921

The original *Shuffle Along* opened in New York City on May 23, 1921, after a series of out-of-town performances in Baltimore; Washington, DC; and across Pennsylvania. The show had a book by Flournoy E. Miller and Aubrey Lyles, who had been performing the vaudeville playlet, *The Mayor of Jimtown*, since 1909. Composer Eubie Blake and lyricist Noble Sissle transformed Miller and Lyles's vaudevillian plot into a revelatory opportunity for jazz dance and song. It was the first successful all-black musical to be produced in New York City since the groundbreaking comedy duo Bert Williams and George Walker staged *Bandanna Land* in 1908.[16] *Shuffle Along*'s book featured a secondary "blocked lovers" plot plopped within a farcical tale of a mayoral race among three men in Jimtown, a small southern town of black residents. In its manifestation of a modern, all-black municipality, *Shuffle Along* staged a temporary utopia with no dialogic references to larger structures of Jim Crow racism. The jokes lightly parodied topical issues such as Prohibition and suffrage. Comical situations and characters' foibles spurred the action. Miller played Steve Jenkins and Lyles played small and scrappy Sam Peck, a "henpecked" husband to a status-conscious suffragette.[17] Jenkins and Peck regularly dip into the till of the general store they run together and get caught in absurd scenarios of deception. In keeping with the tension between spectacle and narrative so common in vaudeville, the first scene of Act 2 culminates in a twenty-minute "comic ballet" boxing match between Miller and Lyles that showcased their physicality, timing, and the expert intimacy of performing together for over a decade.

Shuffle Along combined progressive and regressive elements. Early in Act 1, the romance between the third mayoral candidate, Harry Walton, and the ingénue Jessie Williams staged a revolutionary new form of physical intimacy for the popular stage: a kiss between a black couple in love (figure 2.1). Yet, Harry also sang the wistful "Sing Me to Sleep, Dear Mammy (With a Hush-a-Bye-Pickaninny Tune)" in a downstage area referred to as "Possum Lane."[18]

FIGURE 2.1 The ingénue, Jessie Williams (Lottie Gee), and her suitor, Harry Walton (Roger Matthews), made history as a romantic black couple in the 1921 production of *Shuffle Along*. Billy Rose Theatre Division, New York Public Library. "Scene (suitor and gentlemen chorus) stage production *Shuffle Along.*" COURTESY OF NEW YORK PUBLIC LIBRARY DIGITAL COLLECTIONS, HTTP://DIGITALCOLLECTIONS.NYPL.ORG/ITEMS/7B75EF40-B77E -0131-5AE5-58D385A7BBD01.

The "pick lullaby" was a subgenre of the "coon song" and perpetuated minstrelsy stereotypes of nurturing plantation mammies. *Shuffle Along*'s chorus, in particular, embodied the contradictions between the show's emergent and residual elements.[19] The dancers' physical exuberance was a formal innovation as the women "didn't just promenade like so, oh no! They stomped, shimmied, and shuffled like never before!"[20] The dancers' enthralling movement made them more than interchangeable decorative bodies, which was commonly how chorus members in white revues such as the Ziegfeld Follies were presented. At the same time, colorism was evident in the selection of chorus members, who ranged from very light to medium-toned brown complexions. Still, even the reality of colorism is not the whole picture. Performance historian and theorist Jayna Brown asserts that "it was the dancing chorus that articulated the new urban moment" represented by *Shuffle Along*, not only because of the women's jazz movement *on* stage, but because they brought vernacular dance from social gatherings and clubs to Broadway.[21] On stage and off, they "embodied the pleasurable mobilities of the modern age."[22] In addition, the landmark show led to many new opportunities for the chorus dancers to travel and perform throughout the 1920s and into the 1930s.

Theater historians agree *Shuffle Along* not only established a romance plot between two sympathetic and virtuous black characters but also introduced syncopated jazz to Broadway and partially desegregated audiences because the creative team insisted that a section of the orchestra be reserved for black customers who would otherwise be limited to the balcony.[23] However, in addition to some of the songs, the book also contained performance conventions derived from minstrelsy. Several male characters spoke in dialect, mispronounced words, and used malapropisms. For example, Onions, the grocery store porter, is a standard "shuffling darky" type who avoids work and engages in comic "eccentric dusting."[24] As the comic stars of the show, Miller and Lyles wore blackface makeup to play Steve Jenkins and Sam Peck. According to historian Allen Woll, the comedy duo performed in blackface because, early in their careers, they "discovered that jobs were easier to get if the theatre managers and the audiences assumed they were white men wearing burnt cork makeup. This early adaptation to the demands of the audience became their trademark . . . and they retained their comic masks throughout the 1920s."[25] In this, Miller and Lyles were similar to Bert Williams, who also wore blackface on the Broadway stage, while his partner George Walker did not. Both comedy duos negotiated the profound contradictions of asserting black subjectivity within a white supremacist and capitalist performance context (figure 2.2).[26]

For Wolfe the original *Shuffle Along* was a portal to prominent performers such as Florence Mills and Eubie Blake, as well as to little-known figures from African American performance history, such as the actress and singer Lottie Gee, who originated the role of the ingénue Jessie Williams. Wolfe has identified the dismaying yet productive space between the significance of the original production and its somewhat meager historical record: "I was just intrigued how something could go from being so significant to ending up as someone's footnote, and then that gap . . . seemed to me a musical."[27] It is not that *Shuffle Along* was utterly evacuated from the archive. For instance, Woll dedicates a chapter to the show in his 1989 book *Black Musical Theatre: From "Coontown" to "Dreamgirls."* The PBS miniseries *Broadway: The American Musical*, first broadcast in 2004, features Wolfe discussing the uptown/downtown

FIGURE 2.2 The African American comedy team Flournoy E. Miller (kneeling) and Aubrey Lyles (standing) wearing blackface makeup in the 1921 production of *Shuffle Along*. Billy Rose Theatre Division, New York Public Library. "Scene from the stage production *Shuffle Along*." COURTESY OF NEW YORK PUBLIC LIBRARY DIGITAL COLLECTIONS, HTTP:// DIGITALCOLLECTIONS.NYPL.ORG/ITEMS/FD8EADE0-7598-0131-A70A-58D385A7B928.

cultural exchange that *Shuffle Along* instigated. Nevertheless, the show and its creative team have not become a cultural reference point for musicals of the era such as Kern and Hammerstein's *Show Boat*. Nor has it become readily associated with the famous performers involved. When *Shuffle Along* was known to black Broadway performers, it represented a past to jettison.

Broadway star Billy Porter attended performing arts programs for high school and college during the 1980s and played Lyles in *Shuffle Along . . . and All That Followed*. He cites the songs of *Shuffle Along* as the clearest signal that the show triggered shame: "You know, to be truthfully honest with you, just from reading the song titles on the album cover, me and my black friends, in our naiveté, sort of rejected this show . . . songs like 'Pickaninny Shoes' and 'Bandana Land.' And we heard that there was blackface. And, you know, without context, without historical context to sort of look at it through that lens, we immediately rejected it."[28] In Porter's formulation Wolfe's call to reengage with and ultimately celebrate *Shuffle Along* fostered previously unavailable access to the fraught material. Porter describes *Shuffle Along . . . and All That Followed* as an emollient and an epiphany, calling the show "an amazing journey" that provided him the opportunity to comprehend the significance and complexities of the Jazz Age *Shuffle*. McDonald, who is close in age to Porter, described her own introduction to the material, "I was so intrigued . . . because I didn't know any of this history. And this history, you know, that's a direct line to me as a performer. And the fact that I knew nothing about it, immediately I was just like tell me more, tell me more, tell me more."[29]

Younger members of the cast, who were born in the late 1980s and early 1990s, were equally compelled to connect their personal trajectories to the original *Shuffle Along*. Yet, as with Porter, *Shuffle Along* triggered shame. However, it was a shame for *not* knowing about it. Cast member Adrienne Warren acknowledged, "I didn't know anything about it until I started talking to George about it. And *then* I felt horrible that *I* didn't know this history because it's *my* history, it's all our history."[30] Amber Iman admitted, "It was crazy how stupid we all felt."[31] The cast and creative team's urge to correct the historical record became an almost evangelical motivation for staging *Shuffle Along . . . and All That Followed*. As Iman observed, "That's why it felt so important and so heavy. Because of the amount of material we covered, because we felt like we were doing this for those whose shoulders we stood on. You know, you wanted to make them proud, you wanted to do it justice."[32] Being in the show was not only an opportunity to access an unfamiliar history of black performance. It was also a chance to work with illustrious performers who inspired their own career choices. For Iman, working with McDonald became a life-altering experience: "She's the Goddess. She's the queen of Broadway . . . for so many little brown girls she is the epitome of inspiration and goals. To get to work with her and to get to know her . . . I will never forget [it] in my life."[33] Thus, as much as *Shuffle Along . . . and All That Followed* was aimed at educating Broadway audiences, it also educated its cast, connecting many of them to a performance history that had seemed too far in the past to be accessible.

SHUFFLE ALONG, OR, THE MAKING OF THE MUSICAL SENSATION OF 1921 AND ALL THAT FOLLOWED

Shuffle Along, or, The Making of the Musical Sensation of 1921 and All That Followed opened April 28, 2016, and closed a few months later on July 24, logging one hundred performances after thirty-eight previews. The show intersperses Sissle and Blake's songs within a book that depicts *Shuffle Along*'s unlikely success and the post-*Shuffle* struggles of its creative team. Act 1 encompassed Sissle and Blake meeting Miller and Lyles, securing funding from a white producer, barely scraping by on the road, renovating an inadequate and dilapidated theater in New York City, and finally triumphing. Moving through time and geographical location, supertitles above the proscenium arch informed the audience when and where the action was taking place. Although almost none of the original *Shuffle Along* was staged, Wolfe closed the first act with the show's most recognized hit, "I'm Just Wild about Harry," on a set that replicated the original *Shuffle Along*'s southern setting. Act 2 followed the different trajectories of the creative team and the show's key performers, from the competitive battles that Miller and Lyles fought with Sissle and Blake to Aubrey Lyles's Garveyism and Lottie Gee's perpetual search for an opportunity as sensational as *Shuffle Along*. Returning to his atemporal framing device, a direct address coda from each major character explained their basic biography until the year of their deaths.

Wolfe worked with the original *Shuffle Along* to establish boundaries around the Jazz Age modes of representation the contemporary production would bring to the stage. To emphasize the innovation of the original, Wolfe included the musically innovative numbers from *Shuffle Along* and skipped the minstrelsy-style songs. The operetta ballad "Love Will Find a Way" comes early in the first act of the 1921 show and was sung by the young lovers, Harry Walton and Jessie Williams, that established *Shuffle Along*'s most remarkable plot and character innovation. Setting the scene at the Colonial Theatre in

Baltimore, Wolfe staged the debut of "Love Will Find a Way" as prefaced by a heated debate among *Shuffle Along*'s creative team and cast members about the immediate physical danger of presenting a sincere "love song between a colored man and woman" during the 1920s.[34] Miller, played by Brian Stokes Mitchell, served as a grounding force throughout the production. During the debate, he noted, "As you all know, there's tons of songs celebrating our love of watermelon, Virginny, Dixie, but none celebrating our love of each other."[35] After relaying historical occurrences of mob violence against black performers, Miss Mattie Wilks, played by Amber Iman, observed, "Anything that makes us hopeful and heartfelt instead of beastly and buffoonish is forbidden."[36]

As Lottie Gee playing the role of Jessie Williams, McDonald conveyed deep apprehension about the song. Brandon Victor Dixon was cast as Eubie Blake. As a native of Baltimore, Blake suggested to his collaborators that they wait for New York to include the song. The dangers of the innovation were not only due to the lyric's romantic sentiments, but to the radical decision that the romantic characters would kiss. Physical intimacy was an affront to white audiences' expectations for black characters. As the critic Lester A. Walton put it, when it came to black characters, audiences "thought they have no business being ardent lovers."[37] Wolfe gave the decision of whether to include the song to Miller, who proclaimed, "History is calling! The song goes in tonight!"[38]

Wolfe offered multiple frames for the audience's reception of "Love Will Find a Way." The audience watched *Shuffle Along*'s creative team watching from the wings, thus emphasizing the anxiety of the historical moment. Not only did the audience watch them watching, but other cast members narrated every move McDonald as Lottie Gee as Jessie Williams made: "She's reaching out! She's . . . touching his hand! He's touching hers."[39] Another character noted with glad surprise, "The audience, they're listening!" Wolfe's frames triangulate the event. The audience heard the romantic ballad but saw a comic counterpoint in Lottie Gee and her scene partner's wary expressions as they keep an active lookout for as escape route even as they perform smitten dedication. Simultaneously, the anxiety of the stage-right characters dissecting the scene moment by moment located the high-stakes reality of the original. Through dialogue and staging, Wolfe and the performers created a transtemporal interrogation of the song and its embodied performance. Rather than simply a triumphant affirmation of black Americans' right to romantic love, the scene is transformed by the weight of historic, symbolic, and actual violence, forcing audiences to grapple with that reality in tandem with the pleasure and immediacy of McDonald's vocal range and comic capabilities.

In addition to "Sing Me to Sleep, Dear Mammy (With a Hush-a-Bye-Pickaninny Tune)," Wolfe omitted "Pickaninny Shoes." The omission of the songs is significant because of their connection to the contemporary production's scenic design by Santo Loquasto. In an apparent visual reference to the grocery store set of the original *Shuffle Along*, Loquasto dotted the walls of Sissle and Blake's imagined rehearsal room with faded print advertisements for soap. In doing so, he activated the ghosts of commercial representation of blackness. Late Victorian and early twentieth-century soap advertisements celebrated whiteness as a hygienic ideal and often objectified black children as dirty creatures verging on the inhuman.[40] Among the rehearsal room ads, the Fairbank Company's iconic Gold Dust Twins appeared. As a proprietor of lard and then soap, the Fairbank Company depicted pickaninnies to sell its popular Fairy Soap and Gold Dust Washing Powder. Fairbank's Gold Dust Twins were black imps, nude from the waist up, who cavorted while they cleaned. Advertising copy invited consumers to "Let the Gold Dust Twins Do Your Work" and asked beleaguered women, "Are you a slave to housework? Gold Dust has done more than anything else to emancipate women from the back-breaking burdens of the household."[41] In that case, the history of chattel slavery translated to ad copy humor directed at white women. In 1921, of course, slavery was not a distant legacy but a firm memory for many black Americans.

The rehearsal room was important for Wolfe's staging of other *Shuffle Along* numbers including "I'm Just Simply Full of Jazz" and "Honeysuckle Time," which Wolfe intertwined with the initial flirtation between Lottie Gee and Eubie Blake. Gee let down her guard and learned her moves, Blake tickled out a new tune, and they were surrounded by the specter of casual consumption of dehumanized, commodified blackness. Painted as faded rectangles that blur into the temporary architecture of the rehearsal room walls, the historically significant advertisements may very well have gone unnoticed (or unseen for those in the balcony) by the majority of audience members. Yet, they were an important example of the many instances of historical knowledge layered into the live moment of performance in Wolfe's musical. By locating the advertisements in the rehearsal room, the scenic design emphasized the ways identity is rehearsed in interior architectural space for an external presentation, as well as the way racist ideologies were rehearsed and performed through the consumption of consumer goods. In a contemporary moment framed by history, McDonald and Dixon perform Gee and Blake's human connection within this context of commodification.

The rehearsal scene's representation of commodification took place in the inherently commercial context of Broadway. As David Savran notes, "the musical is first and foremost a product of the marketplace in which the aesthetic is always—and unpredictably—overdetermined by economic relations and interests."[42] Broadway audiences have household incomes far above the national average and are 75 percent white.[43] That makes its audiences whiter than the demographics of the nation and much whiter than the population of New York City. While Broadway audiences are technically a minority in that their wealth and whiteness represent a small percentage of the nation's demographics, they are majoritarian in how their purchasing power determines what succeeds on the Great White Way.

Shuffle Along . . . and All That Followed addressed the overdetermining structure of the original *Shuffle Along*'s need to please white audiences in order to be a financial hit while actively referring to the contemporary audience demographics. Wolfe extended the past into the present, utilizing the words and gesture of a white character to point out that his show also depended on a white audience to fill the seats of the Music Box Theatre. *Shuffle Along . . . and All That Followed* implicated the contemporary audience's connection with the 1920s performance context via a light tone. A telegram tap-danced and spoken by Sam, the white liaison between *Shuffle Along*'s creative team and white producer John Cort, notes: "Hearing great things about *Shuffle*. STOP. Now to see how the show plays in front of all audiences, i.e. . . ." After uttering "i.e.," Sam Ashmanskas, who played the character Sam, gestured to the house and knowing laughter rippled through the audience. The fact of the 1921 majority white audience did not need to be named because the 2016 audience, myself included, provided the same information with our bodies in our seats. Although this transtemporal collapsing had a real politics to it, the moment went over easily.

Later in the show, Wolfe induced audience wincing by addressing the fact that celebrating black talent can be very much in line with white supremacy. The thirteen-member chorus dramatized the original *Shuffle Along*'s three-week tour through Pennsylvania in choreography that echoed the rhythms of the railroad in a piece *New York Times* critic-at-large Wesley Morris described as having "the most erotic, insane, violent, crazy energy."[44] As the dancers travel their "graveyard tour" of Pennsylvania, the president of the railway, as a huge fan of *Shuffle Along*, offered the cast and crew their own private car. He exclaimed, "I say, I've seen a nigger show or two before in my day, but this one's one of the best!" Miller and Lyles process the politics of accepting such an offer (Lyles notes the private car "wasn't free" to which Miller responds, "Nothing is"). In this moment, Wolfe was careful not to implicate the contemporary audience, relegating a spoken racial slur to a fleeting caricature of ignorant whiteness and containing it as one of many moral compromises the production faced on the road.

While the notion of an all-purpose white antagonist might seem facile, Ashmanskas's multiple roles point to the consistent and unyielding structures of white dominance that *Shuffle Along* faced. In addition, whereas the lack of white characters in previous works by Wolfe, such as *Noise/Funk*, can arguably make the behavior of the black characters read as individual pathologies,[45] playing a producer, train engineer, and journalist, Ashmanskas's multiple permutations of racism and menace forced the audience to have several confrontations with whiteness. Wolfe returned to the specter of the majority white audience with a haunting by the controversial white Harlem Renaissance enthusiast Carl Van Vechten. He appeared as a character in Act 2 and seemed to curse the creative team with the condemnation "They won't remember you!" As *Shuffle Along . . . and All That Followed* got closer to its closing date, this scene took on an increasingly grotesque quality that collapsed past into present in a mode quite opposite Wolfe's recuperative transtemporal strategy.

GESTATIONAL TEMPORALITY AND CAPITALIST CALENDAR TEMPORALITY

For a show that took up temporality as a dramatic material with which to work, *Shuffle Along . . . and All That Followed* experienced a harsh and immediate temporal pivot due to the 2016 Tony Awards. The awards have a major impact on the financial stability and longevity of shows on Broadway, as research shows that, not surprisingly, "winning nominations have a stronger effect than losing nominations" on post-awards success.[46] Therefore, the timeframe from the weeks just before nominations (announced in May) to the evening of the awards in June exists in a compressed capitalist temporality during which information and maneuvering for beneficial positions occurs at an accelerated pace. In late April 2016, producer Scott Rudin argued that *Shuffle Along . . . and All That Followed* should be categorized as a revival rather than a new musical because the songs were by Sissle and Blake. However, citing Wolfe's new book, the Tony Awards committee ruled that the show was a new musical and would therefore be in the same Best New Musical category as the phenomenally famous hip-hop musical *Hamilton*, which received a record-breaking sixteen nominations.

Each day seemed to bring an update in the midst of the high-stakes Tony Awards season. On May 10 McDonald announced her surprise pregnancy via a tweet that read: "Who knew that tap dancing during perimenopause could lead to pregnancy?"[47] Interestingly, McDonald chose to foreground her stage of life cycle. At age forty-five, she was ten years older than what obstetricians consider "advanced maternal age." The surprise was twofold. There was the surprise that it had happened when it did, as well as that the pregnancy had happened at all. The news caused scheduling changes, including a delay in McDonald's engagement in London, for which she had already planned to temporarily leave *Shuffle Along . . . and All That Followed*. However, the switch kept McDonald in the show for a longer period of time in the short term, which benefited the show. Although the performers' union Actors' Equity Association has no parental leave policy, McDonald was able to arrange for a leave from the show because of the power of her fame and name recognition. She continued to deliver her characterization of Lottie Gee with piquant humor, growing belly and all, and audiences knew she would temporarily leave the show in late July.

The cast of *Shuffle Along . . . and All That Followed* performed on the Tony Award broadcast, including McDonald in a royal blue velvet dress kicking high while pregnant. However, the show did not take home any awards. Less than two weeks later came the surprise news that the show would close in one month. Despite the fact that the show had been grossing over $900,000 a week to houses filled to 99 percent capacity or higher, the producers decided to shutter the $12-million production, presumably because advance sales were low for the dates after McDonald's departure, even though there were plans to create a feature dance with Glover and replace McDonald with Grammy-winner Rhiannon Giddens. Iman describes the shock of the one-month timeframe: "I was standing next to my friend Christian and I remember distinctly grabbing his arm and I don't know if I held my breath or I didn't have any breath in my body but it was like 'what is going on here?'"[48] The announcement intensified the urgency of the cast and crew's pedagogical mission as they realized, "we have this important story to tell and a limited amount of time in which to do it."[49]

Megaproducer Scott Rudin used McDonald's star status to substantiate his claim that her pregnancy necessitated the show's closing. His press release stated, "Audra McDonald is the biggest star on Broadway, and audiences have been clamoring to see her in this role since the first preview of *Shuffle Along* in March of this year. . . . It has, however, become clear that the need for Audra to take a prolonged and unexpected hiatus from the show has determined the unfortunate inevitability of our running at a loss for significantly longer than the show can responsibly absorb."[50] Rudin's scapegoating of McDonald's pregnancy framed two temporalities as existing in utter opposition: that of gestation versus investment recuperation. Rudin's rhetorical move underscores how the calendar capitalism of Broadway's temporal regime regulates *all* performers, but particularly women who might or do become pregnant. As the sociologist Barbara Adam notes, "birthing, feeding and caring—all key features of maternal times—have to be given whatever amount of time they need. Such times, therefore, are constituted outside the commodified, rationalized clock time of employment relations."[51] Because of this opposition, Rudin was able to present McDonald's pregnancy as impossible to work around. His binary temporal thesis neglected to mention the costs of bankrolling a show with a twenty-four-member chorus and top industry talent, the challenge of recuperating producers' investments with the Music Box Theatre's comparatively small number of seats, and the fact that the show won none of its ten Tony Award nominations.

The debate over whether McDonald's pregnancy actually prompted the closing depends on whether one views *Shuffle Along . . . and All That Followed* as a star vehicle for McDonald or an ensemble piece. On the one hand, it is difficult to argue that anything with McDonald in it is *not* a star vehicle since many consider the six-time Tony winner to be "Broadway's greatest star singer, possibly ever."[52] On the other hand, it is perhaps equally difficult to argue that a show with Mitchell, Porter, Dixon, and Joshua Henry is fundamentally dependent on another performer. Although it seems clear that McDonald's temporary leave was consequential, it was not the only factor. As I have argued elsewhere:

> The protrusion of pregnancy on the professional stage makes it an easy target but imagine a scenario where the density of factors that lead a show to close were honestly accounted for. What if the press release said, "Unfortunately, this is a hugely expensive show to run. It has a lot of stars and a large chorus and the staging is complex. It didn't win the awards we hoped it would win. The producers are nervous about advance sales." Imagine a world where a host of complex capitalist decisions didn't come down on one woman's body.[53]

Rudin further negotiated McDonald's womb as a capitalist territory by suing the show's insurer, Lloyd's of London, for not recouping the show's losses, contending McDonald's pregnancy caused her to "abandon" the show due to the "accident" of perimenopausal conception.[54] Lloyd's investigated McDonald and accused her of knowing about her pregnancy in February, before the policy was written in March.[55] Thus, their application of exacting calendar time to McDonald's gestational temporality was deployed as a capitalist strategy to recoup losses. Rudin's abrupt decision suggested a devastating circular temporality to the show in which Wolfe and Glover's affirming and energizing transtemporal musical wound up restaging the power dynamics of a century past.

BROADWAY FOR BLACK LIVES MATTER

> You hear people blasting "What's Going On" by Marvin Gaye and it's 20-whatever year that was.... At the moment I was like, "What year is it that I'm walking through the streets and it feels like this?"
>
> AMBER IMAN

A third concurrent temporality is crucial to understanding the temporal politics of *Shuffle Along . . . and All That Followed*. This section's epigraph comes from an April 2017 interview I conducted with cast member Amber Iman. She describes the bewildering temporal suspension that seemed to envelop Harlem on July 13, 2013, when it was announced that George Zimmerman was acquitted of all charges for shooting seventeen-year-old Trayvon Martin the previous year in Sanford, Florida. In Iman's perception of time, a day in the second decade of the new millennium conjured the atmosphere and aurality of civil rights–era strife. Not only did Iman question the verdict's place in calendar time but, in her recollection, the specific year of the Zimmerman verdict escaped her because of the annual, monthly, or even daily distress of racist violence. That is, collective trauma collapsed forty years and befogged four years. Iman experienced asphyxia and psychological paralysis: "I felt like the breath got taken from me, my chest was incredibly tight and it was this feeling of powerlessness, complete powerlessness. I felt 'I am black in America and I can do absolutely nothing about what's happening and we're all walking around with targets on our backs.'"[56] With Iman's acute sense of vulnerability, the verdict also provoked temporal consternation regarding black Americans' future. Iman saw "people walk around hopeless and confused and lost and dazed and wondering, 'what happens next?'"[57]

Trayvon Martin's murder and Zimmerman's acquittal are frequently identified as the instigating traumas provoking the social justice movement #BlackLivesMatter. In her book *From #BlackLivesMatter to Black Liberation*, African American studies scholar Keeanga-Yamahtta Taylor charts the United States' "culture of racism" through different historical eras, tying the nation's contemporary crisis of antiblack violence directly to the failed promise of the end of the Civil War. Focusing on the 2015 death of Freddie Gray in Baltimore, Maryland, Taylor observes that 150 years has not managed to deliver citizenship in the form of legal justice and physical autonomy to black Americans: "The distance from the end of the Civil War, with the birth of Black citizenship and civil rights, to the state-sanctioned beating and torture of Freddie Gray constitutes *the gap* between formal equality before the law and the self-determination and self-possession inherent in actual freedom—the right to be free from oppression, the right to make determinations about your life free from duress, coercion, or threat of harm."[58] Here we see racial time once again being expressed in spatial terms: gaps in justice, gaps in theater archives, gaps in collective memories.

From 2014 to 2016, consecutive summers were indelibly marked by national headlines about antiblack violence as digital cell phone footage of murders circulated and news coverage proliferated.[59] For three years, Iman's activist urge incubated as her career accelerated, stalled, and accelerated again when she was cast in *Shuffle Along . . . and All That Followed*. In early July 2016, less than two weeks after the show's closing announcement, Alton Sterling and Philando Castile were killed by police officers in Louisiana and Minnesota, respectively. Castile's girlfriend, Diamond Reynolds, utilized Facebook Live to show the world what was happening in that moment. This included Officer Jeronimo Yanez swearing with his gun drawn, Castile bleeding out, and Reynolds's measured response to Yanez's directives while giving the plaintive commentary, "Oh my God, please don't tell me he's dead. Please don't tell me my boyfriend just went like that."[60] Footage of Castile's death, Reynolds's real-time response, and the knowledge that Reynolds was arrested and her four-year-old daughter witnessed everything, spurred national despondence and fresh rage at the familiarity of escalating police violence leading to a black civilian's murder. The names Philando Castile and Alton Sterling replaced the names Sandra Bland and Samuel DuBose from summer 2015, replacing the names Eric Garner and Michael Brown from summer 2014. A feeling of perpetual crisis pervaded, a feeling that the nation was caught in a temporal loop, replaying scene after scene of extrajudicial antiblack violence.

In the aftermath of Castile's and Sterling's murders, Iman found being part of the black cast of *Shuffle Along . . . and All That Followed* to be personally and politically transformative: "To work on a show like *Shuffle Along* and be surrounded by veterans, an older generation of folks. . . . We sat at their feet and asked them what to do. I remember distinctly sitting in Billy Porter's dressing room and he just shaking his head and looking at me and me shaking my head . . . trying to figure out what to do."[61] This intergenerational reciprocity was comforting and motivating. Iman converted her feeling of powerlessness into action. She used social media to mobilize, posting a call on Facebook for fellow performers to somehow address the crisis of violence against black Americans by asking "Where is Broadway for Black Lives Matter?"[62] In tandem with intergenerational connection and political crisis, Iman identifies a temporally situated personal motivation for her turn to activism in the summer of 2016: "I think I spent maybe the last ten or so years of my life being obsessed with working. 'What show am I going to be in and how am I going to pay my bills?' The older I got—as if I'm fifty!—but the older I got I was like, 'Is this it? Like, is this all my life is going to be? Just waiting for the next script, waiting for the next show?' And I wanted to find a way to kind of take control of my life. And I just started looking for a purpose, a real purpose in my life."[63] The political context intertwined with Iman's own lifecycle and the process of maturing from a young, struggling performer to a sense of self that included connecting with and acting beyond the immediacy of professional theater demands.

From Iman's initial expression of frustration came a collective push to organize a free concert and conversation event. Broadway for Black Lives Matter took place August 1, 2016, at Columbia University in New York City, one week after the closing of *Shuffle Along . . . and All That Followed*. The night included an astounding array of activists and performers sharing perspectives, suggesting strategies for social justice, and creating community. Audra McDonald and Brian Stokes Mitchell took the podium at the beginning of the evening, explaining the direct connection between the original *Shuffle Along*, *Shuffle Along . . . and All That Followed* and Black Lives Matter:

> This evening is a result of activism—of a desire to do something. For the past many months, we have been involved in a show called *Shuffle Along*. A group of African-American artists in 1921 got together and created something that was bigger than the sum of its parts, a show that changed Broadway

and the world, by being one of the forces that paved the way for the Harlem Renaissance, and while we were doing this show, we were witness to the many disturbing acts that were happening in our present-day world. Acts that have continued to demonstrate the need and amplify the voice of the Black Lives Matter movement.[64]

McDonald and Mitchell connected the original *Shuffle Along* to its Jazz Age era and named the show's culturally transformative impact, identifying that transformation as part of the motivation for the *Shuffle Along . . . and All That Followed* cast and crew members organizing Broadway for Black Lives Matter. Connecting the original show to contemporary activism was significant because the original *Shuffle Along* was long remembered, if it was remembered at all, as a jazzy dance comedy that retained too many remnants of minstrelsy to be something to celebrate. Iman and her colleagues' work can be seen as part of the "third-wave women of color feminist-scholars' and artists' signature practice of recuperation and restoration" that Soyica Colbert, Douglas A. Jones Jr., and Shane Vogel use to describe the site-specific work of conceptual artist Simone Leigh. As an event that both comforted and coalesced, Broadway for Black Lives Matter was that very "mending—of what has been forgotten, overlooked, misremembered, suppressed, or denied" of which Colbert, Jones, and Vogel write. It was "time as a manner of attention."[65]

BROADWAY ADVOCACY COALITION

The response to Broadway for Black Lives Matter showed Iman and her colleagues that, as artists, there was a place for them in activism but they "needed to figure out how to use [their] voices."[66] After such a stirring and successful evening, the organizers were faced with the question of futurity. As swing performer Britton Smith notes, "We felt like it was time to solidify what was next."[67] The group of six organizers, all black and all millennials, asked themselves how they could go forward in time and build on the evening's profound energy and enthusiasm. They asked themselves, their peers, and fellow artists what they saw as missing in their communities, neighborhoods, and society.

In response, Iman and her co-organizers decided to shift from a social justice platform to an emphasis on community engagement. To signal this more expansive approach, Broadway for Black Lives Matter transformed into the Broadway Advocacy Coalition (BAC), originally taking up the idea of connecting artistry and activism into #artivism. Iman notes that the decision to change the name was based on emphasizing inclusivity, as they discovered that Black Lives Matter was seen by some as exclusionary.[68] Although this could be interpreted as a step back from a decisive political agenda, it was also a self-protective move in that, as Iman puts it, "we didn't want to have to spend most of our time making other people feel comfortable."[69] The BAC tried to initiate the Invitation, "a monthly event series blending performances and discussions rooted in history, advocacy, and policy to build fundamental change."[70] For instance, the April 2017 gathering addressed "incarceration and the social justice system—how people directly affected by the criminal legal system collaborate to decarcerate prisons and rebuild communities."[71] The BAC is an ambiguous afterlife of both *Shuffle Along . . . and All That Followed* and the Broadway for Black Lives Matter event. The group's effort to balance digital connectivity and event-driven social justice work was difficult to sustain due to the geographical dispersion and diverse professional commitments of the organizers. Its timeline of events has been sporadic and, in its most recent transformation, race and social justice are not overt topics. As of fall 2018, the BAC works with the mission of "Building the capacity of advocates, students, artists, organizations and communities to use the arts as an integral part of their social change work. We believe that placing Artistry at the center of solving today's most pressing issues will create a new type of dialogue and impact."[72] With slated classes for artist engagement at Columbia University, the BAC's life and afterlife are uncharted. Broadway for Black Lives Matter and the BAC can be viewed as an intergenerational response among black performers that extends the transtemporal modes of *Shuffle Along . . . and All That Followed* in continuing the pedagogical motivations of the short-lived but significant show, prompting audiences to think about how much has and has not changed in nearly one hundred years of political and performance history.

Shuffle Along should not be forgotten twice. George C. Wolfe and Savion Glover's *Shuffle Along, or, The Making of the Musical Sensation of 1921 and All That Followed* deployed a transtemporal mode of performance that used tap pedagogy to educate cast members and audiences about a landmark production little known to those outside of scholars who study the Harlem Renaissance and/or musical theater history, staging the professional success and personal costs of working within Broadway's racial time, that is, the racist and exploitive majoritarian structures of commercial Broadway and Jim Crow. Foregrounding the concurrent temporalities concentrically circling Wolfe's work opens it to an expansive analysis, emphatically showing that *Shuffle*

Along... and All That Followed cannot be considered just another Broadway failure. In fact, its brief run compounded the contemporary show's temporal connections with the original as it came to increasingly comment on contemporary economic and racial dynamics within and beyond the show itself.

NOTES

I thank the editors and anonymous reviewers for their valuable suggestions and am grateful to Elizabeth L. Wollman, Nicole Lee, Joanna Dee Das, and Kevin James Burke for reading chapter drafts and offering encouragement. Emily Clark provided crucial expertise on tap dancing. I dedicate this chapter to Xavier and Tariq Drayton, survivors and thrivers.

1   L. Hughes, *Big Sea*, 223.
2   See chapters 5–7 in Woll, *Black Musical Theatre*.
3   Woll, *Black Musical Theatre*, 60.
4   Richardson, "'Time Is Out of Joint,'" 308. Richardson tracks four types of "analytical foci": story time, text time, stage time, and the metatemporal.
5   Walsh describes the significance of the actor's body in history plays: "It is the animated body of the player who represents an absent being; in history plays, this means the actor who is a present-tense, living and breathing stand-in for a missing historical personage." See Walsh, "Theatrical Temporality," 66.
6   See C. Young, "Don't Blame Pregnancy."
7   Hanchard, "Afro-Modernity," 253.
8   Krasner connects the significance of the Tulsa Race Massacre to *Shuffle Along*. See Krasner, *A Beautiful Pageant*, 242–43. This long-neglected part of the nation's history has recently received increased attention. See D. Brown, "They Was Killing Black People," and D. Brown, "Olivia Hooker."
9   See Hartman on afterlife not being "an antiquarian obsession with bygone days or the burden of a too-long memory, but because black lives are still imperiled and devalued by a racial calculus and a political arithmetic that were entrenched centuries ago." Hartman, *Lose Your Mother*, 6. Also discussed in the introduction to this volume.
10 "Bring in 'da Noise, Bring in 'da Funk."
11 Hill, *Tap Dancing America*, 70.
12 Hill also describes the dancing of *Shuffle Along* as "the aural and corporal synergy of black rhythm, more swift, subtle, and propulsive than what had previously been heard." Hill, *Tap Dancing America*, 70.
13 "Remixing *Shuffle Along*."
14 Specific steps identified by Emily Clark, email correspondence.

15 Tap historian Brian Seibert refers to "the kinesthetics of hearing: the way that hearing is a kind of touch, blasts of air knocking against the eardrum." See Seibert, *What the Eye Hears*, 5.

16 Krasner, *Resistance, Parody, and Double Consciousness*, 151.

17 Krasner, *A Beautiful Pageant*, 249.

18 Miller et al., *Shuffle Along* libretto, 44.

19 R. Williams, *Marxism and Literature*, 121–27.

20 *Shuffle Along . . . and All That Followed*, performance.

21 J. Brown, *Babylon Girls*, 198.

22 J. Brown, *Babylon Girls*, 190.

23 See Woll, *Black Musical Theatre*, and Krasner, *A Beautiful Pageant*.

24 Miller, et al., *Shuffle Along* libretto, 22.

25 Woll, *Black Musical Theatre*, 60.

26 For analysis of how Williams and Walker negotiated the complexities of presenting their comedy on commercial Broadway and appealing to white audiences, see D. Brooks, *Bodies in Dissent*, and Krasner, *Resistance, Parody, and Double Consciousness*.

27 "Audra McDonald and George C. Wolfe Interview."

28 "Remixing *Shuffle Along*." The *Shuffle Along* song is titled "Bandana Days."

29 "Remixing *Shuffle Along*."

30 "*Shuffle Along*," *Theater Talk*.

31 Iman, interview.

32 Iman, interview.

33 Iman, interview.

34 *Shuffle Along . . . and All That Followed*, performance.

35 *Shuffle Along . . . and All That Followed*, performance.

36 *Shuffle Along . . . and All That Followed*, performance.

37 Lester A. Walton, "'Shuffle Along' Latest Musical Gem to Invade Broadway," *New York Age*, June 4, 1921, quoted in Krasner, *A Beautiful Pageant*, 253.

38 *Shuffle Along . . . and All That Followed*, performance.

39 *Shuffle Along . . . and All That Followed*, performance.

40 See McClintock, *Imperial Leather*, and Amato, "The White Elephant in London."

41 Undated advertisement.

42 Savran, "Toward a Historiography," 213.

43 "One quarter of all tickets were purchased by non-Caucasian theatregoers. Of theatregoers age 25 or older, 81% had completed college and 41% had earned a graduate degree. The average annual household income of the Broadway theatregoer was $222,120." *Demographics of the Broadway Audience*.

44 "Audra McDonald and George C. Wolfe Interview."

45 For instance, Terry-Morgan critiques the "Street Corner Symphony" in *Noise/Funk*: "'Street Corner Symphony' tells the downside of the story, but does not

reveal the beauty making and durability of these Black folks, as it did in act one. Against drug infestation, municipal neglect, White gentrification, and economic strangulation, Black Harlemites are still fighting the Great Battle. The cosmic power of 'Da Beat needs to be reinforced in this section so that the audience is not left thinking these Black folks are solely responsible for their demoralized condition." Terry-Morgan, "Noise/Funk," 683.

46 Kulmatitskiy et al., "Survival of Broadway Shows," 123.

47 McDonald, Twitter post.

48 Iman, interview.

49 Iman, interview.

50 "*Shuffle Along* Sets Sudden Broadway Closing."

51 Adam, *Timewatch*, 95.

52 Green, "Anxiety and Ecstasy."

53 C. Young, "Don't Blame Pregnancy."

54 Hershberg, "Audra McDonald Stars in New Law Suit."

55 Hershberg, "New Claims in Audra McDonald Case."

56 Iman, interview.

57 Iman, interview.

58 Taylor, *From #BlackLivesMatter*, 192. Emphasis mine.

59 State and vigilante violence certainly happens at any time of year and many high-profile cases have not happened in the summer. My point is that during the summers 2013–2016, antiblack violence became consistent topics of national conversation and crisis. In particular, August 2014 saw a month of clashes between protesters and the Ferguson, Missouri, police after Officer Darren Wilson shot eighteen-year-old Michael Brown and Brown's body was left in the street for hours on August 9. For more on the meaning and impact of the unrest in Ferguson, see Taylor, *From #BlackLivesMatter*.

60 Reynolds, Facebook Live Video.

61 Iman, interview.

62 "How Amber Iman Created Broadway for Black Lives Matter."

63 "How Amber Iman Created Broadway for Black Lives Matter."

64 Gioia, "Why Black Lives Matter."

65 See the introduction to this volume.

66 Iman, interview.

67 Broadway Advocacy Coalition. In 2020, the BAC updated its mission and staff; many of the founding members remain on the board of directors and board of advisors.

68 Iman, interview.

69 Iman, interview.

70 Broadway Advocacy Coalition.

71 Broadway Advocacy Coalition.

72 Broadway Advocacy Coalition.

A Sonic Treatise of Futurity

Universes' Party People

With its signature Afro-diasporic musical aesthetic, the New York–based poetic theater ensemble Universes produces a theatrical experience that is first and foremost auditory. Recurring sound-making strategies such as a cappella harmonies, salsa riffs, rapping, hand clapping, fist slapping, stepping, beatboxing, scratching effects, and looping techniques surface across Universes' body of work and its performers' bodies. In *Party People* (2016), the ensemble deploys a rhythmic matrix of vocals inflected with hip-hop, gospel, and blues to stage the history of two of the most radical organizations of color that have remained in the periphery of America's cultural history—that of the Black Panther Party (BPP) and Young Lords Party (YLP).[1]

In this chapter, I critically listen to how Universes' *Party People* uses the technologies of sampling and beatboxing to perform the loop, a sonic-temporal strategy that sounds out the radicalisms of blacks and Latinxs in the 1960s and 1970s and reconfigures the temporal logic of history, performance, and race.[2] Developed by pioneering DJs such as Kool Herc and Grandmaster

Flash, the loop enacts an alternative sense of time: one of rupture, suspensions, and new continuities. Instead of being constrained by the temporal emplotment and rhythm of the original music production and following its predetermined linear path, the loop manipulates musical temporality into a different flow, one that overturns preestablished hierarchies and allows for circularity. The loop is more than a mode of simple repetition: it produces a new compositional logic that disrupts the linearity of the past with indefinite movement. In *Party People* Universes loops the sampling of phrases, sounds, and beatboxing to evoke the Black Panthers' and Young Lords' struggle for freedom and wholesale social change.

Drawing on José Esteban Muñoz's concept of queer futurity and Tina Campt's black feminist futurity, I argue that in using the loop Universes produces a sonic treatise of futurity that makes audible the Black Panthers' and Young Lords' moments of radical protest and coalition-building. For Muñoz a queer futurity favors acts of resistance, refusal, and rejection that engage with the *then* and *there* and eschews the *here* and *now*.[3] "What we need to know," he writes, "is that queerness is not yet here but it approaches like a crashing wave of potentiality."[4] He pushes us to consider how we can craft queer utopic spaces that at once negate what is and welcome what could and should be. A queer aesthetic, Muñoz contends, is not an individual act, but a collective one that distorts time—its past, present, and future—as a means of leading us to emancipatory possibilities, allowing for us to dream and enact new and better realities.

For Campt a grammar of black feminist futurity performs "a future that hasn't yet happened but must. . . . It's a politics of pre-figuration that involves living the future *now*—as imperative rather than subjunctive—as a striving for the future you want to see, right now, in the present."[5] Turning our attention to the practice of listening to images, Campt asks us to imagine how black refusal and black resistance might sound. In imagining the sound of agency, defiance, and fugitivity, Campt locates the aspirational aesthetic of survival, upward mobility, and potentiality against the disposability of black lives that don't seem to matter.[6] From Campt we learn that in order to enact the practice of fugitivity, which she defines as a form of refusal with a commitment to survival, one must perform a future that has not yet arrived and place it in the *now*. Both Muñoz and Campt stretch time by taking the now beyond its present moment. Instead of focusing on what now is, we must listen and see the potentiality of what now can become.

With this in mind, I propose that in using hip-hop techniques such as sampling, beatboxing, and looping, Universes composes a sonic treatise of futurity, aural arrangements that enflesh both the disruption of systemic violence and the coalition-building between and among communities of color. Instead of relying on technologies to create the loop that is a customary practice in hip-hop music, Universes enfleshes the loop as a means of creating conduits of knowledge that work toward creating a more equitable future. Building on the decolonial project of Elisa Facio and Irene Lara, who coin the term "enflesh," I call attention to the embodiment of sound that puts minoritarian knowledge into practice, interrogates the past, and alters power relationships of dominance. Facio and Lara's call to enflesh is more than just acting; it is a call to flesh the spirit and spirit the flesh with deep consideration to social, environmental, and global justice as well as the well-being of all communities and of all life.[7] Enfleshing is a radical form of embodiment, one that engages with the futurity of communities of color and makes audible a future full of potentialities and possibilities, which given the context of today's antiblack and anti-immigrant sentiment can be difficult to imagine.

In *Party People* Universes gives bodily form to the memories of the Black Panthers and Young Lords as well as the many spirits of members who have long passed or are still in the struggle. The collective sounds out the radical past of the Black Panthers and Young Lords to bring attention to civil right activism then and now. Emerging against the 1960s backdrop of social and economic crises inflicting many American cities, the Young Lords and Black Panthers combined community-based efforts (like those of Simone Leigh's *Free People's Medical Clinic* and Theaster Gates's *Dorchester Projects* discussed in this volume's introduction) with critiques of capitalism and the role of the state. They challenged the perception that urban poverty was a racial phenomenon and instead offered a theoretical analysis of how mid-century structural racism and poverty begat deindustrialization, urban decline, unemployment, segregated housing, segregated public schools, and an ailing public healthcare system that drastically impacted communities of color.[8]

Disenchanted by the failure to enforce the victories of the civil rights movement and frustrated by the government's inability to offer solutions to entrenched social problems, the Young Lords and Black Panthers fought to protect and preserve their communities. Both organizations put forth a vision of potentiality—taking pride in their culture, history, and identity while also focusing on what they could do to gain access to resources. Amid the harsh reality of white supremacy, state violence, and racialized capitalist inequality, the Black Panthers and the Young Lords energized, galvanized, and inspired people from all walks of life to reconsider how American society valued the lives of blacks, Latinxs, and other disenfranchised groups, who shared similar histories of oppression and colonialism.

The historical conditions of the sixties and seventies resonate loudly with America's antiblack and anti-immigrant sentiment today. Universes was founded in the Bronx, New York, in 1995. The spatial and temporal origins of the ensemble greatly shaped their aesthetics. Because the Bronx is known as the birthplace of hip-hop, it is not surprising that Universes energizes their soundscape with the sonic texture and contours of this rich, innovative cultural form. In the mid-1990s, the Bronx faced a disproportionately high concentration of poverty and unemployment. Along with economic depression, Universes contended with the political climate of the time: the intensive criminalization of youth of color and resultant ascent of mass incarceration. Three years before the official founding of Universes, the US Department of Justice released a report in 1992 stating that "there is no better way to reduce crime than to identify, target, and incapacitate those hardened criminals who commit staggering numbers of violent crimes whenever they are on the streets."[9] The practice of enforcement and punishment emphasized "tough on crime" policies and largely rejected rehabilitation.[10]

As artists of color who came of age in the eighties and nineties in this milieu, the eventual founders of Universes endured the paradoxical circumstances of living under state surveillance and abandonment.[11] Their work pushes the boundaries of conventional American theater practices by drawing on urban poetry and music as well as Afro-diasporic performance traditions. From unveiling the machinations of race, politics, and history during the Nuyorican poetry scene of the 1970s (*Slanguage*, 2001) to the impact of Hurricane Katrina in New Orleans and beyond (*Ameriville*, 2005), Universes' cutting-edge theater grapples with histories of oppression that have impacted black and Latinx communities in order to spark new conversations about what it means to be an American citizen.

Commissioned by the Oregon Shakespeare Festival's (OSF) United States History Cycle, a ten-year initiative aimed to produce original works focused on the theme of "American Revolutions," Universes developed *Party People*.[12] The words "cycle" and "revolution" in the title of this initiative inhabits another temporal dimension, that of repetition and disruption, which is significant to Universes' sonic strategy. While both words capture the reoccurring sequence of events over a period of time, "revolution" brings into sharper focus how insurgences, uprisings, and rebellions are recurring events that disrupt the course of history. Furthermore, while *Party People* lives in the cycle of American revolutions, it works to coexist within a present of racial justice.

Between 2009 and 2016, Universes developed and wrote *Party People* during a time when anti-immigrant policies such as Arizona's State Bill 1070 and House Bill 2282 were passed.[13] Etched into the public consciousness were also the fatal shootings of Trayvon Martin, Michael Brown, and Tamir Rice, among others, and the birth of the Black Lives Matter movement. While Universes does not specifically focus on any one incident, *Party People* must be heard in the context of this larger racial justice movement. Universes offers a sonic treatise of futurity that fights against antiblack and anti-immigrant acts of violence prevailing then and now, serving as a model for younger generations on how to achieve a more equitable future.[14]

THE REVOLUTION MUST BE HEARD

Emerging during the federal government's escalating disinvestment and displacement of working-class communities of color in the 1970s, particularly areas such as the South Bronx, hip-hop calls attention to urban blight and lived despair. Like the Black Panthers and Young Lords, hip-hop stems from youths' desires to rebuild their community amid years of urban decay. As Mark Anthony Neal observes, hip-hop culture "was representative of a concerted effort by youth urban blacks [and I would add other youth of color and poor youths] to use mass-culture to facilitate communal discourse across a fractured and dislocated national community."[15] Collectively, the dreams and desires of belonging in America were expressed through the cultural phenomenon of hip-hop music.

The complex rhythmic layering in hip-hop, along with its oral, collective, and participatory dimensions that derive from African music traditions, challenge Western notions of musical conventions and social order. Since its inception, hip-hop has often been perceived as incomprehensible and unintelligible and thus dismissed as noise. Rendering hip-hop as noise, Jennifer Stoever argues, is not simply personal or individual reasoning but is symptomatic of how the American listening ear processes dominant ways of sounding as the default and alternate ways of sounding as aberrant.[16] The legacy of slavery and the enforcement of Jim Crow laws have profoundly shaped our listening practices, which, in turn, impact how raced subjects imagine themselves and how they must navigate society. Since both the ear and eye adhere to the racialization of the Other, performing bodies of color on the stage will "never really lose their referent" as racial Other; thus, listeners might only hear hip-hop music—the rapping, scratching, and beatboxing—as noise and decide to tune it out or police it.[17]

This perception of hip-hop as noise is not entirely wrong; the sonic aesthetic of hip-hop is in fact often noisy and rough. Rappers spit poetics into a mic, DJs scratch records creating a new compositional logic, and beatboxers use their lips and tongue to create an aerodynamic amalgam of sound and breath ventriloquizing musical instruments. Max Roach reminds us that "the thing that frightened people about hip hop was they heard rhythm—rhythm for rhythm's sake. Hip hop lives in the world of sound—not the world music—and that's why it's so revolutionary."[18] Given hip-hop's distinct urban Afro-diasporic and Latinx sociopolitical contexts, it must be understood as an oppositional cultural form that centers self-determination, resistance, and black and brown freedom.

While some critics and theatergoers see the dynamic sonic components of Universes' work as groundbreaking, others don't quite know what to make of them. Some critics perceive Universes' hip-hop soundscape as simply unintelligible, excessive noise.[19] Galen Workman's theater review offers some context for why the soundscape of *Party People* is unintelligible to certain audience members:

> The approach, the music, and execution stirred pasty-skinned, hip-hop hating, old fogy me. . . . I feel defensive about liking the production so much because many of my friends find fault with the music, the repetitiveness of some of the themes, the unexplained stories, the missing call to specific action. . . . I think my friends' unease stems in part from their (and my) unfamiliarity with the way *Party People* is thrown at us. As Oregon Shakespeare Festival's Claudia Alick mused, with *Party People* my friends and I are experiencing something like what kids of color feel when they walk into a classic evening of Shakespeare.[20]

Workman observes that his lack of understanding stems from how he has been socialized to listen to white music as normative and perceive hip-hop as Other, even as he denaturalizes artistic "genius."

Workman's self-reflexive review calls on audiences to "listen in detail" to the racial past, present, and future. To listen in detail, as Alexandra T. Vazquez posits, is "not archeological work done to reconstruct the past," but rather an approach of understanding the ways that music and sounds reflect the complex and entangled histories of colonialism, racism, and slavery.[21] When we listen in detail, we train the ear to hear difference and make audible the histories that have been "left behind from a near past."[22] These newly heard soundscapes serve as "disruptive fissures that crack" dominant narratives.[23]

When we listen more closely to the details, we not only make sense of what we hear, but also call attention to the practice of listening—how we listen and experience the contours and texture of sounds. When approached through its detail, sound is not simply discussed in the context of its musicality, but what sound does to the listener and how it moves them. As Roshanak Kheshti reminds us, "what is felt on the flesh, tasted on the tongue, and imagined in the psyche" is how listeners materialize sound and music.[24] Putting careful attention to detail makes audible the feelings evoked by performers, the audience's reception, and the interaction between the community and performer, which may slip by undetected.[25] The goal is not to excavate or capture sound, but to index the sonic impact throughout time and note the effects at the moment, while also imagining its past and future assembly yet to be heard.[26] Similar to the language of Shakespeare that demands readers and spectators embrace the multidimensional meanings of words and phrases, Universes charges the language of *Party People* with acoustic and poetic depth. To make sense of Universes' rhythmic hip-hop matrix, we must listen in detail—failure to do so hinders our ability to hear the revolution in the Black Panthers' and Young Lords' rally for freedom.[27]

SOUND AND TIME AS MECHANISMS OF OPPRESSION AND LIBERATION

Critical race studies often attends to how white supremacy manipulates sound and time as separate mechanisms of domination and hegemony, but time and sound are inextricably linked. For instance, for over two centuries the enterprise of slavery determined the lives of blacks in the West. In order to annihilate black personhood and its sense of autonomy, whites controlled the time and sound of black people. For instance, masters and overseers micromanaged enslaved people's time: from when they worked, ate, took breaks, slept, played music, or worshipped. Michael Hanchard explains this temporal manipulation as "racial time," the unequal temporal access to institutions, goods, services, resources, power, and knowledge.[28] Enslaved and colonized people combatted white temporal dominance by constructing their own temporality. They pretended to be ill, feigned ignorance, or broke their instruments to slow down their pace of work.[29] These individual and collective acts worked toward an autonomous temporality that liberated the master–slave relationship, which Hanchard refers to as "temporal freedom."[30]

While Hanchard calls attention to efforts to combat practices of stolen time in slavery and its aftermath, historian Mark Smith turns to the deployment of sound as a mechanism for reinforcing and dismantling white dominance. A well-managed plantation, for instance, established an aural social order. Communication among enslaved people was strictly limited. Religious gatherings or any type of convening were either prohibited or supervised. As Smith explains, the sounds of chains dragging on dirt roads, the snarling barks of hound dogs chasing runaways, and the violent whip lashings asserted an aural dominance that instilled fear and powerlessness, hindered aspirations, and dehumanized enslaved people.[31] To resist their exploitation, enslaved people would create their own sonic strategies such as silence, drumming, spirituals, and work songs. These strategies helped enslaved people to communicate with each other and convey coded information to escape or rebel, denying whites the satisfaction of the enslaved simply submitting to subordination.

Sound studies has shown how race indelibly shapes how we listen to sound, but the field remains a largely white, ableist, masculinist, technological, and presentist enterprise in its orientation. As Gustavus Stadler's provocative post in the *Sounding Out!* blog (2015) argues, sound studies nods to the lived socially constructed categories of gender, race, ethnicity, religion, disability, citizenship, and personhood but does not necessarily engage it. In recent years, however, there has been a growing body of sonic scholarship foregrounding various modalities of social difference that offer trailblazing accounts of sound's role in the racial history of the United States and beyond. This work harkens our ears toward understanding fault lines of power surrounding categories of difference and reveals fissures in the hegemony of repetition in performance studies and sound studies.[32]

For instance, Fred Moten carefully listens to the phonic breaks in radical black aesthetics that materialize the visual, breaks that allow for chronicling the resistant and disruptive sounds of freedom that have been muted from the archives of experience and language.[33] In a special issue of *American Quarterly* called "Sound Clash: Listening to American Studies" (2012), guest editors Kara Keeling and Josh Kun remind us to listen to the sound of citizenship, nation building, and racial formation.[34] Inspired by W. E. B. Du Bois, Stoever offers the term "sonic color line" to think about how racism and racialism impact listening practices and their politics.[35] Similarly, Nina Sun Eidsheim examines how listeners carry a series of assumptions about race depending on the vocal timbre.[36] Scholarly paradigms such as Vazquez's "listening in detail," Deborah Vargas's "musical dissonance," and Dolores Inés Casillas's "radio listening tactics" train the ear to decipher the Latinx sonic strategies deployed in music, recordings, and radio shows.[37]

This scholarship reveals the importance of moving beyond regarding sound as a purely aesthetic object of study to explore the ways sound inaugurates bodies and power to produce meaning across different temporalities. One direction this effort reveals is to listen to the processes of creating and arranging sound in the theater, to attend to what Ross Brown and Mladen Ovadija call "dramaturgy of sound."[38] Amplifying sound-making and listening practices expands the space of theatrical performance to include the sounding body, recorded sounds, and other phonic traces on and off the theatrical stage. I listen in detail to how the Black Panthers and Young Lords created sonic-temporal strategies to combat racism and white dominance and how Universes then reconstitutes them so as to make audible black and Latinx activism in American history in order to compose a sonic treatise of futurity.

The production of sonic and temporal strategies that worked to dismantle oppressive power structures was central to the civil rights movement and other black/Latinx freedom struggles. Revolutionary nationalist organizations like the Black Panthers and Young Lords sought to break free from the strictures of time and sound that the larger society placed on their communities. Founded in 1966 by Huey P. Newton and Bobby Seale and located in Oakland, California, the Black Panther Party espoused a strategy of armed self-defense to combat systemic poverty, educational disparities, underemployment, and police brutality faced by black communities.[39] Inspired by Malcolm X's Pan-Africanist perspective, Frantz Fanon's anticolonial approach, and Marxist ideologies, the BPP saw their efforts as a national endeavor advocating for the rights of black people in the United States that would swell to a worldwide effort of liberation for all oppressed people in the world.[40]

The BPP's radical tactic of armed self-defense and organizing "community survival programs" along with their militant sartorial aesthetics liberated them from the temporal constraint of waiting for protection and provisional services.[41] While civil rights organizations such as the National Association for the Advancement of Colored People, the National Urban League, the Congress of Racial Equality, and the Student Nonviolent Coordinating Committee sought racial justice through nonviolent and legal tactics, the BPP used militant action and rhetorical styles to fight against police brutality and other social inequities.[42] Instead of sit-ins, they took over public spaces. Instead of wearing suits or dresses that adhered to a politics of respectability and civility, they carried loaded firearms and wore Afros, black berets, black leather jackets, and powder-blue shirts to signify revolution.[43]

They also took matters into their own hands when they organized community survival programs aimed to end state-sanctioned violence against their community, alleviate economic distress for poor and working-class African Americans, and affirm the ethic of self-determination. The first BPP survival program addressed police aggression in East Oakland, California, by creating a civilian patrol unit to monitor police arrests and defend community residents against police aggression. What first began as one local organization soon became a national network of sixty-eight BPP chapters providing community services including free breakfast programs for schoolchildren, an ambulance service, and a lead-poisoning detection program, among other initiatives.[44] The Black Panthers aimed to eradicate waiting for such services to meet immediate needs of their community, thus recharging time with agency, action, and change.

The BPP set an exemplary model of radical activism that was instrumental for the evolution of the Young Lords. As the BPP took root and spread, their discourse and politics resonated with many Puerto Ricans and other people of color; in fact, several Puerto Ricans became active in the New York chapter of the BPP.[45] Originally started as a street gang in Chicago's Lincoln Park neighborhood in 1959 to defend Puerto Rican neighborhoods from rival Italian, Appalachian, and Latinx gangs, the Young Lords, under the leadership of José "Cha Cha" Jiménez, shifted toward an activist agenda and became the Young Lords Organization.[46] YLO worked in alliance with the BPP and other Black Power advocates.[47]

Fashioning itself after the BPP, the YLO used nationalism and self-determination as their entry point and took on a similar sartorial aesthetic. However, the YLO brought particular attention to the colonial relationship between Puerto Rico and the United States. They worked on Puerto Rican radical ethnic nationalism and liberation on the island and in the mainland while also honoring their Puerto Rican black and indigenous culture.[48] While Puerto Rican nationalism was a driving force in the organization, it was a multiracial and multiethnic group. In New York City "approximately 30 percent of the organization's membership was composed of African Americans and non–Puerto Rican Latinos," which points to their revolutionary tactics of coalition-building.[49]

Akin to the BPP's survival programs that reduced the amount of time their community had to wait for certain protection and provisions, the Chicago

YLO met the needs of their community by organizing protests against police misconduct, occupying Armitage Church to establish a day-care and health clinic, and stopping an urban renewal plan in the Lincoln Park neighborhood that would have resulted in the displacement of many Puerto Ricans and other Latinx people.[50] Sister organizations began to form in other cities. In New York City, the Lords renamed YLO the Young Lords Party (YLP).[51] They offered educational classes, free breakfast programs for poor children, drug detoxification programs, and garbage clean-up programs, and they monitored police activity in an attempt to curb police brutality.

Inspired by the Black Panthers' guerilla tactics, the YLP staged a series of "offensives," including piling and setting ablaze a large heap of garbage on Third Avenue, taking over the First Spanish Methodist Church on 111th Street and Lexington Avenue, running a free children's program, and seizing hospital equipment and moving it to areas where it was most needed.[52] They also conducted free testing for lead poisoning and tuberculosis as well as organized food and health drives in New York's Puerto Rican communities. Their offensives and social service programs sought to attend to the most urgent needs of the poor and people of color, drawing media attention to not only race-based social inequalities but also the ways the government had neglected people of color and the spaces they inhabit. Such efforts were undoubtedly instrumental in catapulting young Puerto Ricans of the sixties into radical politics.[53]

Like the Black Panthers, the Young Lords' sartorial aesthetic also included wearing Afros, military fatigues, leather jackets, shades, and berets. However, the Lords accessorized their outfits with items that accentuated their Puerto Rican identity. Pinned on the berets was a button of a fist holding a rifle with the Spanish phrase "Tengo Puerto Rico en mi corazón [I have Puerto Rico in my heart]." More than militant, the Young Lords' style was what Frances Negrón-Muntaner calls "a look of sovereignty," a way of being, dressing, and moving the body that denoted the Young Lords as autonomous political actors exercising self-governance and full citizenry.[54] Every aspect of the outfit screamed defiance. They also wore Puerto Rican flags on all parts of their clothing. Adorning their bodies with the Puerto Rican flag was a way of protesting against US colonial authority, since it was illegal during the first half of the twentieth century to publicly display it.[55] Together the Young Lords' sartorial aesthetic was part and parcel of their disruption of time and sound oppression. Their warrior-like uniform removed the colonial stigma of Puerto Ricans as docile, passive, and disposable subjects and transformed Puerto Rican subjectivity into a portrayal of strength, honor, and resilience.[56]

The US government perceived the activism of groups like the Black Panthers and the Young Lords as a threat and, consequently, established regimes of aural and temporal repression to monitor and inhibit their efforts. Started in 1956 under J. Edgar Hoover's leadership, the FBI's Counter-Intelligence Program (COINTELPRO) policed the ideas and activities of many radical collectives by disrupting and neutralizing their activities. By the 1960s, Hoover expanded the COINTELPRO's charge to "counteract domestic terrorism and conduct investigations of individuals and organizations who threatened terroristic violence," among whom he included the BPP and YLO.[57] In addition to monitoring the Panthers' and Lords' every move, from where they went to what they said, COINTELPRO used aural and temporal tactics of repression including harassment, intimidation, wiretapping, infiltration, smear campaigns, and blackmail to imprison anyone who seriously challenged the status quo of racism, militarism, and capitalism in American society.[58] These tactics at the end of the day were about managing and controlling the time and sound of the BPP and YLO. At times COINTELPRO went as far as murdering members, as was the case of Black Panther Fred Hampton.[59] In the name of law and order, COINTELPRO disrupted, infiltrated, and discredited the activism of the BPP and YLO, working to strip away any modicum of temporal, spatial, and aural autonomy: its aim was to prevent them from speaking out against social injustices and enacting social change.

Bobby Seale, a cofounder of the BPP, shifted the appropriation of time from a collective effort to an intellectual endeavor with his book *Seize the Time: The Story of the Black Panther Party and Huey Newton* (1970). Arthur Goldberg, a reporter for the *San Francisco Bay Guardian*, recorded *Seize the Time* while Seale was in jail and under threat of two major political trials in 1969 and 1970, both of which he eventually won. With the goal of setting the record straight and restoring the historical roots of the BPP, Seale lays down his voice in the tape recording rather than first putting his thoughts on the page.

As a recording that one could pause, play, and rewind, Seale's recorded voice begs us to listen a little harder to how he deploys sound and time to combat white supremacy. If we "listen in detail," as Vazquez proposes, Seale sets up the concept of seizing time not solely as a temporal strategy but also as a sonic strategy. Goldberg, who at the time was the editor of *Ramparts* magazine, had the audio transcribed and sent back to Seale, who then put on the final touches. While the recording of *Seize the Time* is not readily available or archived in an institution, in the introduction of his book Seale signals the urgency of capturing his voice on tape to assure that his ideas were disseminated since his life was in danger.[60] As readers, we are left to imagine the sonic residuals in his writing—the all-out protest voice that jumps off the page and does not conform to racial inequities or wait for others to enact social change. If we listen in detail, we hear his impassioned call to appropriate time and eradicate racial time. As he states in the conclusion of his book:

> We know that as a people, we must seize our time. . . . Huey P. Newton seized the time when he moved and put the BPP into motion. . . . The time is *now* to wage relentless revolutionary struggle against the fascist, avaricious, demagogic ruling class and their lowlife, sadistic pigs. Power to the People! Seize the Time!

His call to seize the time is an exhortation to take hold of the opportunity and fight against the persistent repetitions of oppression, which he underscores in his book with a fierce militant tone through a final capitalized inscription—SEIZE THE TIME.[61]

The concept of seizing time was front and center when Elaine Brown performed the Black Power jazz poetry song titled "Seize the Time" at a rally held at Oakland's Bobby Hutton Memorial Park on November 12, 1969.[62] A year later, she released a revolutionary album with the same title. Brown's recording captures "the feelings of the Black and Party," and invites listeners to learn the words of the songs as they are printed on the inside of the cover so that they can have a deeper understanding of the BPP's poetry.[63] Brown uses her singing voice as a tool for moving the needle toward equity and social justice. On the back of her album she reminds us:

> Songs, like all art forms, are an expression of the feelings and thoughts, the desires and hopes, and so forth, of a people. . . . A song cannot change a situation, because songs do not live or breathe. People do. And so the songs in this album are a statement—by, of and for the people. . . . And that, in fact, we have always had the power to do it. The power to determine our destinies as human beings and not allow them to be determined by the few men who now determine them. . . . But the power only belongs to all of us, not just some or one but all. And that was the trick. That was thing that we never understood. And that is what these songs make.

The articulation and circulation of the concept "seize the time," both textually in Seale's book and sonically in Brown's performances in rallies, demonstrations, and album recordings, puts a halt to the cycle of temporal and aural repression by mobilizing readers and listeners to reclaim and bestow time with new values, beliefs, expressions, and, most importantly, a futurity of equitable possibilities that rupture the blunt repetitions of power.

Similarly, in titling their bilingual newspaper and local weekly radio show *Pa'lante*, meaning forward and onward in Spanish, the Young Lords also affirm a futurity of progress. Often used in rallies and demonstrations to mobilize the collective, the word works against the idea of the colonial subject as docile and passive, and refuses the notion of racial time. Just as the word "Pa'lante" is charged with social change and social action, using the mediums of newspapers and radio shows as powerful tools for community education and change created pathways of futurity. Both the newspaper and radio stations included local, national, and international news, updates about the movement, editorials, and creative writing. The Young Lords directed the ear to listen to the sounds of revolutionaries spreading information, politically educating the public about the movement and organizing the community to action. Their use of various mediums of circulation and dissemination added to their futurity, as it became a means for economic stability and provided longevity for both organizations.

Collectively, the Black Panthers' and Young Lords' sonic-temporal tactics put Muñoz and Campt's notions of futurity into practice. These radical organizations attempted to break the white supremacist yoke of time and sound as means to create emancipatory possibilities. They came up with sonic strategies in slogans and songs, and used radio stations and albums to encourage the masses to take hold of their own time and propel themselves forward to enact new and better realities. They created frameworks in their survival programs and offensives that placed people of color outside of the function of "white time," working to reduce the waiting period not only of accessing the necessary civic services but also of attaining human rights. Time seizure or appropriation, as Hanchard calls it, refers to moments when collectives such as the Lords and Panthers use the time of a racial subject and its related institutions for the purposes of affecting positive change for their communities. They put into the present a future they wanted to see. Instead of waiting for social reform from the state, the YLP and BPP seized time and sped up the pace of social equity by challenging the discriminatory practices of employment, education, housing, the health-care system, and the criminal justice system.[64] While Black Panthers and Young Lords could not regain the time stolen or lost by the history of racism, the YLP and BPP guerilla tactics attempted to "eradicate the chasm of racial time"—the perpetual state of waiting in limbo—by

FIGURE 3.1 *Party People* at the Public Theater, 2016. Malik (Christopher Livingston) and Jimmy (William Ruiz, aka Ninja) prepare for the opening of their performance installation. PHOTO BY JOAN MARCUS. COURTESY OF JOAN MARCUS.

making human rights, goods, and services readily accessible.[65] In essence, the Black Panthers and the Young Lords produced embodied pathways of futurity that made visible and audible their liberation from colonial and racist structures of power.

PLAY, REWIND, REPLAY: LOOPING THE REVOLUTION

I now move to examine how Universes' *Party People* uses the history of the BPP and YLP to reconstitute live and embodied sonic-temporal strategies to teach and incite today's generation to pursue social justice. To date, plays about the Black Panthers or Young Lords engage with the personal and cultural history of one or the other group, but rarely engage with the shared history of these organizations.[66] Drawing on over twenty interviews conducted by Universes with members of the Black Panthers and Young Lords, *Party People* follows the story of Malik, who also uses the name Mk Ultra, and his Latino friend Jimmy, two young countercultural artists (figure 3.1).[67] Both are tethered to the history of the radical past of the 1960s and '70s. Jimmy is the nephew of Tito, a former Young Lords Party member still involved in union organizing and a reentry program for inmates, and Malik is a Panther cub who has never seen his father anywhere but in jail and visits him in prison to maintain their relationship. Like the members of Universes who conducted interviews to develop *Party People*, Jimmy and Malik also interviewed numerous Panthers and Lords and use them to create a multimedia installation exhibition called "Party People." Malik and Jimmy invite former members to the gallery opening and set up the exhibit in such a way that their invitees are not merely attendees but the very subjects of the exhibit. The opening of the exhibit in *Party People* ultimately becomes a critical moment not only for the curators who embrace the unique opportunity to reunite members of both parties, but also for the revolutionaries who have not seen each other in over twenty-five years with old rivalries still intact. Additionally, as part of the exhibit, Jimmy appears as a quasi-television host and clown provocateur named Primo, wearing a red Ronald McDonald wig and bulbous red nose, relentlessly asking the invitees incendiary questions that both spotlight their activism as Black Panthers and Young Lords and pick at the scabs of old wounds.

As audience members settle in their seats to see *Party People*, the two young artists silently work on their multimedia performance art exhibit: Jimmy edits video interviews on his laptop, while Malik watches over his shoulder. From the outset, the audience witnesses Malik and Jimmy constructing a historical narrative of the Panthers and Lords.[68] Unlike the Panthers and Lords who were surveilled by authorities, Malik and Jimmy are DJs with complete control over time, sound, and space, as they cut sections of the film, rearrange them, and dispose of sections that no longer serve them.

As soon as the house lights go down, we are pulled into an audiovisual montage of excerpted interview recordings of Black Panthers and Young Lords displayed on several mounted monitors. We meet Helita, Maruca, and Tito, former members of the Young Lords, as well as Blue, Amira, and Omar, all former members of the Black Panthers. The recordings are not actual archival footage of the Panthers or Lords, but of the actors playing the roles. As the audiovisual montage runs, the actors gradually assemble on stage one by one. Eventually, we hear the loop, samples of isolated phrases excerpted from the interviews that Universes reuses and seamlessly sutures to create another compositional logic. As Joseph Glenn Schloss explains, looping is the art of "creating a cycle out of linearly conceived melody."[69] Originally the sequence of the excerpted recorded interviews had their own linearity and melody, but once it was reduced to a set of phrases and then looped, it imparted a new compositional logic of the revolution.[70]

At this point, we only hear a technologically produced loop, drawing our attention to the practice of generating a sample-based track through electronic devices. If we listen a little harder to the loop, we learn about the sonic-temporal strategies of fighting for social equity used by the Black Panthers and the Young Lords in the seventies. However, the sonic message quickly changes when the actors speak over the loop and on top of each other, creating an enfleshed loop composed of phrases:

> *Tenant's rights . . .*
> *We opened up free clinics . . .*
> *Because no one would deal with the rats and roaches . . .*
> *. . . picking up the garbage . . .*
> *The police violence against us was out of control . . .*
> *It was Viet Nam, man!*
> *If you go, you can be an American!*[71]

Universes uses the technologically produced loop to reconfigure the radical past by overlaying the enfleshed loop into the present, creating sonic and temporal fragments of repetition and that repetition's disruption.

There is a strange rhythmic dissonance and melodic discontinuity upon hearing the two loops harmonize and collide. This new compositional logic not only reveals the legacy of these radical groups, but it also mars the revolution with chaos and agony revealing its traumatic vestiges. As performed in *Party People*, the traumatic past—COINTELPRO's coercion and disinformation including charges made against members and sowing suspicion within the organization and within both groups—continues to haunt the lives of Panthers and Lords. What were once stories about the revolution become a rapid whirlwind of words played over each other, reducing it to mere noise. The static television screen amplifies the noise even louder with the outbursts of words here and there by actors. Yet it is this incomprehensible noise that evokes the relentless dedication, passion, and labor-intensive work of resistance and activism by the BPS and YLS. These loops are loops of history. We hear the fervor and urgency of the black/Latinx freedom struggles, the angst of racial inequality, police brutality, unfair housing practices, and poverty experienced by the working class and people of color during that time, and the pain and chaos that comes with being a revolutionary.

If we listen in detail, we can understand the beginning of the play as a metatheatrical moment in which Universes trains the audience's ears in how to listen to the difference between a loop mediated through technologies of sampling, cutting, and splicing and a loop mediated through the theatrics of the body. The performance of both loops reveals that a revolution needs technology and the live body to sustain its momentum. If we listen even harder, we also hear history as loops, reminding us that the past does not so much live in the then, but it lives in the now and into the future. Performance, as many argue, is repetition, but not all performance repeats itself by framing itself as repetition. Universes uses the loops to frame repetition as repetition across time, repeating itself referentially. The past echoes in the present and the present reverberates in the past as the actors enflesh the memories of Panthers' and Lords' activism.[72] The loop is a methodology of enfleshing the radical revolution then and now. The metatheatrical work of Universes lies in referential repetition so as to teach the next generation about the various sonic-temporal strategies composed of an aesthetic of violent rupture and coalitional suture.

LOOPING THE RUPTURE: "MOTHERFUCKER" AND GUNSHOTS

Universes creates the most audible sonic rupture in the play with the ear-splitting thunderous looping of gunshots and eruptive looping of the word "motherfucker" altering the rhythm and flow of the play. The looping of "motherfucker" and the gunshots jams the smooth progression of time, disrupting the temporal and sonic dimensions of white supremacy. Following the staging of the technologically mediated loop and the enfleshed loop, audiences witness Malik in flesh and live video feed enunciating the word "motherfucker" several times. The first time the audience hears him curse, it is shocking, but then there are giggles. The funny moment immediately diffuses as he repeats "motherfucker" each time louder and more aggressively. As Seale writes in *Seize the Time*, "motherfucker" has multiple meanings. "With the rising consciousness of black people learning about Black History in general," the word acquires a positive connotation as a "real complimentary statement to a brother or even a sister" as opposed to when used by the master or by the black boys of the ghettos.[73] What at first seems like a joke immediately becomes a rupture or crisis of sorts.[74] The meaning of "motherfucker" shifts as Malik first delivers the word with a sort of ambiguous humor and then gradually he delivers the word carrying more of a confrontational or menacing tone.

We quickly learn that Malik's vocal eruptions of "motherfucker" are all part of his rehearsal: he is in the middle of practicing how to properly say the word "motherfucker" as the son of a Black Panther. As a narrator reconstructing the historical narrative of the Lords and Panthers, Malik steps out of his performance and directly explains to the audience why he rehearses this word. He shares with the audience that ever since he was a child, he studied the Panthers' every move—how they sounded, walked, and dressed. He would play, rewind, and replay old videos of the Panthers as he obsessively rehearsed their "I don't take no shit" facial expression, the "get out of my way" bop, and the raising of the Black Power fist and would tirelessly practice saying "motherfucker" for hours to make sure "he would use it with purpose, as a noun, a verb, an adjective, and a subject."[75]

This opening charges the entirety of the play with temporal and sonic layers of repetition and disruption. When Malik enfleshes the Panthers through sound, he transgresses the temporal boundaries of the past and present. He plays, rewinds, and replays over and over again old footage of the Panthers, creating a tapestry of sound, music, and events that reshuffle the revolution of the sixties and the activism of today. This is another metatheatrical moment. In *Party People* the audience witnesses Malik rehearsing, which temporally bounds the scene in repetition, and then there is the repetition of "motherfucker," which I am referring to as the loop. Similar to the opening scene, here the mediated and live body come face to face. Malik again manipulates time and sound, but in this scene the motherfucker loop is an embodied repetition of self-referencing and enfleshment of the BPS and YLS. The loop amplifies the double-consciousness of being a contemporary black young man and the son of a Panther who desires to carry forth the legacy of the organization. The loop links Malik to the past and allows him to travel across time referencing himself while also enfleshing the BPS and YLS.

Just as the motherfucker loop echoes a temporal awareness of the past and present, so does the looping of gunshots. The audience cringes to the hard-piercing bullet sounds. In this moment of trying to make sense of what has happened or will happen as a consequence of the shooting gun, the audience toggles between different temporalities. It takes us back to December 4, 1969, when the Chicago Police opened fire for seven minutes, about eighty-three to ninety shots, at the Black Panthers' apartment quarters, killing Fred Hampton, the chapter founder and chairman. While the looping of gunshots acoustically evokes the dismantling of the Panthers and Lords and the memory of fallen comrades, it also strongly resonates with the contemporary moment.

Gun symbolism suffuses much of hip-hop music and culture today and yet it confronts and contends with the consequences of gun violence. The repetition of the gunshots registers the disproportionate number of young men of color today as gun victims under the hands of police authorities.[76] The repetition of the gunshots makes audible the transtemporal violent resonance of the past and the present. The gunshot directly resonates with the present moment, as the entire ensemble, with the exception of Jimmy and Malik, who are representative of the next generation, ducks and falls to the ground. This final image on stage of Malik and Jimmy in search for answers of a radical history they know through books but are unable to grasp fully leaves the audience with more questions than answers.

Galvanized by social injustices, young people in today's America organize to protest hate, racism, xenophobia, the prison system, sexism, police brutality, voter suppression, and economic inequality. Yet many young activists are still not fully aware of the ties that bind today's movements with those that came before. The history of groups like the Black Panthers and Young Lords, who militantly pushed back, has been erased from American history curricula. When mentioning them at all, media portrays these revolutionary groups as hate groups, terrorists, or gangs. As such, Malik's vocal looping of "motherfucker" and his enfleshment of the Panthers, execution of the facial expression and walk, writes history within the key and time signature of radical people of color, affirming their presence, participation, and contribution in American history, refusing to be silenced, erased, or forgotten by a system that has refused Malik's very existence and the existence of blacks in general.[77]

Despite Malik's commitment to embodying the Panthers, Malik's dad bluntly reminds him, "Boy, you ain't no Panther." That is, regardless of how many times he plays, rewinds, and replays the revolution and correctly executes all the moves, he will never be a Panther. On the one hand, Malik's enfleshment of the Panthers refuses to accept the erasure of blacks throughout history. On the other hand, Malik refuses to accept his father's erasure of him trying to uphold a legacy he inherited. Feeling that his performance has failed, he digs deeper into the radical past to understand what happens to the ones who, like him, came after the civil rights movement and contemporaneous freedom struggles. Malik, as a representative of the younger generation, refuses to be erased and refuses to be perceived as a failure.[78] His persistence to "get it right" and comprehend the Panthers works to affirm the visibility and audibility of black futurity, shifting it from violence and death to potentiality and livelihood. While Malik's dad undermines Malik's effort to enflesh the

Panther, Jimmy, who walks in on his rehearsal, applauds his performance and asks him if it is going to be part of the exhibition. Malik responds affirmatively and then eagerly shares the final version of the video footage he created, which we now hear as the sonic treatise of futurity whose enfleshed composition we have witnessed in this performance.

RUPTURING THE REVOLUTION IN REPEAT MODE

If Universes' use of looping makes a call for America to listen to the radical history of its blacks and Latinxs, beatboxing serves as a sonic rupture of repetition modeled on enfleshed revolutionary action. This rupturing is reminiscent of hip-hop's aesthetic, which mirrors the profound social dislocation and alternative ways people managed and contested the social circumstance.[79] Hip-hop aficionados often credit the birth of hip-hop to DJs who began to rap while sampling, mixing, looping, and scratching on turntables to accentuate, repeat, or isolate the beat and encourage breakdancing. Faced with the challenge of not owning or even affording beat machines, samplers, or sound synthesizers, hip-hop practitioners created the vocal percussion art form of beatboxing.[80] Musicians use their lips, cheeks, tongues, and throats to imitate the sound of drum machines, drums, and other percussion instruments as well as the simultaneous imitation of bass lines, melodies, and vocals to create an illusion of polyphonic music.[81]

Following the sonic rupture of gunshots, the ensemble physically rises up to beatboxing and rapping. Jimmy beatboxes, enhancing the sonic texture and temporal dimensionality of *Party People*. Sonically, beatboxing is an embodied way of looping the break. The portion of the song that DJs often loop is known as "the break," a moment during the song where all the musical elements from the vocals to the bass lines disappear for a period of time, with the exception of the percussion. When the DJ seamlessly loops the break, it becomes the song itself and the party people go wild on the dance floor. Beatboxing becomes such an essential element in *Party People* that Universes phonetically transcribes the sound of beatboxing. For instance, when Jimmy beatboxes, the script reads:

PFF T P K
T KEU KPFF K
T K (X3)
PFF K PFFK PFF P K K.[82]

This phonetic transcription of the beatboxing creates a sound narrative that matches or approximates beatboxing, making it legible to the ear and allowing readers to imagine the vocal performance. While phonetically annotated, the transcription cannot possibly capture all of the beatboxer's aerodynamic choreography. The spacing between letters attempts to transcribe the continuous flow of sound and breathing patterns, but the aggression or high-pitch sounds of an exhale or inhale are not encapsulated in the beatbox notes.

As the beatboxer, Jimmy creates various drum tracks by looping and recombining six letters. The percussive punch of "P" generates the sound of the kick drum, while "PF" produces the sound of the snare and "T" generates the sound of a closed hi-hat. These three linguistic sounds produced by the vocal tract require an affricate articulation of both lips, which means that the beatboxer must first entirely stop the airflow, then press their lips to create a constructed channel and produce an airflow with turbulence.[83] The phonation of these sounds is voiceless and egressive. That is, they are produced without vibrations of the vocal cords and the air flows outward. The "K" sound offers a clicking sound or inward clap snare. Instead of a voiceless, egressive airflow, the "K" requires a voiceless ingressive airflow, where the beatboxer inhales and the tongue body makes a constriction against the palate creating a click's characteristic of smacking or popping.[84] These beatboxing sounds of "P," "T," and "PF" evoke temporal movements of continuous rupture that does not halt progression, but alters its speed. That is, beatboxing is progression of time with disruption in repeat mode.

In addition to considering the semantic and logistic elements of beatboxing, it is important to account for who is making the sound of the body, what they are doing, how they are interacting, and their social relations. While Jimmy beatboxes, the older generation in the cast slowly rises up from the gunshots, stressing how the younger generation must proceed by creating ruptures within the revolution to craft a better future. Universes resounds the revolution of the Black Panthers and the Young Lords through beatboxing. Hearing the beatboxing, members of the ensemble, who had fallen on the ground to hide from the gunshots, rise up singing the gospel lyrics "I HIDE I RISE I CRY I SURVIVE WHAT HISTORY DOESN'T TELL YOU IS THAT I BLEED RED LIKE YOU. WILL YOU RISE WITH ME IN DARKEST NIGHT? ARE YOU WILLING TO SACRIFICE YOUR LIFE?" Jimmy's aerodynamic choreographic beatboxing serves as the rhythmic foundation for the gospel song. He simulates drum sounds as well as bass lines, melodies, and vocals. This polyphonic movement and ruptures help the revolution move forward. Universes reminds us that sounding out radicalism not only loops the revolution but offers the sonic-temporal strategy of continuous disruption: the rupturing of the revolution on repeat mode. White supremacy actively controls and quiets the voices of marginalized communities, but if we listen in detail the sonic-temporal strategy of beatboxing allows marginalized communities to make noise without using their words. Beatboxing thus radicalizes our ears to strive for a better future now.

LOOPING US INTO THE FUTURE

Understanding the transgressive artistry of looping allows for a more complex listening of how and why Universes incorporates this sonic-temporal strategy. The use of looping sounds (gunshots), words (motherfucker), and phrases (Tenants' rights . . . / . . . picking up the garbage) in *Party People* is a sonic intervention making audible the agency, defiance, and perseverance of the Panthers and Lords. In contrast to the ways COINTELPRO suppressed the social and political activities of these two radical organizations of color, Universes' sonic-temporal strategy of looping, rooted in Afro-diasporic practices, renders a sonic treatise of futurity that enfleshes the radicalism of the Young Lords and the Black Panthers—the violence and coalition building—and the making of a more inclusive and equitable tomorrow. Universes' sonic treatise of futurity operates as a site of agency and activism, enfleshing the often-neglected history of communities of color—their experiences, struggles, and dreams—into the aural imagination of today's America. More than honoring the Black Panthers and the Young Lords, *Party People* offers the sonic-temporal strategy of looping as means of dreaming and enfleshing emancipatory possibilities, repositioning disenfranchised communities as agentive citizens who make a more just world, galvanize the radical present toward change, and fuel the future with potentiality.

Through looping, Universes' sonic treatise of futurity makes audible the radicalism of the Black Panthers, putting sonic pressure on historical linearity and amplifying the disruption in the cycle of history. Toggling back and forth between the late 1960s and the contemporary moment, Universes resounds how these radical organizations live in our collective memory. Jimmy and Malik's multimedia exhibit makes audibly palpable the rallies of freedom spearheaded by the Panthers and Lords, and attempts to prove to the older generation that they, the younger generation, are as informed, passionate, and revolutionary.

Looping, however, does not solely live in the past: it dislodges the radical history of the '60s and '70s from its temporality and reveals the past's ongoing relevance to the present. Present, past, and future sonically intersect, collide, and coexist to create alternative temporal logics of race. Instead of the racial time of waiting, *Party People* proposes looping to reduce waiting time by constantly referring to and disrupting the cycle of white supremacy. Coincidentally, the same injustices that drive the older generation to fight against inequities motivate the younger generation. By the end of the performance, Jimmy and Malik realize that this event not only has given them the opportunity to gain a deeper understanding of the history, but also has made them keenly aware of the emotional fractures and wounds of the past that are far from healed. We listen to the memories of the Black Panthers and Young Lords as well as the legacy of slavery and its long-lasting trauma. Jimmy and Malik learn about the inner thoughts of the party leaders and the younger generation, they learn how revolution worked then for party members, and they learn how revolution looks for the younger generation. As a result, Jimmy and Malik broach more intimate relationships with members of the Black Panthers and Young Lords. More than anything, the performance expresses the violence and loss that comes as a result of the societal disinvestment of communities of color and the aesthetic practices that might mend or restore such loss.

Universes does not stay stuck in the then and now, but disrupts the past and present with a futurity that renders youths of color as agents of change. In order to incite social change, heal, and restore hope in the political imagination of Jimmy and Malik, the younger generation, Universes' hip-hop sound-making practices—looping, rapping, and beatboxing—teach us not only that we must recall the history of the Black Panthers and Young Lords, but also that we must embody temporal forms within the revolution other than repetition and disruption. Universes' use of looping, rapping, and beatboxing in *Party People* punctuates the history of the Black Panthers and Young Lords with a disruptive and disrupted repetition in an effort to create a communal discourse around radicalism as well as inform and mobilize youths of color today. In order to create a more equitable future, we must put disruption on repeat mode to reignite the spirit of social change and activism. Whereas traditional American history often occludes race, Universes' persistence to sound out the radical past of communities of color accrues the significance of race in America's history. Universes counters the rise of antiblack and anti-immigrant sentiment with their sonic treatise of futurity. They resound dispossessed people as agents of change, recalibrating America's history to include minoritarian histories much needed for the eyes and ears of the younger generation.

NOTES

1 Initially, Huey P. Newton and Bobby Seale, the founders of the organization, named it the Black Panther Party for Self Defense and Justice but in 1968 shortened it to the Black Panther Party (Wilson, *Black Panther Party*, 10). For a comprehensive study of the Black Panther Party, see Alkebulan, *Survival Pending Revolution*; Jones, *Black Panther Party Reconsidered*; Ogbar, *Black Power*; Wilson, *Black Panther Party*.

2 In "¡Oye, Oye!" P. Herrera and McMahon take a sonic turn and make a call to pump up the volume to the ways Latinx theater artists make difference audible and use sonic strategies to claim space, citizenship, and belonging.

3 Muñoz, *Cruising Utopia*.

4 Muñoz, *Cruising Utopia*, 185.

5 Campt, *Listening to Images*, 17.

6 Campt, *Listening to Images*, 107.

7 Facio and Lara, *Fleshing the Spirit*, loc. 262 out of 6607, Kindle.

8 Fernandez, "Young Lords," 153.

9 Barr, introductory letter, ii. https://www.ncjrs.gov/pdffiles1/Digitization /139583NCJRS.pdf, accessed January 1, 2019.

10 For scholarship on mass incarceration, see M. Alexander, *New Jim Crow*; Pager, *Marked*; and Stevenson, *Just Mercy*.

11 In *Can't Stop Won't Stop*, Chang offers two terms to understand the forces that shaped the post–civil rights, hip-hop generation: "the politics of abandonment" and "the politics of containment." For the hip-hop generation, America's equal opportunity ideology was nonexistent, as they were drastically affected by postindustrial economic restructuring and the intensive criminalization of youth of color. As a result of deindustrialization, poor communities of color were abandoned. There were dramatic declines in manufacturing and blue-collar employment in major American cities, and erosions in tax revenue, which resulted in cuts in education and support services for urban youth. At the same time, youths of color faced governmental and state containment as politicians ran on "tough on crime" platforms that represented them as dangerous predators, and prison industries stepped in to provide the economic boost needed with the flight of manufacturing industries from urban centers.

12 The OSF initiative started in 2008. By the end of the initiative, up to thirty-seven new plays would be developed. Some of the most notables include *Roe* by Lisa Loomer, *Indecent* by Paula Vogel, *The Liquid Plain* by Naomi Wallace, and *Sweat* by Lynn Nottage.

13 While State Bill 1070 declares the lack of proper immigration paperwork a mis-
    demeanor, House Bill 2282 prohibits public schools from including any courses
    that promote the overthrow of the US government or resentment toward a race
    or class of people. These bills along with past legal practices such as propositions
    187 and 227, which denied undocumented individuals the right to health care
    and education, and eliminated bilingual education in the classroom, respectively,
    target Latino immigrants and attempt to erase the histories of resistance by mar-
    ginalized communities.

14 Unless otherwise noted, the author bases this analysis on the original version of
    Party People, which premiered at the Oregon Shakespeare Festival on July 3, 2012,
    and ran through November 3, 2013. During this time, the play was published
    through Kindle Direct Publishing, July 26, 2012. Since then *Party* has been rede-
    veloped for Berkeley Rep's Thrust Theatre, where it ran from October 24, 2014,
    through November 23, 2014. Most recently, *Party People* had a successful run
    at the Public Theatre November 1 through December 11, 2016, and it coincided
    with the fiftieth anniversary of the founding of the Black Panther Party for Self
    Defense.

15 Neal, *Soul Babies*, 371.

16 Stoever, *Sonic Color Line*, 14.

17 Stoever, *Sonic Color Line*, 12.

18 Owen, "Fab 5 Freddy and Max Roach."

19 Ross, "Active History on Stage."

20 Workman, "*Party People*."

21 Vazquez, *Listening in Detail*, 8.

22 Vazquez, *Listening in Detail*, 8.

23 Vazquez, *Listening in Detail*, 20.

24 Kheshti, "Touching Listening," 714.

25 Vazquez, *Listening in Detail*, 10; 39.

26 Vazquez, *Listening in Detail*, 21.

27 Martin Luther King Jr.'s speech "A Testament of Hope" (1968) resonates strongly
    here. "The black revolution," as King states, "is much more than a struggle for the
    rights of Negroes. It is forcing America to face all its interrelated flaws—racism,
    poverty, militarism, and materialism. It is exposing evils that are rooted deeply in
    the whole structure of our society . . . and suggests that radical reconstruction of
    society is the real issue to be faced." King, *Testament of Hope*, 315.

28 Hanchard, "Afro-Modernity," 253.

29 Samuels offers a deeper understanding of how disabled folks bend the clock to
    meet their bodies and mind rather than bending their bodies and mind to meet
    the clock. How might these moments of feigning illness to break away from the
    micromanagement of enslaved people's time might be understood through the
    lens of crip time? Samuels, "Six Ways of Looking at Crip Time."

30 Hanchard, "Afro-Modernity," 255.

31 Stadler, "On Whiteness and Sound Studies." M. Smith's study of sound as an "index of identity" in nineteenth-century America, for example, suggests how "nineteenth-century ideas of progress were linked to sounds of work and industry (the cadence of hammers), how plantations ran according to an aural social order of managed sound and noise, and how racial and ethnic otherness, while so traditionally rooted in visual terrains of exclusion and biological racism, were also aurally constructed, from the 'whoops' and 'peals' of Native American 'savagery' to the incomprehensible 'noise' of black speech and black song." As Smith argues, "If we listen to antebellum America, we hear that modernity, capitalism, freedom, and constructions of gender, class, and otherness had distinct and meaningful aural components. It also suggests that workers, black and white, understood the power of silence and the control of sound as tools of effective resistance to their enslavement and exploitation." "Listening to the Heard Worlds," 158.

32 D. Brooks and Kheshti, "Social Space of Sound."

33 Moten, *In the Break*.

34 Keeling and Kun, "Introduction."

35 Stoever, *Sonic Color Line*.

36 Eidsheim, *Race of Sound*.

37 Vasquez, Listening in Detail; Vargas, *Dissonant Divas*; Casillas, *Sounds of Belonging*.

38 R. Brown, *Sound*, 206; Ovadija, *Dramaturgy of Sound*, 16.

39 Malcolm X, Deacons for Defense and Justice (a southern African American civil rights group), and Black Liberation Army were predecessors of the Black Panther Party that made a call for self-defense. For an examination of the Black Panther Party's distinctly revolutionary tactics and the role of state violence, see Y. Williams and Lazerow, *In Search of the Black Panther Party*; and Austin, *Up against the Wall*.

40 With the expanding Cold War in the Third World, the Black Panther Party cultivated international alliances with Algeria and revolutionary governments such as Cuba, North Korea, China, North Vietnam, and the People's Republic of the Congo. The Black Panthers began to practice intercommunalism, which called for an international coalition strategy to hinder the worldwide imperialistic empire building project. See Malloy, *Out of Oakland*, 3, 27. For more on the international efforts of the Black Panther Party, see Bloom and Martin, *Black against Empire*; Clemons and Jones, "Global Solidarity"; Jeffries, *Huey P. Newton*; Kelley, "Stormy Weather"; and Reitan, "Cuba, the Black Panther Party, and the U.S. Black Movement."

41 Spencer, *Revolution Has Come*, 117.

42 In 1967 the Student Nonviolent Coordinating Committee and the Black Panther Party briefly joined forces. See Wilson, *Black Panther Party*, 11.

43 For more on sartorial black aesthetics, see Ongiri, *Spectacular Blackness.*

44 For scholarship on the activism of local Black Panther chapters throughout America, see Jeffries, *Black Panther Party in a City near You*; Jeffries, *On the Ground*; Murch, *Living for the City*; J. Williams, *From the Bullet to the Ballot*; Y. Williams, *Black Politics/White Power*; Y. Williams and Lazerow, *Liberated Territory*; and Witt, *Black Panthers in the Midwest.*

45 Many Puerto Ricans joined the efforts of other civil rights organizations such as the Student Nonviolent Coordinating Committee (SNCC) or the Congress of Racial Equality. See Ogbar, *Black Power*, 151.

46 While in jail in the summer of 1968, Cha Cha Jiménez was exposed to the writings of Malcolm X, the Black Panthers, Mao, and other philosophical and political texts by fellow inmates from the Nation of Islam. See Lazú, "Chicago Young Lords," 34, and Ogbar, *Black Power*, 154.

47 Ogbar, *Black Power*, 158.

48 Ogbar, *Black Power*, 156.

49 Fernandez, "Young Lords," 146.

50 Fernandez, "Young Lords," 143.

51 In May 1970, the New York chapter of the YLO split from the Chicago YLO and became the Young Lord Party (Lazú, "Chicago Young Lords," 33). For additional context on the Young Lords Party, see Fernandez, "Between Social Service Reform and Revolutionary Politics"; Enck-Wanzer, *Young Lords*, which offers a collection of significant primary sources with foreword by former Lords Iris Morales and Denise Oliver-Pérez.

52 The Young Lords named their organizing tactics after the Vietnamese Tet Offensive because of their grassroots, well-coordinated organizing that resulted in mass action. The Tet Offensive was a coordinated series of North Vietnamese attacks against South Vietnam that forced the collapse of the government and army of Nguyen Van Thieu, and resulted in the United States scaling back its involvement in the Vietnam War.

53 Torres, "Introduction," 7, and Lazú, "Chicago Young Lords," 30.

54 Negrón-Muntaner, "Look of Sovereignty," 17.

55 Negrón-Muntaner, "Look of Sovereignty," 12–13.

56 Negrón-Muntaner, "Look of Sovereignty," 14.

57 Federal Bureau of Investigation, FBI director to all offices; Federal Bureau of Investigation, G. C. Moore to W. C. Sullivan.

58 *Hampton v. Hanrahan*, 600 F.2d 600 (1979). In April of 1979 the Seventh Circuit Court of Appeals found that the FBI defendants and their government lawyers obstructed justice by suppressing the BPP files. Most significantly, the Court of Appeals also concluded that there was serious evidence to support that the FBI planned and executed the Fred Hampton raid and had participated in a "conspiracy designed to subvert and eliminate the Black Panther Party and its

members," thereby suppressing a "vital radical Black political organization." Also see National Lawyers Guild, *Counter-Intelligence*.

59 Haas, *Assassination of Fred Hampton*.

60 Seale, *Seize the Time*, viii.

61 Seale, *Seize the Time*, 429.

62 The rally was hosted by Masai Hewitt, minister of education of the Black Panther Party. Along with Elaine Brown, other speakers included Angela Davis; Terence Hallinan, attorney and anti-war activist; and Charles Garry, the Black Panthers' attorney, who related a message from Bobby Seale. "Black Panther Rally at Bobby Hutton Memorial Park."

63 E. Brown, *Seize the Time*.

64 Brittney Cooper posits that "the racial struggles we are experiencing are clashes over time and space. . . . Those in power dictate the pace of the workday. They dictate how much money our time is worth" ("Racial Politics of Time") Similarly posited in Lipsitz, *How Racism Takes Place*.

65 Hanchard, "Afro-Modernity," 256.

66 Roger Guenveur Smith's one-man play *A Huey P. Newton Story* (1996), for instance, examines the Black Panthers cofounder. Jacqui Lazú's "El Bloque, a Young Lords Story" (2007) focuses on how the Young Lords gang in Chicago's Lincoln Park transformed into a national human rights organization and mobilized Puerto Ricans and other marginalized communities during the civil rights movement. Jacqueline Wade's *Black Panther Women* (2016) brings to life the African American women who joined the Black Panther Party and sought to transform a system of racial oppression.

67 Universes conducted interviews between 2009 and 2012 with founding Black Panther Party member Bobby Seale; former members David Hilliard, Emory Douglas, Billy X Jennings, and Ericka Huggins; and Young Lords cofounder Jose Cha Cha Jimenez and members Felipe Luciano and Iris Morales.

68 The published version of *Party People* in 2012 differs from the 2016 New York premiere at the Public Theatre.

69 Schloss, *Making Beats*, 138.

70 Schloss, *Making Beats*, 138.

71 Universes, *Party*, loc. 38–48, Kindle.

72 I am inspired by the decolonial project of Facio and Lara, who call to flesh the spirit and spirit the flesh. "The fleshing of the spirit and the spiriting of the flesh," as they argue, "are linked intrinsically to social, environmental and global justice, to the well-being of us as women, to our communities and all of life, to all of our relations." I use the word "enflesh" to stress how Universes gives bodily form to the memories of the Black Panthers and Young Lords as well as the many spirits of members who have long passed or are still in the struggle. *Fleshing the Spirit*, loc. 263, Kindle.

73 Seale, *Seize the Time*, 408.

74 Christol discusses the use of the word "motherfucker" in Bobby Seale's *Seize the Time: The Story of the Black Panther Party and Huey Newton* as symbolic of a rupture or crisis.

75 In the production at the Public in 2016 the opening scene begins with the vocal performance of "motherfucker"; however, in the 2012 published script, the play begins with Jimmy and Malik silently working on their Black Panthers and Young Lords multimedia performance art exhibit. The monologue appears in both the production and published version, loc. 122–140, Kindle.

76 History.com Editors, "Police Kill Two Members."

77 I am thinking about how Campt and Moten deal with acts of refusal. In *Listening to Images* Campt calls attention to the "quotidian practices of refusal" by dispossessed people. Similarly, in *In the Break* Moten argues that since Western theory has never kept the black body in mind and has excluded it from the system, black performance asserts the existence of a black subject (13–14). Both Campt and Moten see blackness as something "fugitive," an ongoing refusal of standards imposed by white supremacy. This refusal to be silenced and erased is the premise of Party People. See also Coleman, "Practices of Refusal in Images."

78 Malik and Jimmy stand for the post–civil rights generation and are composite characters based on the experiences of members in Universes.

79 Gosa and Nielson, *Hip Hop and Obama Reader*, 13; Chang, *Total Chaos*, x; Rose, *Black Noise*, 39.

80 Smalls explains that "beatboxing, like the other elements of hip hop, is an art form influenced by multiply sound genealogies, including French troubadours, North Indian 'vocal bols,' West African ritual music, jazz, blues, barbershop quartets, and Japanese technology (Roland drum)." "'Make the Music with Your Mouth.'" Also see TyTe and White Noise, "Part 2: Old Skool."

81 Stowell and Plumbley, "Characteristics of the Beatboxing Vocal Style"; Kapur, Benning, and Tzanetakis, "Query-by-Beatboxing."

82 Universes, *Party*, loc. 79–80, Kindle.

83 Blaylock, Patil, Greer, and Narayanan, "Sounds of the Human Vocal Tract," 2288. Included in this study is a table of beatboxing sounds that appear linguistic with a description of them.

84 Blaylock, Patil, Greer, and Narayanan, "Sounds of the Human Vocal Tract," 2288.

PART II
CHOREO-
CHRONOGRAPHIES

Joe Louis's Utopic Glitch

In this chapter, I consider the ways that black bodies can call forth utopic disjunctures in time. To do so, I turn to two archives of movement. My first and primary archive lies in sports reporters' narration of the boxer Joe Louis (World Heavyweight Champion, 1937–1949); my second supporting archive lies in a lineage of dance and its respective narration. In both of these discursive archives, movement begets in its viewers the impression of intertwining animal and mechanical aesthetics, reflecting the imbrication of the primitive and modern that characterizes twentieth-century artistic production across aesthetic forms. Unlike other aesthetic forms, though, movement arts not only are preoccupied with time, but are themselves time-based: they are the unfolding of gesture in time. Movement artists' utilizations of animal and mechanical tropes can thus signify on two levels: first, they may address the animal and mechanical as time-based ideas of historical progression (the presumed development from the primitive to the modern); second, they may mobilize the animal and mechanical as embodiments of durational gesture. In other words, movement artists can perform the ways that an animal and a machine move differently in time.

Louis's archive suggests that, when suspended between these normally disjunctive regimes of timekeeping, a body might enact a utopic temporality that is neither animal nor mechanical, neither past nor future—and yet is all of it, too. Therefore, in what follows I will propose Louis's performance as one of utopic "glitch"—the embodied performance of an error or bug in a system. As artist and researcher Andrew Brooks describes, "the glitch involves encouraging or amplifying the failure of technologies and systems. Claiming aberration and failure as sites of creation, glitch artists and musicians create unstable systems that allow for emergent and distributed forms of agency. Paradoxical in nature, the glitch is inevitable yet unexpected, tiny yet disruptive. It is an art form that amplifies noise both literally and conceptually."[1] Brooks names as qualities of the glitch an inherent instability, the amplification of system failures, and emergent and distributed agency—all qualities that resound in descriptions of Louis's inhabitation of discordant time signatures and the black public's empathetic response. Louis's movement aesthetics activated his position as subject and object, thing and flesh, such that Louis was at once a figure of animalistic machinery and the ambassadorial hope of his people. Louis generated an incredible affective response in his fans, and I will argue that the media vehicles that carried Louis's performed glitch into American homes facilitated Americans' intensely emotional response by allowing his movements to exert a kinesthetic claim on viewers. Few Americans saw Louis in action. Instead, newspaper and radio coverage offered Americans a proprioceptive experience of Louis's movement, an experience that was all the more e/affective for being communal.

Descriptions of the public's radio-based encounter with Louis suggest the kind of hopeful, life-affirming potentiality that is utopia for José Esteban Muñoz. Muñoz particularly embraces the idea of utopia for queer and minoritarian subjects as a way into political possibility and as a reaffirmation of life, both now and in a future that can be better. Utopia is not, for Muñoz, a purely speculative nonplace, nor is it an actualized and inhabitable social structure. Utopia is instead a fleeting image of the possible which resides in the quotidian—a glimmer of futurity glimpsed with life-sustaining effect. It is "a certain mode of nonbeing that is eminent, a thing that is present but not actually existing in the present tense."[2] Utopia urges the present into "relation [with] the alternative temporal and spatial maps provided by a perception of past and future affective worlds."[3] For Muñoz, then, the past, present, and future might signal to each other from their respective places—meaning that, even while each is itself a vibrant world or dimension, their places are relatively fixed.

I will hew close to Muñoz's theorization of the utopic in its fleetingness, in its potentiality, and in its quotidian home. But I am less interested in the future and the past as distant beacons that signal to those trapped in the present and more concerned with how utopia's ephemeral potentiality might rupture the sense of the future, past, and present as stable markers at all. Might some performances or aesthetics disrupt linear, progressive regimes of time, forging a utopic temporality that is fleeting but that is also deeply presentist rather than future oriented (in that the future is not a different location at all)?

If Louis issued glimmers of the utopic that reorganized or ruptured traditional time, perhaps this offered his base a more livable present (even if it was also short lived)—surely no small thing in the wake of what Christina Sharpe has called "antiblackness as total climate."[4] Sharpe's analysis begs the question of how one should live if the present is merely the place where a brutal past meets the likelihood of a nonfuture. Jasmine Johnson's chapter in this volume, "Sorrow's Swing," offers one answer, showing that the buoyancy of black vernacular dance is black mourning set in motion. Johnson takes up an instance in which blackness is constructed through a corporeal assertion that acknowledges the burden of antiblackness and insists upon black life in the face of that burden. In taking up Louis, I turn to another such corporeal assertion, this one focused on interrupting the conscription of blackness into dominant and oppressive temporal structures. Louis's archive suggests that one answer to Sharpe lies in a present that contains fleeting encounters with alternative embodiments—encounters in which race is not abandoned for the sake of freedom but rather used to disrupt the time sheets of nonfreedom. Therefore, I begin with the fleeting, utopian moment.

"There was never a Harlem like the Harlem of last night," trumpeted the *Daily Worker* on June 23, 1938, the day after world heavyweight champion Joe Louis defeated German boxer Max Schmeling. "Take a dozen Harlem Christmases, a score of New Year's eves, a bushel of July 4th's and maybe—yes maybe—you get a faint glimpse of the idea."[5] The Louis–Schmeling fight carried the emotional burden of the approaching World War, and Americans of all stripes cheered for Louis in spite of the color line. But as the *Daily Worker* implied in locating the heart of the festivities in Harlem—where Seventh Avenue was closed from 125th to 145th to accommodate the revelry[6]—Joe Louis held special significance for black Americans. For them, Joe Louis was an outsized figure of hopefulness and potentiality both before and after the moment of impending war.

During the five years between 1933 and 1938 Louis appeared on the front page three times more than anyone else in the widely read African American periodical the *Chicago Defender*, with Emperor Haile Selassie of Ethiopia coming in at a distant second—during years which included the Italian invasion of Ethiopia. (Louis had eighty mentions, Selassie twenty-four.)[7] Over forty-three songs were recorded about Louis, in which he was compared to heroic figures such as Samson, Hercules, Moses, and John Henry.[8] Authors such as Ralph Ellison, Langston Hughes, and Chester Himes mentioned Louis in their works. Richard Wright, Marcus Garvey, and Martin Luther King Jr. each used Louis to illustrate their divergent political agendas. Autobiographies—including those of Miles Davis, Maya Angelou, Malcolm X, and Jimmy Carter—routinely recount listening to Louis fights on the radio, or the feeling of a city when he won.

Newspapers also reported the transformations that swept cities when Louis prevailed. The black newspaper *Philadelphia Tribune* recounted an important Louis victory in this way:

> Negroes from every point of the American compass converged in a great swirl of plunging, dodging men and women, whooping for dear life. Their life flowed together, they were complete to themselves, merged into one body of song, with joyous hearts furnishing drum beats. . . . They swayed i[n] time to the one theme that ran like a steady, glowing thread through the hilarious mob, turning loose everything they had. . . . True, prior to the fight life had dwelt in every fiber of Harlem: yet hardly life—rather the promise of it . . . if Joe won! . . . Even in those hall bedrooms, so familiar to human interest stories—the iron bed, wash-stand, and slop-jar kind—the dinginess of the surroundings were forgotten. The residents therein were King and Queen for a day.[9]

Accounts of Louis victories invariably convey a sense of electric joy. In the passage above, the author is explicit about Louis acting as a catalyst: his win enlivens the very fiber of Harlem, which otherwise lay as dormant potential trapped in the effects of dingy rooms. The result reads as utopic, not only in terms of individual joy—which is present in the swirl of countless black people from every point on the American compass—but also in the way this diverse community is transformed into a flowing body (figure 4.1). This utopic expression is both visual and aural, with unity forged in song and in heart/drum beats as well as through glowing thread. It transforms the present quotidian (iron bed, washstand) into the backdrop of royals. Furthermore, this feeling of hilarious joy colors the newspaper reportage, as the author attempts to render the experience poetically rather than in dispassionate observational tones.

FIGURE 4.1 Harlem residents celebrate after Joe Louis's first-round KO of Max Schmeling, June 22, 1938. *NEW YORK DAILY NEWS* ARCHIVE/GETTY IMAGES.

It was the same in every city, and—significantly—was experienced as equally powerful by black and white observers. British journalist Alistair Cooke was in Baltimore watching a Fats Waller show on the night Joe Louis became heavyweight champion. Cooke described hearing a distant rumble that approached like a wave until it drowned out even the band, finally crashing into the club as a chaotic rumpus "like Christmas Eve in darkest Africa." "For one night," he said, "in all the lurid dark-towns of America, the black man was king."[10]

Repeated references to the crowning of the common black man (and woman) through Louis, the joy that pulses through mobs of people, the enlivening thrum that reached into unremarkable cold-water flats—this affective glow stands in marked contrast to the figure of Louis himself. Louis was a famously inexpressive figure, and the press also commented extensively—even obsessively—about this quality of Louis's performative self (figure 4.2). Yet in *both* the dominant press and the black press, descriptions linked Louis's expressionlessness to his movement qualities in the ring, and these movements were, in turn, described as mechanical, animalistic, or both.

FIGURE 4.2 Joe Louis walking with his wife, Marva Trotter Louis, in Harlem, September 25, 1935. BETTMANN/GETTY IMAGES.

On the side of the deadpan as an expression of the animal, there are instances such as the following:

> "Stinging" Louis is like flicking a sleeping lion with a whip. Where Dempsey, stung, charges in wildly, Louis . . . moves inexorably in on that deadly stalk of his—his "dead pan" face showing none of the fire behind it.[11]

> "The best nickname for Joe Louis," says one who has known him well for the last year, "is Black Leopard." . . . "I like the name Black Leopard because . . . this is the untamable, dead-pan actor of the jungle whose main thrill in life is a chance to rip and tear. The main thrill Joe Louis knows is knocking someone out as quickly as he can land either right or left— without any change in expression."[12]

In both of these passages, Louis is compared to a jungle cat. Cats bore a special relationship to the black body during the early twentieth century, when the "jungle" symbolized the colonial project, exoticism, and "primitivist" aesthetics (such as those underwriting the "Voodoo Macbeth" of 1936). Cobras and other striking snakes also loom large in descriptions of Louis. One might anticipate animal metaphors for black boxers in particular, given the well-known and long-standing stereotype of African Americans as bestial and unevolved (and some newspaper reports certainly did suggest that Louis was not particularly smart). Yet in drawing the comparison to large cats in particular, journalists linked Louis to creatures generally regarded as intelligent—or at least wily—though this intelligence might live in the body more than in the brain.[13]

Beyond a general reference to jungle animals, though, both of these quotations focus on *particular* movement qualities: on the one hand a "deadly stalk" that carries connotations of sly, lurking slowness; on the other, a desire to rip and tear that is related, instead, to fast or savage abandon. These passages also gesture toward unpredictability—Louis can move left or right, or go from sleeping to tearing lion, with no telling change of expression.

Yet even as some reports interpret Louis's movement through the trope of the jungle cat, others do so through the figure of the automaton:

> Joe Louis' training camp at Pompton Lakes, N.J. is a busy workshop where the finishing touches are being put on a great fighting machine. By the time Chief Engineer John Roxborough and Master Mechanic Jack Blackburn finish oiling and polishing the automaton from Detroit, he may not be the consummate fighting machine he will be some day, but he will be tuned and adjusted to destroy Ponderous Primo Carnera when they meet June 25.[14]

> The poker-faced Louis, standing in midring while his beaten foe was being led to his corner, accepted the cheers of the crowd with no emotion. He stood there, his face expressionless while Referee McGarrity raised his right arm. Then he shuffled off to his corner to receive the grins and handshakes of his handlers. There wasn't a drop of perspiration on Louis' brow.[15]

In these passages, Louis is described as expressionless, emotionless, and machinelike. In the second passage, he doesn't walk, but shuffles. Given the surrounding description of him without emotion or agency (especially in the way he stands waiting for McGarrity to raise his arm or to blankly receive praise), it's clear this isn't the shuffle of soft-shoe but of a machine—one might imagine the stiff walk adopted as a convention of Frankenstein's monster in movies, a walk meant to show him as built. The first quotation is much clearer in the purpose to which Louis has been built (and by whom).

Images of the metallurgic are employed often with boxers; a "hammering" punch, for example, is a long-standing descriptor. Yet, notably, descriptions of Louis absent the human agent. A hammer, in other words, requires a human operator—a person to swing the hammer and provide it its force. A machine may have an engineer and a mechanic, but once it is turned on, it does its own work, requiring little or no humanity. As automaton, Louis is described as mechanized in just this way.

Robots and automatons were a natural preoccupation of the machine age, when Americans worried about the effects of machines on their subjectivity as their work was sped and regulated in new ways.[16] Yet the black body as automated machine carries a special significance in the American imagination. Beyond the general objectification that accompanied slave status, we might consider Alan L. Olmstead and Paul W. Rhode's hypothesis, taken up by Edward E. Baptist, that the average amount of cotton picked per day per slave tripled between 1810 and 1860.[17] In other words, while American production as a whole sped *because* of machinery, black American production had (already) sped *as* machinery. Surely this allows us to consider the metaphorical implications of the black body as not simply employing mechanical methods, but being mechanized *in and of itself*.

Black Americans might then be uniquely poised to offer aesthetic interpretations of the machine age, and this is indeed what Joel Dinerstein proposes in his work *Swinging the Machine*. Dinerstein's book "reveal[s] how the presence (or 'voice') of machinery became integral to the cultural production of African American storytellers, dancers, blues singers and jazz musicians" through a process he calls the "techno-dialogic."[18] He sees the techno-dialogic at work especially in swing music—in its big band musical forms, in the dances that accompanied it, and in the subjects (namely John Henry) that preoccupied it. In each of the cultural forms he analyzes, Dinerstein sees reflected the aesthetic elements that social theorist Stuart Chase advocated in his 1929 work *Men and Machines*: "mass, size, speed, fleeting images, repetition, sharpness of line; oral experiences of the staccato, precise timing and rhythm of completed operation"[19]—a list that makes boxing seem suddenly like a perfect modern aesthetic form.

Moreover, Dinerstein's descriptions of machine aesthetics suggest the primitive as the ghost in the machine. Throughout *Swinging the Machine*, Dinerstein cites white observers of black cultural production whose assessments of black machine aesthetics he finds valuable *in spite* of their primitivism.[20] He urges his readers to look past the fact that these commentators associated blackness with wildness, abandon, nature, or irrationality, and notice *instead* blackness's performance of machine aesthetics. One senses Dinerstein insulates black subjects from observers' accusations of primitivism in order to assert their full, modern humanity—an instinct with which I can sympathize. Yet as Shane Vogel has shown, sometimes these other, less respectable aesthetic associations were exactly what black cultural makers were after.[21] Certainly, primitivism could *also* be racist projection. But to insist that it must be overstates respectability's hold on the African American aesthetic imagination. It also undercuts the mutual imbrication of the modern and the primitive that is a constant thread of the modernist cultural production of the early twentieth century.[22]

Unsure whether what they saw in Louis's movement was more machine or jungle animal, sportswriters refused to pick a favorite, insisting instead that Louis was somehow both. Here's an illustrative quotation, which appeared in the first book-length biography of Louis, in 1936:

> Joe Louis . . . might be likened to a combination panther and polar bear; he is ice cold under every stress in the ring. Even more he is a pugilistic robot, a living thing of gears and levers, of bearings and coils and pistons, the human machine—but what a machine! Physically we see six feet and one inch of athletic manhood so molded in streamline smoothness it is ideal for shedding punches. . . . The Ring Robot . . . , if you take him apart to find the mechanism [in] back of his tremendous punching ability, must reveal an abundance of steel in the muscles. How otherwise can one account for the tremendous recoil in the impact of his blow?[23]

This bizarre quotation is representative of descriptions of Louis not only in its choice of referent images—that is, a panther and a machine—but in its toggling between them. Over and over, across years and media sources, descriptions of Louis are framed in animalistic terms, especially using animals of colonized places that were seen as more "primitive" and exotic. At the same time, *and sometimes within the same sentence*, Louis is described as a machine. At times such descriptions are predictably racist in the ways they marshal the nonhuman, yet at other times journalists apply these tropes in laudatory tones. Black journalists also employed (and collapsed) these twinned tropes to describe—and honor—Louis's fighting prowess, suggesting these descriptors resonated with black readerships as well as white ones.

As an example of this toggling in the black press, William Nunn of the *Pitts-burgh Courier* wrote:

> Louis, last night, was a superb fighting machine. He went out to "shoot the works" in the first round. His attack was cold, calculating, merciless. As Bob Murphy said, "For the remainder of the 10-round battle, Louis moved after his foe with the relentless shuffle of a crazed animal moving through the canebrakes. There was a weave, a bob of the head, and then unchained lightning flashing through the glow."[24]

Nunn's description evokes the tropics, as Louis moves as an animal moves through cane (presumably as the cat to which the press so often referred). But there is also explicit mention of a fighting machine—and it is cold and calculating. "Merciless" might refer to either machinery or the indifferent predator—as, indeed, might this unchained lightning, which is both electrical, like machinery, and untethered, like a beast.

Some of these observations originated, Nunn acknowledges, from Bob Murphy, editor of the *Detroit Evening Times*. But in seconding Murphy's description through his citation, Nunn paints Louis as both animal and automaton, primitive fighter and calculated machine, for the black readership of the *Pittsburgh Courier*. And he kept up the refrain, a few months later describing a fight in vivid present tense: "Carnera comes to his feet to meet the relentless 'fighting automaton' who has battered him to the floor. His arms are hanging low, as he backs around the ring. Like a panther, stalking his prey, Joe Louis comes in again!"[25] A few months after that: "Max Baer, the 'in-and-out' champion, will meet a perfect 'fighting machine' 'neath the glare of the calcium floodlights at Yankee Stadium come Tuesday night, September 24. He'll meet a demon of the ring . . . a cold-blooded, ruthless, cool, calculating 'killer.' . . . He'll face a man transformed into a venomous jungle beast."[26] In each of these quotes, Nunn toggles with stunning rapidity between Louis as automaton and Louis as jungle beast.

While Nunn was perhaps the most constant employer of these paradoxical discourses in the black press, he was hardly the only one. Bill Gibson of the *Baltimore Afro-American*, for example, described Louis's fight against Max Baer by saying:

> It was like having a gun on a big-game hunt and then suddenly discovering that you had left the shells at home. It was the case of an unarmed man treading into a nest of machine-gunners. So fast and furious did the

piston-like arms of Louis release their dynamite on the face and body of Baer that it was well nigh impossible to count the blows. It was open season for Baer-hunting and Louis took full advantage.[27]

Here Louis transforms from the presumed prey of the elephant-gun into the embodied nest of machine gunners (men and guns both), then into the pistons releasing dynamite, then into a hunter. A mere three sentences later, Gibson wrote, "Like a slinking, blood-thirsty tiger, the Brown Bomber, who by his showing earned the modified title of 'Brown Embalmer,' staked his prey. His deliberation was uncanny, and as in his other major engagements, it threw fear into the heart and soul of his opponent." Bomber, embalmer, blood-thirsty tiger, all within the span of a sentence.

In their utilization of these tropes, the sportswriters who translated their visual impressions of Louis provide yet another instance in which the primitive and the modern act as intertwined, coconstitutive phenomenon—a long, cross-disciplinary project in which the global north invented (and periodically overhauled) the so-called primitive in order to define and negotiate its own position in the industrializing world. Tracing the contours of the modern and the primitive was an especially generative preoccupation for artists and writers (as well as the collectors and editors whose curatorial hands bolstered their cultural import).

For some, the colonized or racialized other represented a human idyll—a primeval vestige still blessedly connected to earth and to gods, an uncontaminated fount from which we might drink—in limited doses—to reconnect with innocence or mysticism. This view underwrote much of the levity of the Jazz Age, as well as the change in Western artistic styles sparked by Picasso's famous encounter with African masks at the Trocadéro Museum in 1917. For others, natives in their irrational savagery were the perfect models for existence in a brutal modern world, or as a cure for bourgeois ennui—hence the manifesto of the Italian futurists simultaneously praised gleaming machines and war and primordial elements. Surrealists, too, often embraced a darker primitive imaginary.[28] Whether idealizing the other as a source of innocence or barbarity, though, it was clear "they" were not "us" (or at least not as "we" are today)—not rational, not civilized, not modern, not mechanized.

Black American cultural production of the twentieth century self-consciously entered this fray, situated, as it was, on the fault line of blackness's presumed primitivism and America's assumed modernism. In negotiating their response to blackness's persistent conscription into this entanglement, many artists preferred a side. Some black artists asserted their place in modernity's future through a purposeful embrace of the machine. As Dinerstein has convincingly argued, this can be seen in the driving beat of swing music or in the "torque, wheel, and precision" of the lindy hop's gyrations (to name two examples).[29] Other black artists, however, embraced a more primitivist view of themselves. Zora Neale Hurston offers a signature instance of this in "How It Feels to Be Colored Me":

> The orchestra grows rambunctious, rears on its hind legs and attacks the tonal veil with primitive fury, rending it, clawing it until it breaks through to the jungle beyond. I follow those heathens—follow them exultingly. I dance wildly inside myself; I yell, I whoop; I shake my assegai above my head, I hurl it true to the mark *yeeeeooww!* I am in the jungle and living in the jungle way. My face is painted red and yellow, and my body is painted blue. My pulse is throbbing like a war drum. I want to slaughter something—give pain, give death to what, I do not know. But the piece ends. The men of the orchestra wipe their lips and rest their fingers. I creep back slowly to the veneer we call civilization with the last tone.[30]

Hurston explicitly embraces the primitive jungle and its animality, and she implicitly limns its temporal frame. Her use of "creep back" articulates the primitive as outside of the here and now, and the labeling of civilization as a veneer suggests the temporal layering of progressivist time. The dyad of primitive/modern pertains, even if one might move between them.

By contrast, Louis—as Nunn, Gibson, and others present him—corporeally asserts his *simultaneous* belonging to both animal and mechanical time. Moreover, his movement-based intervention stakes its own claim about the modern/primitive entanglement as one *of* time. As reported by the most expert watchers of his day, Louis embodied a temporality that was both, *and neither,* primitive yesteryear and/nor technological future; both *and neither* pre- and/nor posthuman, thereby unfurling the black body across time.

As mentioned at the outset, the mechanistic and animalistic bear different relationships to timekeeping.[31] This is true as they manifest in conceptions of progressive, evolutionary eras—that is, in the idea that the animalistic is tied to an earlier and less evolved moment of human development (for better or worse). But, as one can see in the earlier descriptions of Louis, the animal and mechanical also bear different relationships to time in the ways their movements play out rhythmically or durationally. The mechanistic is above all characterized by regularity—a reliable, unceasing beat that came to be insinuated into the human body during the age of industrialization.[32] The animalistic, on the other hand—especially as embodied by the jungle cat—is about explosive movement out of stillness or stalking; an unpredictable surprise of movement that is anything but regulated. The optimal assertion of modernist aesthetics in movement, then, finds ways of interweaving these two interpretations of time. And the optimal *black* assertion of modernist aesthetics in movement is to suspend the black body between modernism's poles, allowing the black body to flicker between them.

Louis appeared to slip the yoke of what dance scholar Thomas DeFrantz has called "legitimate corporality" by dislocating the black body within time's usual fences—enacting his own glitch. Louis offered his audience a vision of what it might look like to signal against the regimes of time and timekeeping that would trap the black subject between the ticking modern future and the timeless African past.[33] While this experience was available to all Americans, it held special significance for black Americans due to their particular relationship with animal and mechanical temporal regimes. I therefore think that Louis can be seen to embody a messianic time, as Walter Benjamin describes it—ruptural, immediate, qualitative, and sort of quantum in its historical movement.

Benjamin's philosophy refuses the concept of mankind's historical progress, which, he says, "cannot be sundered from the concept of its progression through a homogenous, empty time."[34] Rather than an empty, forward-moving expanse, Benjamin frames all of human history as miniscule—a nanosecond in the history of the universe.[35] This historical condensation—all of human time in such close proximity—facilitates the eruption of the messianic moment: "the 'time of the now,'" he says, "is shot through with chips of Messianic time."[36] Benjamin makes the recognition and redemption of "the presence of the now" the true calling of the historical materialist.[37] The historical materialist "takes cognizance of [messianic time] in order to blast a specific era out of the homogenous course of history—blasting a specific life out of the era or a specific work out of the lifework. . . . The nourishing fruit of the historically understood contains time as a precious but tasteless seed."[38] Through its blasting cognition, historical materialism does not so much reconstruct the past as construct it anew in relation to the present. "Historicism gives the 'eternal' image *of* the past," says Benjamin; "historical materialism supplies a unique experience *with* the past [emphasis added]."[39] The messianic brings forth the latent but unactualized potential of what has been. The newly realized can appear in the form of a dialectical image, which is not the return of what was before but instead a *"renewed presentation* of what was never really present before."[40] In the flash of the dialectical image—here, the visions of Louis's movement, which reference but are not of a primitive past—"the historical index of the images not only says that they belong to a particular time; it says, above all, that they attain to legibility only at a particular time."[41] I'll return to the particular legibility of Louis as a product of a historical moment shortly.

First it's worth noting that the future doesn't obtain much in Benjamin. Indeed, he criticizes social democracy for "assign[ing] to the working class the role of the redeemer of future generations, in this way cutting the sinews of its greatest strength . . . , [for their hatred and their spirit of sacrifice] are nourished by the image of enslaved ancestors rather than that of liberated grandchildren."[42] But what of those rarely written into the progress of homogenous time, and rarely cast as redeemers of the future? What of those grandchildren unlikely to be more liberated than the children of the current present? This is where, in combatting the historical nonfuture diagnosed by Sharpe, Benjamin's presentist philosophy productively meets Muñoz's not-yet-here. When one brings Benjamin's commitment to the dead into conversation with the minoritarian strategies for utopian futures Muñoz names, one finds that the messianic rupture of the present might contain redemptive potential for the inevitable violences of the future as well as those of the past. If the dense seed of the messianic present can encase the not-yet-here as well as the has-been, the messianic now might redeem the unborn as well as the already-dead—not because the future will be progress (a concept that would rely on homogenous time) but rather because we can suppose, given the stature of our human history in the universe, that it *won't* be.

This wasn't Benjamin's ultimate concern—for him the messianic, in its fullness, would bring about the theological end of time: "Only a redeemed mankind receives the fullness of its past," he said; "only for a redeemed mankind has its past become citable in all its moments."[43] Still, as Stéphane Symons summarizes, this doesn't mean "there are no anticipations of this suspension which are, themselves, already visible in history."[44] Rather, the messianic moment's citational power might harken to the future, too.

If Lee Edelman or Sharpe would point out the limits of that futurity for the minoritarian subject (and Muñoz takes as one of his prompts Edelman doing just that), Benjamin's philosophy is also haunted by the oppressed, by the enslaved ancestors and the past sufferings rendered mute in the course of homogenous historical time.[45] Indeed, it is the oppressed who have the power to call down (or up) the messianic now; "their incapacity to testify to what was [and will be] done to them, becomes sign of the (historical) condition that is in need of (divine) redemption."[46] For those presently consigned to the historical realm, caught between oppressive past and grim future, this may seem like small consolation. *So*, Louis's glitch might suggest, *don't (only) be caught there.*

Other instances of this ruptural timekeeping can be found in Louis's day, and in our own. Take, for example, the dance stylings of eccentric dancer Earl "Snake Hips" Tucker, a contemporary of Louis.[47] Tucker is linked to the primitive, as is clear from his name. Dance historians Marshall and Jean Stearns described Tucker's dance as one "in which the loins [were] undulated in a very un-European fashion."[48] The Stearnses' assertion pits Tucker's movement self-consciously against European movement, though it does some of its work through nonspecific suggestion. Duke Ellington, who performed with Tucker, was less reserved, saying Tucker's dance originated in "tide-water Maryland . . . , one of those primitive lost colonies where they practice pagan rituals and their dancing style evolved from religious seizures."[49] Ritual, excess, and altered states inform Tucker's dance in this estimation.

The Stearnses wrote that Tucker had a "disengaged and a menacing air, like a sleeping volcano, which seemed to give audiences the feeling that he was a cobra and they were mice"; as with Louis, the cobra, as an exotic animal, signals the black body. Yet they also described him as having a "baleful, hypnotic stare"—an erasure of emotion that tips toward the mechanical.[50] Moreover, Tucker's dance routines could also enact the mechanical, as we see in footage from Tucker's brief appearance in Duke Ellington's short film *Symphony in Black: A Rhapsody of Negro Life* (1935).

The first clear image of Tucker, which is composed as a long body shot from above, shows him dancing "snake hips." It's followed by images of his lower legs and feet, with a line of chorus girls in feathered headdresses silhouetted across them. The women never quite coalesce into an "indissoluble girl cluster," as Siegfried Kracauer described the Tiller Girls' dancing aesthetic.[51] Yet while the Tiller Girls' geometric perfection was intended to be seen from aerial heights (a quality exploited by Busby Berkeley, Louis's contemporary, in his cinematic iteration of such dance), the women supporting Tucker's number instead offer a close-up, zoomed-in view. They still give the impression of "a machine of girls"[52]—but in this case, the impression is that they are the gears that drive Tucker's legs. The next shot of Tucker is from below, with a couple at a cabaret table now obscuring the lower part of his body—then once again, a cut to the chorus girls superimposed over those legs. Finally, we see

Tucker doing an iteration of the tremble. Tucker's upper body remains frozen as his legs shake him in an in-place circle like a wind-up figure.

Tucker has been claimed as a progenitor by contemporary street dancers who recognize a lineage from Tucker's dance stylings to their own. Several commenters on YouTube footage of Tucker's performance in the short film *Crazy House* (1930) recognize "pop and lock" in Tucker's belly roll, wherein he falls to an uncanny angle at the limit of a hip extension, then pulls himself up to fall to the other side.[53] An interweaving of animal and mechanical movements also links Tucker's eccentric dance with today's street dance styles like Bone Breaking (or Flex) and Memphis Jookin. Dancers at times enact machinelike qualities, moving with fluidity to a hard stop, as though having reached the end of a mechanical extension. This movement quality evokes the engineered and inanimate (i.e., "the robot").[54] Dancers also index the motion of the automaton, or explicitly humanoid machine, perhaps most clearly in moments where it appears to break, collapsing a joint at a time into unlikely angles. Organic collapse is not achieved in this breakage; rather, it evokes rigid forms dangling from mechanized joints. At the same time, contemporary dance also depends on the animal in a number of ways: stalk-and-pounce movements that combine gliding control with quick, unexpected explosions of speed (this is the inverse of the machine gliding to hard stop), near-falls or flips that depend upon catlike agility for recovery or transition, or inhuman movements that nevertheless trade in animal rather than mechanical possibilities—movements that dancers will call "the fish" or "the octopus," for example.

Predictably, writers who describe street dance inevitably toggle between the mechanistic and animalistic in their descriptions, mirroring the ways newspapers attempted to report the aesthetics of Louis's movement. Describing Memphis Jookin, for example, the *New York Times* writer Alastair Macaulay writes:

> Frequently a current of isolated impulses passes in sequence down a dancer's arm: you see each component—the wrist, the forearm, the elbow, each shoulder—but you see also the snakelike rippling fluency that turns these staccato effects into a legato current. Sometimes upper and lower body move at the same time, sometimes with seeming independence; at other times a phrase jumps from lower to upper, or vice versa.[55]

In this passage, "snakelike" is explicitly animalistic, while "component" evokes the mechanized. "Current" might refer to water (primordial force) or to electricity (enlivening force of the machine); this ambiguity redoubles the sense of admixture.[56]

Like the earlier writers struggling to name what they saw in Louis's boxing, writers on contemporary street dance struggle to name the aesthetics of disjunctive temporality, most often, though not only, rendering it in the form of slow motion rather than lightning-fast strikes. One of the most masterful workers of this effect is Storyboard P, a dancer of Flex. Indeed, an article about Storyboard P in the *New Yorker* was titled "The Impossible Body." As its author Jonah Weiner explains, "Although Storyboard can twist, curve, and crumple his body with a calligrapher's control, he likes to disrupt fluid motion with tremors and twitches, so that he appears to flicker, like a figure in a zoetrope."[57] Against fluid motion—the smoothness of hydraulics come to mind—Storyboard introduces tremors and twitches. Tremors and twitches are the organic body's own small glitches, the tiny disruptions which highlight failure and error in a system. The effect of this is like a zoetrope—that simple Victorian movement machine that sent human and animal bodies into magical, flickering motion. Weiner goes on to explain that Storyboard P employs a style known as "animation." As one fellow dancer describes, Storyboard P has pushed the effect to the point where he can appear to be "glitching"— embodying an irregularity in time.[58]

Sound scholar Caleb Kelly has described the work of the glitch as one of "cracking" media; similarly, Louis's aesthetic embodiment of divergent time signatures cracked the medium of time, introducing error to time systems that would consign the black subject to a prehistoric ahistory or yoke him to the regimentation of modern time.[59] Louis signaled *between* the empty and homogenous time signatures foisted onto the black subject (where the empty might stand for prehistoric nontime and the homogenous for the regimentation of modern labor). Signaling both, Louis overloaded the system.

Furthermore, through the radio commentary of his fights, Louis was able to act as an agent for others to experience something of this glitch—and recall that Brooks's definition of the glitch encompassed the amplification of noise and the distribution of agency. Accounts of the affective power of Louis fights suggest a messianic cracking open of the present as a powerful restorative in a climate of terrible past and likely terrible future.

Relatively few Americans were lucky enough to watch Louis in action— even fewer with a view that could accommodate close observance. Most boxing fans in the 1930s were introduced to fighters through newspapers, got blow-by-blows of fights from radio announcers, and then enjoyed more colorful written accounts in newspapers the next day. As Louis was receiving regular newspaper coverage throughout the incredible string of victories

FIGURE 4.3 Joe Louis flexing his back muscles, April 4, 1935. COURTESY OF THE *DETROIT NEWS*.

that installed him as a cultural icon, sports pages played a formative role in how Louis was fashioned in iconicity. Stated simply, newspapers told Americans what they were "seeing" when they listened to a Louis fight. Or, more intriguingly, newspapers told Americans what they were *feeling* when they listened to a Louis fight, for blow-by-blow radio commentary invites a kind of proprioception—the sensory perception of muscles and ligaments (figure 4.3).

John Martin, the formidable American dance critic and theorist, referred to proprioception as "movement sense," and theorized its role in the spectatorship of dance.[60] Though Martin is rightly criticized on many fronts—a strong racial bias not least among them—models for understanding movement spectatorship remain indebted to his observations. Martin believed that proper dance spectatorship was underpinned by an organically triggered metakinesis rooted both in our prior muscular experience (that is, our movement sense) *and* in a process of "inner mimicry" (the mimetic translation of the physical world into our own bodies, such that we straighten when standing before a tall building, or interpret a rock as standing or lying based on a physiological mirroring). Martin believed that if inner mimicry resulted from even the inanimate object, the muscular sympathy triggered by observing a moving human body was all the more powerful.[61] And because Martin believed that emotional memories were at their core physical memories, he believed they could be triggered when watching dance. He summarized the quick transition thus:

> We shall cease to be mere spectators and become participants in the movement that is presented to us, and though to all outward appearances we shall be sitting quietly in our chairs, we shall nevertheless be dancing synthetically with all our musculature. Naturally these motor responses are registered by our movement-sense receptors, and awaken appropriate emotional associations akin to those which have animated the dancer in the first place. It is the dancer's whole function to lead us into imitating his actions with our faculty for inner mimicry in order that we may experience his feelings. Facts he could tell us, but feelings he cannot convey in any other way than by arousing them in us through sympathetic action.[62]

It is farfetched to imagine that emotional and physical lives are so perfectly aligned across race, class, and gender that an intended emotion can be automatically triggered by muscular sympathy. Still, the viewer's matrix of emotional and bodily sensation remains an ongoing concern of movement scholarship.[63] *Something* bodily transpires when watching dance, and it often has an emotional correlative. The sticky points consist in what crosses bodies, how, and how to name that thing or process. Deidre Sklar uses the term "empathic kinesthetic perception" to describe a metakinetic process that maintains difference. She writes (emphasis mine):

> Empathic kinesthetic perception suggests a combination of mimesis and empathy. Paradoxically, *it implies that one has to close one's eyes to look at movement, ignoring its visual effects and concentrating instead on feeling oneself to be in the other's body, moving.* Whereas visual perception implies an "object" to be perceived from a distance with the eyes alone, empathic kinesthetic perception implies a bridging between subjectivities. This kind of "connected knowing" produces a very intimate kind of knowledge, a taste of those ineffable movement experiences that can't be easily put into words. Paradoxically, as feminist psychologist Judith Jordan points out, the kind of temporary joining that occurs in empathy produces not a blurry merger but an articulated perception of differences.[64]

Though Sklar wrote this as part of an article about cross-cultural witnessing of dance, it carries profound implications for the intraracial witness of Joe Louis's movement through the quotidian vector of the radio. As mentioned above, blow-by-blow commentary is deeply proprioceptive. Culturally, we honor sports commentary's metakinetic power all the time—whenever characters in movies and plays and commercials imagine themselves as athletic figures *and then self-narrate* the action as they pretend to swing a bat or shadowbox ("and the crowd goes wild!"). Radio commentary invites us to feel ourselves in the position of the actor who is narrated, to feel their movement in our own, still muscles. Most writers on dance's kinesthetic sympathies (or empathies) focus on vision as vehicle—yet Sklar here suggests a bypassing of optic witness, thereby opening up kinesthetic empathy as a critical apparatus. Indeed, Sklar suggests that this effect might be all the more powerful for being unsighted: one has to close one's eyes to look at movement, ignoring its visual effects and concentrating instead on feeling oneself to be in the other's body, moving.

If Louis's radio listeners experienced empathic kinesthetic perception as they listened to the fight, perhaps they experienced not only the feeling of punching and footwork, but also the *timing* of that feeling of punching and footwork, which was the timing of the glitch. Sklar's theory, in other words, provides for the "emergent and distributed agency" of the glitch to spread to the public, where it could manipulate the temporal and corporeal coordinates of Louis's fans. Perhaps the elation of Louis victories came not only through the defeat of white opponents, but through the tiny embodied error that let black bodies signal against the timekeeping regimes under which they normally labored (perhaps made all the more acute through the highly regimented three-minute rounds of the ring). This might explain the joyous collapse of time that appears in the quotations at the beginning of this chapter—a dozen Christmases, a score of New Year's eves, a bushel of July 4ths, all rolled into one. Moreover, it helps account for the unity of rhythm in elation that characterizes the celebration: "Their life flowed together," the reporter wrote, "they were complete to themselves, merged into one body of song, with joyous hearts furnishing drum beats. . . . They swayed i[n] time to the one theme that ran like a steady, glowing thread through the hilarious mob, turning loose everything they had." The one theme that ran through the crowd, I think, was the erroneous, embodied eruption of a messianic time, a utopic and fleeting and *now*.

Richard Wright described a Louis victory by saying, "Four centuries of oppression, of frustrated hopes, of black bitterness, felt even in the bones of the bewildered young rose to the surface. Yes unconsciously they had imputed to the brawny image of Joe Louis all the balked dreams of revenge, all the secretly visualized images of retaliation AND HE HAD WON!"[65] What I'm suggesting is that in fact Louis imputed to the bones of all those bewildered youth the feeling of having fought that fight, and having done so with an efficient mechanical precision, an animal ferocity, and a cool, inscrutable face. Louis offered the average Great Migration black man or woman the feeling of utopic potentiality in which neither the mechanistic modern nor the animalistic primitive ruled, but both existed in the same "impossible" body. As the descriptions of Harlem after Louis victories indicate, these men and women experienced a joyful and communal telescoping of time. It was, too, a kaleidoscopic swirl, a glowing thrum connecting everything and everyone in a fleeting but profound cracking open of the present. It was a fleeting glimpse of the utopic, not as a future or past horizon, but in the present of the glitching black body.

NOTES

1 A. Brooks, "Glitch/Failure," 37–40.
2 Muñoz, *Cruising Utopia*, 9.
3 Muñoz, *Cruising Utopia*, 27.
4 Sharpe, *In the Wake*, 21.
5 Quoted in Roberts, *Joe Louis*, 170–71.
6 "Harlem Celebrants."
7 Boddy, *Boxing*, 305.
8 Roberts, *Joe Louis*, 103.
9 Evans, "Joe Louis Revenge."
10 Cooke, *Letter from America*, 19.
11 O'Connell, "Many Like Baer." This information is credited as coming from another black boxer, one "Tigah" Henderson. As his name suggests, the association of black boxers with jungle cats went well beyond the individual figure of Louis. Tigers are, of course, of Asia and not Africa. Yet the representational structures of the early twentieth century reveal a certain fungibility of dark-skinned Africa and Asia, such that Helen Bannerman's South Asian *Little Black Sambo* (1899) could become conflated with African Americans. Given the fungibility surrounding ideas of jungle and primitive, the actual provenance of tigers matters less here than the associative register.
12 Rice, "Another Nickname."
13 While reporters frequently described boxers of any race in animalistic terms—a "mule kick" of a punch, for example—the tropes of tigers, panthers, and cobras are held especially for black boxers.

14 McCormick, "Joe Louis Perfects Two-Fisted Body Attack."

15 Dunkley, "Joe Louis Stops Levinsky."

16 Seltzer, *Bodies and Machines*, 13.

17 The underlying cause of this increase is contested between the authors, though neither position undercuts my point. Baptist, *The Half Has Never Been Told*; Olmstead and Rhode, "Wait a Cotton Pickin' Minute," 525.

18 Dinerstein, *Swinging the Machine*, 126.

19 Dinerstein, *Swinging the Machine*, 11–12.

20 Dinerstein, *Swinging the Machine*. 72. See also 154–55, 274, 306.

21 Vogel, *Scene of Harlem Cabaret*.

22 See, as a start, Rubin, *"Primitivism" in 20th Century Art*; Archer-Straw, *Negrophilia*; Manning, *Modern Dance, Negro Dance*; Grossman, *Man Ray, African Art, and the Modernist Lens*; Cheng, *Second Skin*.

23 Van Every, *Joe Louis*, 118.

24 Nunn, "We Looked at the Next Heavyweight Champ." Nunn was a black reporter (and father of actor William Goldwyn "Bill" Nunn III).

25 Nunn, "Bill Nunn Writes His Story."

26 Nunn, "*Courier* Scoops Field Again!"

27 Gibson, "Louis, Uncrowned Champ," 2.

28 For example, see the art journal *Documents* edited by Georges Bataille.

29 Dinerstein, *Swinging the Machine*, 266.

30 Hurston, "How It Feels to Be Colored Me," 826–29; for further discussion of the primitive in cabaret culture, see Vogel, *Scene of Harlem Cabaret*.

31 Also important is their differing relationships to learned versus innate skills or knowledge. The mechanical is teachable and reproducible. The animal is innate and, ergo, in terms of primitivism/modernism, in line with those narratives that cast African American expression as natural and therefore unskilled.

32 Dinerstein, *Swinging the Machine*. Dinerstein rightly reminds readers of Picabia's artwork, for example, and its conflation of the American body and machines.

33 DeFrantz, "The Black Beat Made Visible," 71.

34 Benjamin, "Theses on the Philosophy of History," 261.

35 Benjamin, "Theses on the Philosophy of History," 263.

36 Benjamin, "Theses on the Philosophy of History," 263.

37 Benjamin, "Theses on the Philosophy of History," 261.

38 Benjamin, "Theses on the Philosophy of History," 263.

39 Benjamin, "Theses on the Philosophy of History," 262.

40 Symons, "Benjamin's Philosophy of History," 22.

41 Benjamin in the *Arcades Project*, as quoted in Symons, 24.

42 Benjamin, "Theses on the Philosophy of History," 260.

43 Benjamin, "Theses on the Philosophy of History," 254.

44 Symons, "Benjamin's Philosophy of History," 38.

45 Edelman, *No Future*.

46 Symons, "Benjamin's Philosophy of History," 36.

47 Snake Hips Tucker was born in 1905, Josephine Baker in 1906, and Joe Louis in 1914. Hurston was born in 1891—though she routinely took a decade off her age.

48 The Stearnses recount an evening in the 1950s spent demonstrating and discussing dance with Asadata Dafora (Sierra Leone), Geoffrey Holder (Trinidad), and Al Minns and Leon James (the Savoy in New York City). Holder and Dafora recognized Tucker's dance style and concurred that it was known as the Congo in both Trinidad and in Africa. The Memphis Jook dancer Lil Buck continues a sense of lineage, naming Tucker as a forbear alongside the Nicholas Brothers and Fred Astaire. Women are noticeably absent from this lineage, although Tucker had a number of female dancing partners, at least one of whom was called "Miss Snake Hips"—suggesting she, too, performed a similar style. Stearns and Stearns, *Jazz Dance*; Kourlas, "Lil Buck and Jon Boogz."

49 Stearns and Stearns, *Jazz Dance*, 235.

50 Stearns and Stearns, *Jazz Dance*, 236–37. In interpreting the hypnotic as mechanical, I'm thinking of cultural instances, like the *Manchurian Candidate* (1959), in which hypnotism is linked to the technology of "brain washing" and results in robotic action. One can also call to mind the cultural trope of inducing hypnosis through the (mechanistic) swing of a (mechanical) watch. Still, hypnotism is an interesting cultural hinge in its dual animal and mechanical signification. Rudyard Kipling's "Kaa's Hunting" (1893), for example, suggests hypnotism as an animal, rather than mechanical, trick. Moreover, Franz Mesmer, pioneer of hypnotism, based his theories in "animal magnetism."

51 Kracauer, "The Mass Ornament."

52 Cheng, *Second Skin*, 122.

53 The Stearnses analyze Tucker's usual dance routine as five main movements: Spanking the Baby, Snake Hips, the Charleston, the Belly Roll, and the Tremble. Each of these Tucker modulated, starting small and growing gradually larger and more shocking. Cummings, *Crazy House*; Martin, *The Champ*.

54 For more on the racialized history of robots, see especially Chude-Sokei, *Sound of Culture*.

55 Macaulay, "On Point."

56 This is not the only article to reference snakelike, rather than catlike, movement. See, for example, Hoby, "Storyboard P." Some journalists, such as Rice, also invoked the snake while describing Louis.

57 Weiner, "Impossible Body," 23.

58 Weiner, "Impossible Body," 23.

59 Kelly, *Cracked Media*, 9.

60 John Martin, *Dance in Theory*, 13.

61 John Martin, *Dance in Theory*, 17–25.

62 John Martin, *Dance in Theory*, 23.

63 Foster, *Choreographing Empathy*; Watching Dance Project.

64 Sklar, "Five Premises," 30–32.

65 R. Wright, "Joe Louis Uncovers Dynamite," 18–19.

Sorrow's Swing

Flying Lotus's video "Never Catch Me" (from the 2014 album *You're Dead*), directed by Hiro Murai and choreographed by Keone and Mari Madrid, opens to a window covered by a gauzy white curtain. As the camera pulls away, a room materializes. A closed casket sits parked in the floor's center. The camera retreats further; a small bouquet and vase stand atop a wooden table. The room is still; unless the casket is inhabited, the room is empty.

In one protracted shot the camera continues exploring the shape of this area against the soundscape of soft chimes. It lets us into a small church room with caramel carpet, wooden benches, and a single podium. The camera exits and we move with it down a red velvet aisle. A black woman wearing a hat the shape of Saturn moves down the walk path. We follow her as the scene is made available to us: a memorial in remembrance of two black children.

The mourners' seating arrangement suggests an occasion of paying respects: a wake. Black folks sit scattered throughout the pews like an abacus. The children's personalities are introduced to the viewer through belongings arranged carefully around their caskets: stuffed animals, ballet slippers softened from use, and smiling photos of these two siblings, perhaps. Lying in one casket, the young boy wears a suit. He holds a single unbloomed calla lily across his sternum. In the casket next to him, the young girl has on a sparkly teal dress. Her nails are painted, each finger a slightly different hue of pink, her small hands wrapped around a white tulip in emergent bloom.

The pastor carries forth as the lyrics swell in both volume and cadence. In this scene, a future is being memorialized through the reckoning of these children's abbreviated past.

Kendrick Lamar's lyrics drum as the boy's eyes flash open.

Lookin' down on my soul now
Tell me I'm in control now
Tell me I can live long and I can live wrong and I can live right
And I can sing songs and I can unite with you that I love, you that I like
Look at my life and tell me I fight.[1]

Both children wake, ascend, and lift out of the caskets. Without acknowledgment from those in the pews (the mourners' faces do not change, their bodies remain facing forward), the two phantoms perform an eccentric dance number. They make their way out of the dim church and onto a sunlit playground, eventually diving into and driving off in the hearse scheduled to take them away as corpses and not conductors.

At first consideration, Hiro Murai's inclusion of this buoyant dance form (historically attributed to black adults performing adolescence) within the somber context of a memorial service might appear unfit. Is not a funeral an unlikely occasion for black jubilee?

Exploring the relationship between death and subjectivity in twentieth-century American literature and culture, Sharon Holland has argued that black subjectivities are intimately connected to death. In *Raising the Dead: Readings of Death and (Black) Subjectivity* (2000), she argues that death is not fully past nor eventual, but lives perpetually. For Holland, "death is the absolute mirror of life, not its grotesque refraction."[2] With this in mind, how does "Never Catch Me" and the eccentric dance it features speak to African Americans' intimacy with mourning? What, I ask, is the relationship between this upbeat movement genre and the persistence of black precarity? In "Never Catch Me," two dead black children revive in order to exercise the fullness of their bodies' capacity to move. Is the point here that black children are especially at risk of premature death? Is it that black joy (often presumed to be the primary source of black social dance) perpetually prevails? Or that the afterlife is the only free place for black kids? Put differently: Is "Never Catch Me" remonstrance, celebration, or eulogy?

In light of these questions, this chapter explores the relationship between eccentric dance, black adolescence, and mourning. Popularized through vaudeville and minstrel shows, eccentric dance is marked by its rhythmic lilt, playful theatricality, physical pliability, and ephebism. I situate the eccentric dance tradition alongside W. E. B. Du Bois's language around death and José Esteban Muñoz's theory of "feeling brown." In so doing, I argue (1) that this dance form speaks to the complexities around adult performances of primitivism and black adolescence and (2) that eccentric dance is a performance mode through which the time of black mourning is embodied as a swing.

Black vernacular dance has been historically misunderstood as inherent, unmediated, and without choreographic intention. As a result, black dance has been oversimplified by white audiences who have misinterpreted black people's virtuosic dancing as evidence of essential culture, rather than as innovative and performative.[3] "The scholarly literature of African American culture has largely ignored the central role of dance in secular cultural institutions," Katrina Hazzard-Gordon argues. She continues: "The literature on popular entertainment . . . by and large views black expression as exotic variations of corresponding white forms."[4] Moving away from readings that interpret black vernacular dance as corollary to Europeanist dance modes, as a practice of racial transcendence, or as simple care-freedom or jest, this chapter meditates on a rhythm of sorrow. In so doing, I frame eccentric dance specifically, and black social dance generally, as choreographically intentional, innovative, and upbeat not in spite of black people's subjection to racial violence but through a reckoning with that violence itself.

I turn to the dance of Josephine Baker and Earl "Snake Hips" Tucker to illustrate the ways notions of adolescence and primitivism frame how eccentric dance was understood. The success of these two figures hinged on their performances of black immaturity, corporeal unreliability, and stunted growth. I circle back to Flying Lotus to argue that the choreographic performance in "Never Catch Me" extends a different iteration of eccentric dance, as it features children performing within a scene wherein the precarity of black life is not ghosted, but made literal through the site of funeral. As a result, "Never Catch Me" upends the temporal expectations historically mapped onto this dance form. Rather than framing eccentric dance as primitive and therefore of the past, "Never Catch Me" frames eccentric dance as a reckoning with the uncertainty of futures for black children.

Understanding the bodily work that unfolds in "Never Catch Me" requires situating its movement within the eccentric dance tradition. Popularized through vaudeville and minstrel shows and reaching its height in the 1920s and '30s, eccentric dance introduced one component of black social dance (individual flair in relation to the shared choreography of the group) to the concert stage. Breaking from the conventions of line dancing (a genre marked by choreographic uniformity) eccentric dance wed unexpected movements, embodied idiosyncrasy, and comedic grace. Eccentric dance depended on a dancer's ability to invent a singular and kooky iteration of a personalized technique.

Eccentric dance was not an ahistorical or random performance innovation. Its emergence was tied to both white expectations of black performers during the interwar years and the economic constraints that influenced black performers' professional choices. The term "eccentric," as Brian Harker has written, gained wider use in the 1920s and was first used to qualify a particular type of jazz music. It was sometimes referred to as "trick playing," as unorthodox sonic arrangement, as comedic, or to signal a novel approach to music making itself. Eccentric dance made visible the sonic conventions of the time. "In breaking out of the chorus and articulating bodily difference rather than uniformity," Harker writes, "eccentric dancers gained popularity as self-choreographers, rather than pupils."[5] Even with the Charleston, which developed into a partnering dance in the mid-1920s, eccentric dance's choreographic lilt, partnership/solo dyad, and wedding of ballroom and tap provided an occasion for black dancers to test the limits of their innovation alongside the dependability of a dance union. In other words, one could "break away" from a partnered dance to innovate and test new moves, and then return to that partner for the safety of shared rhythm. Eccentric dancers scouted the body's choreographic reservoir to render new embodied lexicons.

Although dependent on dancers' expression of individuality, eccentric dance holds a technique: in it, waists refuse to announce in which direction they are heading to next and limbs move like ropes, slack in one moment, taut in the next. Like Harker, dance scholars Jean Stearns and Marshall Stearns interpret eccentric dance as movement inextricably connected to jazz. About this movement genre they write that it "may include elements of contortionist, legomania, and shake dancing, although these styles frequently overlap with others, and a dancer can combine something in all of them."[6] Ultimately, eccentric dance required that performers offer a unique and previously unseen dance lexicon, rather than privileging the repetition, imitation, and mastery of prior choreographic phrases.

African American dancers performed eccentric dance to, in part, secure employment while managing expectations that they execute a more pronounced eccentricity than their white contemporaries.[7] As Lynne Emery writes, "Blacks were *expected* to be eccentric: to combine rhythm, speed, durability, freak diversions, and the low comedy stereotypes indicative of an 'exotic' heritage. From these limitations, the Afro-American fashioned a vernacular art form of extraordinary creativity and innovation."[8]

Creative innovation is tied to material imperatives; thus, financial incentives for black performance must be held in tandem with the artistic innovations of black cultural producers. Within the context of line dance, "standing out" (to use the backdrop of a chorus line on which to cast one's performative difference) was a way for black performers to be noticed. Moreover, eccentric dance was also tied to the promise of future employment. In other words, a dancer had to "stand out" in order to find and keep a job. Economic imperatives influenced the evolution of the genre. Indeed, as Stearns and Stearns point out, it is "perhaps because they had to be outstanding to get a job" that "Negro dancers were occasionally eccentric to the point of no return."[9] Black eccentric dancers practiced originality as a rule, precisely because they could not economically afford to blend in and simply repeat a choreographic precedent.

No two performers better represent the eccentric dance tradition in the popular imagination than Josephine Baker (1906–75) and Earl "Snake Hips" Tucker (1905–37). Both extended original choreographic lexicons; both, albeit differently, depended on a performance of black primitivism for their choreographic success.

The subject of more than twenty biographies, the details of Baker's life are well documented.[10] St. Louis–born Baker was a black American chorus girl, dancer, choreographer, and activist who traveled extensively in Europe as a headliner. One of four children, Baker herself emphasized the racial violence that she and her siblings endured while growing up. Her family's financial insecurity compelled Baker to leave school at eight years old in order to take a job and help support the household. She worked as a maid, a caretaker for children, and as a domestic worker. Baker's admiration for performance developed as she studied vaudeville theater dancers. At fifteen she would join a traveling troupe. When that troupe dissolved, she gathered what money she had saved, bought a ticket to New York, and dove into theatrical performance and dance. She auditioned for *Shuffle Along*; too young to join the chorus she worked instead as a dresser. But Baker eventually made her way onto the stage after she petitioned to stand in for a pregnant "chorus girl" who consequently left the show. In this context, Baker's career (joining a chorus only to stand out and apart from it) began. "She was noticed by the audience who responded enthusiastically to her antics," Edward Thorpe writes, "and the management paid her the astronomical fee of 125 dollars a week to continue her chorus-line clowning."[11] From her early performances through a robust international career, readings of Baker have "remain[ed] tethered to the vexed poles of vilification and veneration."[12]

Notions of the primitive black girl served as a recurring trope during the modern age, and Baker's goofy enactment of black adolescence hinged on her performance of a seemingly compulsive choreographic unreliability.[13] White audiences "consumed the pleasure of an unruly black female other,"[14] while black audiences mobilized her performance of primitivism to reshape the meaning of American blackness. As Jayna Brown has written, "enactments of 'primitive joy' were rituals of racial reclamation for an urban black populace seeking to redefine the terms of their racial inheritance in their struggle for modern freedoms."[15] Readings of eccentric dancers like Baker evoke a double meaning of primitive as, on the one hand, natural and without mediation/training and, on the other hand, pure. Nadine George-Graves explicates this tension in her essay "'Just Like Being at the Zoo': Primitivity and Ragtime Dance." She writes:

> The association between blacks and animals in these dances was seized upon as further evidence that blacks existed at an earlier stage of biological development, somewhere between apes and whites. They were therefore considered cruder, simpler, baser. The irony and complexity is evident, however, in the fact that primitivity was celebrated at the same time it was disparaged.[16]

Baker's performances of primitive kookiness spoke to the association of black people, early biological development, and simplicity. Although she certainly subverted expectations of her performing body, she was also known for crossing her eyes, getting "lost" onstage, and emitting a train of facial expressions that conveyed both humor and ineptitude.[17] Dance scholar Anthea Kraut argues that Baker's performance of childlike confusion characterized her repertoire. "From her early days in *Shuffle Along* to her 1936 appearance in 'The Ziegfeld Follies,'" she writes, "with numbers choreographed by the ballet master George Balanchine, Baker inevitably seemed to forget the steps she had been taught and wound up performing her own idiosyncratic moves in their place."[18] This forgetfulness was not, as audiences believed, innate absent-mindedness, but a performance effect that spoke to the conventions of black eccentric dance at the time.[19]

Baker's performances were rooted in her own understandings of young black female dancers. Brown explains that Baker "remembered the eccentric dancing of black children performers in her routines. Their eye-crossing and angular bodily poses were iconic, and Baker adopted them as her own."[20] Baker's performance of adolescence characterizes her dancing in the 1934 French film *Zou Zou*. In it, she enacts a choreographic flare marked by a kind of evocation of naïveté. The title and texture of her movement gestures toward a performance of adolescence: in "Josephine Baker Dancing with Her Shadow," the dancer performs surprise of her own body's dark cast.

We know less about Baker's contemporary, Earl "Snake Hips" Tucker, whose performances also revealed complicated desires for black primitivism in motion. In Tucker's case, assumptions of black primitivism emerged through a different avenue: the discomfort he conjured in white audiences which rubbed up against desires for a nonthreatening black body in motion. Eccentric dance as iterated through Tucker's body was a performance of evasion, parrying, and escapism.

Born in 1905 in Baltimore, Earl Tucker reached fame through his creation of a dance he honed in the 1920s called "Snake Hips." In 1920 Tucker moved to New York, through his work with the then-traveling May Kemp Show. Tucker developed a choreographic reputation by frequenting Harlem music clubs; he danced at the Savoy Ballroom, Connie's Inn, and the Cotton Club regularly. In 1930 Tucker would exact a two-minute-long set in a short film, *Crazy House*, directed by Benny Rubin. Tucker and his signature movement also appeared in *Symphony in Black: A Rhapsody of Negro Life*, a 1935 musical short starring Duke Ellington. The circulation of these performances introduced Tucker's dancing to audiences beyond those who were present for his live performances.

Eccentric dance's efficacy was best measured by others' inability to locate a move's origins or succeeding direction, and Tucker's dance surely succeeded in this evasion.[21] The Snake Hips dance draws from embodied repertoires popularized during the interwar period, principally the shimmy and the Lindy

Hop. Ultimately known as the "Human Boa Constrictor," Tucker came to be referred to as "Snake Hips" because of his serpentine-like slink of the body. Collapsing the hips like a lawn chair in one moment, and plunging the body down and up with an accordion-like ease of a slinky, Tucker capered in ways that were syrupy in one moment and as immediate as breaking glass in the next. Snake Hips was a "torso" dancer, and recollections of his movement reveal the awe, discomfort, and titillation he evoked from audiences. He was described as both "an impossibly primitive dancer" and as enacting a "low down dance."[22]

"All he did," Pigmeat Markham recalled about Tucker, "was bend and wiggle his knees while he mixed up variations on the Quiver and Grind."[23] Yet consider the presumed ease connoted in "all he did" alongside the reflections of another one of Tucker's contemporaries, a man who went by Butterbeans. Butterbeans persuaded Tucker to teach him the Snake Hips technique, but "I never *could* learn it," Butterbeans recalled.[24] While Markham suggests that Tucker merely reworked existing dance moves, Butterbeans's failure to perform the movement suggests the difficulty of the dance. The Snake Hips dance is a writhing twist, a movement quality somewhere between taffy and slinky. Protracted, buoyant, and outstretched, the dance required complete and physical authority over one's body. A snake is known for its glide, but it also educes a threat of potential menace. Will a snake slither past or will it dart? This dichotomy between meander and attack describes the range of Tucker's movement quality.

If, as Anne Cheng argues, Baker's skin functioned more as simulacrum than autobiographic signal (even when she might have approximated an audience's desire for her oft naked body), Tucker's costume was a performance of concealment that also spoke to and differently refused normative expectations for black dancers. Tucker often wore billowing clothes, shirts with puffed sleeves, and a sash or sequined cummerbund around his waist.[25] "I think he came from tide-water Maryland," explained Duke Ellington, who employed Tucker in the early 1920s to support the band's self-described "jungle effects."[26] Ellington explained that "Tucker had . . . a disengaged and a menacing air, like a sleeping volcano, which seemed to give audiences the feeling that he was a cobra and they were mice."[27]

Tucker evoked familiar dance movements in order to interrupt, draw out, or ultimately refuse choreographic expectations. By establishing a choreographic alliteration, Tucker was able to evade audiences, slipping in and out of sight. In this way, he played with viewership: the moment one seems to register what just happened, another trick has already begun. In the 1930 film *Crazy House*, Tucker repeats particular moves only to cut them with a wide lasso of the hips or an unanticipated collapse of the legs. While he embodies the sing song, dancing inside of and even snapping with the upbeat of the rhythm, he also introduces aberrant movements that occupy alternative rhythmic registers. In this sense, Tucker uses the repetition of one movement (a one-leg kick à la the Charleston, for example) in order to establish a pulse that he quickly breaks with a knee-skate on the floor, an elevator-like levitation back to foot, or a final cartwheel forward. His dance tours the rhythmic possibilities inside the score. While Baker's repertoire demonstrated a play with primitivism that sometimes spilled over the racialized and gendered expectations mapped onto her body in motion,[28] Tucker set a choreographically repetitious pace to sever it and refuse audiences' expectations of his bodily direction.

Tucker's and Baker's repertoires reveal the ways that eccentric dance depended on the individuality of the black body in motion, even while that bodily "success" was interpreted as cultural evidence of primitivity and therefore pastness. Each dancer performed a different iteration of eccentricity: for Baker a performance of childlike quirkiness; for Tucker an unpredictable comportment as menacing as it was titillating. Although eccentric dance sometimes conformed to the expectations mapped onto black performers during the early twentieth century, the genre also played with those assumptions to consistently yield new choreographic possibilities. Eccentric dance makes audiences question whether black bodies are made of bones or elastic, of joints or of mash. In this light, black eccentric dancers manipulate time through embodied suspension. They play with imaginings of black pasts in order to invent the present anew.

The choreography performed by Will Simmons and Angela Gibbs in "Never Catch Me" offers a different way to think through eccentric dance precisely because it centers children in motion, rather than the adult figures typically associated with the form. As a result, "Never Catch Me" shifts the temporal expectations mapped onto the movement genre. As Gibbs and Simmons pace down the aisle, pop unexpected joints inside the rhythm, swing between each other, and spin tightly around themselves, they step into and then subvert the church choir's soul clap that windmills their movement. While the eccentricity here is in the play and pliability of choreography, "Never Catch Me" offers a different iteration of eccentric dance: not as adults' negotiation with the past, but as children's embodiment of uncertain black futures. This alternative eccentric dance register is social; its audience is constituted by a community of black people who do not register, what's more are not even seeking, black performance.

SORROW, "FEELING BROWN," AND BLACK MOURNING

In chapter 11 of *The Souls of Black Folk* (1903), sociologist W. E. B. Du Bois writes about personal grief. In "Of the Passing of the First-Born," Du Bois describes the tide of feelings that wash over him as he meditates on the unexpected death of his son, Burghardt Du Bois. The child was born on October 2, 1897, and would die only eighteen months later as a result of diphtheria, a treatable infection made deadly because no white doctors would admit the black baby. "Of the Passing" reads equal parts ache and relief. Before the son dies, Du Bois sees a potential in the boy's birth. He writes: "I too mused above his little white bed; saw the strength of my own arm stretched onward through the ages through the newer strength of his; saw the dream of my black fathers stagger a step onward in the wild phantasm of the world; heard in his baby voice the voice of the Prophet that was to rise within the Veil."[29] Although the arrival of his son instilled pride, Du Bois also understood the fact that racism would have constrained the child's future. With this in mind, the son's passing meant that he was able to escape the violence of antiblackness. This relief, made possible through death, turns Du Bois's paternal gloom into solace. The tragedy crushed Du Bois himself, but on behalf of his dead son Du Bois felt deliverance. He is relieved that his son died "before the world had dubbed [his] ambition insolence, had held [his] ideals unattainable, and taught [him] to cringe and bow."[30] Time had not yet allowed the "second sight" to impact the child's consciousness. "He knew no color-line," Du Bois writes, "and the Veil, though it shadowed him, had not yet darkened half his sun."[31] The fact of infancy meant that the child's "sun" remained uncloaked, even if the child was departed.

Du Bois is not sorrowful for the deceased son, but is some version of the feeling for himself. He addresses the child directly: "Better far this nameless void that stops my life than a sea of sorrow for you."[32] The baby's death does not mean complete deletion: he remains in the parents' lives as a perpetual stop. Thus, those who physically last are unceasingly suspended in their mourning, while the child, through casualty, flees. He writes: "All that day and all that night there sat an awful gladness in my heart . . . and my soul whispers ever to me, saying, 'Not dead, not dead, but escaped; not bond, but free.'"[33]

This simultaneity of stillness and flight, of physical lull and spectral getaway, describes both the temporal register of "Never Catch Me" and the embodied technique of eccentric dance. The here now/gone now of the movements, the impossibility of fully seeing the work and worlds at play, is both the rhythm of black mourning and the technique of eccentric movement. This happens at the level of song and title, as "Never Catch Me" signals perpetual escape. Its elusiveness is also the substance of sorrowful black performance. Importantly, the enactment of dance does not mean full expression or articulation. As Du Bois writes with regard to black music, "In these songs, I have said, the slave spoke to the world. Such a message is naturally veiled and half articulate."[34]

Perhaps "Never Catch Me" is a representation of "feeling brown," a depressive state that José Muñoz outlines in "Feeling Brown, Feeling Down: Latina Affect, the Performativity of Race, and the Depressive Position." Muñoz's critical reading of the work of Chicana multimedia and performance artist Nao Bustamante can help us clarify the relationship between brownness, depression, and performance output. Moving away from clinical definitions of depression, Muñoz describes a depressive position as "brown feeling." Feeling brown "chronicles a certain ethics of the self that is utilized and deployed by people of color and other minoritarian subjects who don't feel quite right within the protocols of normative affect and comportment."[35] He elaborates: "What I am describing as 'feeling brown, feeling down' is a modality of recognizing the racial performativity generated by an affective particularity that is coded to specific historical subjects who can provisionally be recognized by the term Latina."[36] Brownness is not black, nor yet white; neither does it sit neatly at a "center." Rather, brownness for Muñoz is a self-understanding of the unachievability of whiteness.

Feeling "brown" accounts for the condition of having one's feelings perpetually marginalized; feeling "down" is "meant to be a translation of the idea of a depressive position. Thus, down is a way to link position with feeling."[37] Resisting a universalist approach to depression, Muñoz recognizes "feeling down" as both of history and impacted by race, gender, class, and sex. How might brown feelings or down feelings cast elucidative light on the meaning of eccentric dance in "Never Catch Me"?

As Gibbs and Simmons make their way to the courtyard, the church choir's soul clapping and the cadence of jump rope swell into staccato. The pair make their way into the light of day; they reverse the operations of the opening scenes by running through the very chambers we witnessed at the video's start. Simmons and Gibbs seem to skate vertically across the pavement as their movement takes them stage right. Their bodies flow like a carom: catching and recatching the force of movement with their limbs. As they travel across the yard the other children continue their play; they jump rope and clap hands in muted sing song. Finally, these two ghosts dive into the back of a hearse while the playground children dash after them. The black girl is behind the wheel, steering. The black boy perches his head out of the window, sunshine toasting his face. The video ends as it began: with the boy's eyes closing and opening once. But this time: a wide smile stretches across the geography of his face.

In "Never Catch Me" only the youth playing outside eventually recognize the child ghosts. Here, the dance (the way it cuts down the aisle, hurdles over the pews, and chases the sun) reveals a different rendering of eccentric dance, one in which black children, rather than being a kind of caricatured inspiration, are protagonists. What Thomas DeFrantz calls the "black beat made visible" (the ability of black dancers to *be* sound) we might productively apply to "Never Catch Me": here are black children embodying the threat of black death—making it, and the beat, fleshy.[38]

While Eric Ducker of *Fader* writes that "Murai's videos often incorporate elements of horror and science fiction, knocking the perspective of the world askew, but not enough to make it unrelatable," the premise of the scene in "Never Catch Me" (premature black death) is soberingly real.[39] Murai reflects on the reactions of Gibbs's and Simmons's parents at the site of their babies in caskets:

> It was weird for the kids' parents. They were very supportive of the project, but it was a very visceral thing seeing their kids in coffins. As soon as they got there and they saw them in coffins and they saw the photos lined up on the table, they immediately started breaking down and crying, which is a very strange way to start a shoot day. But obviously I totally understand it, I'm sure it's a crazy thing to witness. . . . The kids didn't look at death the same way as their parents did.[40]

This moment signals the familiarity and repetitious fact of deceased black children. While Murai's use of "weird" functions as a signpost for a host of reflexes and responses, this on-set moment embodies a perpetual truth: that living in the afterlife of chattel slavery means death is an ongoing fact of black life.[41] Christina Sharpe elaborates on this condition through her framework of living "in the wake"—a condition shaped by "living the history and present of terror, from slavery to the present, as the ground of our everyday Black existence; living the historically and geographically dis/continuous but always present and endlessly reinvigorated brutality in, and on, our bodies while even as that terror is visited on our bodies the realities of that terror are erased."[42] Thus living in "the wake" means acknowledging, and existing perpetually alongside, death. It is a state of being in the world through a practice of "care-full" engagement with the history of antiblackness.[43] In "Never Catch Me," black children exact eccentric dance to negotiate black living in the wake at the literal site of a wake. By centering black children, not as performance texture but as protagonists, the video inverses Baker and Tucker, for whom eccentric dance was impacted by expectations that black adults perform as children. Eccentric dance, in Murai's performance world, reminds us of the uncertainty of presuming a black future at all.

Murai explains, "The original idea was to do something extremely joyful that felt like a catharsis compared to the setting."[44] Black vernacular dance traditions, however, are not joyful despite brown feelings; they are buoyant because of them. "Never Catch Me" captures the affective particularity and sorrow of blackness. Ghosting shapes black social dance, but so too does an engagement with both the afterlives of slavery and a trust in an otherworldly afterlife. An ultimate belief in, as Kendrick Lamar hails, "that life beyond your own life."[45] Black people dancing, in other words, is not antipodal to sorrow. It is its child.

The final scene in "Never Catch Me" resonates with the concluding moments in *Souls*. Du Bois ends:

> If somewhere in this whirl and chaos of things there dwells Eternal Good . . . America shall rend the Veil and the prisoned shall go free. . . . My children, my little children are singing to the sunshine, and thus they sing: *Let us cheer the weary traveler. Cheer the weary traveler. Let us cheer the weary traveler along the heavenly way.* And the traveler girds himself, and sets his face toward the Morning, and goes his way.[46]

Breaking free from the mourners' grief to dance within the company of other playground children, the two dancers motion toward the sunshine, chase the sun, and cast their faces toward its hugging rays. "Never Catch Me," in this light, is a staging of black life above the veil—a choreography of the Passing of the First Born. It is not that black people can only live in death, but that a performance of black child afterlife reveals just how far the black living are forced to be from "toward the Morning." Like sorrow songs, eccentric dance in "Never Catch Me" "tell[s] in word and music of trouble and exile, of strife and hiding."[47]

Black vernacular dance has always kept time, and eccentric dance as practiced historically and in "Never Catch Me" is no different. In this video, we see the ways black eccentric bodies escape total arrest through choreographic subterfuge. It extends an embodied language that speaks to the black body's capacity to push against the imposition of its limits, even if that limit is physical death. This is the time of eccentric dance: a decisively unruly body, escaping anticipations of its next move. Eccentric dance thus embodies one rhythm of blackness: that black time is both of the past and ongoing. In staging the casket as neither a total obliteration of black life, nor a romantic beginning to an afterlife, "Never Catch Me" acknowledges black mourning as present perfect.

Sorrow, feeling down, and mourning do not only materialize as (affective) anchors dragging African Americans down by the waist. A confrontation with the encroachments on black life, alongside a dance with the dead, emerges as an upbeat, a buoy, and also a swing.

NOTES

1 Flying Lotus, "Never Catch Me."
2 Holland, *Raising the Dead*, 39.
3 See DeFrantz, "Black Bodies Dancing Black Culture"; Gottschild, *Digging the Africanist Present*; Malone, *Steppin' on the Blues*.
4 Hazzard-Gordon, *Jookin'*, xii.
5 Harker, "Louis Armstrong," 71.
6 Stearns and Stearns, *Jazz Dance*, 231. Legomania refers to "a limited type of eccentric dancing sometimes known by the even more restricted term, *rubberlegs*" (236).
7 Emery, *Black Dance*, 344.
8 Emery, *Black Dance*, 344.
9 Stearns and Stearns, *Jazz Dance*, 233.
10 See, e.g., Baker and Chase, *Josephine: The Hungry Heart*; Guterl, *Josephine Baker and the Rainbow Tribe*; Archer-Straw, *Negrophilia*.
11 Thorpe, *Black Dance*, 107.
12 Cheng, *Second Skin*, 3.
13 J. Brown, *Babylon Girls*.
14 Jules-Rosette, *Josephine Baker*, 81.
15 J. Brown, *Babylon Girls*, 193.
16 George-Graves, "'Just Like Being at the Zoo,'" 65.

17 Jules-Rosette, *Josephine Baker*.

18 Kraut, "Between Primitivism and Diaspora," 437.

19 Emery, *Black Dance*, 340.

20 J. Brown, *Babylon Girls*, 109.

21 DeFrantz, "Black Beat Made Visible," 76.

22 DeFrantz, "Black Beat Made Visible," 186–87.

23 Emery, *Black Dance*, 203.

24 Stearns and Stearns, *Jazz Dance*, 238.

25 Cheng, *Second Skin*, 39.

26 Stearns and Stearns, *Jazz Dance*, 235.

27 Stearns and Stearns, *Jazz Dance*, 236.

28 Cheng, *Second Skin*, 62.

29 Du Bois, *Souls of Black Folk*, 173.

30 Du Bois, *Souls of Black Folk*, 174.

31 Du Bois, *Souls of Black Folk*, 173.

32 Du Bois, *Souls of Black Folk*, 174.

33 Du Bois, *Souls of Black Folk*, 173.

34 Du Bois, *Souls of Black Folk*, 209.

35 Muñoz, "Feeling Brown, Feeling Down," 676.

36 Muñoz, "Feeling Brown, Feeling Down," 679.

37 Muñoz, "Feeling Brown, Feeling Down," 679.

38 "The dancing body is itself considered the generative force of movement only through the act of stylization," DeFrantz writes. "In this process of personal invention, the dancer approaches a goal of purity, of expressing the self by manipulating basic movement utterances." "Black Beat Made Visible," 12.

39 Ducker, "Behind the Scenes."

40 Ducker, "Behind the Scenes."

41 Hartman, *Scenes of Subjection*.

42 Sharpe, *In the Wake*, 15.

43 Sharpe, *In the Wake*, 23.

44 Ducker, "Behind the Scenes."

45 Flying Lotus, "Never Catch Me."

46 Du Bois, *Souls of Black Folk*, 216.

47 Du Bois, *Souls of Black Folk*, 210.

Parabolic Moves

Time, Narrative, and Difference in New Circus

The combination of elements that compose *Cuisine et confessions* (*Cooking and Confessions*), a 2014 production by Quebec-based new circus company Sept doigts de la main (Seven Fingers of the Hand), initially seems incongruous and bound to fail. Onstage cooking—of omelets, banana bread, and pasta—mingles with the intimate stories of circus performers, who talk to us about the details of their lives while mixing dough, straining boiling water, and performing strenuous and high-risk acts (figure 6.1). These circus acts run the gamut from acrobatics, aerial work with silks and corde lisse, hand-to-hand, to diabolo, Chinese hoops, juggling, handstands, and trapeze.[1] The stories that emerge amid such strenuous routines are not uniformly entertaining, uplifting, or even coherent: some are absurd and disorienting, while others are dark and tinged with melancholy, despair, and irresolution.[2]

Yet despite (or even because of) this admixture of food memories, circus feats, and storytelling, *Cuisine et confessions* enables a productive investigation

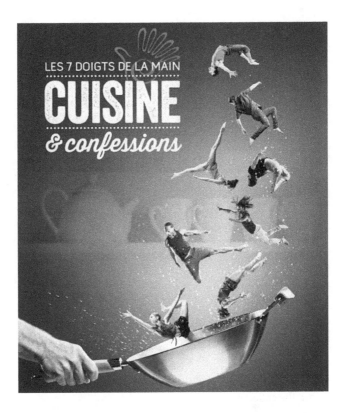

FIGURE 6.1 The promotional flyer for Sept doigts de la main's show
Cuisine et confessions, 2014. FLYER DESIGN BY SOPHIE LECLERC. PHOTO
BY OLIVIER TÉTREAULT.

of minoritarian becoming and offers novel modes of representing difference
in performance. These modes of representation of minoritarian difference
arise through aesthetic and political questions of genre—namely, the piece's
attempt to merge narrative conventions of stage realism with circus aesthetics.
Narrative time collapses in the tension between circus time and lived, or sensory, time: the temporalities of circus, cooking, and memory that dominate
the piece frequently subvert efforts toward verisimilitude, in the act exposing realism's limitations for minoritarian subjects. The outcome of the piece's
contestation between phenomenological and constructed ideas of identity is
that a "minoritarian temporality" is crafted onstage to displace some of the
pitfalls of conventional identitarian representations and to gesture toward
one of the company's central goals: the construction of unity in difference,

FIGURE 6.2 Performer Matías Plaul (Sept doigts de la main) balances on the Chinese pole, 2014. PHOTO BY ALEXANDRE GALLIEZ.

a collaborative project that does not subsume the micropolitics of difference within the collective.

Cuisine et confessions is structured as a disaggregated assemblage of solo performances that touch intimately upon aspects of identity. Race, sex, gender, class, migration, antidictatorship, and other facets of the performers' "real" identities emerge throughout the performance. For example, performer Matías Plaul's solo treats his father's abduction, torture, and disappearance at the hands of the Argentine dictatorship during the Dirty War, and the ways in which his father's absent presence has shaped Plaul's life as an artist and activist (figure 6.2). While Plaul tells his story, he undertakes an intricate and high-stakes Chinese pole routine and prepares, with the help of his cast members, a dish of pasta that he imagines might have been his father's last meal. The colliding temporalities of circus movement and cooking threaten at times to consume the narrative that he is telling.

As such, Plaul's biography is offered to the audience as a series of fragmented vignettes, avoiding a sense of narrative completion or closure. In contrast to his precise movements, his words—the details that he chooses to tell us—almost sound improvised, although they are not. This proto-aleatory sense of chance in Plaul's narrative contrasts with the other rhythms to which his body is beholden—those of the high-stakes feats he performs—and allows for the character to become disaggregated into three bodies: character, performer, and material body. This disaggregation of character further undoes any narrative coherence that we audience members may anticipate. In the unsuturing of narrative and character coherence lies the potential for a new kind of storytelling to emerge, one that I am calling "parabolic" for the ways that Plaul's and other circus performers' bodies enact parabolas, moving arcs in time and space that overtake the nostalgic parables of self that they tell.

Like Plaul's vignette, the nine other solo performances that compose *Cuisine et confessions* center on a performer's memory of a specific food. Some memories exhibit ethnicized overtones (like a memory of borscht performed by Russian-Canadian cast member Anna Kichtchenko), while others seem less programmatic. The choice to center the narrative on a food rather than a person, and to weave a parable around the person's memory of the food, amounts to what I am calling a "paranarrative," in which cooking and eating (as well as circus movement) do the work of explicating character with sensory techniques, displacing a verisimilitudinous narration of identity such as one might find in the "personal monologue" genre. Structured by the temporalities of food, memory, and circus precision, the paranarratives in *Cuisine et confessions* depart from a conventional narrative arc by focusing on an object *beside* those which might populate the field of identitarian difference. For example, the twinned paranarratives of performers Sidney Iking Bateman and Melvin Diggs treat matters of race, gender, and class but displace these categories onto disparately temporalized arcs of cooking and circus that at times seem arbitrary or aleatory. As the solo performances come together, they form a minoritarian temporality that compels the audience to take an active role in stitching together the narrative fragments that emerge. Yet I found that I did not feel compelled to compile the accumulated fragments into a totalizing knowledge of Diggs or Bateman, as I might have in a conventional stage realist work. Rather, when the scene ended abruptly, I was left with an arbitrary "cut" in my meaning-making and tenuous links between memories of food and race, gender, and class.

Such storytelling techniques allow for a parabolic approach (in the dual sense of parabola and parable) to the topics of race, gender, sexuality, class, ideology, and violence. While questions of difference emerge prominently—they are not concealed or effaced—the paranarratives center on memories of the quotidian sensory acts of cooking and eating, shifting the burden of narrative away from revealing identity as a coherent, centralized whole, to be commodified by the audience and absorbed into its hovering, othering gaze. As an audience member, I *was* anticipating a moment of reveal, and the confirmation of my capacity to "know" the other onstage through realist narrative. But my expectations were confounded, happily, by the stories' unwillingness to arrive at such representational completion. In the vignettes, minoritarian temporalities of parabola and curve confront the limitations of a narrative arc of stage realism, refusing to offer the audience a holistic picture of an identity or a life. These paranarratives resist consolidation into a multicultural whole, despite the promise that the piece holds out for such pat resolution.[3] The result, I argue, is that we audience members receive the performers' storytelling parabolically—as a series of elliptical motions that glide purposefully over, under, and around the central conceits of conventional realist parable. These narrative parabolas are in keeping with Plaul's, Bateman's, and Diggs's physical arcs as they propel their bodies into the air in ever-changing trajectories.

The parabolic stories of *Cuisine et confessions* stem in part from the hybrid genre of *nouveau cirque* ("new circus") in which the Seven Fingers of the Hand is working—a genre that is interested in the possibility of stage realist dramaturgical and narrative conventions, but which also confronts the limitations of such conventions for circus performance. As I detail below, *Cuisine et confessions* exemplifies new circus's turns to and away from dramaturgical and narrative conventions of realism. This approach can produce innovative modes of staging minoritarian difference that subvert the twin pitfalls of stage realism and of the circus's legacy of othering and exploiting minoritarian bodies. In *Cuisine et confessions*, the commingling of diverse temporalities destabilizes realism's verisimilitudinous affect. At times the action onstage approaches realist conventions, such as coherent narrative and character-actor parity, while at others the exigencies of circus movement and timing force deviations from these conventions. Such ambivalent play with realism allows for the emergence of new approaches to storytelling. Movements do not equal narratives: tracks of plot, character, and body are off-kilter and disaggregated, unfolding according to disparate temporal rhythms. The disjunctive timing and compensatory focus on a sensory object (food) in lieu of an identity-arc inhibit the coherence of a story of self and the insights that we may glean. Instead, the stories in *Cuisine et confessions* proceed in contingencies of flips and leaps, turns and tightropes, attempted feats successful and failed. Timing upends narrative rather than supporting it: time cannot be leashed to plot or character development but moves in differently scaled parabolas. And such timing creates the potential for new ways of representing minoritarian circus bodies: not in terms of conventional portrayals of minoritarian difference as stagnated, stuck, frozen in time, or "outside of time," in contrast to normative identity's ostensibly ever-evolving, recursive trajectory. Instead, the performance's parabolic play of narrative and time allows the minoritarian bodies onstage to emerge *in time*, in their own time, and in a state of becoming that resists succumbing to identitarian fixity.

THE MULTIPLE TEMPORALITIES OF *CUISINE ET CONFESSIONS*

Charting the distinct temporalities that converge in *Cuisine et confessions*, I note first the sensory time of cooking and eating. Food production and consumption are inexorably bound up in time and phenomenological intention. As Barbara Kirshenblatt-Gimblett notes, "Timing is crucial to the sensory character of food and more specifically to the interaction of the thermal, haptic, and alchemic. . . . The kitchen runs on multiple clocks. Those clocks are set to the conditions of light, heat, cold, air, and agitation."[4] In *Cuisine et confessions*, the quotidian temporalities of food are enacted for us, live, as the artists cook the foods of their memories in the vast Tohu theater, utilizing every component of a set that is also circus lab and functional kitchen.[5] Processes of cooking involve the entire cast: as in symphonic performance, each performer takes up a task that joins with the others to produce a meal. Alongside, and occasionally in tandem with, this sensory temporality is that of circus: split-second choreographies, rhythms of laughter and danger; the near-miss and perfect landing; and an overwhelming sense of bodily risk that pervades each act. New circus is (often pointedly) circus without a net: lacking this fallback, its free falls require precise spatiotemporal calculations and coordination that the artists must embody to avoid injury and death. In the circus feat, the body signifies multiply: as a character (sometimes), a performer, and a vulnerable, fleshy body that succumbs to gravity, falters, and gets hurt.[6]

Finally, the performers' telling of a memory resituates the past in the present, with potentially transformative consequences. Rather than distinguishing and isolating the past from the present, the use of cooking to (re)enact a memory allows the past to be reshaped by the present. For example, when Diggs cooks an omelet with the support of the other performers, he actively reimagines the childhood memory that coalesced around the omelet. He brings this past into a present time to create a new experience, shared between audience and artists, that allows for an active revivification of this past through its (re)telling. The present, then, substitutes for realism's sealed coherence a "realer real": that of the sensory "event time" of here and now. Likewise, when Plaul imagines what his unknown father's last meal might have been, he enacts a new memory to supplant that which he lacks. Together these phenomenological temporalities—running on distinct but sometimes converging tracks—compose a paranarrative that provides each performer with an opportunity to reshape their narrative arc, evading identitarian rigidity while not eliding the fact of difference.

Through this blend of circus, food, and stories—which takes shape in a shared timescape, but gestures to a specific other (inaccessible) time for each artist, triggered by sensory memories—we audience members can participate in the active retelling of the past and come to understand minoritarian difference not as a "what," but as a "when and where," in the words of critical race scholar Michelle Wright.[7] As Wright notes, reifying Blackness—or, I would add, any identitarian category—as "a determinable 'thing,' as a 'what' or 'who' . . . exhibits the unnerving qualities of a mirage: from a distance, it appears clearly cogent, but up close . . . evanesces, revealing no one shared quality that justifies such frequent and assured use of this signifier."[8] While an impulse to define and categorize characteristics of minoritarian identity would seem to provide insights, in fact this definitional or explicative impulse limits our understanding due to its inherently exclusionary nature. Wright asserts, in ways that resonate for an interpretation of minoritarian difference: "The only way to produce a definition of Blackness that is wholly inclusive and nonhierarchical is to understand Blackness as the *intersection* of constructs that locate the Black collective in *history* and in the *specific moment* in which Blackness is being imagined—the 'now' through which all imaginings of Blackness will be mediated."[9]

Wright puts forth a spatiotemporal approach that situates Blackness as both "constructed and phenomenological"—both a set of shared traits and a concept "imagined through individual perceptions in . . . ways" that are contextually contingent.[10] The phenomenology of Blackness—and of minoritarian difference more broadly—departs from a "linear progress narrative" of the historical construct, to manifest in what Wright calls "Epiphenomenal time"—a noncausal temporality of the now through which we interpret the past, present, and future.[11] Wright's Epiphenomenal time is the now of reimagined, aestheticized memory that the artists cook up for us in *Cuisine et confessions.* The multiple temporalities of *Cuisine et confessions* compel spectators and performers alike to inhabit an intersection of history and now. In leaving behind the conventions of narrative coherence for the precarity of the now, the paranarratives of *Cuisine et confessions* enact and embody minoritarian temporalities. Below, I plot theoretical and contextual nodes of Wright's "when and where" for circus bodies, tracing circus's ambivalence around realism, narrative, and otherness. I also bring to bear links between circus bodies and minoritarian bodies, the aesthetics of event time, and thick description of several vignettes in *Cuisine et confessions* to assess the potential of performance to enact a parabolic mode of storytelling that glides over, under, and around identitarian representations onstage, enfolding audiences and artists into communal but contingent acts of meaning-making.

NEW CIRCUS'S TURN TO (AND AWAY FROM) REALIST NARRATIVE

In what ways might circus bodies signify character and narrative *differently* from other performance genres? How is the contemporary genre of new circus approaching the aesthetic challenges of staging minoritarian difference? And how does the example of *Cuisine et confessions* shed light on performance's ability to stage a deconstruction of identity through manipulations of time and movement? To answer these questions, I will briefly contextualize Quebecois new circus before turning to a discussion of the aesthetics and politics of realism, narrative, and temporality as these inform circus practice. Historically, circus has been one of the most clearly othering forms of popular entertainment. Arising through and centered around ethnological pageants and "freak shows," circus has had a pronounced "body problem." This body problem has entailed the representation of its performers as "freaks," androgynes, and other transgressive types that blurred boundaries between human and animal, male and female, and confronted the gazes of curious spectators across Europe and North America, helping these spectators to shore up their sense of the normal through an encounter with othered bodies.[12] Spectacles of otherness thrived on the seeming facticity of the exoticized body, the denuded and measured body made to bear (and bare) the "proof" of its own enfreakment.[13] Entities on display—who were often imperial subjects, people of color, sexual and racial minorities, and people with disabilities—constantly negotiated their subjection to the voyeuristic and colonizing gaze. Circus's othering operated in tandem with traits such as its conventionally disaggregated, non-narrative structure. Nineteenth-century circus focused on spectacle divorced from speech, parading an endless series of types for public consumption. Often this parade had no plot other than a development toward extremes, or a reiteration of white supremacy and Western hegemony.

Circus acts were also historically the province of family troupes—famous acrobatic families, for example. But in the mid- to late twentieth century many of these family networks began to be replaced by institutionalized circus schools boasting marks of nationalist pride. This shift can be seen in the codification of circus acts and apparatuses named for specific nations: for example, the Chinese pole and hoops; Russian bar, cradle, and swing; German wheel; Korean board; and the like. This shift brought with it a change in circus's body problem, from exoticized freak to depersonalized, de-identified automaton.[14] As Roy Gómez-Cruz observes, since the institutionalization of circus training, highly trained, athleticized bodies have become substrates for the contemporary global circus industry. The performer's body is presented as "muted, subsidiary . . . raw material for extreme physical action" by a circus that "values and legitimizes extreme physicality over . . . other expressive strategies."[15] Rigorous training regimes transmute difference into tropes of exoticism or subsume it under costume and makeup. The contemporary reaction to circus's historical body problem, which continues to haunt the form, has not eradicated the problems dogging representations of bodies in performance. Circus bodies are still indiscriminate fodder for fantasy and spectacle, and circus labor is still precarious and largely anonymous. In much contemporary circus—perhaps as an overcompensating measure intended to combat previous othering moves—race, ethnicity, and sexuality are often divorced from social or political context and relocated into a new ethnological fantasy: the Black body as a spectacular aesthetic object, for example, deracinated from a discussion of Blackness per se.

Quebecois new circus has interacted with circus's body problem in a variety of ways. Arising concurrently with and informed by French *nouveau cirque*, Quebec's new circus emerged in the 1970s to gain traction in the 1980s, flourishing in the 1990s.[16] Its most famous icon is Cirque du Soleil (hereafter CdS), founded in 1984.[17] CdS's response to the politics of bodies on display must be understood within a broader aesthetic shift. The aesthetics of new circus depart from historical formats in multiple ways: no animals onstage; elimination of the three-ring model; often no safety nets or harnesses; and a dynamic interdisciplinary engagement with dance, physical theater, and digital, visual, and installation art. Diverse aesthetics and genres mingle freely in Quebec's artistic landscape, amounting to what Charles Batson and others denote the "nouveau bouger montréalais" (new Montreal movement), a corporeal and image-based aesthetics that often highlights abstract or experimental forms.[18]

Historically, circus was structured as a series of feats of progressively augmented skill and risk, and disaggregated numbers separated by acrobatic and clown interludes. Beginning in some ways with CdS's productions, new circus practitioners increasingly turned from this disaggregated format to the construction of circus dramaturgies that seek to communicate a strong, plotted through-line via performers' embodied acts.[19] While narrative in performance may seem in some lights to be a throwback to a pre-postmodern, pre-postdramatic mode, it represents something distinct in circus performance: a departure from the conventional modes of meaning-making that previously characterized the genre. Perhaps beginning with CdS's ventures into diegesis, new circus practitioners are concentrating not only on thematic holism, subtexts, and narrative continuities, but also on the ways that movement can communicate affect through uses of dramaturgy. Yet the new circus companies differ in the kinds of dramaturgies that they seek to depict. CdS productions have avidly cultivated a diegesis that is often at odds with stage realism. Indeed, CdS productions are characterized by their antirealism: elaborate costumes and makeup; fantastical, superhuman characters; pan-ethnic universalism; an Esperanto-like supralinguistic mode; and depersonalized performers, whose characters are prioritized above the thinking and feeling persons that inhabit them.[20] This does not advance circus's engagement with the historical body problem, since such techniques anonymize bodies and elide the fact of difference.

New circus has been bolstered by an infrastructure of pedagogy, dramaturgy, and technical training, which has spurred the rise of new approaches to circus aesthetics. In the decades after CdS's emergence, an expansive culture of experimental and alternative circus activity has grown up around, and split off from, CdS. In part, this is due to the proximity of CdS and Canada's National Circus School (École nationale de cirque, or ENC). Established three years before CdS's founding, the ENC has had a cross-fertilizing effect for both CdS and its range of offshoots and subsidiary ventures. Students from ENC circulate actively among different circus companies, auditioning for CdS, spending time with the company, and defecting to form their own companies or work for others.[21] Several troupes have emerged alongside and in response to CdS, interacting ambivalently with the former's dominant national and international presence. Quebec's current "Big Three" new circus companies, according to Louis Patrick Leroux, are CdS, Cirque Éloize, and Seven Fingers of the Hand.[22]

Seven Fingers of the Hand has absorbed some aspects of CdS's use of dramaturgy and narrative while rejecting others. The seven founders of the company (including Quebecois Canadians and US and French citizens) framed their early mandate as an alternative (or antithesis) to CdS's antirealist style. As Leroux states, in launching their company in 2002, the Seven Fingers "positioned themselves . . . *in reaction* to [CdS's] aestheticized, anonymous seventy-five performers onstage wearing Lycra and heavy stage makeup [as] they had all been when they were working for Cirque du Soleil."[23] In many of its works, the Seven Fingers engages in a process of collective creation that derives its substrates from the intimate personal experiences of participating artists and features minimalist aesthetics. Company members have called this approach a "human scale" (*grandeur de l'homme*).[24] They desired to move past the constraints facing CdS performers, who are often inserted into an overarching thematic arc without interpretive agency, and into a realm of creation emphasizing "aesthetic intimacy and authenticity."[25] The aesthetic of Seven Fingers is often participatory and site-specific and, unlike CdS, incorporates spoken dialogue in the untranslated natal languages of the performers. In *Cuisine et confessions*, for example, performers wear street clothes and tell us their names, delivering their solos in French, English, and Spanish. They build elaborate routines around mundane, quotidian objects, frequently using paranarrative techniques.

Of the company's nearly two dozen productions, at least a third draw upon conventions of stage realism that produce, in the language of its press releases, a sense of "authenticity," "humanness," and insight into "real life."[26] These conventions include an emphasis on the synthesis of actor and role; a coherent narrative plot that unfolds incrementally; and uses of the visually represented body to indicate a holistic identity. But in the work of Seven Fingers, these conventions do not manifest in the same way as they might in a traditional realist stage play. Seven Fingers' uses of realism are informed by at least two factors: first, the company's multidisciplinary aesthetic landscape specific to Quebec, which has often rejected realism; and second, the exigencies of circus praxis itself, which challenge narrative coherence. Even if it were a desideratum, seamlessly coherent realism often proves impossible, due to the ways that the circus body is made to matter differently from the actor's body in stage realism.

In circus, contingencies of risk and timing take precedence over the coherence of actor and character, as well as evolutionary plot development. Injecting realist narrative continuity into circus is not as simple as it may appear. As Leroux notes, circus performers are most often focused on the physical stakes and rhythms structuring their movement, as well as their relationships to their apparatus, and do not tend to draw upon the techniques that theatrical performers have, from Stanislavski on: those of imagining their bodies into a role and a story.[27] Circus temporalities and physical demands would seem to hinder Stanislavski's championed idea of a seamless narrative through-line that develops character in an evolutionary fashion. Yet Seven Fingers and other breakout groups are clearly interested in utilizing narrative and character tropes and conventions borrowed from stage realism. While the company has incorporated many aspects of what we might consider to be stage realism into its productions, these works confront the limitations and challenges of uses of realism in circus—in ways that prove productive for staging minoritarian difference.

PITFALLS OF "HUMAN-SCALED" AESTHETICS

As Batson discusses in his comprehensive profile of the Seven Fingers, the company's use of realist techniques both reveals and mystifies performers' "humanness."[28] The use of a purposefully banal, intimate dramaturgy trafficking in *vérité* contrasts markedly with the performers' extreme physical exertion and bodied brilliance. The incorporation of quotidian aesthetics serves not to make this "realist" circus more relatable but rather to widen the gap between audiences' sense of the performers' humanness and our awe at the superhuman feats of artistry and skill that their bodies undertake. Spectators engage in a multifaceted reception, comprising narcissistic comparison of the performers to ourselves; juxtaposition of "the quotidian 'humans whom we feel we know, who walk, talk, and wrestle with boredom,'" and the "extraordinary" ordeals that they undergo.[29] Yet the company's focus on humanness itself as a kind of topos, developed through realist dramaturgical aesthetics, threatens to become an underexamined humanism no less universalizing than CdS's fantastical antihumanism. The works of Seven Fingers frequently resort to a whitened universal humanism, in which the white cisgendered body is made to stand in for the figure of the human.

The problems with Seven Fingers' uses of universal humanism are part of a more general representational dilemma with realism. Stage realism's problems abound for minoritarian subjects. The very act of exposing oneself onstage for identitarian exhibition, often framed as verisimilitudinous (or the "real"), creates an ossifying trap of visibility that can freeze minoritarian difference into an essentialized identity-as-possession, subjecting the "other" to the viewer's gaze and assimilating difference into a knowable "same."[30] The problems of realism are reminiscent of the linear, causal narrative that Wright exposes as fixing identity categories in place. At issue is the stereotyping, ossifying, and exploitation of multiracial, differently sexed and gendered bodies within a frame marked as realist. Minoritarian subjects—especially "visible minorities," to use the Canadian parlance—are frequently societally overdetermined, both onstage and in everyday encounters. And stage realism's conventions are often deleterious for representations of difference.

Realism can be turned to more complex and varied ends, however. What happens when we allow certain narrative conventions of stage realism to flourish while stifling others? Circus's temporal dimensions can force performing bodies around the pitfalls both of realism and of historical circus's body problem. Seven Fingers' exploration of a human scale as applied to non-white, noncis, nonstraight bodies has been ambivalent at best; nonetheless, *Cuisine et confessions* is one of the most prominent examples of the company's purposeful attention to difference onstage, and perhaps the most overt attempt to investigate representations of racial and sexual difference. The stories in *Cuisine et confessions* tend toward the verisimilitudinous, utilizing food memories as diegetic and dramaturgical fulcrums.[31] Yet the production confronts the pitfalls of stage realism much more actively than does the company's other work, drawing upon new resources to challenge the universal humanist impulses lurking behind realism and bring more useful facets of the real to the fore. The limitations of realism for circus in fact afford fruitful aesthetic and political outcomes for performances of difference, which *Cuisine et confessions* begins to address.

As such, the production's collection of solos embodies concepts of minoritarian time and being advanced by critical theorists whose works traverse race, class, sexuality, and gender.[32] Minoritarian critiques of temporality, while varied, connect at the joint of embodied difference, conceived by dominant societal forces as "out of time" (and place). There is a prevailing conviction that being out of time leads to death—as in Lee Edelman's "no future," or pervasive conceptualizations of the fact of Black death.[33] The queering of minoritarian time can evoke repetition, stagnation, distortion, temporal drag, fast forward, and syncopation. Yet minoritarian (counter)temporality can also contain a liberatory or utopian dimension (the latter not negating the former)—as in queer time, which has helped shape a denormativized understanding of temporality as lived by queer and trans subjects. Another example is the kind of queer futurity—the act of thinking and feeling a "then and there" even in the prison house of the "here and now"—imagined by José Muñoz in *Cruising Utopia*.[34] I propose that, by both offering and obfuscating the telling of a "real" story onstage, the solo performances in *Cuisine et confessions* situate minoritarian subjecthood as a spatiotemporal phenomenon.

In order for this phenomenological subjectivity to emerge, elements of quotidian verisimilitude do not have to flee the scene. Like theater theorist Stanton B. Garner Jr., I am fascinated by performances that attempt to stage a "realer real," an aestheticization of the real. Representation of the real (as in realist theater) "both disguises and foregrounds the sensory channels of theatrical address, and in the slippages and instabilities between these operations it lays a foundation not only for . . . mimetically sealed theatre . . . but for excursions into the sensory field of theatre and its modes of audience, actor, and character experience."[35] This overlayering of reals promises (or threatens) to upstage spectatorial versions of reality by supplanting and usurping our conceits through other bodies, other voices, which compel acknowledgment of their virtuosity and multivocality.[36] Telling a parable in the shape of a parabola opens up possibilities that might not otherwise emerge in a coherent narrative of self, confounding the desires that the genre of realism often conjures in audiences: to see revealed an evolutionary sense of the human, to grasp authenticity of experience, and the like. These desires prove dangerous for those who are consistently excluded from the category of human, those whose bodies are regularly forced into realism's visibility trap.

In the paranarratives of *Cuisine et confessions*, a push toward realness collides with other tenors of the real—the complement of risk, timing, and physicality. This interlarding of diverse realisms and reals creates a newly shaped space for storytelling. Theater's threat of corpsing (a spontaneous outburst of laughter that turns the character into a corpse) touches circus's very different corpse: the prospect of disability, injury, and death. It is possible that the creators of *Cuisine et confessions* did not go into the process of making the piece with the intention to discuss race, gender, sexuality, class, ideology, or anti-oppression movements. But these themes emerge parabolically in the performance by virtue of this overlayering of embodied real(s). In the following sections, I describe moments in the production that offer techniques of parabola, paranarrative, and the creation of minoritarian temporality.

"JE SUIS ARRIVÉ CHEZ LUI À 5H DU MATIN / ET IL M'A PRÉPARÉ DES *EMPANADAS*...."

Paranarrative collision and layering occur in performer Emile Pineault's brief attempt to locate a "self-portrait," which collapses under the futility of "sending my flesh through the meat grinder, diluting my soul in a broth."[37] Abruptly, Pineault ends his speech with the phrase: "I came to his house at five in the morning, and he made me empanadas." The monologue cuts off here; we do not know if Pineault is gesturing toward queer love and sex, family, or all three. But the paranarrative—and the arbitrary feel of the cut, which mocks my spectatorial urge to make concrete meaning—indicates a queer, minoritarian sensibility. Deconstructing identities in representation, African diasporic cultural theorist Stuart Hall describes the working of such a cut in his reinterpretation of Derridean *différance*, glossed as playing on the terms "differ" and "defer." Quoting Christopher Norris, Hall writes, "the idea that meaning is always deferred . . . by the play of signification."[38] *Différance* challenges representation to remain incomplete and "open to being deferred, staggered, serialized."[39] My yearning to interpret what I have seen and heard threatens to impose a "'break' in the infinite semiosis of language" but ultimately does not impinge upon the infinite capacity for difference and deferral.[40] "It only threatens to do so if we mistake this 'cut' of identity—this *positioning*, which makes meaning possible—as a natural and permanent, rather than an arbitrary and contingent 'ending.'"[41] The fundamental disequilibrium between discourse and its interpretation mirrors the relationship between Seven Fingers' paranarratives and our spectatorial perambulations, which seek to glean an interpretation from narratives that are inevitably "beside themselves."

Pineault's monologue, in its play of signification, does not shy away from, but does not overtly signal, the queer male body. Its implication finds an (imperfect) echo in the hand-to-hand duet that follows Pineault's fragmentary speech. Compact and stocky, Pineault appears almost boylike as he enters into a gorgeous and intimate fleshy architectonics with Mishannock Ferrero, his tall and lanky partner. Their same-sex duet traverses dance and acrobatics, involving stylized and anticipated poses as well as unexpected weight-balancing maneuvers, as when the larger Ferrero is carried by Pineault. This duet embodies a parabolic representation of minoritarian sexual difference: a queer, loving, open-ended choreography that does not crystallize into identitarian enunciation. Rather, Pineault's textual and embodied vignette plays in and around categories, showcasing his smallness but also his strength. The object of the paranarrative—the partially excavated sensory memory—and the different rhythms of movement and speech overwhelm any attempt at a direct, evolutionary character development. We receive Pineault's story as a fragmentary process of narration.

Pineault's solo, bound to disparate and intertwined temporalities of circus, food, and memory, builds a minoritarian temporality through its parabolic mode of diegesis. Minoritarian temporality might be understood as the "when and where" of minoritarian subjectivity, which I interpret with respect to queer Argentine poet, sociologist, and activist Néstor Perlongher's concept of "devenires minoritarios" (minoritarian becomings). Perlongher elaborates on Deleuze and Guattari's declaration, in A Thousand Plateaus, that "all becoming is a becoming-minoritarian."[42] Perlongher valorizes the minor and marginal as sites of a transformative politics through Felix Guattari's "'desiring cartography,' based on affect and embodied practice."[43] Perlongher himself embodied such a desiring cartography, cruising Brazil's Praça República in the 1980s and seeking to map space with his body, "the way a surfer rides the waves of a libidinal sea," to reveal "the other Brazil: the Brazil of minoritarian becomings—becoming-black, becoming-woman, becoming-homosexual, becoming-child . . . from processes of marginalization and minoritization."[44] This mobile mapping practice locates a subject in space and time but does not fix or ossify that subject on an identitarian grid.

Pineault offers us an understanding of subjecthood, interpreted through the body, in his tumble into the arms of his partner, and the ways that his body expounds its own narrative in and through such movements. Pineault is thrown upward, pitched off Ferrero's heels for a low and tremulous flip into the air, and nearly falls before he is steadied at the ankles, balanced on Ferrero's fleshly furniture. The sudden insertion of risk reminds us of the fragility of the body interanimating the character that Pineault expresses onstage; the play of balance and counterbalance reassures us as Pineault tries again, launching his small, muscular frame into the air, to land successfully on Ferrero's prostrate form. As an audience member, I am not sure of what I am witnessing, or how to make this parable mean something about Pineault as a person. However, I understand the multilayered movements of the bodies onstage in terms of an oscillating roster of character, performer, and flesh.

In the convergence of multiple temporalities, the body becomes central as the medium of our meaning-making. During Pineault's near-fall, for example, I can see clearly revealed David Graver's overlapping designations of the character body (the persona that Pineault briefly expressed before the microphone), performer body (comprising skill, athleticism, artistry), and fleshy body (the biomaterial of bones, internal organs, musculature, fat, and skin).[45] The performer and fleshy body threaten to upstage the character body, further breaking up the already fragmented, incomplete narrative. These multiple bodies echo Perlongher's sense of the subject as a multiplicity concentrated around "exteriority," "open to the surfaces of contact," rather than "an interiority full of guilt and complexes."[46]

The parabolic techniques employed by the performers in *Cuisine et confessions* are more invested in coincidences, surfaces, and conjunctures than in accessing a mythic and predetermined interiority, or a subject that precedes the scene. In Pineault's solo, the impossibility of the consumable persona, the impressionistic hint of food, and the temporality of circus physics converge in a parabolic time of minoritarian becoming. This becoming does not reach a finitude, or even a plenitude, before it is cut with a segue into an erotic scene involving the larger ensemble. Pineault and Ferrero are joined by the rest of the cast in a strange and sexual configuration, a moving architecture. As performers spin off and balance on each other's flesh, each partnership that emerges from the original coupling embodies trust, danger, balance, reciprocity, timing, and improvisation. The pairs fragment further into less discernible shapes, spinning and quivering, twirling, and melting, as the music fades out. Even while coming together, these bodies disintegrate the fragile story that Pineault has built around a spare framework of words and gestures. The parabolic moves with which Seven Fingers traces paranarratives resemble Deleuze and Guattari's "points of flight," escape routes that implode "normative paradigm[s] of social personality."[47] But they also differ, in that they are not merely points of departure but elliptical swoops and aerial arcs that trace precise (albeit indirect) trajectories, continually thwarted by gravity and chance. Perlongher notes, citing Deleuze, that "becoming isn't moving from one point to another, but rather entering the in-between."[48] I would add that the parabolic movements of minoritarian becoming are about that which is *beside*, or adjacent to, an object that we might call identitarian.

Pineault's body can be described as short and muscular, bearded, youthful, masculine, and white. But how does the paranarrative approach apply to the complex nonwhite bodies onstage? *Cuisine et confessions* offers parabolic approaches to questions of race and racialization, acknowledging much more concretely than the company's other works circus's body problem—the polarization of bodies into othered freaks and depersonalized automata. As a small number of theorists note, circus is a whitewashed landscape, suffering from a relative dearth of nonwhite artists whose skin tones are purposefully made to matter in their artwork, as opposed to simply "existing" or "being there." Even when prominent artists like Robert Lepage have sought to instigate a discussion around questions of racial difference (as in the Lepage/CdS collaboration *Totem* [2010]), the circus frame almost inevitably forces the performers into the realm of exoticized ethnic other.[49] For the relatively small pool of nonwhite circus artists who obtain regular work in the North American and European industry, racial difference is often concealed by costumes and makeup or made to perform freakery and ethnopageantry. By contrast, I felt that embodied Blackness was engaged in *Cuisine et confessions* through a paranarrative sensibility of minoritarian becoming, allowing minoritarian subjects to occupy a place and time, rather than being fixed on a categorical grid outside of time.

In a Chinese hoop, acrobatic, and hand-to-hand duet between Sidney Iking Bateman and Melvin Diggs, both of whom happen to be Black male performers hailing from St. Louis, Missouri, the kinds of subjecthood that Stuart Hall describes come to life. Addressing new representational techniques for postcolonial and diasporic nonwhite Caribbean subjects, Hall frames identity not as a preestablished fact but as a "production," a syncopated process of enunciation in which "who speaks, and the subject who is spoken of, are never identical, never exactly in the same place."[50] Bateman and Diggs, like the other cast members, tell us of their memories centering on foods. These enunciated memories exemplify Hall's insistence that the past cannot be "recovered" but instead must be produced through continual retellings, which figure cultural identity as a "becoming" that belongs "to the future as much as to the past."[51] More substantive than Pineault's monologue, Bateman and Diggs's braided duologue reconfigures memory for minoritarian becoming, revealing "cultural identities [as] . . . the unstable points of identification or suture, which are made, within the discourses of history and culture. Not an essence but a *positioning*."[52]

Choreographed to dual-track voice-overs describing childhood memories, Bateman's and Diggs's moving bodies localize their personae in a spatiotemporal past—St. Louis—and simultaneously in our shared now, in which circus precision, and the performer and fleshy bodies, intrude upon the character body. Bateman and Diggs's scene starts innocuously, seeded by a reference from the production's opening segment. In a bit of script that had before seemed to me superficial and arbitrary, Diggs had noted his favorite food to be "the perfect omelet," and then proceeded to comically describe an omelet that reached transcendental heights of fancy. Now, as the rest of the cast members position Chinese hoops (lightweight, flimsy plywood frames) on the set, Bateman asks us if we want to know why Diggs has chosen this food. While Diggs and Bateman commence an exquisite collaborative choreography—a duet that has them sailing through the frames in synchrony and counterpoint, their bodies arcing into the air with unmatched grace and elegance—Diggs tells us in voice-over that his attachment to omelets comes from his childhood, when on weekends his siblings would leave to see their father, but he would stay at home, because he "didn't have a father to go to." He would come downstairs to an omelet, a sign that his mother "let me know that she was there for me and cared for me." The omelet is for him an act of solidarity and care against the pain of loss. This monologue at first seems more coherent than Pineault's, providing insights about the feeling of being fatherless. Yet it soon begins to fracture into reverberated echoes of disjointed phrases, mixing with Bateman's own childhood memories. Bateman recalls sitting in the parking lot outside of Rally's in St. Louis, eating French fries and reading books with "her," ostensibly a reference to his mother. Bateman tells us that he didn't like reading but did like fries, so the food is a compensatory gesture—just as the comforting omelet soothes Diggs's melancholia regarding his father's absence. The two monologues intertwine as Bateman's and Diggs's bodies do—crisscrossing the space and coming to rest beside each other, flying through the frames, enacting choreographic bits and supporting each other's weight. Yet the voice-overs are not in sync with the circus time: the performers' embodied temporalities are timed to each other, while the soundtrack is timed to the making and enjoyment of food, and the sensory memory that links French fries to books, eggs to parenting (figures 6.3 and 6.4).

In some moments the two timescales converge, but often they are at odds, confounding my attempt to find a beginning, middle, and end. As such, speech

FIGURE 6.3 Performers Melvin Diggs (left) and Sydney Iking Bateman (Sept doigts de la main) leap through Chinese hoops, 2014. PHOTO BY ALEXANDRE GALLIEZ.

FIGURE 6.4 Performers Melvin Diggs (left) and Sydney Iking Bateman (Sept doigts de la main) do parallel flips through Chinese hoops, 2014. PHOTO BY ALEXANDRE GALLIEZ.

and movement structure a dueling duet of paranarratives. The braided monologues blend and dissolve, finally coming together in a clashing, overlapping rumination on St. Louis as a place of "waiting": waiting to die or be put in jail ("It got to a point where it's like, you know what, I will die young, I don't care"), waiting with futility and fatalism—feeling next in line after "my brother or my uncle." The minoritarian time retold in this duet recalls Michael Hanchard's phenomenologically situated "racial time," a disjunctive temporality informed both by the individualized experience of "waiting"—"a time structure that is imposed upon us"—and by the structural project of modernity, which relegates African-descended peoples to a place outside of historical temporality.[53] In both micro- and macropolitical senses, minoritarian subjecthood is experienced phenomenologically as disparate temporality.

Yet if, in racial time, waiting structures life, in circus time bodies do not wait to move; they launch into unhesitating arcs. In this paranarrative, the theme of waiting is altered, subverted, and entangled with happiness, pride, and desire to return to St. Louis, as well as the urge to "get out" from under stagnation's weight and be "free" of the life that friends and relatives have "known . . . for so long, they don't know anything else." Amid conflicting sentiments and repeated phrases—"if something happened to my family"; "never look back"; "the percentage is so small, I'm not willing to take that risk"; and "free"—hangs a nearly indecipherable question about futurity and the possibility of return, of livability, against the specter of Black death. These disconnected, repeating fragments are layered atop one another to create a sonic collage that ultimately refuses to cohere.

Meanwhile, on stage, the stakes and frames get higher: Diggs sets a lightweight hoop high atop the others and approaches it in a leap, missing the opening and causing the frame to collapse. This is our perennial reminder of the fallibility of bodies under duress, the reintrusion of the fleshy body (and its skin acts), which once more breaks up and interrupts the illusion of the character body. Then Diggs retries, and makes it this time—astonishingly, and to spectators' audible gasps. After this spectacular recovery, Bateman completes an equally thrilling leap through the frame, displaying his copious acrobatic skills. Finally the two turn to look at us, breathing and sweating. The nonlinear structure of their scene embodies a queer time of Black survival, in which Blackness takes flight as a "when and where," in effect a "here and now." As C. Riley Snorton notes, "Blackness is . . . marked by psychogeographic proximity, comprised in the 'possibility of existing in the same place in different times.'"[54]

The temporalities that surface in Bateman and Diggs's scene support this reading, yet their synchronous movements also displace a fixed (past) subject into a mobile (present) one. Abruptly, their scene comes to a halt—another semiotic cut—as the music switches unceremoniously into an upbeat rhythm. I am abruptly pulled away from Bateman and Diggs's duologue without fully comprehending it.[55] Yet I come away with a lingering sense of the interplay of character, performer, and fleshy bodies, as well as an understanding of circus timing as permeating and combatting, to some degree, the waiting that has consumed these performers' past lives, and which they confront in the here and now before my witnessing gaze. Bateman's and Diggs's paranarratives embody Hall's argument that identity-as-becoming necessitates an endless play of signification—a play that continues long after the scene ends. For Hall, identity-as-becoming is the only means of subverting colonial oppression of minoritarian groups. Identity-as-becoming is fully implicated in how we reconceptualize the past—a past not given, but always "'after the break,' [and] always constructed through memory, fantasy, narrative and myth."[56]

Here as throughout, paranarrative strategies and parabolic moves offer approaches to the challenge of making sense of minoritarian becoming without fixing meaning in representation. *Cuisine et confessions* is an intersection between event time (composed of the temporalities of circus/food/memory) and the societal forces that seek to fix and stagnate minoritarian difference into a place that is outside of time. Event time offers the possibility of weaving minoritarian subjects back *into time,* through the specific temporalities that their bodies effect. Yet this is not a given. We cannot afford to idealize performance practices, as these practices are not, by virtue of their form alone, venues for remaking the body. On the contrary, as in the example of historical circus, performances often perpetuate and worsen the conditions of visuality and power that limit minoritarian freedoms. Given the vexed medium that is performance, I argue that *Cuisine et confessions* makes inroads into representation of minoritarian difference by foregrounding temporality and continually confusing and conflating the character, performer, and flesh onstage. The focus on embodied temporality throws off our spectatorial ability to extract a consolidated identity from the work, yet it does not make difference disappear.

The prominence of temporality in *Cuisine et confessions* is an effect of performance's capacity to simultaneously exist in time and represent time, as Alice Rayner observes. This duality holds out the possibility for a critical and denaturalizing perspective through the manipulation of performance's temporalities.[57] Rayner notes that we (audiences and artists) "are both in time and made of time," and in experiencing performance together, we can share in the "mutual, subjective creation of the temporal field" through "attention, interest, focus, storytelling, and history-making."[58] While realist time often sutures performer to character within a coherent and familiarized developmentalist narrative, the minoritarian temporalities that emerge in *Cuisine et confessions* offer distinct interpretations of the "real" onstage. They showcase the possibilities for artistic creation to "pla[y] with time" by offering "a specific exchange between the modes of perception," which "highlight[s] the suspension and interplay among time zones."[59] Temporality in aesthetic representation becomes "a *relationship* that includes both objective and subjective conditions . . . that both constitutes and dissolves existence."[60]

One way that performances can play with time, in service of resisting the subject's constitution prior to the event, is through an aleatory approach. While *Cuisine et confessions* is pre edited and not aleatory in its form, some of the textual fragments that get thrown forward incubate a proto-aleatory effect, helping us to see the event as constituting its subjects rather than being preceded by them.[61] In the solos of Pineault, Diggs, and Bateman, I am never quite sure whether (and when) I am witnessing the character, performer, fleshy body, or all three. I am also never certain why particular fragments of text have been selected for narration. I am made aware of the arbitrary nature of each cut that isolates one scene from the next. The scenes' architecture prevents the suturing of performer to character and draws attention to the multiplicity of time. My acts of observational meaning-making necessarily rely on my attention to several temporalities at once. Minoritarian becoming is made possible through parabolic and proto-aleatory techniques in this event time. In the separate but interlinked time-world created by the performance, food's sensorium (in past and present) allows the subjective flow of memory time to intertwine with the precision of circus time, forming a blend that ultimately creates a phenomenological replacement for identitarian coherence. Temporality can then subsume an intersubjective response as the dominant motor of our shared feeling.

"IN FACT, MY FATHER WASN'T JUST DEAD"

In the event time of *Cuisine et confessions*, absent fathers and truncated familial structures are a recurring theme, for which food memories and projections do compensatory work. The theme of absent fathers floats on the surface of the collection of solos, appearing to emerge as a coincidental (and proto-aleatory) effect of the collective creation approach. Yet the thematic continuity provides the audience with connective tissue for the assemblage of parables. Diggs's paranarrative finds an (imperfect) echo in Matías Plaul's testimonial about his missing father, a *desaparecido* tortured and killed by the Argentine dictatorship, missing since January 4, 1977. This story is different from all of those which came before: it takes place in silence, without musical accompaniment, and is narrated in a relatively more coherent fashion, in the genre of *testimonio*. It is initially unclear how Plaul's story fits with the paranarrative mode, but gradually links emerge. His father was abducted en route to dinner with friends, and Plaul, who was eight months old when his father was taken, wonders what his last meal before his murder would have been. Plaul has only "blank pages" where memories might be, but he fills the pages with stories "heard over the years" and childhood drawings in which his father looms large on the page. But the stories, he admits, about the concentration camp into which his father was placed, and his torture and death, are "hard for a young child to understand." The void is so deep as to be nonnavigable with memories alone.

Plaul's story, then, is not a parable about a memory of food, but a reconstruction of an unknown past through the present act of collaborative cooking, a healing ritual. Plaul recasts his father's imaginary last meal as spaghetti. Creating the fictive scene (a lost future past) as the entire cast helps him prepare pasta and vegetables, Plaul says: "Kitchen will smell of tomato sauce . . . full of flour. We will laugh a lot, talking about politics and *fútbol*. And we will play guitar, sing a song, and at the end make a toast." Finally, he imagines: "At one moment, my father will stand up, give us a last kiss, walk to the door, singing with a little smile. . . . He will always be thirty-two years old, younger than me now." In Rayner's theorization, this sense of minoritarian temporality allows for our full, shared experience of time as "a mode or a way of my knowing through which I recognize the way of living presently through my body; in the past through my memory, and towards a future, which is (ultimately) death."[62] Like Pineault, Diggs, and Bateman, Plaul stages the past in the present, removing this past from stagnation through the embodied temporalities of circus and cooking.

Plaul syncopates his story with Chinese pole acts, each calibrated dramaturgically to scenes in the narration. Again, this final solo displays much more character–actor parity. Enacting his father's capture, torture, disappearance, and death, Plaul climbs to the top of the pole, hangs upside down with his crossed ankles supporting his weight, then lets his body free-fall until his head is inches from smashing into the floor. He relaxes and allows his body to slide off the pole, as if melting. Later, when he narrates his father's capture, the other performers mimic a dinner party. Plaul interrupts, running and tumbling, strangling one and beating another. He flees, and several cast members pursue him. Plaul becomes at this moment the character of his father ("a revolutionary, an intellectual, and a member of a communist group") trying to evade kidnappers, shimmying up the pole as his hunters fling themselves onto it. He jumps down again to describe the dinner they'll prepare, then returns to the pole, climbing upward in a methodical crouch, before swaying off in a graceful and perilous backbend, swinging the lower part of his torso and his legs while holding on with both hands. His body billows and stretches outward like a sail. At once he seems to fall suddenly—this fall looks far more uncontrolled than the previous one, and is accompanied by his soft expression: "no, no." At the end we can see that he has had the pole in his grasp the whole time, nestled between his lower arm and side. But from our perspective, it also looks like his body (now gone limp) has been skewered on the shining metal. He stiffens, then softens and lets himself slowly down. The light around him dims and dies (figure 6.5).

In this embodied reenactment of his father's abduction, Plaul does not ask for our pity or empathy, but for solidarity. Solidarity here means unsticking the past from its ossification and introducing speculation into the seemingly sealed-off history—a leap into the present. Plaul also invites the cast to exorcise the past through collective action: performing the realist narrative and cooking pasta and tomato sauce to dispel the intransigence of memory. Plaul's solo recalls Perlongher's theorization of the Southern Cone's antidictatorship movements, which Perlongher links overtly to minoritarian politics of antiracism, feminism, antihomophobia, and social justice. The movements that arose to counter dictatorship constituted "a multiplicity of social outbursts that brandished the values of autonomy and the right to difference. The most blatant expressions of these rebellions came through (and, to a lesser extent, still come from) the so-called 'minority movements': feminist, black, homosexual, free-radio movements, etc.—and more discreet and underground, by way of mutations evident in the realms of habits, daily micropolitics."[63]

While each solo in *Cuisine et confessions* centers on an individual's pursuit of a sensuous food memory, Plaul's solo brings to the fore a subtle theme that I have noticed throughout: the collective project of support, and the embodied structures through which the ensemble physically and figuratively reinforces, supplements, and surrounds each storyteller. Plaul seems very alone at times,

FIGURE 6.5 Performer Matías Plaul (Sept doigts de la main) on the Chinese pole, 2014.
PHOTO BY ALEXANDRE GALLIEZ.

but the cooking of pasta and the careful support of his fellow performers make palpable this solidarity, the sense in which the ensemble comes together to bolster its individual members. This monologue develops into a collective project (to reenact the scene, to make his father's last meal), and cooking creates a coalitional politics that buttresses acts of minoritarian becoming. Each vignette, I realize, is not a solo after all: in fact, the ensemble is always present to provide reinforcement. These mechanisms of care constitute resources that make the piece into a holistic entity, albeit one composed of different perspectives, distinct parabolas. None of the scenes asks to be linked to the others, yet connections arise organically, incidentally, as exterior points of contact on a desiring cartography.

CONCLUSION: SET YOUR WATCHES

Plaul's monologue is set off from the others yet necessitates the presence of his fellow performers to help him enact the trauma of his father's disappearance, and the resolution of a last meal. In this way, the final solo reveals the

stakes of Seven Fingers' project of difference in unity (or unity in difference), a purposeful act of coming together that nonetheless remains fundamentally disaggregated. Perhaps this unity in difference is what ultimately
enables the production's creation of a politics of minoritarian becoming. As
incommensurable and distant as a circus company seems from the antidictatorship movements that Perlongher describes, both projects confront the
challenges of creating a collectivity without losing sight of the molecularity
and micropolitics of individual complexity. The idea of unity in difference
recalls Hall's argument that identity-as-becoming does not rest on continuities but rather resides in the paradox of shared *discontinuities*. The name of
the company, "Seven Fingers of the Hand," refers both to its seven founders
and to its ethico-aesthetic project: unity in difference, and difference exceed-
ing unification. Fingers are connected to but operate semiautonomously from
the hand, and the hand that possesses seven fingers is an anomaly—hence the
impossibility, or near-impossibility, of the coexistence of unity and difference.
In *Cuisine et confessions*, the Seven Fingers seek to build a shared affective
experience across the disparate realities of audiences and performers.

While Hall's (re)conceptualization of *différance* encapsulates the techniques of the paranarratives, Perlongher's embodied mapping is our spectatorial act of interpretation.[64] *Cuisine et confessions* deliberately brings together
discursive and meaning-making realms at the end for a communal transaction. The exchange that transpires between the artists' "instances of discourse"
and our acts of spectatorial interpretation calls for a ritual, one that depends
on food and timing. Thirty-six minutes before the piece's end, performer
Gabriela Parigi had asked us to set our timers for thirty-six minutes: this is
the time that it takes to bake banana bread from Sidney Bateman's recipe.
Throughout Matías Plaul's monologue, the sweet scent of baking bread wafts
inexorably through the auditorium. Our senses are piqued as time elapses.
When Plaul's story concludes, the cast moves solemnly, methodically, re-
arranging and organizing the kitchen/set, cleaning up. Then the music starts
again, a staccato rhythm whose purpose soon becomes clear: it's a clock. We
count down together. This is the communal moment of synchrony: as the
scent permeates our shared space, the production culminates in our readi-
ness to receive the baked bread to be shared among us, served by the performers. The bread is the realization of Seven Fingers' holistic project, a ritual
of distribution and consumption. It is, in fact, the labor of creating a shared
project—the intimate architectonic linkage of bodies in relationships, both
supporting and supported. Eating the bread together incubates a new shared

memory; perhaps we will incorporate the events into our own food-oriented subjectivities, to be thrown forward into future remembrance. I feel, in this final gesture, a visceral and sensual metaphor for the difficult, complex labor of balancing difference with commonality. In this context, a piece like *Cuisine et confessions* presents the possibility to transform how circus can tell stories differently about different bodies in motion and time.

Cuisine et confessions is only one reference point among many in the repertoire of Seven Fingers. As the company expands, its creative team explores approaches that venture more deeply into fantasy and spectacle, including collaborations with CdS and Broadway. This is all acceptable within the realm of new circus, and I would not begrudge the company the chance to try new and different things—to "innovate," in the artistic and entrepreneurial senses. But I think that their collective creation techniques hold the potential to create valuable, unusual pathways around the pervasive body problem and visibility trap, by virtue of this focus on spatiotemporal coordinates of past made now, which arc over and under identity categories. The parabolic moves of *Cuisine et confessions* minimize an imperative to reveal narrative coherence while not evacuating important questions of minoritarian difference that surface in performance. Even if the creators of *Cuisine et confessions* did not intend to touch upon the questions of race, gender, sexuality, class, ideology, and violence that arise in the stories provoked by food memories, coming at the stories via parabolic trajectories that continually land beside themselves in fact strengthens their telling and releases them from fixity. And I confess that I am biased, drawn to investigating works that seek to present a valence of "reality" framed as authentic but also as scripted performance. Perhaps it is through this paradox that we spectators can be productively upended by the "representational and phenomenological instabilities" of the "troubling actuality" of a work like *Cuisine et confessions*, and the minoritarian becomings that it stages.[65]

NOTES

1 These terms are defined in a glossary in Leroux and Batson, *Cirque Global*, 294–307.

2 Indeed, some reviewers thought that the show was uneven and never quite "gelled." See Fricker, "Cuisine and Confessions."

3 See the work of Ferguson (for example, *Aberrations in Black* and *Toward the Reorder of Things*) on the complexities of a multicultural whole and the neoliberal

forces that make this whole cohere. "Multicultural" here might also signal the Canadian state's policy of multiculturalism, which was adopted in 1971 and converted into the Canadian Multiculturalism Act in 1985. I am reluctant, however, to bound the cultural performances in the piece within national borders.

4 Kirshenblatt-Gimblatt, "Making Sense of Food in Performance," 76.

5 Tohu, the theater's name, refers to the expression "tohu-bohu," which means "topsy-turvy, joyful chaos." Thanks to Louis Patrick Leroux for this information.

6 See Graver, "Actor's Bodies."

7 M. Wright, *Physics of Blackness*, 3–4.

8 M. Wright, *Physics of Blackness*, 2.

9 M. Wright, *Physics of Blackness*, 14.

10 M. Wright, *Physics of Blackness*, 4.

11 M. Wright, *Physics of Blackness*, 4.

12 For information on circus history, see, for example, Adams, *E Pluribus Barnum*; Bogdan, *Freak Show*; J. Davis, *Circus Age*.

13 On "the body in the spectacle," see A. Hughes, *Spectacles of Reform*.

14 Hurley, "Multiple Bodies of Cirque du Soleil."

15 Gómez-Cruz, correspondence with the author, May 7, 2017.

16 Cruz, "Contemporary Circus Dramaturgy," 269; Hurley, "Multiple Bodies of Cirque du Soleil," 124.

17 Harvie and Hurley, "States of Play."

18 Batson, "Les 7 doigts de la main," 100; Tembeck, *Danser à Montréal*.

19 Thanks to Louis Patrick Leroux and the Montreal Working Group on Circus/Cirque (http://resonance.hexagram.ca/circus/), whose members have brought to the fore this newfound investment in circus dramaturgy and the construction of narratives by means of circus action.

20 Harvie and Hurley, "States of Play," 312.

21 These defections may be in part due to CdS's grinding tour schedule, low compensation, and poor labor rights for troupe members.

22 Leroux, "Reinventing Tradition," 9.

23 Cruz, "Contemporary Circus Dramaturgy," 270. Emphasis mine.

24 Batson, "Les 7 doigts de la main," 102. Many of the founding members (Shana Carroll, Isabelle Chassé, Patrick Léonard, Gypsy Snider, Sébastien Soldevila, Samuel Tétreault, and Faon Shane) are still with the company.

25 Batson, "Les 7 doigts de la main," 100; Boudreault, "Le cirque parlant des 7 doigts de la main."

26 See the Seven Fingers website for these descriptions and multimedia press materials: http://7doigts.com/spectacles (accessed November 10, 2017). The works of Seven Fingers are quite variable in terms of their style and technique. There is not one unifying approach that characterizes the company's repertoire; this commitment to innovation and changeability is part of the allure. Not all productions follow a realist aesthetic vein. Many are in accordance with the superhuman

aesthetics of CdS, for example. Others are interested in genre-mixing of various kinds: between circus and contemporary dance, for example.

27 See Cruz, "Contemporary Circus Dramaturgy," 269–73.

28 Batson, "Les 7 doigts de la main," 102–4.

29 Batson, "Les 7 doigts de la main," 104–5.

30 See Phelan, *Unmarked*, 2–11, 24–25.

31 *Cuisine et confessions* was codirected by founding members (and life partners) Shana Carroll and Sébastien Soldevila; the artists who premiered the work, and whose stories populated it, are mostly ENC graduates: Sidney Iking Bateman (USA); Danica Gagnon-Plamondon (Canada); Melvin Diggs (USA); Mishannock Ferrero (USA/Sweden); Anna Kichtchenko (Russia); Emile Pineault (Canada). Matías Plaul, Pablo Prámparo, and Gabriela Parigi (all from Argentina) were trained at La Arena.

32 For a perhaps oversimplified list of examples among the many notable scholars: on sexuality and gender, see Jack Halberstam, José Muñoz, Kathryn Bond Stockton, Elizabeth Freeman, Lee Edelman, Leo Bersani; on critical race studies, Michelle Wright, Richard Iton, Barnard Hesse, Harvey Young, Hortense Spillers, Michael Hanchard; in the intersections and interstices, Christina Sharpe, Fred Moten, Katherine McKittrick, Rinaldo Walcott, C. Riley Snorton, E. Patrick Johnson, Mae Henderson.

33 See, among the plethora of studies that link death to minoritarian difference, Edelman, *No Future*; Holland, *Raising the Dead*.

34 Muñoz, *Cruising Utopia*, 1; see also Freccero's survey of queer temporality in scholarship, "Queer Times."

35 Garner, "Sensing Realism," 121.

36 Garner, "Sensing Realism"; see also Rivera-Servera, "Moving from Realism."

37 "Comme si je pouvais simplifier mon être en quelques ingrédients, passer ma chair au moulin à viande, diluer mon âme dans le bouillon. Il n'y a pas de recette pour l'amour, pour la création, pour le bonheur" (Carroll and Soldevila, *Sept doigts de la main*, 57:51).

38 Christopher Norris, qtd. in Hall, "Cultural Identity and Diaspora," 239.

39 Hall, "Cultural Identity and Diaspora," 239.

40 Hall, "Cultural Identity and Diaspora," 240.

41 Hall, "Cultural Identity and Diaspora," 240.

42 Deleuze and Guattari, *Thousand Plateaus*, 291.

43 Perlongher and Díaz, "Minoritarian Becomings."

44 Perlongher and Díaz, "Minoritarian Becomings."

45 Graver, "Actor's Bodies."

46 Perlongher and Díaz, "Minoritarian Becomings."

47 Perlongher and Díaz, "Minoritarian Becomings."

48 Perlongher and Díaz, "Minoritarian Becomings."

49 See Fricker's excellent intervention, "'Somewhere between Science and Legend.'"

50 Hall, "Cultural Identity and Diaspora," 234.

51 Hall, "Cultural Identity and Diaspora," 236.

52 Hall, "Cultural Identity and Diaspora," 236. Emphasis in original.

53 Hanchard, "Afro-Modernity," 251–53.

54 Snorton, "What More Can I Say?"

55 Despite repeated attempts, I was unable to interview Bateman and Diggs.

56 Hall, "Cultural Identity and Diaspora," 237.

57 Rayner, "Keeping Time."

58 Rayner, "Keeping Time," 34.

59 Rayner, "Keeping Time," 34.

60 Rayner, "Keeping Time," 35. Emphasis mine.

61 This thesis is also present in Fischer-Lichte, *Transformative Power of Performance*.

62 Rayner, "Keeping Time," 35.

63 Perlongher and Díaz, "Minoritarian Becomings."

64 Hall's reading of Derridean *différance* shares points in common with Perlongher's reinterpretation of Deleuze and Guattari, and not just for the two theorists' parallel processes of minoritarian reenvisioning—a crucial move that we must honor, not only as the application of a (white, European) school of theory, but as an act of fashioning in itself, which exposes Deleuze's and Derrida's "borrowing" from nonwhite, non-Western theorists (for example, Deleuze's debt to Édouard Glissant).

65 Garner, *Sensing Realism*, 120.

Choreographing Time Travel

Rethinking Ritual through Korean Diasporic Performance

There was a woman with long black hair that seemed to stretch from the depths of the ocean, Korean diasporic multimedia performance artist Dohee Lee recalls. The woman spoke but her words were indiscernible. "She just dropped bells [i]n my hands and that vibrated my whole body, so I had to dance. I had to sing," explains Lee. "When I woke up, I realized I was dancing. I was singing."[1] The woman in the dream turned out to be Mago, a creator goddess in Korean mythology. Lee's journey to decipher this figure led to deeper understanding of the myth's connection to Korean shamanism and of the histories of Lee's family on Jeju Island in South Korea. These revelations manifested in *MAGO* (2014), a ritual performance that integrates movement, sound, film and motion graphics, site-specific installation, and Korean mythology with the tumultuous history of state-sanctioned violence on Jeju Island.[2] "In the performance, I'm reflecting on ancient times, on history, on our ancestors' lives, as well as the present," ruminates Lee. "So it's a piece that's also about time travel."[3]

In this chapter I discuss how the utilization and re-visioning of Korean mythology and performance practices allow Lee to "time travel," playing with different timescales, linear and cyclic, that interface with contrasting states of being. The performance engenders representational time travel—the experience of multiple temporal arrangements in a performance space that kindles transtemporal connections with histories of social and political violence and ecological destruction and concomitant experiences of displacement, resilience, and community. In doing so, MAGO shows the cyclical nature of state-sanctioned violence in particular and the need for reconnection to mythic and indigenous knowledge. Lee's performance provides a living blueprint for how to reinvigorate ritual performance as an ethical critical praxis of reckoning with histories of violence wrought upon bodies and the earth. The method of this reinvigoration pivots on an overlaid temporal logic: where ancient time, mythic time, present, past, and the future commingle as manifested in techniques of movement, breath, sound, and visual imagery. By ancient time, I am referring to a historical pastness that is centuries removed from the present of the artist. For Lee, ancient time blends into mythic time, which is otherworldly and connected to the beginning of the world and the ongoing communing with spirits. Through time travel, Lee foregrounds Korean practices of healing and sustainability that recenter women's experiences. Through MAGO, Lee invites the audience to consider a womanist ritualized practice of temporal commingling, a linear temporal map (ancient time–past–present–future) meshed with a cosmic cyclic map (mythic time), as a survival tactic for negotiating the condition of social and political precarity. In other words, Lee deploys ritual performance as a way for the audience to open themselves to suspension that is anticipatory in the Muñozian sense.

Born in South Korea, Lee trained at the master level in traditional Korean dance, singing, and percussive music rooted in shamanism. Since moving to Oakland in 2002, she has committed herself to integrating Korean performance practices with contemporary dance, sound and vocal experimentation, and video art. "Every time is different," explains Lee, "but I follow the form of Korean rituals combined with modern approaches of movement, music, visuals, sets, costumes, installation and technology."[4] In creating her immersive ritualized theatrical performancescapes, Lee collaborates with sound designers, musicians, costume designers, and visual and new media artists. Her collaborators over the years have included artists like Anna Halprin, the Kronos Quartet, and the Degenerate Art Ensemble. Lee is the recipient of numerous prestigious awards that reflect the multidisciplinary scope of her work, including a Guggenheim Fellowship, the Herb Alpert Award in the Arts for Music Composition, the Doris Duke Impact Award for Multidisciplinary Performance, and a Kenneth Rainin Foundation New and Experimental Work Grant, among others.

For Lee, MAGO has been a deeply personal artistic project and journey. When she moved to the Bay Area, Lee became curious about the history of her new home, the people who once inhabited the land, and the belief systems of these people, leading Lee to ask, "What is home? What does it mean to belong where you are?"[5] This questioning led Lee to meditate on her own homeland, Jeju Island, and its unique histories and cultural practices. Initiated by her dream of the woman from the ocean, Lee decided to visit her birthplace of Jeju Island to learn about local shamanic rituals, meet with villagers, and explore the mythology around Mago. In describing what is at the heart of MAGO, Lee explains, "It's about my hometown, Jeju Island, South Korea, and my ancestors and the present issues that people are dealing with there. I took my personal story and created a mythological journey—like a superhero story."[6] Ritual performance is the imagined space where the ordinary becomes extraordinary, where mortals can experience suprahuman powers of invoking and embodying multiple temporalities. Lee brings the characterological potential of ritual performance to the audience where we follow her on this journey.

Lee developed MAGO during a two-year residency at the Yerba Buena Center for the Arts (YBCA) in San Francisco, working with a team of collaborators that included Adria Otte on the development of the sound score and Donald Swearingen with other sound design, Steven Sanchez on animation, David Szlasa on visual images and video art, and Alenka Loesch on costume design. Premiering on November 14, 2014, at YBCA, MAGO toured nationally afterward. As part of her process of developing MAGO, Lee led a series of workshops and site-specific seasonal rituals in and around the YBCA complex. For example, in a winter ritual that extended for eight hours, Lee invited participants to line up and name an ancestor they wished to remember, while Lee channeled the emotions felt between herself and the participants through singing, chanting, and movement.[7] "With these seasonal rituals, I could feel the potential of creating a new performance from the experience of traditional, modern and contemporary practices," shares Lee.[8] This amalgamation of the traditional with the modern and contemporary is at the heart of Lee's practice.[9]

My analysis of MAGO departs from theories of ritual that have pervaded performance studies, in which the teleology of ritual privileges reintegration (whether in social and cultural rituals or aesthetic works that function ritualistically). In his conceptualization of social and cultural processes as "social dramas," as initially inspired by Ndembu rituals, Victor Turner articulates the four phases of social dramas as a breach, crisis, redressive actions, and reintegration.[10] A linear temporal logic underpins Turner's view of ritualistic processes that culminate in some kind of resolution.[11] Turner fixates on liminality, which occurs in the middle part of a social drama, as "that time and space betwixt and between one context of meaning and action and another."[12] Expanding his reading of liminality, as having a more circumscribed potential in tribal and agrarian rituals, Turner coined the term "liminoid" to talk about leisure activities such as aesthetic performances, "as being more often the creation of individual than of collective inspiration and critical rather than furthering the purposes of the existing social order."[13] A Turner-influenced separation of liminoid activities from the realm of ritual liminality fails to capture the world-making possibilities of ritualized performances by artists of color.[14] Aesthetic performances like MAGO do not simply have ritualistic characteristics; they do more than function ritualistically. They are rituals in the artist's eyes that are a mode of survival.

Lee's ritual practice takes the form of multimedia performances that draw on indigenous Korean practices and experiment with new styles and techniques. Further, her ritual performances engage with contemporary social and political issues. "I was very interested in a new form of ritual that makes sense in this moment in time, that acts as a go-between when it comes to reconciling ancient times and the present," she explains.[15] We find in MAGO a prime example of how Lee conceives of this new ritual practice as aesthetically experimental, temporally fluid, and politically engaged. "I believe that art has the power to creatively confront our struggles—to regain our strength and to take action," she explains. "That is why my creative journey is centered in ritual. I dedicate my performance as a ritual to not only discover my own history and myth, but also invite others to discover their own."[16] For Lee, a performance like MAGO is a ritual, particularly in the sense that there is a kind of spiritual communing for a collective in a process of transformation. Yet, that transformation is stalled in the face of social and political precarity.

Instead the audience lingers in a condition of suspension, marking a shift from a Gennep-cum-Turner view of liminality as a temporary phase of transition. They are invited to dwell in deferral, a condition of suspension, like particles floating in a viscous mixture. In other words, Lee takes a Muñozian approach to ritual performances, positing the difficulty and impossibility of reintegration in the "here and now's totalizing rendering of reality," to borrow Muñoz's language, and yet holding on to potentiality.[17] For Muñoz, "a potentiality is a certain mode of nonbeing that is eminent, a thing that is present but not actually existing in the present tense."[18] In Lee's performance, the seeds of that potentiality lurk in multiple times and spaces, below and above, in the histories, images, and breathing techniques of those who traverse the ocean floor or in animals that fly through the skies and sit perched in trees. As such, Lee presents us with figures like sea divers and crows as paragons of caretaking and witnessing. The ocean and the sky are more than just metaphors; they are heuristic orientations for how to navigate social and political precarity. This suspension is more than just a temporary phase; it is a way of being in the world long after the performance ends.

Influenced by Korean shamanic rituals, MAGO loosely follows a Korean ritual structure: summoning the memories and spirits of the ancestors, communing with them, and then releasing the spirits and purging pent-up emotions in the participants. "The work itself will be a cleansing/purging ritual," Lee explained in an early interview about the piece, "an intensely personal journey of birth, self-discovery, confrontation, actions, and rebirth, and like all of my work, will embrace spirituality, politics and healing."[19] However, the performance does not culminate in the usual "release." The work is organized into six chapters centered on Lee's performance of six female figures: Mago, Karma, Grandmother, Lee as herself, Crow, and the warrior Ara. "Lee sees herself as inhabiting the archetypal realm of the shape-shifter," writes Nirmala Nataraj, "the one who leads viewers through the performance in a ritualistic process."[20] The performer who shifts shape has unique powers. "Performance," writes Dwight Conquergood, "privileges threshold-crossing, shape-shifting, and boundary-violating figures, such as shamans, tricksters, and jokers, who value the carnivalesque over the canonical, the transformative over the normative, the mobile over the monumental."[21] Lee not only embodies characterological transformations; she makes possible temporal crossings. Through her shape-shifting performance, Lee leads the audience on a journey across seas, historical periods, psychospiritual realms, and dreamscapes.

In the opening scene, Lee takes on the character of Mago—summoning this mythic figure into the space and bringing to the surface submerged memories of violence. The sound of water dripping echoes as if in a cave (figure 7.1). A figure with her back slightly stooped steadily makes her way up to the top of a white cubic platform. Lee is dressed in a crumpled white-sheened *hanbok* with its long, flowing skirt and large billowing sleeves, her face covered with a wooden mask of a woman with an angular nose and black braid draped across the top of her head. Twenty feet behind Lee a long white banner sweeps down from the ceiling with a projection of a milky jade-colored holographic mask hovering toward the top, indecipherable markings resembling prehistoric writing occupying the rest of the banner. Lee calls on the audience—which surrounds her, sitting to either side of the long, rectangular clearing that she traverses in the Grand Lobby of the YBCA—to join the ritual performance.

The mythic figure of Mago is the foundation for Lee's performance, serving as a kind of spirit guide for her. Embodying Mago also allows Lee to amalgamate multiple temporalities. "Mago taught me about connection," ruminates Lee, "connection between myself and the land, between the spirits, between ancestors and the past, and between other people."[22] In Korean mythology, Magohalmi (Grandmother Mago) was a "giant goddess who created all of nature and its geographical formation of this universe."[23] The giant goddess walked across the sea and created mountains and islands with mud from her skirt, according to the legend.[24] Over centuries Koreans focused more on re-telling myths about male ancestors, so many Koreans might know the name but not attribute any significant mythical actions to Mago, and some might not have even heard of the name. In Korean mythology Tangun is considered the first ancestor, but Lee wondered about the mother of Tangun. "I [was] digging into that lineage, and then I found Mago."[25] Lee's digging primarily involved reading books and searching for internet material that mentioned Mago, even in passing.[26] The motifs of Mago, as Nami Lee explains, are also found in the Jeju Island legend of Son-moon-dae-halmang, a Mago-like goddess.[27] In making this connection, Dohee Lee muses that "you can realize . . . how much one figure as a[n] energy form has so many different names."[28] Discovering Mago for Lee kindled a desire to recuperate the myths that have helped people make sense of their world and to recenter the forgotten women at the center of these stories. "The people valued these [mythic] figures," explains Lee, "and this value gains meaning and importance over time and that

FIGURE 7.1 Dohee Lee embodies the Mago character, 2014. PHOTO BY PAK HAN. COURTESY OF PAK HAN.

myth can become a blueprint for how to protect and sustain the community."[29] By community, Lee refers not simply to a Korean diasporic community but to any local community.

Through costuming and video art, Lee represents the character of Mago as temporally fluid: both ancient and young, present in the here-and-now of the performance space and spectral through the video art in other scenes. Lee's stooped posture and slow movement suggest an elderly body marked by the passage of time, while her wooden mask is that of the *gaksi*, or young bride, whose youthfulness is marked by red-colored lips and a long braid draped across the top of the forehead, distinct from the tight bun-style of elderly Korean women. The gaksi is a stock character in the Korean traditional *Hahoe* mask dance dramas and an avatar of a tutelary goddess, one that protects humanity.[30] A holographic image of this mask reappears throughout the performance—puncturing the temporal span of each chapter with the spectral presence of the mythic figure of Mago.

The white color of Lee's hanbok, or traditional Korean dress, has varied cultural referents, pointing to the multifaceted role that Lee plays in this ritual performance. The white color of Lee's hanbok brings to mind how Koreans, traditionally known as "white clad folk," have worn white clothes since ancient times because "they thought white symbolized the light of the sun and so considered this color sacred," as N. Choi puts it.[31] The outfit also brings to mind the attire of shamans. "In Korea, shamans and other religious figures often wear white ceremonial robes," writes Bong-Ha Seo, "which have much the same meanings as when white is worn by the general population: absoluteness, sacredness, and purity; or for mourning clothes, grief and sadness."[32] Lee's donning of the white hanbok is also an expression of sacredness and purity and of mourning—giving Lee's character an ancient quality and foreshadowing the sense of loss over the destruction on the island.

Lee's voice inflections convey a gynocentric vision of creation that extends from Mago to the sea divers on Jeju Island, which is an important spatial referent in the performance. With its lush forested interior landscape, pristine beaches, and unique volcanic rock formations, Jeju Island is a popular vacation and honeymoon destination for Koreans. Most famously, Jeju is home to the *haenyeo*, women—including Lee's own grandmother—who for generations have worked as "deep-sea divers, who submerge as much as 200 feet without oxygen tanks to collect abalone, urchin and shellfish in the coral reefs, and who work through their 70s."[33] These female sea divers are the economic and social backbone of the society on the island. A bell rings and Lee moves from mythic time into human time, as mythic past and island traditions merge. Lee begins to sing tones suggested by the bells. Her voice rises and falls as she makes a whistling downward glissando, "WHOoooooo" sound, multiple times and sings before she removes the mask. The whistling sound is Lee's riff on *soombisori* (breath sound) of Jeju's female sea divers. Soombisori will return as the motif for the music later in the performance and will be juxtaposed against moving images of the sea divers in the ocean. The sound of soombisori emitted from a body representing Mago conveys Lee's contention that the Jeju sea divers are descendants of Mago, whom she refers to as the "mother of the universe."[34] In choosing this lineage for the sea divers, Lee elevates the haenyeo as mythic-like figures. They mother the universe through sustainability practices as they traverse the ocean floor and responsibly gather sea life for consumption.

The performance moves from one act of creation (the world) to another (birth), each of which has its own scale of time. Whereas the temporality of gestation of a human being spans roughly nine months, the temporality of creation is boundless. Lee transforms into the character of Karma, who straddles life and death. Karma is not necessarily from Korean mythology, but a reflection of the Buddhist concept of karma. A cyclical temporality is at the heart of the concept of karma. Lee sees Karma, like Mago, as a force who gives birth to humanity, deciding who will be reborn. Both figures dictate the timescales of living beings, doing so in manners that are not linear. Lee's heavy, labored breathing at the beginning of her Karma performance, what she calls the "breath of past life," gives sonic and physical form to the metaphorical taking in and expelling of the past lives of humanity into new forms. As her body begins to shake and her facial expressions contort, Lee enacts possession, much like a shaman who enters a trancelike state and is taken over by a spirit. Throughout the performance, a shaking or trembling movement or clockwise twirling evoke shamanic ritual movements that signify the beginning of a trance or possession. In Jai Arun Ravine's conversation with Lee, Lee shared that "in traditional Korean shamanic ritual, the way of communicating with spirits is vibration."[35] Lee's vibrational movement suggests that she may be symbolically being taken over by the spirit of Karma, communicating with Karma, or going through the beginning pangs of birth; it may be that all of this is happening. The facial gestures of pain, discomfort, and anger transition into the animation of the seeds of future life on her dress as the seeds undulate and Lee emits a dolphinesque squeal-like cry. The grotesque blending of Lee's squeal with the surprising sight of miniature felt fetus-shaped dolls under the top layer of her skirt transitions into a tender moment where Lee rolls up part of her skirt and cradles it like a baby. In this scene, Lee invites the audience to experience multiple affective registers of unease, bewilderment, surprise, and warmth.

After Lee portrays Mago and Karma, the audience moves to the Forum, a multipurpose performance space, and sits on risers fanning the stage. In this scene that Lee describes as "remembering my grandmother," she calls to mind not just her own grandmother but also the generations of women sea divers and even the Grandmother goddess of the sea.[36] There is a sense of multilayered temporalities embodied in the different generations of women evoked: Mago and Karma, Lee's grandmother, and sea divers. In foregrounding and celebrating female elders, both mythic and human, Lee conveys how knowledge of one's ancestral histories and mythic traditions can recenter and guide the self. Sitting center stage Lee dons a white dress with cap sleeves and a long flowing skirt, a modern take on the hanbok; strips of long vertical cloth with names in black ink run down the front of her skirt. These are the names of those killed in a massacre on Jeju Island, which I explain in more detail later. She is seated upstage of a long white cloth that extends toward the audience. Lee's white dress visually connects her with the character of Mago from the first chapter of the performance. The long cloth on the floor brings to mind the long white cloths used in a shamanic ritual movement to signify the passageways between worlds. Ravine describes it as a "long river of cloth" that "symbolizes waterways and their relationship to the haenyeo [sea divers], who dive all day and then return home to their children and grandchildren."[37] The long cloth onstage extends out toward the audience, inviting them into the ritual—conveying a desire to connect the worlds within the performancescape of MAGO with the world of the audience. Lee's ritual performance transforms the robe from between worlds to between performer and the audience.

Though the visual imagery grounds this scene in the recent past, Lee's portrayal of her grandmother and a shaman blur the temporal demarcations of this scene; simultaneity is an important temporal mode in the performance. Behind Lee, long white curtains form a central vertical screen flanked by two large horizontal screens. "Grandmother," whispers Lee in English (figure 7.2). A fog horn rings and she begins singing in a style that combines elegiac p'ansori operatic singing with Lee's imitation of the whistling soombisori of the sea divers in Jeju. On the screen stage right, a grainy video of a shaman holding a ritual on a cliff overlooking the ocean plays, while a video of a flat boat with a large sail with three people onboard moves across the screen. On the center panel a large flame flickers. For the first time in the performance, video footage of life on Jeju Island is shown, marking a transition from representations of ancient time through the stylized performances of Lee as Mago and Karma to what Lee calls the "recent past." The video of the ritual likely depicts an annual shamanic rite held in the spring in which the divers appeal to the Grandmother goddess of the sea for their safety. "During this ritual," writes Chul-in Yoo, "all divers are descendants of the goddess and bond together as children of the same ancestor. They scatter millet on the waters and pray for a plentiful harvest."[38] Though this is a moment in the performance when the "liminoid" aspects of MAGO separate from its function as a ritual, this is precisely Lee's point. Her ritual performance is not like a traditional shamanic ritual; it is a new form that merges the traditional with the modern and contemporary.

In the same vein of aesthetic commingling, Lee merges the characters of her grandmother and a shaman figure in her performance. The headdress on Lee and the shaman in the video are similar; Lee is not only channeling her grandmother but also performing as a shaman. Similar to Lee's veneration of sea divers as mythic-like figures, Lee elevates her grandmother as a spiritual figure, similar to a shaman in annual spring rites on the island who appeals

FIGURE 7.2 Dohee Lee performs the Grandmother character, 2014. PHOTO BY PAK HAN. COURTESY OF PAK HAN.

for the safety of the divers. Lee's grandmother is her protector. She slowly steps from side to side, while lifting one arm in the air and twirls clockwise—making her way along the cloth as she moves closer to the audience. In her twirling, Lee employs the shamanic movement of possession, symbolically inviting the spirit of her grandmother, the Grandmother goddess, and perhaps others to enter her body.

Lee's riff on the sea divers' soombisori embodies generational circularity and continuity. She calls out the whistling sound of the sea divers in a more melodic way, and the sound of other whistling echoes back. In between singing, she makes her own version of soombisori; the whistling sound and singing echo in the space, surprising Lee when she hears it. After Lee heard the free divers' soombisori, she knew that it would become the motif for the music in this scene.[39] The breathing technique of rapid expiration known as soombisori occurs because the free divers use no breathing apparatus. Their "wheezy whistling gasp" upon emerging from the water has a high frequency that can be easily heard over the noise of the waves.[40] "To the trained ear of a haenyeo," writes Mikhail Karikis, "each s[oo]mbisori has a distinctive sound; it is thus a unique acoustic structure, a sonorous 'identity card' for each haenyeo, which is produced in the individual mouth and body of each woman."[41] It is a social sound shared by divers not only to identify themselves and acknowledge each other, but also to keep track of each other for survival in the murky, choppy waters. Soombisori is also "trans-generationally transmitted," writes Karikis, "creating an inter-generational sonic bond that ties the community and functions as a sonic signifier of their professional identity."[42] Though Lee is alone onstage, the echoing of her singing and whistling creates a chorus of soombisori, the sound of survival and community.

The playing of moving images of sea divers on the screens depicts how the women are caretakers of the ocean, using eco-friendly harvesting methods to sustain the marine life around the island.[43] The video shows the women in full-body black wet suits jumping into the water and exploring the bottom of the ocean for marine life to harvest. While Lee sings a tribute song to the female sea divers of Jeju in Korean, the moving images of the sea divers in the ocean are superimposed with the translated text of her song: "Sea of Jeju / float that boat / row its oars / speedily / oh wind, oh wind / do not blow / the sea gleaning boat is leaving / to glean / go in the sea / the buoy / your life line / leaving behind a fresh-born babe / go in the sea / ceasing to breath[e] / the haenyo's exhale." Lee calls upon the sea and wind to tend to the boats and divers who risk their lives in the choppy waters with only buoys marking their presence under the sea. She also notes the sacrifice many of these women made at the beginning of their diving careers when they left behind their babies.

Lee's performance of three maternal figures—Mago, Karma, and Grandmother—illuminates her desire to recuperate a gynocentric vision of creation and care of the earth. These female figures birth and care for humans and live harmoniously with the natural elements. The sound of crickets can be heard, and a graphic of a night sky packed with stars appears on the side screens while a silhouette of a bare tree appears against a cosmos of blue stars on the central screen. Lee places the bundle on her back, lovingly caressing the baby on her back. On the screen stage left, a holographic faded image of Mago's mask appears—as if Mago is looking down at Lee as she cares for the baby— and then Lee disappears through the middle screen. Lee's gesture of mothering echoes the previous scene with Karma cradling a baby formed from the cloth of her skirt; these babies beckon future possibility. At the same time, the spectral presence of Mago symbolically layers ancient and mythic time over the past. This layering manifests Lee's conception of time as cyclical and concentric where subjects experience ancient time, mythic time, the past, and the present simultaneously.

As much as *MAGO* is about female mythic, ancestral, and historical figures, the performance also pivots on the question of how to reckon with the legacy of state-sanctioned violence and ecological destruction on the island. "We urgently need myths and rituals to regain what we have lost in this destruction," writes Lee in the program. "How can we remember the songs of our ancestors, the words that they spoke, their care of the land, people and spirits?"[44] Lee shows how militarism and political strife have damaged the world created by Mago and Karma and cared for by the haenyeo. After a scene where Lee performs as her "present self" on a journey through an idyllic landscape evoking the rural countryside of Jeju, the performance transitions to menacing images of danger and death, which are in stark contrast to the previous scene's images of the vivacity and resilience of the sea divers. The world of Mago is in danger. Images of an old man in traditional Korean clothes sitting next to a Korean man in a military uniform, a young Korean child looking frightenedly at the camera, a white military officer with dark glasses, and a dead Korean person's face surrounded by flowers in a coffin alternate on the screens as flames dance across the images. While there is little historical specificity to the images, what does come through is the encroachment of militarism on life in Korea, a threat to a traditional way of life and to the next generation.

Through *MAGO* Lee seeks to make her audience confront and witness a collapsing of time between different historical periods wrought by continuing structures of violence. In Lee's politically engaged ritual performance, she deals with legacies of the Jeju massacres and the impact of the building of a US naval base on the island. When Lee returned to Jeju to learn more about Korean mythology, shamanic rituals on the island, and the issues facing Jeju residents, she confronted a deep silence harbored in her own family. She recalls the "thick silence felt in my grandparent's traditional *jogajip* home— silent memories of past tragedies."[45] Lee is referring to the most devastating trauma of Jeju's past tragedies: the state-sponsored massacres and atrocities that took place between 1948 and 1954 in response to an armed uprising on the island.[46] Residents took to the streets on April 3, 1948, to protest elections and the development of a new separate government in South Korea under the tutelage of the US military, leading to years of fighting between local insurgents, police, and Korean military.[47] Hun Joon Kim writes that the Korean government's "counterinsurgency strategy was extremely brutal, involving mass arrests and detentions, forced relocations, torture, indiscriminate killings, and many large-scale massacres of civilians."[48] "The Jeju massacres," writes Howard French, "were part of a particularly brutal effort by the government in the southern part of Korea to root out those it suspected of being Communists on the eve of the country's civil war."[49] The violence resulted in 25,000 to 30,000 deaths, about 10 percent of the population on the island.[50] After fifty years of public silence surrounding the massacres, the Korean government established a truth commission in 2000.[51]

As part of her research, Lee visited massacre sites, and she saw connections between the massacres on Jeju Island and recent events, as the South Korean government has quelled local protests in Jeju's Gangjeong Village against the building of a US naval base on the island. Lee refers to naval base–related protests and incidents in Gangjeong Village as "another 4.3 incident," referring to April 3, when the uprising began.[52] "My eyes traveled back to the ocean, where new military development is once again destroying the land and people," writes Lee. "Drills cut into ancient volcanic stone and families, neighbors and villages divided again. Sixty years. It still continues."[53] Ravine writes, "The construction of the base is eroding the island's ecosystem and many aspects of traditional culture on Jeju, among them the practices of the haenyeo."[54] As we will see in MAGO, these histories of state-sanctioned violence and the threat to the island's ecosystem by the building of the naval base and an indigenous way of living are deeply intertwined.

Breath and sound convey the overlaid temporal logics of the piece. As tiny white petals begin to cascade down the black screens, only Lee's heaving can be heard. This is a moment when it becomes clear how breath is deeply cyclical in MAGO. Her labored breathing evokes the labored exhalation of Karma in a previous scene, making one wonder what will be revealed or birthed through the repetition of time. Will it be new life? Will it be death? "Over sixty years," Lee whispers, "it still continues." She whimpers and then makes a shushing sound. "Over sixty years," she repeats, "it still, it still continues." Here Lee links the 4.3 Massacre—"sasam, the Jeju massacre, April 3, 1948. Families, neighbors and villages divided" (as explained the program notes)—to the current encroachment of US militarism on the life of Jeju Island.[55] Lee steps onto a stump center stage and lets out a rhythmic moaning sound. She raises her hands to the sky, first the right hand as if supplicating to the heavens. A black stump with large tentacles for roots descends above her. Everything is dark except for the petals cascading down the screens behind her. Bells tinkle, a distinctive sound from a shamanic ritual and evocative of Lee's catalyzing dream, and Lee slowly and deliberately brings her arms and hands together.

FIGURE 7.3 Spirit characters approach Dohee Lee, 2014. PHOTO BY PAK HAN. COURTESY OF PAK HAN.

She seems to be in a trance as she gradually spreads her hands out with the palms open as if trying to hold the weight of the world in her hands. In gestures usually not used in a shamanic ritual, Lee calls out to spirits to join her (figure 7.3).

The audience is invited to join in this part of the ritual performance as living puppets when they don paper masks to the accompaniment of spirits. Nine performers known as the "spirits" march slowly onstage toward Lee. They are wearing long-sleeved white shirts and pants with white paper masks over their faces. To the steady beat of a drum, they march upstage and Lee disappears through the center curtain/screen. A chorus of four spirit musicians dressed in long blue coats makes its way onstage from the sides. They play brass and woodwind instruments, which are played by expiration of breath, linking these instruments to soombisori and Lee's breath-centric performance. An image of the masks, white rectangles with angular cutouts, is projected on the street; these are the same masks on each audience member's chair.[56] "Wear your mask" reads a subtitle on the screen. The white paper masks bring to mind *nukjeon*, a paper puppet in the shape of a human body with simple cutout facial features. These puppets are often used in Korean shamanic rituals to represent the spirits of the deceased. The performers in *MAGO* bring to life these puppets in a ritual for the dead. The spirits slowly march downstage, alternately turning to different sides and kneeling, looking out as if surveying the audience and the land. Images of a foggy forest appear on the screens, so it is not clear if the spirits are viewing the aftermath of a fire or the thickness of a foggy day. The witnesses, or spirits, then move into a triangular formation and kneel on one knee. As they rise, a flock of black crows perched in a tangle of tree branches becomes visible on the screens. Alternate realities and timelines—the aftermath of the encroachment of militarism on the island or an ethereal world—are presented to the audience.

Crows play an important role in *MAGO* as witnesses to the long cycle of violence on the island. Lee visited several massacre sites on Jeju Island as she was researching *MAGO*, and she found herself each time in the "company of a murder of crows."[57] In the program, she writes:

> It seemed to me that they were witnesses and protectors of the land and lost souls. Watching me, piercing me with their gaze and asking, "What did you see?" "What did you hear?" My eyes traveled back to the ocean, where new military development is once against destroying the land and people. Drills cut into ancient volcanic stone and families, neighbors and villages divided again. Sixty years. It still continues.[58]

Lee views the crows on the island as "witnesses and protectors" that incite her to reflect on the island's histories of state-sanctioned violence against the land and its people. When she takes on the role of Crow, Lee becomes both witness and protector, calling upon other witnesses—including the audience—to join her.

In the performance Lee blurs the line between human and animal, conveying how the crow has capabilities that humans have seemed to lack in their suppression of memories of the massacres. She slowly emerges from the center curtain dressed in a sleeveless black top with a deep V-neck and black pants overlaid with a white skirt. A carmine underskirt is visible beneath the white, and beneath the top layer a cluster of felt seed pods hangs. Feathers frame part of her face, and her costume is an amalgamation of her previous costumes as Mago, Karma, Grandmother, and herself. The sounds of crows cawing fill the space as the spirits disperse. With her arms elevated, Lee draws her hands together to form a beak and make jabbing motions. She twirls clockwise and counterclockwise multiple times as she glides across the stage and juts her head like a bird. After the fog clears in the projection on the screens a flock of crows nesting in trees becomes visible, eventually transitioning into animated images of white silhouettes of crows flying across the screens. In a distorted metallic-sounding voice, she whispers indecipherably (with subtitles projected on the screens)

Oh! I can hear a voice
There was a woman
she is calling us
it is time to gather
from the south, north, east, and west
let's bring them all.

Lee as Crow is calling out to other crows to gather for a ritual. It is unclear whom the woman referenced is, but I surmise that it may be Mago.

Titled "Invited Ritual—Crow," the scene then unfolds as a kind of council of crows gathering to report back on what they have seen around the world. After stomping and gesticulating energetically by throwing her arms out rhythmically to the music, Lee calls out in English, "Everyone here? / Is everyone here?" Each time Lee asks a question, crows caw in response. "What about east? That's it? What about east? Is everyone here? What about west? Yeah? What about north?" Suddenly the screen changes from the birds to fast-moving storm clouds. Lee stops moving and quietly implores, "So, what did you see? What did you see?" The previous images of the frightened Korean child, the white military officer, and the pair of Korean men flicker on the screens as Lee continues her series of questions, linking this moment to the performance's earlier scene of danger and death when these same images were projected to show the encroachment of militarism on life in Korea. The images then change to still photographs of Palestinian refugees crowded into a bus, dead bodies on the ground, children lined up against a wall, Jewish people with the star of David on their jackets, sea divers in Jeju wading through the water, a video of bombs dropping from an airplane and of a mushroom cloud, young Vietnamese children walking down a road, and countless others. The atemporal playing of mostly iconic images of the violence of settler colonialism, the Holocaust, the dropping of atomic bombs during World War II, and the American War in Vietnam conveys the interconnectedness between acts of state-sanctioned violence and the cyclical nature of this kind of destruction, though I would have liked to have seen a more sustained and nuanced treatment of these images. Lee's juxtaposition of these violent photographs with everyday life images from Jeju Island communicates her contention that the threat to the livelihood of haenyeo from the building of the US naval base is another form of state-sanctioned violence.

In using a call-and-response, Lee highlights a distinctive quality of ritual, the dialogic relationship between the performer and audience. Lee's repeated questions of "what did you hear" and "what did you see" begin to generate responses: these range from a voice-over that declares fragmented sentences such as "one of the greatest genocides of the twentieth century" and "millions dying," to audience members who call out, "I heard guns firing," "houses burning down," and "I saw the blood." Lee approaches the first row, directly facing the audience, and points to the audience as she asks them what they saw. This kind of direct physical invitation (both eye contact and digital gesticulation) and verbal invitation prompt certain members of the audience to bridge the gap between watching a performance and witnessing violence—joining the council of crows as witnesses to histories of state-sanctioned violence. "For Lee," writes Crystal Mun-Hye Baik, "this reciprocated practice of listening and responding enacts moments of self-reflexivity by allowing the audience to identify distinct modes of racialized and gendered violence that stretch beyond the borders of Jeju. These recounted incidences—the terrifying experiences of militarized warfare, racial oppression, and settler occupation—are not isolated, nor are they exceptional."[59]

This is a critical moment in the performance when Lee directly addresses her audience, urging them to participate in the ritual of confronting the past. As Nataraj writes, "The ritual itself is an important active process. It's about connecting, processing, confronting and reconciling the things that we experience."[60] "Speak up," commands Lee, "We never talk about it. What did you see? What did you hear? What about you? What about you? What about everyone?" After the video transitions to images of moving clouds, Lee calls out more emphatically, "Open your eyes. Open your eyes. Open your ears. Open your eyes. Open your eyes. Open your eyes. Open your ears. Open your eyes. Open your ears. Open your eyes. Let's bring the heart back." A holographic image of the Mago mask reappears on the screen stage left and floats against the moving images of storm clouds. The spectral presence of Mago once again symbolically layers ancient and mythic time over the past, present, and future—creating the sense that Mago is ever present.

FIGURE 7.4 Dohee Lee performs with drummers, 2014. PHOTO BY PAK HAN. COURTESY OF PAK HAN.

RESUSCITATING THE HEART

As a tonal shift happens when the drums are brought on, time shifts from a more historically specific moment to one that is more ancient and mythic, evoking the primordial. After Lee calls out to "bring the heart back," she gestures out toward the audience as four female Asian American drummers drag eleven *buk* drums on stands center stage forming a semicircle (figure 7.4). Known as the "Crow Warriors," these women join Lee in a boisterous and thunderous playing of the large round buk, one of the four central instruments in Korean traditional *p'ungmul* drumming. Video images of water cascading vertically and horizontally fill the screens; there is not uniform movement of water but a wild cascade of water, evoking the temporal collisions in the performance. The coordinated pounding of the drums is meant to be a call to action, like the playing of a war drum, to spur on the audience to prepare for battle. Further, the beating of the drums is like resuscitating the heart, asking the audience what it may mean to be reconnected and brought to life with the heartbeat of one's ancestral traditions. That the drummers are an ensemble as opposed to a solo performer conveys the importance of a collective in grappling with histories of violence and finding ways to move forward. Most important, Lee places the power to resuscitate the heart in the hands of women.

In the final scene of *MAGO*, the audience returns to the physical space where the ritual performance began, illuminating Lee's cyclic use of space and time. The audience waits in the lobby space where Lee emerges as Ara the future warrior, a metaphor for the sea divers.[61] "To me divers are the warriors," explains Lee, "this dive[r] as a warrior comes out [to] the world to confront it."[62] Lee plays a stringed fretboard instrument she designed with vertical and horizontal strings that emits high-pitched harp-like music, what Lee refers to as Ara's weapon. She leads the audience in a chanting call-and-response ("Oohahahah") with the participation of the nine spirits. In Korean she sings, "The ocean. My homeland, Jeju, my land. I share the pain and suffering with you." What is most significant about this final scene is Lee's decision to present the performing arts—"music and dance," she explains—as her/our weapon: "This is our weapon and we keep, keep going [at] it."[63] There is not a sense of closure or reintegration at the end of Lee's ritual performance. Having invited the audience into a condition of suspension, she reminds them that the work is continual. Central to this work is the reinvigoration of mythic narratives, ancestral histories, indigenous traditions, silenced memories, and stories.

"My creative process is that the story itself becomes the medicine," explains Lee. "Medicine is inside of the pain, inside of tears, inside of struggles. That is why I think sharing and speaking stories is a powerful method to take action."[64] As a reimagining and staging of time travel, *MAGO* fosters a critical space for "sharing and speaking" the stories of mythic figures and suppressed histories and reclaiming women-centered indigenous practices. Through *MAGO* Lee illuminates the urgent need for "myths and rituals to regain what we have lost in this destruction."[65] The performance imagines and stages time travel through ancient time, mythic time, the past, the present, and the future by using visual, sonic, and embodied techniques. The physical and visual presence of the six female figures allows for multiple temporal arrangements to exist in the performance space. This puts into practice Lee's belief that "we always live in the mythical time and past time and present time and they lead us to the future, all the time."[66] However, the seeming linearity of the time travel is punctured by the spectral presence of Mago through video imagery, shamanic ritual movement, and haenyeo-inspired breathing technique that Lee uses throughout the performance. Mythic and ancient time collide into the present, past, and future. This commingling of temporalities inspired by female figures puts forth her contention of the need for recuperating a gynocentric vision of the world in order to impede the repetition of histories of state-sanctioned violence. "This is the time when you see that this whole of the society is collapsing because [of] the patriarchal system," explains Lee. "So this is the time [for] matriarchal power to come back."[67] As such, Lee seeks to communicate the vitality of women and their indigenous practices for survival and the unearthing of interred histories. As ritual performance, MAGO invites the audience to meditate on what it may mean to join far-flung communities across space and time in these excavations and to reclaim one's own ancestral histories and practices. While MAGO illuminates the simultaneity of different temporal arrangements, Lee's ritual performance is predominantly future-beckoning with an orientation toward kindling care *for* women-centered indigenous practices and *of* the earth and its inhabitants.

NOTES

1   D. Lee, interview with author.
2   Jeju Island is off the southern tip of South Korea.
3   As quoted in Nataraj, "MAGO Project."
4   Fong, "Chapter Two."
5   As quoted in Nataraj, "MAGO Project."
6   Fong, "Chapter One."
7   Yong, "Artist to Artist"; Howard, "'ARA Gut.'"
8   As quoted in Yong, "Artist to Artist."
9   Anna Halprin is one of Lee's greatest influences. Lee teaches at the Tamalpa Institute, cofounded by Halprin, and has collaborated with Halprin.
10 Turner, *Dramas, Fields, and Metaphors*, 37–42.
11 "In keeping with my explicit comparison of the temporal structure of certain types of social processes with that of dramas on the stage, with their acts and scenes, I saw the phases of social dramas as cumulating to a climax," writes Turner. See Turner, *Dramas, Fields, and Metaphors*, 43.
12 Arnold Van Gennep's articulation of the liminal in the three phases of rites of passage as separation, transition, and incorporation influenced Turner's conceptualization of liminality. See Turner, *From Ritual to Theatre*, 24–27, 113.
13 Turner, *From Ritual to Theatre*, 41, 113.
14 "Ritual liminality, therefore," writes Turner, "contains the potentiality for cultural innovation, as well as the means of effecting structural transformations within a relatively stable sociocultural system." See Turner, *From Ritual to Theatre*, 85. Elam has a similar contention. In his study of Luis Valdez's El Teatro Campesino and Amiri Baraka's Black Revolutionary Theater, he argues that ritual processes

were "critical elements in the social protest performances of El Teatro and the BRT." El Teatro and BRT "infused the 'liminoid realm of theater' with elements of the liminal." See Elam, *Taking It to the Streets*, 13, 16.

15 D. Lee, "MAGO Project."

16 Yerba Buena Center for the Arts, *Playbill*.

17 Muñoz, *Crusing Utopia*, 1.

18 Muñoz, *Crusing Utopia*, 9.

19 D. Lee, "MAGO Project."

20 Nataraj, "MAGO Project."

21 Conquergood, "Of Caravans and Carnivals," 138.

22 Nataraj, "MAGO Project."

23 *Encyclopedia of Korean Folk Literature*, 27.

24 *Encyclopedia of Korean Folk Literature*, 27–28.

25 D. Lee, interview with author.

26 One book Lee credits in particular is Park's *Budoji*, a controversial book on ancient Korean history that describes the era of Mago. For a summary of *Budoji* and description of the legend of Mago, see N. Lee, "Reflections on Mago," 765–77.

27 N. Lee, "Reflections on Mago," 769.

28 D. Lee, interview with author.

29 Fong, "Chapter One."

30 Chon, *Korean Mask Dance Dramas*, 112–13. For more on the masks, see Cho, *Traditional Korean Theatre*, 116–19.

31 Choi, *Josen Sang-sik Mun-dab*, 47. As quoted in Seo, "White Hanbok," 123.

32 Seo, "White Hanbok," 124.

33 Ravine, "Resonance and Resistance."

34 D. Lee, interview with author.

35 Ravine, "Resonance and Resistance."

36 Lee is referring to Son-moon-dae-halmang, a Mago-like goddess. D. Lee, interview with author.

37 Ravine, "Resonance and Resistance."

38 Yoo, "Hardy Divers Gather Seafood," 17.

39 Fong, "Chapter Two."

40 Karikis, "Artist's Statement."

41 Karikis, "Artist's Statement."

42 Karikis, "Artist's Statement."

43 Yoo, "Hardy Divers Gather Seafood," 17.

44 Yerba Buena Center for the Arts, *Playbill*.

45 Yerba Buena Center for the Arts, *Playbill*.

46 French, "South Koreans Seek Truth."

47 For a more detailed account of the uprising, see H. J. Kim, *Massacres at Mt. Halla*, 13–37. For more on the question of American responsibility, see Merrill, "Cheju-do Rebellion," 196.

48 H. J. Kim, *Massacres at Mt. Halla*, 2.

49 French, "South Koreans Seek Truth."

50 H. J. Kim, *Massacres at Mt.* Halla, 2, 12.

51 For more on the Korean truth commission, see H. J. Kim, *Massacres at Mt. Halla*.

52 D. Lee, "SPEAK."

53 Yerba Buena Center for the Arts, *Playbill*, 5.

54 Ravine, "Resonance and Resistance."

55 Yerba Buena Center for the Arts, *Playbill*, 5.

56 The use of white masks also brings to mind the work of Anna Halprin. See Worth and Poynor, *Anna Halprin*, 135.

57 Yerba Buena Center for the Arts, *Playbill*, 5.

58 Yerba Buena Center for the Arts, *Playbill*, 5.

59 Baik, "*MAGO* and Communal Ritual," 10–11.

60 Nataraj, "MAGO Project."

61 Ara is the Korean goddess of tears. See D. Lee, ARA Project.

62 D. Lee, interview with author.

63 D. Lee, interview with author.

64 Fong, "Chapter One."

65 Yerba Buena Center for the Arts, *Playbill*, 5.

66 D. Lee, interview with author.

67 D. Lee, interview with author.

PART III
TEMPORAL (IM)MOBILITIES

DWELLING OUT OF TIME

Repetition demands
the new.

JACQUES LACAN

The future belongs
to ghosts.

JACQUES DERRIDA,
IN *GHOST DANCE*

Carceral Space-Times and *The House That Herman Built*

"What kind of house does a man who has lived in a six-by-nine-foot-cell for over thirty years dream of?" *The House That Herman Built* (2006), a collaboration between artist-activist Jackie Sumell and Herman Wallace, the latter of whom spent over forty years in solitary confinement in Louisiana State Penitentiary, began with this question.[1] Starting in 2002, the two corresponded, and, together, Sumell and Wallace designed a dream home in response to the prompt. The home is around 3,200 square feet in total, designed to take up the space in the world that Wallace cannot.[2] Aside from a few luxuries, the large two-story structure they dreamed of emphasizes functionality. It includes several guestrooms and open spaces to host gatherings. The outside areas are replete with flowers and greenery, and the inside is colorful and decorative. Wallace and Sumell draw on Wallace's personal background in the decoration, incorporating African art and the iconography of the Black Panther Party. The building has yet to be constructed, but Sumell exactingly produced digital and miniature models.

To complete the project, Sumell and Wallace wrote each other, spoke on the telephone, and engaged in visits, amassing more than three hundred letters and an extensive archive of blueprints, designs, architectural drawings, and photographs. Sumell gathered these materials—including thirty-nine drawings, two models, a life-size replica of Wallace's solitary cell, a CGI animated film, and a published book—into an art installation at the Akademie Schloss Solitude in Stuttgart, Germany, in 2006.[3] Since then, Sumell has exhibited *The House That Herman Built* twenty times in a dozen different countries. Occupying an entire room of a gallery, it is a multimedia exhibition staging Wallace's and Sumell's labors. Posted on the walls are informative graphics and timelines about mass incarceration, solitary confinement, and Wallace's life. A miniature wooden model of Wallace's dream home sits on a pedestal, and a digital model is projected. Printouts of the blueprints for the house are also displayed for the viewers' perusal (figure 8.1).

As the exhibition explores, Herman Wallace's days were repeated with unimaginable regularity for four decades. His space and time were restricted and controlled in solitary confinement, imbuing his material reality with the traumas of regulation, violence, and privation. The piece has been described as a kind of memory house—a mnemonic technique first developed by Cicero. What is remembered when the dream home exists both in the mind and in the world? Considering the extraordinary space-time of Wallace's incarceration foregrounds the spatiotemporal aspects of the art piece itself. Time might be thought of as a theory of capture, and art, crafted within confinement, dreams of freedom. The performance of Blackness this conceptual art project exhibits starts in the prison, an institution that constructs the space and time of its subjects through repetition. To follow the movement the editors trace in the introduction to this volume: *The House That Herman Built* moves beyond repetition and performs the time of dreaming both within and outside of confinement.

Wallace's body, within the context of the prison, offers an occasion to rethink the relationship between race and performance as a spatiotemporal category—an occasion deeply informed by inquiries into materiality in studies of both race and performance. For example, we find this inquiry in the interpellative psychological mechanisms described by Frantz Fanon, the hybridic cultural archeology of Paul Gilroy, performance's ontology as disappearance theorized by Peggy Phelan, the analysis of objects and subjects across time

FIGURE 8.1 The exhibition at the American Visionary Art Museum in Baltimore, 2015, with a miniature model of the house and replica of Wallace's solitary confinement cell. COURTESY OF JACKIE SUMELL.

inter(in)animated by Rebecca Schneider, and the phenomenology of Blackness discussed by Harvey Young.[4] Each of these accounts offers a different notion of how performance and/or race assume and/or resist materialization over time. A contested terrain, materialization in these accounts is figured—correctly, I think—as a kind of trauma. This chapter considers how the space-time of race and performance subtends a spectral materialization called the incarcerated body. Focusing on the performance of artmaking by an incarcerated body can help unpack how the space-time of trauma informs the materialization of the raced body—especially in the United States, where the modern history of imprisonment is tied to the history of racism. Trauma and racism materialize in space and time through a repetition that mirrors imprisonment and performance. Yet artworks like *The House That Herman Built*, which was crafted in part from inside a literal cage, reenvision the relationship between race and performance as not solely comprising the prison of repetition.

We might think of the body's materialization not only or simply as the result of biological presence or phenomenological thickness—sedimented through a history of habits, behaviors, and performances—but as composed of phantasmal realities, as Gayle Salamon argues in *Assuming a Body*. Salamon theorizes a materiality that is constructed by various surfaces: phantom, physical, affective, social, and historical.[5] Bodily coherence and legibility, then, are the result of an assemblage of mechanisms, visible and invisible, material and immaterial, fictitious and factual. In Salamon's words, "one is not born a body, one becomes one."[6] The prison misapprehends this becoming. The carceral system—working in tandem with white supremacy—assumes and thus constructs the materiality of bodies of Black subjects as ghostly.

The American prison performs like a haunted house. The prison *possesses* its subjects, foreclosing on their futurity in a repeated performance of the past. This chapter concludes that the temporality of *The House That Herman Built* re-members the subject's encasement in the space-time of trauma—itself a repetition—but with a difference. This difference is that art, as dreaming, crafts for the imprisoned subject a new futurity. If the prison forecloses on the subject's future, then this dreaming performs a rupture in that foreclosure. By materializing a temporal rupture in the repetition of the performance of the law, the dream-time of making art functions as activism.

The prison mimics the space-time of the theater, in which ghosts return to influence our understanding of past, present, and future. Since its earliest days, the American prison was regarded as an exemplary spectacle of modern punishment. Some prisons were even constructed including special openings so that public audiences might gather and watch the prisoners at work.[7] These punishment practices served as a kind of pornographic spectacle, staged for the benefit of outsiders. The prison figures futurity itself as "restored behavior." In Richard Schechner's words, "Restored behavior is living behavior treated as a film director treats a string of film. These strips of behavior can be rearranged or reconstructed; they are independent of the causal systems (social, psychological, technological) that brought them into existence. They have a life of their own."[8] To be trapped in the prison's repetition is to have no future. Or perhaps it is more accurate to say, following Derrida, that futurity belongs to the prison's ghosts that draw from strips of existence to piece together previously scripted acts.[9] The rehabilitation promised by incarceration, then, lies at the center of several vectors of performance across time, and is determined to be completed when the subject fits adequately within a fully restored sequence of behavioral strips.

Carceral subjects have agency, of course, but inasmuch as they also have materiality, the conditions of their formation as subjects are the effects of highly concentrated and reiterated relations of power. Particularly in the setting of the penitentiary, which structures the circulation of power through regulation and labor extraction, we can see how the body is both a doing and a thing done—to adapt Elin Diamond's formulation.[10] The imprisoned body is both performing and is itself a performance. In the accounts of both Judith Butler (1993) and Maurice Merleau-Ponty (1945), the body emerges not solely from biology or individual performance, but in a more complex engagement between sociality, imagination, history, and flesh.[11]

Butler's work in particular demonstrates how categories like sex and race function as bodily ideals materialized through time. The court and its rulings, inasmuch as they stand in for the "temporalized regulation of signification" of the symbolic realm, extend Butler's theory.[12] What could be more performative—and yet more terrifyingly *real*—than the prison sentence? The iteration of this sentence over time makes bodies come to matter, in the symbolic construction of the law. The word of the sentence marks the body, constructing it through symbolic violence. "'Race' is thus thinkable as a kind of speech act," as Ann Pellegrini says.[13] Through iterative ritual, such as those mythic performances that suffuse the courtroom—comprising robes, hallowed texts and precedents, and formalized proceedings—the law discursively contributes to the materialization of the imprisoned body. The law's physical and affective violence completes the process in prison. Banishment and social exclusion are themselves ancient rituals of world-making. In the introduction to this volume, the editors examine how care and attention might augment repetition as the temporality of race and performance. In prison, the incarcerated are subject to unwanted care and oppressive attention.

Wallace is an all-too-common figure in the history of the United States: a Black man captured and socially disabled in isolation, his space and time constricted and controlled. His story dramatizes the unsettling and brutal conditions of criminal justice in the United States. In 1971 Wallace and Albert Woodfox were convicted of armed robbery and sentenced to serve twenty-five years in Louisiana State Penitentiary, commonly known as Angola.[14] They studied politics, organized a chapter of the Black Panther Party, and fought for prison reform. Their thoughtful petitions were treated with hostility by prison authorities.[15]

In 1972 they were convicted of murdering a corrections officer named Brent Miller, and they were placed in solitary confinement.[16] Neither of the men could have possibly committed the crime. The evidence presented against them was dubious, at best: the state offered no physical evidence and the witness who claimed to see the crime was legally blind. Even Miller's wife later expressed regret over the conviction. Around the same time, Robert King was also placed in solitary confinement in connection with the murder, despite the fact that he was not even in Angola at the time. King served twenty-nine years in solitary and was eventually released from prison after he was exonerated. Woodfox and Wallace both served over forty-one years. Woodfox remained in Angola until February 2016, when he was released, and lives currently a free man. Wallace was released October 1, 2013, on humanitarian grounds, and he died three days later of liver cancer. For the majority of his life, he lived twenty-three hours a day in a six-by-nine-foot cell containing a cot, a sink, and a toilet.[17] The figures of the "Angola 3," as they came to be known, capture the racist violence at the heart of punitive incarceration, and its simultaneously arbitrary and pernicious effects on human life.[18] The length and severity of their punishment, and the speciousness of their convictions, sparked an international movement to free them.

The story of mass incarceration repeats across infinite bodies. Indeed, imprisonment itself models a structure of repetition. Paradoxically, though captured in an unchanging, institutionalized present, American prisoners are also bonded to the racist past of the penitentiary: its direct historical outgrowth from chattel slavery. As scholars such as Angela Davis, Michelle Alexander, and Ruth Wilson Gilmore have demonstrated, the system today is subtended by the histories of convict leasing, black codes, lynching, Jim Crow, and endemic police brutality and income inequality.[19] Since the 1970s rates and populations of imprisonment have exploded in the United States independently of rates of crime—which have remained steady. The United States currently incarcerates more people than any other country in history, comprising only 5 percent of the world's population, but confining over 21 percent of its prisoners. In terms of numbers, we have surpassed Stalin's gulags—that other carceral chimera of history.[20]

African Americans are incarcerated at more than five times the rate of whites. If people of color were imprisoned at the rates whites are, the US prison population would decrease by more than 40 percent. Yet we would still imprison more than any other nation. Prison labor is legalized slavery, and incarcerated people make pennies on the hour for working in farming, manufacturing, and service industries. The prison boom is not only limited to men: rates of imprisonment for women are increasing faster than those of any other demographic group. The horror of these statistics is compounded by the real experience of those living in prison, documented in prison literature collections like *Fourth City*.[21] Overcrowding and institutional brutality, combined with systematic erosion of prison reforms (such as education and mental health care), make incarceration a living hell. The temporal experience of the typical American prisoner is embroiled in monotonous repetition without change. The prison reperforms a kind of demonic afterlife of those state-sanctioned racist terrors that are frequently considered abolished in popular discourses. Mass incarceration reenacts in the present the labor extraction of slavery and the regulatory power structure of Jim Crow.

Angola is the largest maximum-security penitentiary in the United States. Founded in 1869, the prison continues the history of racial exploitation on which it was built, drawing the current operations of the prison in a counterpoint structure with the twenty-first-century present and the nineteenth-century past. Angola currently incarcerates over six thousand men, around 80 percent of whom are African American. At eighteen thousand acres, the prison is larger than the island of Manhattan. Located in a remote area thirty miles from the nearest town, the Mississippi River bounds "The Farm" on three sides, and has threatened to flood the institution during bad weather. Angola itself was once a plantation and has gained notoriety for carrying on this legacy of brutality and racism. It still bears the name of the African country from which most of the slaves were taken. It has also been known as the "Alcatraz of the South" and "the bloodiest prison in America." Angola mostly comprises farmland, and the prisoners are kept in several housing units dispersed around the grounds, called "camps." The camps vary in security level, including both lower-security dormitories and a death row. Twice a year, the facility hosts a rodeo, which gathers thousands of audience members to the prison. On these occasions, the institution's normal vectors of surveillance and discipline intensify as the prisoners become objects for touristic amusement. In addition to working in other more typical prison manufacturing industries, prisoners at Angola tend around 2,300 head of cattle, and crops of wheat, corn, soybeans, and cotton. These products are used to sustain the prison itself and are also sold for a profit. Like the practice of convict-leasing, the farm runs on a trustee system. Incarcerated people are drafted to supervise the labor of their peers. Historian of Deep South punishment David Oshinsky observed that Angola is a holdover from before the civil rights era, calling the prison a "state of mind." In many ways, it operates under the most insidious form of penal nostalgia.[22] It is what Achille Mbembe calls a "death-world": "[a form] of social existence in which vast populations are subjected to conditions of life conferring upon them the status of living dead."[23]

I turn to the prison as a critical site for discussing how the space-time of race is performed in part because of this history of violence. The temporality of incarcerated people is *arrested* in a state of suspended animation. As the nonincarcerated world shifts and changes—for the most part—in the passage of time, what we might understand as the normative milieu of temporal transformation, the time of the American prisoner remains locked in a loop, rehearsing centuries-old cycles of retributive pain. In this way, the prison serves as a space of temporal regulation. In terms of spatial regulation, incarcerated people are controlled by physically restraining their sociality—who they interact with, and when and where these interactions occur. Given the theory of materialization outlined above—in which the body is understood as a spatiotemporal construction performed in collaboration, concert, and conflict with others—in the constrained sociality of solitary confinement, how does the body come to matter?

For Colin Dayan, the imprisoned body is the "flesh-and-bones ghost": the living dead. In *The Law Is a White Dog*, Dayan examines how the state makes and destroys its "negative persons" in the rituals of the law, through its symbolic regulatory practices—a kind of necromancy.[24] In Dayan's account, the prison sentence is a speech act with chthonic power to isolate the body and transform living subjects into phantoms. In this way, Dayan offers a way to think through the temporally constrained sociality of prisoners, in addition to the spatial restrictions of confinement.[25] She theorizes civil death thusly:

> The convict, though actually a living being, is not only dead but also buried by the law. The body is there, but restrained in prison. The external physical conditions are clear. The internal spiritual state is not. The physical person (solely body and appetite) has no personhood (the social and civic components of personal identity). What kind of spectral form remains? . . . What is more pressing, more spectacular than the realm of the flesh-and-bones ghost, the palpable specter watching over its own perpetual degradation?[26]

Dayan teases out the spatiotemporal contradictions posed by the body of the incarcerated: at the same time that the bare body is living, breathing, and eating, the person's social and civic identity is restricted. The body in prison is embroiled in a process of resurrection, an ongoing rehearsal of the past. Spatial techniques of capture, segregation, and isolation combine with the temporalities of duration, stasis, repetition, and reiteration in the prison sentence. As the material of the body degrades, undergoes disappearance even, the spectral subject waits and watches in attendance. Because of its interment in the haunted prison house, the carceral body is ghostly, even to the subject himself.[27] *The House That Herman Built* repurposes the spectrality of imprisonment. Wallace haunts the exhibit. His physical body, still locked away, is never present with the models of the home and other displays. Yet the work makes material those social and oneiric aspects of his identity for the spectator. This inversion of the prison's necromancy somehow makes Wallace's ghost *more* real, *more* present, than we would otherwise think of him in his solitary cell.

This phantom materiality is both a product of history and also history's return in the present. The mechanism of solitary confinement, by severing the prisoner's social ties, serves to disable his claims to being a fully living subject. Without social connection and community, he assumes the materiality of a ghost, only visible in the imaginations of those who might remember his visage—including the imprisoned himself. As his physical body ages in incarceration, his "personhood," defined by Dayan as those aspects of being that are tied to external interaction, is frozen in time.[28] To return to Herman Wallace, the person who first entered the solitary cell in 1972 watches over the biological body's degradation. In addition, this spectral effect characterizes his physical body as a Black man in a prison thick with racist history. Blackness, in prison, is a returning. Wallace's body is trapped in a vortex of haunted matter, comprising histories of capture, bondage, and terror. His sociality, limited and channeled by the encounter with the violent apparatus of the institution, in fact comes to be defined by communion with the ghosts of memory and history. All this talk of ghouls and ghosts recalls both Alice Rayner and Marvin Carlson, whose interrogations of theater and performance conclude that these are the privileged realms for thinking through the spectral.[29] We might also think of examples from dramatic literature of ghostly returns, resurrections, and possessions, such as the Negro Resurrectionist from *Venus* by Suzan-Lori Parks.[30] In part serving as a kind of emcee for the play, the Negro Resurrectionist not only digs up cadavers to sell for science, but also digs up old stories to share with the audience. The character guides spectators through the play by announcing scene titles and providing contextual information. The Negro Resurrectionist's disinterment of the story of Saartje Baartman emphasizes our distance from history—what Parks sees as the "dismemberment" of certain figures and stories. The prison misapprehends the revivification of history, dismembering the histories of Black people, mobilizing history's performative dimension to pillory bodies in the haunted present.

Haunting and repetition are also the temporalities of trauma, according to Freud.[31] He describes trauma as an unending, uncontrollable return that comes to possess the subject. The traumatized body behaves in unpredictable and often inexplicable ways, often betraying conscious command, manifesting physical symptoms that can only be corrected through treatment. The phenomenon of trauma is characterized through temporal confusion, during which the subject may not understand *when* they are, and these symptoms are experienced spatially as well: *Where am I?* Anecdotal and clinical accounts of traumatic recurrence describe the subject being transported or visited back in time *and* place. The space-time of trauma is a haunted house, a structure within which the traumatized subject is trapped, lost within its walls and hallways, visited by past specters. As one might infer from theories of the haunting of performance, the theater is one example of how the ghostly space-time of trauma is codified. The prison is another.

It's no wonder then that Wallace and Sumell's work took the forms of both social practice and architecture. Just as clinicians like Bessel van der Kolk attempt to "rewrite" the traumatized brain through embodied therapeutic practices, so too do Sumell/Wallace attempt to reimagine the materiality of the incarcerated subject's body through the dream-time of architectural collaboration.[32] The sociality of their collaboration tells the story of how art dreams of and crafts a new futurity for a subject whose embodied future is foreclosed by the prison. The dream house endeavors to replace the haunted house. Sumell and Wallace endeavor to rewrite his sentence of solitary confinement.

I first encountered the work at a talk Sumell gave at a conference focused on prison art and activism at Rutgers in October 2014, almost exactly a year after Wallace died. Sumell is an American multidisciplinary artist and activist who works on institutional racism and the abuses of the criminal justice system. Her work connects mindfulness studies and social sculpture. A white woman, she grew up on Long Island where she was the first girl in New York State to play tackle football in an all-boys league. In 2001, while working on her MFA at Stanford University, Sumell organized "The No Bush Project" to protest the presidency of George W. Bush, specifically his systematic erosion of prochoice laws.[33] She issued a call to her female friends and acquaintances to shave their pubic hair and mail it to her. Once she had gathered 538 samples, representing the Electoral College, she displayed them as part of the National Organization for Women's April 22 march on the National Mall in Washington, DC.[34] Already in this project, we can see elements that she later employs in *The House That Herman Built*: social protest, collaboration across distance and time, a "literal" approach to conceptual art, and an emphasis on materiality.[35]

As a graduate student studying art, she was first inspired to write to Wallace after attending a talk by Robert King. When he opened the floor up to questions and comments from the audience, no one said anything. The stories he told and the experiences he shared stunned the room into silence. Suddenly, Sumell blurted out, "What can I do?" King answered, "Write my comrades." Resigning to do just that, Sumell began corresponding with both Wallace and Woodfox.[36] Her first letter to them was itself a kind of art project about time: she duct-taped a disposable camera to her arm and set her watch alarm to sound every hour in a day. When the watch beeped, she snapped a random, unfocused picture with the camera. She developed the film, compiled the twenty-four snapshots, and sent them to Angola with the message "*To Mr. Woodfox* and *To Mr. Wallace—here are 24 hours in my simple life.*" The durative nature of this project resembles in some ways a performance art piece: the aesthetic quality of the photo is incidental relative to the fact of its recording her life. She used technological capture in order to materialize the hours of her life for sharing. This piece makes time matter.

I remember distinctly the conceptual shift that formed the center of that talk at Rutgers. She articulated a theory of the "human doing" in contrast to the "human being." We might read in this the conviction that it is through human action that newness, resistance, and change are possible. Her linguistic shift also marks a shift in the temporality of how she conceives of human subjectivity. Subjectivity is no longer something one *is*, but an ongoing process, an unfinished project to be committed to over and over again. This is in contrast to how the spatiotemporal project of the penitentiary functions to assume bodies, organizing them into discrete categories determined not only by gender, race, ethnic, and religious markers, but also by a single past action, the legal consequences of which result in a predetermined sentence of time. If, following Rayner—as the editors of this volume suggest—we understand time as modality, as adverb, rather than as linear or circular, then Sumell and Wallace's collaboration to craft his dream home re-members the materiality of the body in the imperfect tense, something that in English might sound like "human doing."[37] The imperfect might characterize the temporality of dreaming, according to Bert States.[38] It is a kind of time travel, within which the past is revisited, the present restaged, and the future recalled. Dreams, through the time of the imperfect tense, muddy and render abstract the beginnings and

FIGURE 8.2 Detail of the miniature on display in the Royal College of London, 2009.
COURTESY OF JACKIE SUMELL.

ends of things. To extend this claim: in prison, the time of producing art itself is performed as a dreaming.

The House That Herman Built itself remains a dreaming (figure 8.2). Houses are meant to be walked through and lived in, but at this moment, one cannot walk through the house as a complete, live experience. What is left out of the experience? What might have Wallace's house smelled like or sounded like? Herman's house only exists digitally, in virtual space. One must imagine walking through the house. I myself have not had the opportunity to see *The House That Herman Built* as it was first exhibited in Stuttgart, or subsequently when Sumell toured it around galleries internationally. As Sarah Bay-Cheng has argued, digital mediation does not necessarily limit the audience's reception of a work of art.[39] In fact, it can enhance one's affective and intellectual understanding—particularly in this case, given the fact that the *only* way to visit the house that Sumell and Wallace designed is virtually.[40] Even when exhibited in a gallery, the project requires that the audience make a kind of imaginative journey into Wallace's dreams. This virtual proximity paired with haptic distance is part and parcel of the work's message. Wallace is removed physically from the outside world, but his house can travel internationally.

Much of the exhibition's content is brilliantly depicted in the PBS film *Herman's House*.[41] The documentary, produced and directed by Angad Bhalla, follows Sumell as she exhibits in galleries around the world and as she struggles to gather the resources in order to realize Wallace's architectural plans. The story is punctuated by phone interviews with Wallace himself, whose disembodied voice functions as a kind of meditative narration, and with interviews with various other people in Wallace's life, including his sister Vicky, Robert King, activist Malik Rahim—who first introduced Wallace to the Black Panthers—and several others. In one of the most interesting scenes of the film, Bhalla interviews several prison architects, who explain the history and logic behind prison design, and also provide their analysis of the blueprints to Wallace's house. They are astonished—one man calls it "bourgeois"—and nearly unanimously remark on the lack of "free-flowing space." They call it "oppressive" and note that certain aspects of the house seem constricting, possibly even carceral, and that they would have expected a person who had been imprisoned as long as Wallace to dream up something more open. One architect goes so far as to compare the dining room of Wallace's home to a prison day room, wherein inmates congregate. The architects' surprise at the design is telling, because it reveals a profound connection—or perhaps disconnection—between the planning of a prison's construction and its psychophysical effect on the confined. The fact that the design of the dream home resembles Wallace's surroundings should not be shocking at all. In the film, Wallace himself seems taken aback that someone would have such surprise at the design. In his narration after the architect scene, he states, "You look at that house; you're looking at me."[42] The house is a projection of his innermost desires and sensations, which are deeply influenced by his lived surroundings.

The temporality of dreaming itself constitutes an imperfect return to memory: both traumatic and salutary. The time of making art, as a dreaming, approaches materializing in the world what Toni Morrison called "rememory." In literature, Morrison's story of the house at 124 Bluestone Road, from *Beloved*, is perhaps the most significant example of how the traumas, memories, histories, and fantasies of Blackness are restaged in haunting material form.[43] Part of what is relevant to my inquiry is that Morrison employs the form of a house to re-member the past with a difference. This house is also haunted. I am reminded of the oft-quoted speech by Sethe, on time:

It's so hard for me to believe in it. Some things go. Pass on. Some things just stay. I used to think it was my rememory. You know. Some things you

FIGURE 8.3 Computer-aided design of the front of the home, with wraparound porch, balcony, and lush gardens. COURTESY OF JACKIE SUMELL.

> forget. Other things you never do. But it's not. Places, places are still there. If a house burns down, it's gone, but the place—the picture of it—stays, and not just in my rememory, but out there, in the world. What I remember is a picture floating around out there outside my head. I mean, even if I don't think it, even if I die, the picture of what I did, or knew, or saw is still out there. Right in the place where it happened.[44]

Sethe's rememory materializes things that have passed, but, also, a place remembers a picture in the world. It is difficult for Sethe to believe in time because things remain, refusing to truly pass on. Rememory's capacity for materialization makes linear time itself suspect. *The House* also re-members in some ways the space-time of Wallace's incarceration, but it does so with a twist. This difference foregrounds Wallace's desires, agency, and life as an activist.

As a way to frame a virtual tour of Wallace's home, it is useful to recall Anne Cheng's similar exploration of Josephine Baker's imaginary dream house, designed by Alfred Loos.[45] For Cheng, Loos's design reveals a great deal about how the architect, as a middle-aged white European man, perceived Baker—and, indeed, his relationship with her. But what might the rooms of *The House That Herman Built* reveal about Wallace, who had a hand in designing them? What do they say about the relationship between Sumell and Wallace? Cheng's meditations on how Loos translated Baker's sexual and racial identity into the "dreamed covering" of the architecture help unpack some of Wallace's designs, particularly his more extravagant inclusions: these include

FIGURE 8.4 Computer-aided design of the main room, including the "wall of revolutionary fame," featuring images of Gabriel Prosser, Denmark Vesey, Nat Turner, John Brown, and Harriet Tubman. COURTESY OF JACKIE SUMELL.

the seventies-style kitchen, painted yellow, with sprinklers in the ceiling, and a master bedroom, which takes up much of the second floor of the house, furnished with a king-size bed and decorated with African art, a chandelier, and a mirrored ceiling. French doors open onto a large balcony, packed with flowers. Inside the master bathroom is a six-by-nine-foot hot tub, the same size as the cell he lived in for four decades. Adopting Cheng's theoretical lens, we might understand the design as a kind of inversion of the public inside the private.[46] These rooms, typically domestic space, hidden from the world, are in *The House* directed outward, putting Wallace's tastes and passions on display. They serve to exhibit the wealth of his imagination, and the rich cultural traditions closest to his heart.

When one enters from the birch wraparound porch, one sees that the first floor is divided into several rooms which branch off the main sitting room through a set of corridors (figure 8.3). There is one bathroom, two guest bedrooms, and a hobby shop. The furniture is made of either mahogany or pecan. In the interest of security, Wallace includes a gun closet and an escape tunnel. There is also a long room with a conference table, with one wall dedicated to five carefully selected historical figures: Gabriel Prosser, Denmark Vesey, Nat Turner, John Brown, and Harriet Tubman (figure 8.4). Their portraits hang in a line on this "wall of revolutionary fame." Wallace wants to memorialize these abolitionists in part as a tribute to the Black Panther Party.

The Black Panther Party for Self Defense was the most visible element of the Black Power and Black Nationalist movements. Founded in 1966 by Huey Newton and Bobby Seale, the party arose in the immediate wake of desegregation and the victories of civil rights activists.[47] The party responded to the charge that Black people not only should win the rights of citizenship, but also should gain real economic and political power. The Black Panther Party believed in community self-determination and, for example, organized community services to feed starving children for free. Newton and Seale were deeply influenced by the ideas of Malcolm X; they believed armed struggle was necessary to bring about the cultural transformation necessary to end racism and bring about equality. They believed in self-determination and self-defense, especially regarding encounters with police. The Black Panthers' thinking also grew out of the postcolonial tradition: they figured America as occupied territory, with police and government entities acting as colonizing forces, and Blacks and other minority communities as the oppressed. Indeed, the Black Panthers saw themselves as an international movement, collaborating with domestic antiwar organizations and anti-imperialist movements abroad.

The Black Panthers were involved in antiprison, decarceration, and abolitionist efforts. For example, Seale made a brief appearance at the Attica uprising, and the Panthers' influence is clear both in the rebellion's militancy and in its demands for autonomy and justice for incarcerated peoples. Angela Davis, one of the intellectual leaders of the prison abolitionist movement, was also affiliated with the Panthers. As Dan Berger, Mariame Kaba, and David Stein say, in their recent *Jacobin* article "What Abolitionists Do" (2017), abolitionists are not zealous utopians, letting the perfect be the enemy of the good.[48] Abolitionists are after "non-reformist reforms": they "have insisted on reforms that reduce rather than strengthen the scale and scope of policing, imprisonment, and surveillance." These reforms include many things that are not only pragmatic, but already central tenets of activists concerned with policing and incarceration, such as ending cash bail, solitary confinement, and the death penalty; stopping new prison construction; decriminalizing drug use and sex work; and improving conditions for those living in prison. Contemporary prison abolitionists follow in the tradition of the Panthers because they share the overarching goal of seizing power to improve material conditions for people in the wake of historical injustice.

This goal is apparent in Wallace's participation in the collaboration with Sumell. Never expecting that he would be released to live in the house that he designed, Wallace intended that it be used as a community center, a "people's house," as he calls it.[49] Specifically, he wanted it to function as a place where at-risk youth in New Orleans might be mentored to avoid committing the crimes that led to his imprisonment in the first place. His dream to construct a public, communal space contrasts with and stems from the claustrophobia of his solitary confinement. Imprisoned in an oppressive individual cell, Wallace desires a space for sociality and communion, education, and conviviality. The logic of this dream flies in the face of the individualizing logic of penal confinement. Imagination is always larger than physicality, and the interplay between the two reveals dynamic potentials in human creativity. The piece might be said to enact the radically moral world-making Elaine Scarry describes in *The Body in Pain* (1988):

> While imagining may entail a revolution of the entire order of things, the eclipse of the given by a *total reinvention of the world*, an artifact (a relocated piece of coal, a sentence, a cup, a piece of lace) is *a fragment of world alteration*. Imagining a city, the human being "makes" a house; imagining a political utopia, he or she instead helps to build a country; imagining the elimination of suffering from the world, the person instead nurses a friend back to health.[50]

Scarry describes how world-making manifests through artmaking. Wallace dreamed of the world the Black Panthers struggled for, and designed a home in service of it.

I now turn to another encounter, bound up with questions of trauma, that elucidates how the dreaming encounter between Sumell and Wallace functions as a fragment of world alteration: that is the oft-discussed story of the dream of the burning child. Freud first analyzed this narrative as an example of how dreams serve as both wish-fulfillment and to protect the sleeper from waking.[51] In the story, a father, bereaving the recent loss of his child, takes his leave of the body for a while. He retires to an adjoining room to get some sleep, leaving an old man to watch over the corpse. The father drifts off to sleep, and dreams that the ghost of his child comes to visit him, shakes his arm, and says, "Father, don't you see? I'm burning." The father wakes in a fright to discover that the old man next door has shirked his duties and fallen asleep himself, and a candle has tumbled onto the death-bed, burning both the sheets and the body. Freud reasons that the dream does two things: it fulfills the father's wish to have his son alive again—at least momentarily—and it also serves to postpone awakening, keeping the dreamer asleep for a little longer.[52] The father, smelling smoke in his sleep, manifests the scenario of the dream so that the smell functions within the dream diegetically, rather than disrupt the sleeper.

Famously, Lacan reread the dream and, in pointing to the fact that the return of the dead child in fact does *not* prolong sleep but actually precipitates the father's awakening, describes how the return presages Freud's later work on repetition and trauma.[53] The father's awakening is too late to save the burning child, which repeats his own lack of understanding, failure to save, and overall "too lateness" in protecting his real child from death. Cathy Caruth, performing a further rereading, takes the dream as an ethical lesson. Awakening represents in some ways a central problematic in regard to trauma.[54] Despite the fact that "To awaken is . . . precisely to awaken only to one's repetition of a previous failure to see in time," we have a responsibility to attend to that which we will always already have failed to see and to know.[55] For Caruth, trauma poses ethical questions in the domain of history. One awakens to a call one can only hear when sleeping, when dreaming. In other words, becoming "woke"—to take up contemporary social justice vernacular—means one has already arrived too late. She extends Freud to say that trauma is not solely repetition, but in fact a deferral, a belatedness, a never-quite-here. The actual traumatic event then is unreachable and unknowable, except as ghostly return—which recalls my earlier commentary on the space-time of race in the context of imprisonment. Trauma represents, in Caruth's understanding, an ethical imperative to bear witness in the future to those events in history which threaten to be forgotten. *The House That Herman Built* then functions as an act of witness and a dream.

Wallace's dream house similarly says, "wake up, leave me, survive; survive to tell the story."[56] It does not attempt to engender an empathetic audience— though that may occur regardless—but to gather those who might survive to bear witness. Sumell, like the father, is "woke" in a way that is like the "performance of a speaking."[57] The futurity of the dreaming of their artistic collaboration lives in this passing on of the story. This piece performs dreaming in order to awaken an audience. Even though they cannot fully awaken to the trauma itself, they might approach its truth by telling the story of the dream in the future. The piece as a dreaming re-members Wallace—mourns him, grieves for him. This dreaming, which necessarily fails to materialize liberation, nevertheless approaches freedom by rupturing the foreclosure of the future effected in incarceration. If the temporality of dreaming is in some sense a repetition of the past, then it does not do so without performing some difference, some "departure" as Caruth says.[58] The rupture of making art is just such a departure.

Sumell continues her abolitionist art works. In 2011, she collaborated with Albert Woodfox while he was still incarcerated to publish in *TDR* "Prison Industrial Complexity," which is an abolitionist crossword puzzle.[59] It confronts the player with a black and white grid, and they must fill it in with their own knowledge about mass incarceration. This word game further emphasizes how art offers audiences a situation in which to play with the legal mechanisms of the racist criminal justice system. The clues include "Hunger strike that swept across 11 prisons in California in 2011 started here" and "30% of immigrant detainees are held in this US state." In solving the puzzle, the player dwells with the historical realities of American penality. The project takes the form of a playful diversion but encourages serious thought on human suffering. It is a seductive political provocation.

Today, Sumell focuses on the Solitary Garden Project, which asks, "Can you imagine a landscape without prisons?" Sumell corresponds with prisoners currently locked in solitary confinement to plant gardens outside the walls based on their designs. She is currently working to implement this program nationally, teaching others how to cross the prison threshold and start their own solitary gardens.[60] This project adapts her work with Herman Wallace, expanding it into the field of eco-art. Surrounding his dream home are abundant trees and three gardens of gardenias, carnations, and tulips, which are the "easiest for [him] to imagine." This detail was particularly important for Wallace, who wanted visitors to "smile and walk through flowers all year long." Sumell continues today the hope of his desire. In the Solitary Garden Project, she connects prison abolitionist struggles and climate change, emphasizing that both affect the marginalized and disenfranchised most dramatically. What else is a garden but a dream for the future? Like houses, gardens are how dreams come to matter. Though composed of repetition, the reiterated acts of making a garden, like digging, weeding, and watering, proffer a break in the temporality of return by promising a new future.

NOTES

1 Sumell, *The House That Herman Built*.
2 Bhalla, *Herman's House*.
3 Bhalla, *Herman's House*.
4 Fanon, *Black Skin, White Masks*; Gilroy, *Black Atlantic*; Phelan, *Unmarked*; Schneider, *Performing Remains*; H. Young, *Embodying Black Experience*.
5 Salamon, *Assuming a Body*.
6 Salamon, *Assuming a Body*, 24.

7 Tocci, *The Proscenium Cage*, 1.

8 Schechner, *Between Theater and Anthropology*, 35.

9 Derrida, in McMullen, *Ghost Dance*.

10 Diamond, introduction, 4–5.

11 Butler, *Bodies That Matter*; Merleau-Ponty, *Phenomenology of Perception*.

12 Butler, *Bodies That Matter*, xxix.

13 Ann Pellegrini, *Performance Anxieties*, 98.

14 O'Halligan, *Angola 3*; Carleton, *Politics and Punishment*.

15 Bloom and Martin, *Black against Empire*; Woodfox and Sumell, "Prison Industrial Complexity," 2–3.

16 O'Halligan, *Angola 3*.

17 Woodfox and Sumell, "Prison Industrial Complexity."

18 O'Halligan, *Angola 3*.

19 A. Davis, *Are Prisons Obsolete?*; M. Alexander, *New Jim Crow*; Gilmore, *Golden Gulag*.

20 Christie, *Crime Control as Industry*.

21 Larson, *Fourth City*.

22 Oshinsky, "View from Inside."

23 Mbembe, *Necropolitics*, 40.

24 Dayan, *Law Is a White Dog*.

25 Dayan, *Law Is a White Dog*

26 Dayan, *Law Is a White Dog*, 57.

27 A personal anecdote: In my experience as a volunteer teaching artist in a prison, incarcerated people have several times told me they feel like zombies. One man described how he knows he is aging, but at the same time he feels his old self, the person who first entered prison years before, watching over him.

28 Dayan, *Law Is a White Dog*.

29 Rayner, *Ghosts*; Carlson, *Haunted Stage*.

30 Parks, *Venus*.

31 Freud, *Beyond the Pleasure Principle*.

32 Van der Kolk, *Body Keeps the Score*.

33 Morgan, "Bush's Public Enemy No. 1."

34 Morgan, "Bush's Public Enemy No. 1."

35 "The Project That Inspired the Film."

36 Bhalla, *Herman's House*.

37 Rayner, "Keeping Time."

38 States, *Seeing in the Dark*, 8–10.

39 Bay-Cheng, "Theater Is Media," 27–41.

40 Bay-Cheng, "Theater Is Media."

41 Bhalla, *Herman's House*.

42 Bhalla, *Herman's House*.

43 Morrison, *Beloved.*

44 Morrison, *Beloved*, 35–34.

45 Cheng, *Second Skin.*

46 Cheng, *Second Skin.*

47 Bloom and Martin, *Black against Empire.*

48 Berger, Kaba, and Stein, "What Abolitionists Do."

49 Bhalla, *Herman's House.*

50 Scarry, *Body in Pain*, 171.

51 Freud, *Beyond the Pleasure Principle.*

52 Freud, *Beyond the Pleasure Principle.*

53 Lacan, *Seminar of Jacques Lacan.*

54 Cathy Caruth, *Unclaimed Experience.*

55 Caruth, *Unclaimed Experience*, 103.

56 Caruth, *Unclaimed Experience*, 109.

57 Caruth, *Unclaimed Experience*, 110.

58 Caruth, *Unclaimed Experience*, 110.

59 Woodfox and Sumell, "Prison Industrial Complexity," 2–3.

60 Solitary Gardens.

Performance Interventions

Natality and Carceral Feminism

in Contemporary India

Maya Krishna Rao, a classically trained solo performer, begins her performance piece, *Walk*, poised with an elevated foot gesture as if to take a step. A haunting musical score complements her simultaneously brisk and lithe performance across multiple public spaces in New Delhi and beyond. A brief ten-minute piece, *Walk* was created in response to the gang rape and ensuing murder of Jyoti Singh, a medical intern, on a moving bus on December 16, 2012, in New Delhi. The event provoked widespread ire and led to protests across India, and subsequent far-reaching legislative amendments.[1]

Jasmeen Patheja, performance and conceptual artist, began the Blank Noise Project as an art student in Srishti Institute of Art, Design, and Technology, Bangalore, in 2003 to reclaim city streets for women. A public art project, Blank Noise approaches chronic street sexual harassment in Bangalore by opening up spaces for public conversations through creative and playful interventions that aim to shift public attitudes and generate discussions about desires and boundaries.

Moving away from carceral feminist solutions, Maya Rao and Jasmeen Patheja use performance as a mode to initiate transformations in social and cultural attitudes toward gender and sexuality. While judicial dramas that play out in the courtroom focus on the accused, attuned as they are to the presumption of innocence, performance offers a unique avenue to address the survivor's experiences of trauma and resilience.[2] Liberal legalism focuses on the defendant's presumption of innocence, and courtroom proceedings marshal evidence and witness testimonies to either convict or exonerate him/her. Performance, on the other hand, opens up an opportunity to explore gendered experiences of traumatic violations and survival.

While theories of performativity have explored the question of iteration and repetition in the formation of subjectivity, this chapter focuses on newness as holding potential to interrupt the iterative consolidation of misogyny in India. Drawing on Hannah Arendt's conception of natality, I examine creative interventions that unsettle legal and public discourses of sexuality and foster new imaginaries of desire and freedom. Arendt argues, "Action has the closest connection with the human condition of natality. . . . In this sense of initiative, an element of action, and therefore of natality, is inherent in all human activities. Moreover, since action is the political activity par excellence, natality, and not mortality, may be the central category of political, as distinguished from metaphysical, thought."[3] Arendt's conception of natality departs from the Heideggerian "being-toward-death," a radical finitude that draws Dasein away from its inauthentic immersion in everyday life.[4] Focusing on natality, rather than mortality, allows for a consideration of creative interventions that engender new public imaginaries and socialities.

The unpredictable force of protests in the public sphere and subsequent possibilities for renewed legal and social gender arrangements allow us to turn our attention to the natal, rather than mortal, implications of the violent acts and their subsequent repercussions. The affective force of the widespread protests that followed Jyoti Singh's violent rape and murder generated significant legal amendments.

By focusing on renewal, Rao and Patheja turn their gaze away from victimhood and mortality to regenerate female empowerment and feminist solidarities through the political work of friendship. Rao's performance extends friendship as support from intimate partner violence and urges survivors to walk alongside friends, exemplifying notions of negative and positive freedom.

Dispelling damaging stereotypes that disable communication, Blank Noise proffers friendship across chiasmic gender and class positions. Marking a turn away from temporal discussions of liveness that are invested in questions of disappearance, vanishing, and a Heideggerian being-toward-death, these horizontal gestures of friendship and solidarity not only spatialize liveness but also focus on the power of performance to bring new solidarities into being. Moving away from discourses of victimhood, Rao and Patheja also distance themselves from petitions for increased legal mechanisms to redress sexual violence. Through acts of natality—affirmative, playful, and creative performance tactics that enable women to take initiative and reclaim their cities and their streets—Rao and Patheja shift the focus from the suffering, violated woman to a renewal of public cultural practices.

While acknowledging the important strides made through feminist legal activism, this chapter argues that the recourse to liberal legalism normatively regulates and produces the law's properly injured subjects. How does an ideology of freedom and liberty propagated by liberal legalism and its advocates obfuscate unequal and unfree conditions, extend the powers of the privileged, and entrench inequities of those beyond its pale? How have recent challenges by feminist and queer activists upset the teleology of legal "due process" through the instantaneous justice provided by naming and shaming perpetrators of sexual harassment on social media? In the wake of powerful global #metoo movements, how have survivors returned to the jagged shards of traumatic memory to recount inassimilable narratives of sexual violation? Liberal legalism's teleology of "due process" has too often let down its victims and proven to be deficient and incapable of adequately responding to the proliferating, routine, and ubiquitous experiences of sexual violation in India today.

As feminist strategy and activism rethink their approaches to what constitutes justice for survivors of gender violence, there is an opportunity to move beyond punitive state outcomes to encompass broader notions of justice, including an expansive approach to restorative justice. Drawing on Foucauldian conceptions of governmentality, which disperses government beyond the state to the banal operations of everyday life, Janet Halley has critiqued "governance feminism," a feminist justice project that has moved off the streets and has thoroughly interpenetrated the state.[5] Her conception of "the state," however, is not circumscribed to courts, legislatures, and police, but also to the ways in which policing, with threat of legal reprisals, operates across schools, health-care institutions, places of work, and even the home. According to Halley, governance feminism has both a will to power and actual power, "from the

White House to corporate boardroom to minute power dynamics that Foucault included in his theory of the governance of self." In her words, "Feminism may face powers greater than its own in its constant involvement with its opponents; but it deals with them in the very terms of power."[6] Governance feminism, according to Brown and Halley, "should be hypothesized as rife with normative categories, indeed as powerfully productive discourses that draw their normativity from widely dispersed sites in the culture, economy, and polity."[7]

The reliance on legal recourse in feminist movements consolidates and provides social sanction for the carceral state in neoliberal India. While allied to governance feminism, but turning to liberal legalism as panacea for sexual violence, carceral feminism describes a worldview that seeks recourse to the criminal justice system to address issues of gender-based crimes that range from sexual assault to domestic violence. However, in reaching out to policing, prosecution, and imprisonment as the primary solutions to gender-based violence, carceral feminists overlook the ways in which police and prisons and a deeply flawed criminal justice system inflict violence and further empower and entrench a casteist and punitive state.

Building on the pioneering scholarship and activism of Angela Davis and Michelle Alexander, arguments against carceral feminism pay particular attention to the ways in which the criminal justice system is complicit in the perpetuation and legitimation of a racist state.[8] By making retributive justice, incarceration, policing, and surveillance central to redress of gender violence, other interventions such as rehabilitation, community education, and long-term organizing are discouraged. Victoria Law argues that carceral feminism ignores the ways in which race, class, gender identity, and immigration status leave certain women more vulnerable to violence and that greater criminalization often places these same women at risk of state violence.[9] By relying solely on a criminalized response, carceral feminism fails to address these social and economic inequities, let alone advocate for policies that ensure women are not economically dependent on abusive partners.

THE TIME OF/FOR JUSTICE

The brutal sexual and, ultimately, fatal assault of Jyoti Singh by six men on a moving bus in New Delhi was a flashpoint to address the chronic problem of sexual violence in Indian society. The incident took place late one evening on

December 16, 2012, when a twenty-three-year-old medical intern, Jyoti Singh, and her friend Awindra Pandey were offered and accepted a ride back home on a bus after watching a film at a movie theater. The six occupants on the bus were out on a "joyride" and deceitfully cajoled the two to board the bus by promising them a ride home. The occupants beat her friend unconscious and sexually assaulted and violated Singh, including inserting a metal rod in her vagina, after which they dumped the two, naked, on the cold Delhi streets. After eleven days in emergency care in New Delhi, Singh was transferred to a hospital in Singapore, where she eventually succumbed to her injuries. The accused were arrested and charged with sexual assault and murder. One of the accused, Ram Singh, died in police custody. Another defendant was a juvenile and given a maximum sentence of three years' imprisonment in a reform facility. The remaining four defendants went on trial in a fast-track court, were convicted of rape and murder, and were sentenced to death. In May 2017 India's Supreme Court upheld the death sentence for the four men.

Why did this particular case capture the attention not only of the nation but also of the international community? What can we learn from the temporal logic of this case? The progressivist teleology of the upwardly mobile young woman whose aspirations are thwarted is particularly well suited to mobilize an account of the dark, dangerous, and unruly passions of unmodern India. Poulami Roychowdhury examines the ways in which the gang rape of Jyoti Singh is mobilized to circulate the narrative of culture clash of two Indias—one modern and the other traditional.[10] She points out that despite the presumption of class hierarchy, however, the assailants and their victim were from very similar class and caste backgrounds. Roychowdhury argues that the violation of a woman coded as not only modern and rights-bearing citizen but also as unfettered consumer of a globalizing India is internationally legible and justifies political and legal interventions that confirm orientalist conceptions of nonmodern and uncivilized third world nations. Such tropes rehearse colonialist stereotypes of unruly non-Western societies where brown women require international intervention and rescue from rapacious brown men in their own societies.

The question of time, pragmatic, juridical, and conceptual, has also been central to rethinking justice for victims of sexual assault. Pragmatically, as a result of the protests, a judicial committee was set up to study and make recommendations for legal amendments for quicker investigation and prosecution of sex offenders. Some critics have pointed out that similar cases in the past have failed to garner public attention and expedite the unrelenting slowness of the legal process.[11] The fatal assault on the moving bus ignited protests across India and catalyzed legal alacrity. The Justice J. S. Verma Committee report was submitted swiftly after twenty-nine days, after considering eighty thousand suggestions received during the period. The Justice Verma Committee report indicated that failures on the part of the government and police were the root cause behind crimes against women.[12]

The legal amendments in the wake of the Jyoti Singh case provided a rethinking of the way in which rape itself is situated within teleological discourses about marriageability and progeny. Rape laws had hitherto borne the imprint of patriarchal teleology of succession. A new law was introduced that said that penetration of a woman by a foreign object, and not necessarily a penis, would constitute rape. The J. S. Verma Committee report expanded the crime of rape to include any nonconsensual penetration of a sexual nature.[13]

Feminist scholar and legal activist Flavia Agnes argues that in any other case of physical assault, use of a weapon would be "aggravated assault," while in rape, penetrating a woman with rods, sticks, and the like, as opposed to a penis, were seen (in the previous law) as less culpable offences.[14] From this point of view, the penis is the only threat to patriliny, not any other part of the body or any other object. Agnes concludes that when contemporary commentators see forced oral sex as somehow a smaller crime than "real" rape, they contribute, wittingly or unwittingly, to this patriarchal understanding of sexual violation. The law, therefore, only recognizes penile penetration of the vagina as rape, while other forms of penetration came under "outraging a woman's modesty," a considerably lesser crime.

According to feminist theorist, Nivedita Menon, "The notion that 'strict rape' or 'penetration' can be said to have happened only with peno-vaginal penetration is a patriarchal one, based on preserving the body of the woman for patrilineal succession. Such an understanding sees the harm of rape as lying in the potential for (illegitimate) pregnancy, and the subversion of patriliny."[15] The primary threat of rape, in this conception, is to a linear unfolding of progressive heteronormative time, which produces a crisis in patriliny. By insisting that forcible insertion of foreign objects into female orifices constitutes rape, the focus shifted from the instrument of violation to the integrity of the violated body.

The legal amendments following the Justice Verma Committee report enabled a major rethinking of rape by wresting it away from patriarchal discourses surrounding female honor (*izzat*) where women are imagined as symbolic of family or community value. Moving toward conceptions of "consent" meant imagining her as a rights-bearing subject under law—as a citizen and not only as a symbol of family or community value. Moreover, consent acknowledged women's desire and agency in participation in sexual activity.

But what constitutes consent? How do we determine when a line is crossed from consenting to relenting to sexual encounters? The question of consent had emerged decades earlier in the notable Mathura Rape Case in 1972 where a young Dalit girl, between fourteen and sixteen years of age, was raped by two policemen in the precincts of the police station in Chandrapur district, Maharashtra. The Sessions Court found the defendants not guilty. According to their rationale, since Mathura was "habituated to sexual intercourse," her consent was voluntary; under the circumstances only sexual intercourse could be proved and not rape. The Bombay High Court, however, ruled that submission due to fear or intimidation cannot constitute consent, and overturned this judgment and sentenced the accused. Unfortunately, the Supreme Court did not demonstrate the sagacity of the High Court and again overturned its verdict and acquitted the accused policemen. According to the Supreme Court verdict, consent was established because Mathura raised no alarm, did not fight off her aggressors, did not have any bruises, which suggested that she did not struggle and hence her body did not proffer evidence consistent with violent rape. The judge noted, "Because she was used to sex, she might have incited the cops [they were drunk on duty] to have intercourse with her."[16] Rape, in this formulation, can only occur when it constitutes a "first time"; every subsequent time is automatically presumed consensual. Moreover, she is accused of having "incited the cops," thus in a predictably misogynist move, the judgment blames the victim for luring the perpetrator.

This verdict generated a wave of protests and subsequent legal amendments. A group of law professors were vocal in their challenge and wrote an open letter to the Supreme Court, "Consent involves submission, but the converse is not necessarily true. . . . From the facts of case, all that is established is submission, and not consent. . . . Is the taboo against pre-marital sex so strong as to provide a license to Indian police to rape young girls?"[17] The case vividly reveals the imbrication of juridical and disciplinary discourses. She is presumed promiscuous, and as an impoverished Dalit girl, she is denied the category of "victim," which is reserved for upper-caste, Hindu women. The effects of law can be complex, contingent, and shifting; the legal apparatus, in this case, not only withholds justice but also attempts to produce regulated subjects and disciplined populations.[18] This case exposes the thorough enmeshment of legal cultures in caste, class, and gender privilege.

As with the case of Jyoti Singh, the Mathura verdict also generated public furor. The key difference, however, was that while in Mathura's case, the protests pointed to the police as perpetrators and the law as abetting and complicit in the crime against Mathura, forty years later in Jyoti Singh's case, the police and the legal system are considered the guarantors and protectors of upwardly mobile, urban women, imagined increasingly as "victims" of sex crimes committed by unmodern migrant men.

CLASS, POWER, AND SEXUAL ENTITLEMENT

The two distinct time signatures of quotidian misogyny, on the one hand, and the temporality of law in responding to sexual crimes, on the other, both exacerbate gender injustice. The legal amendments following the J. S. Verma Committee Report, however, had brisk and significant impact on the routine misogyny practiced not only in rural or nonmodern contexts but also within "liberal" urban society. Three recent high-profile cases of "progressive," liberal Indian men, journalist Tarun Tejpal, climate scientist R. K. Pachauri, and *Dastangoi* performer Mahmood Farooqui, who are each imbricated in public scandals of sexual abuse ranging from harassment to rape, further illuminate the pervasive and entrenched misogyny within liberal sections of society.[19]

Unlike the case of Jyoti Singh, each case cited above involves a high-profile "progressive," "global" Indian. The apprehended men have been celebrated for giving voice to the disenfranchised through their work in investigative journalism, climate change, and minoritarian performance. Each of the men ostensibly abused his position of power over their survivors/complainants— two were in immediate positions of leadership (Tejpal and Pachauri), while Farooqui was offering research information/advice to a young American PhD scholar.[20]

The question of what constitutes consent was succinctly captured in the judgment in the case of Mahmood Farooqui, who allegedly forced oral sex on an unconsenting American visiting research scholar. The verdict found the defendant guilty and according to newly amended rape laws sentenced Farooqui to seven years in prison.[21] The verdict cited Clause 2 of Section 375, "The essence of rape is absence of consent. Consent means an intelligent, positive concurrence of the woman."[22] This verdict makes clear the distinction between relenting under pressure and affirmatively consenting to sexual intercourse, and represents a significant shift from patriarchal discourses surrounding woman's honor or marriageability and situates consent within the realm of her own sexual agency. However, in 2017, the Delhi High Court acquitted Farooqui of rape.

The Jyoti Singh case, and the ways in which it changed rape laws in India, directly impacted the prosecution of elite liberal perpetrators. However, feminist debates diverged in their approach to grappling with sexual violence in contemporary India. While feminist legal scholars such as Pratiksha Baxi and Mihira Sood offer nuanced arguments about the centrality of the legal process in changing rape culture, others such as Flavia Agnes and Manisha Sethi express reservations about the increasing ways in which feminism is articulated through a carceral register.[23]

In India, an outspoken critic of carceral feminism, Agnes, discusses the limitations of a carceral approach to gender-based crimes:

> I have always been against stringent punishment, either as retributive justice or for its deterrent value. It is obvious that the rationale of deterrence has not worked, though my position has been unpalatable for many within the women's movement. . . . I also do not believe that only when the accused is given maximum punishment is the victim able to overcome the trauma of rape. It is necessary to delink the two. . . . Women want justice but all survivors do not necessarily want to surrender to the complex machinations of the law and become helpless within its processes. Restorative justice can also be a way for women to regain their sense of autonomy, integrity and dignity.[24]

How do sexual and carceral politics intertwine to become the dominant form to redress sexual violence, and what alternative social visions are obscured by this carceral turn in feminist activism? How can a performative turn to reshaping public cultures point a way beyond legal channels to secure sexual and gender justice? Wendy Brown and Janet Halley remind us that legalism deploys liberalism as a normativizing, regulatory form of power. They explore "how the act of making justice claims in the language of liberal legalism shapes us as justice-worthy subjects."[25] While legal petitions for redress saturate contemporary political life, justice cannot be reduced to legalism. Rao and Patheja's artistic endeavors offer alternative ways to envisage and shape social justice that exceed legalistic rationalities. Through their performance interventions, these feminist performers tackle issues of endemic gender violence in Indian society.

The creative interventions of Maya Rao and Jasmeen Patheja exemplify what Hannah Arendt describes as natality in politics: the promise of initiation and renewal, which enables human beings to begin something anew. As she theorizes, action is the supreme mode for citizens engaging in the public sphere, and this ability to act is rooted in natality. In the words of Arendt, "the new beginning inherent in birth can make itself felt in the world only because the newcomer possesses the capacity of beginning something anew, that is, of acting."[26] Through their performance interventions, Rao and Patheja introduce newness into the public sphere, inspire new friendships, and initiate transformations in public cultural attitudes.

Rao first performed *Walk* at midnight on December 31, 2012, in New Delhi, just two days after Jyoti Singh succumbed to her injuries.[27] Performed at Jawaharlal Nehru University campus, well known for its radical student politics, *Walk* enjoined the students to join in a procession that led from the university to a few miles outside the campus to the bus stop, from which Jyoti Singh and her friend had boarded the fateful bus, which became the site of her rape and murder.

Rao trained as a classical Kathakali performer, then taught at the National School of Drama in New Delhi, before starting her career as a solo performer. Performing solo in the mid-eighties was uncommon in India but Rao is an iconoclastic practitioner who evolved her own theatrical idiom. Her solo pieces tackle intense and serious subjects such as the subcontinental partition and its violent aftermath; Rao adapted Manto's short story *Khol Do* into a searing nonverbal solo performance. More recently in June 2017, Rao performed *In the Name of a Cow*, in New Delhi's public square, Jantar Mantar, where a crowd of protestors rallied under the banner "Not in My Name" to verbally and performatively dissent against the fatal lynching by right-wing Hindu extremists of Junaid Khan, a young sixteen-year-old Muslim boy, who allegedly ate beef on a train on June 22, 2017.

Rao is also a celebrated comedic performer whose cabaret pieces such as *Deep Fried Jam*, *The Non Stop Feel Good Show*, and *Quality Street* are biting indictments of contemporary liberalized India. Drawing her audiences into her powerful magnetic field, Rao uses irony and humor in her cabaret performances to offer acerbic social critiques on a range of topics from urban consumerism to everyday sexism in contemporary India. A charismatic and audacious performer, Rao exudes raw energy, courage, humor, and candor that unsettles social conventions.

Walk, an improvisational performance piece, combines poetry, movement, and music to summon feminist solidarities and inspire a new movement for gender justice. In its call to reclaim city streets and urban nightscapes, *Walk* urges its audience to walk as fellow performers and practice what feminist activist Kavita Krishnan calls *bekhauf azaadi*, or fearless freedom.[28] The freedom that Rao envisions in her performance does not seek police protection for vulnerable women but rather insists, in an Arendtian vein, that newness or natality produces political action; taking initiative for social justice discloses the capacity for freedom.

In a poetic idiom, Rao stutters then utters, "I want to, can I, should I, will I . . . walk? . . . I want to walk the streets at two, three, and four in the morning, to sit on a bus, walk on the street, to lie in a park, I try not to be afraid of the dark." In faltering, hesitant words, Rao conveys the diffidence and uneasiness women experience in urban nightscapes. Rao's halting words grow gradually resolute as she empowers her audience with the promise of companionship: "Will you walk? Will you walk? I'll walk with you, don't walk with him, I'll talk with you, I'll walk with you." The repetition of the word "walk" gathers an affective resonance that builds into a crescendo, inciting audiences to move out of their passivity and stirring them to act in collective rage. Extending solidarity to survivors of sexual violence, *Walk* is a rousing summons to action that encourages survivors to move from the isolation of victimhood to the solace and support of feminist friendships.

Furthermore, Rao reminds her audience of the power of protest marches. In the wake of student protests and backlash from the government, Rao performs on the Jawaharlal Nehru University campus in New Delhi in 2015 and refers to the 2012 marches for justice for Jyoti Singh:

In December we walked for justice
So we got a law
February 2013
That's all it takes
It only takes a walk.

Here Rao cites her own prior performance and the power of protest marches to create new laws that may better serve women. Rao does not dismiss legal channels as a viable route to secure justice. However, the performance piece exceeds a narrow pursuit for legal remedies and holds out a sense of imaginative amplitude in its envisioning of gender justice. It gathers its power from the forging of solidarities through live, political actions. Rather than dwelling on the victimhood of Jyoti Singh, Rao's piece offers a creative response, or what Bonnie Honig would describe as "a natal's pleasure-based counter to grief that supplements solidarity forged in sorrow and points in the direction of generative action rather than ruminative reflection or ethical orientation."[29] It is in newness or natality, forged through creative intervention, that feminist performance reorients its politics. Public cultures can be reimagined and reshaped through creative acts of recuperation, solidarity, and friendship.

Describing the first iteration of *Walk*, participant and theater scholar Bishnupriya Dutt writes, "Speaking as one who participated, I found the experience of collective walking mesmerizing. With a music track in the background, Rao set a pace for the rhythm of the walk and we all moved together to that rhythm. . . . For those of us who had participated in the extraordinarily emotionally and literally moving moment of 31 December, *Walk* would never lose its collective spirit."[30] Dutt recollects the event as "mesmerizing," foregrounding the power of the piece to draw the individual spectator out of her narrow self-interest into a larger, affectively charged civic *philia* of political action. This is precisely the power of natality, a renewed political capacity for understanding how we hold each other, of spatializing the temporal, and recognizing the latitudinal dimensions of the live moment. While the focus on disappearance and radical finitude in discussions on liveness awakens one from the torpor of an inauthentic existence, approaching the heinous rape and murder through natal acts of collective solidarity reignites our horizontal sense of togetherness, as an act of profound holding and being held by one another.

Walk addresses a variety of sexual abuses ranging from incest and domestic violence to marital rape and sexual harassment in workplace and public spaces, and in the process illuminates the pervasiveness of sexual violence toward women in contemporary India. While occasioned by the case of Jyoti Singh, the piece reflects on the ubiquity of sexual violations, most often within the precincts of home and family. Rao emphasizes sexual violence in intimate spaces and makes visible the multiple scenes of violation that depart from dominant conceptions of rural migrants as primary perpetrators of sexual violence in the city. Bringing marital rape into visibility, Rao cautions her audience:

> *A man who can't sit next to a woman right*
> *A man who can't lie next to his wife right*
> *Ask her before they have sex tonight—don't walk with him.*
> *Roll out of bed, just walk tonight.*

FIGURE 9.1 Maya Krishna Rao performs *Walk* at the International Theatre Festival of Kerala, Thrissur, Kerala, January 2018. PHOTO BY JOSE FARINHA.

By bringing the question of consent up front—"Just ask her," she says in English and follows it up in Hindi, "Pooch to lo"—Rao insists that we attend to scenes of violation that occur between intimate partners, within families, and other encounters that, while far more pervasive, are seldom reported and often suppressed and censored from the public sphere. These violations are perpetrated not by "outsiders" from which middle-class feminist organizing would seek the police to secure them, but by members of one's own family.

Performed in a variety of public spaces from New Delhi streets to Jantar Mantar, the Jaipur literary festival, and the Jawarharlal Nehru University campus, *Walk* is a piece that inspires spectators with an awakening of their collective power as citizens to initiate legal, cultural, and social transformations in urban spaces (figure 9.1). Rao's performance is remarkable in the ways in which it draws its utopian energy from the power of solidarity to remake public cultures at large. In the process, it avoids portraying women as victims subordinated to sexual dominance seeking narrow legal redress to the problem of sexual violence. Rather, it views the criminal justice system itself ambivalently and the police as complicit in the ubiquitous violence against women. As Rao expresses,

Just give me a cop that listens to what I say to him
Just give me a book so when I speak he will write what I say to him
And just perchance if I cannot say and he saw,
Will he write what he saw?
Give me that cop, give me that law,
Let me just live, live, live,
Let me live free.

By bringing together legal acts of testimony, witnessing, and accountability, Rao underlines the entanglement of agential subjecthood and institutional subjection in generating new possibilities of freedom for women.

BANALITY OF HARASSMENT

While Maya Rao's *Walk* derives from a volatile instance of sexual violence, Jasmeen Patheja's artworks focus on endemic sexual harassment in India. A visual and performance artist, Patheja faced sexual harassment, euphemistically referred to as "eve-teasing," as a child growing up in Calcutta. She recalls that she would frequently be harassed while in her school uniform on her way to and from school. Patheja initiated the Blank Noise Project in 2003 when she was an art student at Srishti School of Art Design and Technology in Bangalore, India. Blank Noise attempts to build a network of "Action-heroes," or volunteers, across genders, sexualities, and classes, who will creatively grapple with the problem of sexual harassment. Patheja was recently awarded the International Award for Public Art, a Sino-American initiative that annually recognizes work aimed at changing civic engagement across the world.

Patheja is emphatic that the performance interventions she stages at multiple sites across Bangalore are not intended as adversarial or antagonistic to men. Rather, she attempts to reconfigure affective experiences of fear and vulnerability into less threatening encounters between sexual subjects in the city. In the words of Patheja,

No woman of any age, colour or character ever "asks for it." Every single day, women in Bengaluru, India, and many parts of the world invest so much time thinking how and with whom to step out of home, and where to go. Everything revolves around the notion of security, which leads to policing and controlling the movement of women. We want a world that is free from fear. A world that is free of warnings that don't falsify safety with women's bodies being controlled. The discourse should be about enabling them to live without fear, without having to clench their fist and having to carry the weight of fear on their back.[31]

Reiterating the importance of bekhauf azzadi, or fearless freedom, Patheja wants to redraw the affective map of the city. Patheja's community art projects attempt to reclaim city streets for women to inhabit and traverse urban public spaces without gendered anxieties of sexual harassment or assault.

In 2005 Blank Noise recruited twelve performers through text messages to stand at a busy red light traffic junction in Bangalore city with each performer bearing a letter that was pasted on their T-shirt that together read Y R U L O O K I N G A T M E. Some volunteers held out posters detailing laws against street harassment.[32] In the words of Patheja, "We are committed to tackling and shifting the fear-based relationship women have been taught to have with their cities."[33] These artivist projects stoke the curiosity of passersby through their creative interventions and new forms of public protest.

Through online campaigns such as *I Never Ask for It*, Blank Noise asks women to recollect their experiences of sexual harassment and send in an item of clothing they wore during the incident of harassment. Building a material archive of clothing offers an alternative record: the pieces of clothing constitute public testimonies of sexual harassment. Blank Noise displays these articles of clothing on their website to comment on misogynist attitudes that blame and shame victims of sexual harassment for dressing provocatively thereby enticing and inviting unwanted attention.

Patheja's performance interventions are multidimensional and incorporate some legal measures into her artivist projects. For example, through the use of cell-phone text-message technology, Patheja has developed a way to feed text messages into a database that links to police reporting systems. "This will enable lawmakers to take simple steps, such as, changing the lights in a particular area or posting extra security personnel."[34] Patheja, like Rao, does not set up a false dichotomy between choosing and rejecting legal avenues for gender justice. While they are critical of a criminal justice system that regulates women's behavior, their feminist approach foregrounds the amplitude and heterogeneity in creative initiatives that deploy multiple strategies, including legal measures, to instigate larger social and cultural transformations in Indian society.

Urban studies scholar Hemangini Gupta participated in Blank Noise's street performance of YRULOOKINGATME. As she describes it, "Blank Noise interventions are built on the individual dreams of participants, inviting them to express their desires and to use these as the bedrock for future interventions. The emphasis of the collective is to engage in moments of disruption and play on city streets that build an archive of individual testimonials (related to street harassment and utopic visions of urban space) and use these to design activist interventions."[35] Gupta connects feminist desires to circulate freely in public spaces to neoliberal practices of risk-taking, consumption, and individual freedom. For Gupta such acts of feminist artivism suggest a brand of neoliberal feminism, which "assume individual responsibility to transform public spaces by emphasizing their personal desires and dreams as the basis for their articulation of feminist freedom."[36] K. Frances Lieder, on the other hand, cautions against flattening out the potential of such feminist interventions. In her study of "Why Loiter" performance practices in Mumbai, Lieder foregrounds the collective solidarity in these exercises, which lays the ground to prefigure a politics that rehearses and embodies the desired society. For Lieder such performances charge public space with "the purpose of circulating different affective norms."[37] Emphasizing the role of creativity within these political actions, Lieder demonstrates the ways in which performances deploy affect to prefigure and reimagine future publics.

It is important to note that while these creative interventions are situated within a neoliberal ferment, they also exceed them.[38] These playful, ephemeral, creative interruptions to routinized sexism are akin to Debord's detournement—a temporary and playful rerouting of the norm through audacious tactics, which offer a glimpse into alternative arrangements of desire and sociality in the urban nightscape.[39]

Patheja's performance interventions actively attempt to reshape public cultural attitudes to gender. Her work with transportation service workers at bus and railway stations, bus drivers, and traffic police attempts to shift passive public attitudes toward sexual harassment in public spaces. The campaign *Walk Alone* resonates with Maya Rao's performance piece *Walk*. With the Hindi words *Akeli, Awara, Azaad* (Alone, Vagabond, Free), Patheja's art projects attempt to empower women to take back their streets and reclaim their public space. One volunteer, Satya Gummuluri, with Blank Noise's project *Walk Alone*, describes her experience thus: "When I feel anxious on desolate streets, I give myself a little talk, telling myself that I am creating an image in people's minds that it's normal for a woman to be out on her own even if it's

FIGURE 9.2 *Talk to Me*, Yelahanka, Bangalore, 2012. PHOTO BY JASMEEN PATHEJA.

late. In a way, I'm shaking up the socio-cultural perceptions associated with it."[40] Here, participants are encouraged to recalibrate their habituated affective responses to urban nightscapes, while also serving as role models for others. In this way, performers deliberately undertake the work of remapping the affective contours of their cities.

In 2012 Blank Noise's public art project *Talk to Me* occurred in Bangalore. *Talk to Me*, or *Yelahanka Action Heroes*, recruited a group of nineteen students to identify a particular street in the town of Yelahanka, which was popularly referred to as "Rapist's Lane" and had acquired a reputation of being an "unsafe space" (figure 9.2). This street was poorly lit at night, had no commercial activity, and men would frequently sit in their cars in the evening and drink alcohol, which disconcerted passersby. Blank Noise attempted to bridge socioeconomic divides by bringing female students into conversation, over tea and samosas, with the inhabitants of the street. The premise was that familiarity could dispel fear and apprehension. For Patheja, conversations enable people to work through stereotypes via a process that encourages openness and vulnerability. Across a table, over a cup of tea and samosas, two strangers, a student and a resident, conversed on a range of topics from fear to love to life. At the end of the conversation, the Action Hero gifted a flower to the person across the table. While Patheja mines the heteronormative clichés of boy-meets-girl encounters, the interclass encounters between men and women from vastly different socioeconomic spheres generated unpredictable effects, in some cases opening up spaces for greater dialogue.

For Patheja, the simple adventure of a purposeful conversation, undertaken with curiosity, could leave behind an enduring trace. Yet, even in these encounters conversations don't always proceed as planned. One participant, Action Hero Astha, conveys her ambivalence:

> The conversation picked up at absolutely random topics and because we had a language barrier I was surprised to see for how long it went on. We majorly spoke about love and how it affects life. What I learnt about the person was that he was really sweet in the beginning and even towards the end but *his intention towards me changed.* He seemed to be a very emotionally sensitive person, who has family responsibilities. He is a person who works according to his will and mood. He makes sure he does things he loves to do, in order to be happy. What I learnt about myself was that I could actually ever speak my heart out in front of a stranger. I always knew that I could make conversation, but I let go this time. Even though we hardly understood what each other said, I think we spent a good time. *His change in behaviour and his courage was the only thing that really surprised and disappointed me* [italics mine].[41]

We are not clear about what in her conversation partner's behavior disappointed Action Hero Astha. It is even more difficult to determine if the "disappointing" behavior constituted sexual harassment. Action Hero Astha succinctly conveys the range of her conversation from insights into her own capacities to learning about her partner's opinions. She was surprised by her sense of freedom and her ability to speak in an unrestrained way with a stranger. At least momentarily, it appears she was able to exceed regulatory prohibitions that may curtail her freedom and expect her, as a "woman," to behave in ways consistent with social norms. However, she is also taken aback when she observes a change in the converser's intention and behavior. Remarkably, her disappointment does not lead her to reject this man, castigate him, or undermine the *Talk to Me* project. Despite some negative feelings, she refuses to imagine herself as subordinated or victimized in her encounter and relates her experience in a generally optimistic way. Action Hero Astha conveys a sense of affective amplitude in her encounter and exposes the possibility that pleasure and risk, excitement and disappointment can reside in a single experience.

Although these ventures may entail risky encounters, Blank Noise's gesture of friendship attempts to remake public cultures through creative play. *Talk to Me* enabled women to sit across from strangers and initiate conversations and thus remake gender relations by relaxing the normative and disciplinary production of middle-class femininity in contemporary Indian society. Their performance interventions echo Brown and Halley's reminder: "If feminism once aimed to make women the sexual equals of men, this aim contains the complex social, psychological, and political project of making gender differently, and not simply the legal one of protecting (historically and culturally produced) vulnerable women from (historically and culturally produced) rapacious men."[42] Simply by seating female art students across a table from men from a lower socioeconomic position and initiating conversation that dispels gendered urban anxiety begins a process of loosening social stereotypes. Blank Noise finds spaces to dislodge the saturation of legalistic claims of victimhood, and introduce newness, pleasure, and risk into cross-class urban encounters.

As we can see from the performance interventions of Maya Rao and Blank Noise, legal recourse does not have to be the only avenue for social and gender justice. Indeed, legalism is never circumscribed to the courts and the criminal justice system. Its effects disseminate in regulatively producing a conception of "woman" marked through caste, religion, region, and class privilege, making invisible the routine sexual violations perpetrated through caste, religious, and military violence. Legal and disciplinary discourses are co-imbricated, and this constitutes the very conditions for who we are and what we do. Circulating in public culture, the effects of legal discourses regulate social relations and normatively produce subject positions. Feminist legal activism, in a carceral register, fails to address the myriad forms of violence faced by women disadvantaged by race, class, caste, ethnicity, and region, including police violence and mass incarceration.

The creative interventions by performers Rao and Patheja take up but also look beyond the law and its delineation of injured subjects to find new and creative ways to engage with the entrenched sexism and gender violence in contemporary India. They extend the steadying hand of friendship by reducing the isolation and disorientation that such violations can bring and affirming the empowering solace found in solidarity. Rao, Patheja, and other artists exemplify ways in which feminist interventions in the public sphere need to reach beyond legal solutions and engage and shift public culture at large. Such performances do not foreclose dialogue enacted through legal fiat, but rather engender newness through playful and creative imaginations of alternative gender, social, and political arrangements.

1 For a detailed discussion of the performative strategies used during these protests, including an analysis of Maya Rao's *Walk*, see Dutt, "Performing Resistance with Maya Rao."

2 I thank David Sklansky for pointing this out to me.

3 Arendt, *Human Condition*, 9.

4 For Arendt, the preoccupation with mortality situates Heidegger's thought within the Western metaphysical tradition. In its focus on radical finitude as the temporal limit which proffers an authentic existence, Heidegger, even if critical of Platonic metaphysics of presence, is still operating within a Western metaphysical paradigm, and disregards the relational dynamics that constitute subjects and publics.

5 Halley, *Split Decisions*.

6 Halley, *Split Decisions*, 22.

7 Brown and Halley, *Left Legalism/Left Critique*, 24.

8 See A. Davis, *Are Prisons Obsolete?*, and M. Alexander, *New Jim Crow*.

9 Law, "Against Carceral Feminism."

10 Poulami Roychowdhury, "The Delhi Gang Rape," 282–92.

11 For example, the eleven perpetrators who raped Muslim woman, Bilkis Bano in the 2002 Gujarat pogrom were finally convicted in 2012 and given a life-imprisonment sentence. The Mumbai High Court upheld the conviction in 2017 after the defendants appealed the verdict. As a result, Bilkis Bano had to wait fifteen years to see her perpetrators brought to justice.

12 Judicial discretion in sentencing had come under scrutiny: sentences had been routinely reduced based on a number of factors such as a woman's past sexual history, her marital status, etc. Following the 2013 guidelines, the sentence for rape was fixed at seven years.

13 Rape is defined under s. 375(d) IPC: "wherein a man is said to commit *rape* if he applies his mouth to the vagina, anus, urethra of a woman against her will and without her consent."

14 See Agnes's interview in Badhwar, "Can't Compare Brutal Gang-Rape with Forced Oral Sex."

15 Menon and Devika, "Mahmood Farooqui Rape Conviction."

16 Haksar "Human Rights Lawyering," 132.

17 Haksar, "Human Rights Lawyering," 132–33. Writers included Professors Upendra Baxi, Raghunath Kelkar, Lotika Sarkar, and Vasudha Dhagamwar, among others.

18 On the regulatory capacities of legalism, see Brown and Halley, *Left Legalism/Left Critique*, 11

19 Tarun Tejpal is a pioneering investigative journalist and former editor in chief of *Tehelka*, a magazine that had produced an entire special issue on violence against

women. R. K. Pachauri is considered one of the foremost scientists of climate change in the world. Former Rhodes scholar, Mahmood Farooqui is an Indian performer, writer, and director. He specializes in *Dastangoi*, a sixteenth-century Urdu oral performance form.

20 The Sexual Harassment of Women at Workplace (Prevention, Prohibition, and Redressal) Act, 2013, is a legislative act in India that seeks to protect women from sexual harassment at their place of work. This statute superseded the Vishakha Guidelines for prevention of sexual harassment introduced by the Supreme Court of India.

21 During the trial, the victim said she didn't resist the rape because she was reminded of the violent murder of Jyoti Singh Pandey, the 2012 Delhi gang-rape victim. Vrinda Grover, the legal counsel for the victim, said, "She has stated before this court, during the recording of the evidence, that she was reminded of the documentary of the Nirbhaya case, where the rapist had said that if the victim had not struggled, she would have survived. The accused (Farooqui) applied force and pushed her down. She then froze. She knew if she resisted the rape upon her, the consequence would be worse" (Sacks, "Indian Director Mahmood Farooqui Convicted").

22 Gaur, *Textbook on the Indian Penal Code*, 649.

23 Baxi, "'Carceral Feminism' as Judicial Bias." See also Sood, "Why the Backlash against the Mahmood Farooqui Judgment Is Manipulative and Dangerous," and Sethi, "Why the Mahmood Farooqui Judgment Is Deeply Flawed."

24 Badhwar, "Can't Compare Brutal Gang-Rape with Forced Oral Sex."

25 Brown and Halley, *Left Legalism/Left Critique*, 17.

26 Arendt, *Human Condition*, 9.

27 In the wake of the December 2013 Supreme Court ruling that recriminalized homosexuality in India, Maya Rao revised *Walk* to bring a range of violations— legal, sexual harassment, and overt physical violence—under scrutiny, thus building affiliations between gender and queer justice. In 2018 the Supreme Court struck down Section 377 of the Indian Penal Code as unconstitutional.

28 Krishnan, secretary of All India Progressive Women's Association, writes, "In the wake of the anti-rape movement that followed December 16, 2012, the streets of Delhi and many other parts of India had resounded with the voices of women declaring 'Don't take away our freedoms in the name of "protection"—protect our right to fearless, fullest freedom instead.' Those women had raised their voice demanding freedom from sexual violence—and also freedom from rape culture that advices women to dress decently to avoid rape; and freedom from the khap panchayats, freedom even from the restrictions imposed by one's own fathers and brothers." See Krishnan, "Rape and Rakhi."

29 Honig, "Antigone's Two Laws," 9.

30 Dutt, "Performing Resistance with Maya Rao," 378.

31 Patheja, "Challenge Is in Developing Empathy."
32 See Gupta, "One Night Stand on the Streets."
33 Pal, "Reclaiming the Streets."
34 Pal, "Reclaiming the Streets."
35 Gupta, "Taking Action," 161–62.
36 Gupta, "Taking Action," 165.
37 Lieder, "Performing Loitering Feminist Protest," 159
38 Gupta, "Taking Action."
39 See Debord, *Society of the Spectacle*.
40 Blank Noise website.
41 Blank Noise website.
42 Brown and Halley, *Left Legalism/Left Critique*, 20.

I really insist on saying it: it's a gay man or a queer person photographing the male body. It's important. That's why I insist it's very important for me to stand behind the images and to reveal myself as the photographer. The queer aspect and the queer aesthetic will be more evident in a certain way . . . so these documentations are not like "throwing a stone and hiding your hand."

JOSUÉ AZOR

Witnessing Queer Flights

Josué Azor's Lougawou *Images and Antihomosexual Unrest in Haiti*

A TELLING OBJECT

A photograph in Josué Azor's *Noctambules: Queer Nightlife* series (figure 10.1) pulls our focus to its bottom edge, to a cracked windshield, a time postviolence. Long threads fan out from a heavily damaged circular center. An invisible exterior light source casts silver threads on the cracks and accentuates the person's furrowed brows, sullen or questioning eyes reflected in the rearview mirror. Part of the person's forehead, their[1] almond-shaped eyes, eyebrows, and a small ear occupy half of the slim rearview mirror. The light also bathes the left side of the neck in soft focus. Barely illuminated ahead, outside of the car, is a white structure with vertical lines and a taller multicolored one on the side of the passenger. Magnified, these structures appear to be a gate and a wall. Let us take a step back. Behind closed gates, inside of a car damaged by a weighty object, sits Josué Azor with

FIGURE 10.1 *Noctambules* series, *Queer Nightlife*, 2013. COURTESY OF JOSUÉ AZOR.

the photograph's subject. Given the position of the shot, a driver must also be there. On the other side of the wall, a group of fifty to a hundred enraged Haitians are protesting a gay interracial engagement ceremony by hurling rocks, Molotov cocktails, and insults at celebrants. Depicting guests' escape from the harrowing scene of the August 10, 2013, festivities in Port-au-Prince, Azor's image stages queers' significance in narratives of acceleration and deceleration in Haitian temporality. It illustrates an altercation three years following the January 12, 2010, earthquake, which extinguished 250,000 lives and was marked "year zero" by national and foreign media to institute a new Haitian and international calendar for the reconstruction, sanitization, and development of Haiti.

The photographic subjects represent same-sex-desiring persons scapegoated for provoking the cataclysm. By claiming time away to celebrate, the partygoers challenge two centuries of Haiti's heteromasculinist expressions of nationality (for example, the iconicity of Toussaint L'Ouverture and Jean-Jacques Dessalines), and by encouraging alternative forms of Haitian personhoods, the subjects contest time-spaces in which identity is constructed, or imagined, through formations other than those sanctioned by representatives and protectors of the nation-state. Their transgression and reinvention of normalized expectations demand they master deflective strategies such as nocturnal gatherings that challenge heteronormative practices. These gatherings fueled massive incivility and violence for four months preceding the engagement ceremony. Not only does the photograph's composition steer viewers to this interpretation, but also the crack on the windshield clearly signals the impact of corrective measures inflicted on brazen and demonstrative lesbian, gay, bisexual, transgender, and intersex (LGBTI) Haitians.

How do creative practices in Haiti cultivate epistemologies that alter toxic representations of nonconforming Haitian bodies? The photographs serve as an alternative mode of representation that captures bodies in dissent, to borrow a phrase from Daphne Brooks, that helps develop futures loosened from the limitations of institutional expectations of gender and sexual codes of conduct.[2] This analysis emerged from my engagement with Azor's photographic series—*Noctambules, Gason Solid*, and *Erotes*—beginning in 2013. Self-taught freelance Haitian artist-activist Azor documents queer self-conception in the underground spaces of gender- and sexuality-nonconforming Haitians in the aftermath of the January 12, 2010, earthquake. Born in 1986, the photographer has exhibited regularly in Haiti and abroad. To support his artistic pursuits, he has also worked for Haiti's Fondation SEROvie which, since 1998, provides psychosocial support and sexual health education to Haiti's LGBTI population. There, Azor managed a fhi360/Linkages health program, which endeavored to improve most-at-risk populations' access to health services and care. Alongside a cohort of queer activists, Azor fashions alternative visions of prescribed gender and sexual identities in Haiti. However he is the only "out" witness, one determined to alter transparent depictions of the queer Haitian person. Azor creates opaque images of his subjects that "displace all reduction" of their lives.[3] His technique deliberately fragments body parts, excavates subversive gender and sexual figurations, blurs time indicators and spatial markers, and transposes photographic styles. His queer photodocumentary projects "activate creative linguistic [and embodied] maneuvers to destabilize assumptive representations that [Haitian queers] are transparent and predictable," recycled in Haitian social life, media, and political and religious discourses.[4] These are restorative dynamics of *dedouble* that sharply critique conceptions of "whole" national identities and resist any justification of his collaborators' sense of time and world-making methods. The photographs restore the spirit of insurgency and unruliness animating all Haitians as they indict the exclusionary logic of homophobes and transphobes that cast these bodies out of the Haitian collective. Azor's visual practice claims that earnest and productive dialogue is attainable only if it revolves around majoritarians' willingness to accept human and nonhuman phenomena that surpass comprehension, as generations of revolutionary Haitians have demanded.

Viewers are invited to become accustomed over time to the unapologetic difference of Azor's subjects, an engagement with queer bodies and social spheres that would strengthen the foundation of relations between conforming and nonconforming Haitians. The series illustrate that "relation is learning more and more and more to go beyond judgments into the unexpected dark of art's upsurgings. Its beauty springs from the stable and unstable, from the deviance of many particular poetics and the clairvoyance of a relational poetics. The more things it standardizes into a state of lethargy, the more a rebellious consciousness arises."[5] Displayed online and in physical spaces, Azor's photographs out Haitian institutions' physical and psychological violence against men, women, male-women, and female-men read as abnormal, grotesque, off-kilter, and norm-breaking.[6] In so doing, he intervenes in the heteronormative logics that organize national time and its institutions and offers, instead, a relational time that emphasizes collectivity and care.

This chapter indexes how Azor imagines and images Haitian men and male-women bullied by homophobes and transphobes into retreating to their towns' outskirts and underground spaces. It also documents how they charge forward by contributing to an archive that engages in a tumultuous journey of image articulation and disarticulation through embodied representations of the Haitian Kreyòl vernacular *dedouble*. I first overheard the term at a dance, when a same-sex-desiring man complimented another: Fi a telman danse, li dedouble sou moun (Girlfriend danced so much, she dedouble on us). My field collaborator Jean Wesler Louis-Jean further elaborated: one partakes in dedouble when he or she appears to metamorphose in moments of joy (like the embodied elation the two men expressed above) or duress. "Kó w rete la. Nanm ou ale on lòt kote," he continued. The body stays here still while the soul travels. "Gen de fwa se komsi ou wè lot pesonalite moun la." Sometimes it's as if you see a person's other personalities.[7] Later, my conversations with a cross-section of Haitians supported his suggestions of dedouble performances. Dedouble is the literal or symbolic practice of teleportation and metamorphosis. For Francophone Haitians, *dédoubler* is "to split or to divide into two," while *se dédoubler* is to self-double, to be outside of or in proximity to oneself.[8] One could understand it as a mode to produce relation. Popular lore proudly attributes dedouble qualities to eighteenth-century maroons of the Bizango secret society, without naming it so. Insurgent Haitian men endowed with Africanist ancestral power flashed through time and space to evade, resist, and defeat

French Emperor Napoleon Bonaparte's army. Dedouble enabled the formerly enslaved to take ownership of their lives and their side of Hispaniola. Its use in a dance by a gay man claims the performance of dedouble as a disruptive revolutionary act that reorganizes national time. A purpose of this chapter is to identify how performances of dedouble actualize mutually affective processes of evocation (attention to long-standing terrors that haunt contemporary realities) and provocation (a critical persistence to expose and work through those violations). Azor points the lens at self-possessed lives to remedy unjust practices, envision opportunities of solidarity and being alongside other Haitians, and set a course for queerly paced futures.

This chapter argues that those who dedouble reimagine and rearrange conceptions of space *and* time. Their leaps through performances of gender and sexualities break some Haitians' romanticization of normative time-spaces that suppress the dialogic realities of nonnormative insights. More directly, their bodily shifts also instantiate alternative developmental through-lines that give rise to a Haitian who sees themself as self-possessed and fully realized. These temporal shifts nuance facile comprehension of the quotidian for their interlocutors, viewers, or witnesses who experience practices that operate on multiple registers, and reflect more accurately the ways Haitians evaluate and contend with systems of power and annihilation. Those who dedouble teleport through the fraught intersections that all hemispheric Americans must navigate to locate themselves within colonial, anticolonial, and postcolonial histories and experiences.[9] They refute "heterogeneous temporal scales" resulting from a European imperialist dictate of time that lionizes its own modernity and humanity by discarding other ways of being, behaving, and acting in the world as prehistorical or prehuman.[10] Dedouble, an embodied theory of the people, critically recognizes cotemporal performances that link spatially and temporally distanced groups and their practices, as it elucidates minoritarian embodied histories, collective memories, and formulations of time that eschew, reconfigure, or bypass dominant groups' sanctions.

In this light, drawing from a range of critical ethnographic methodologies and modes of analysis, this chapter explores performances of dedouble in which Azor depicts queer Haitians suspended in moments of flight: how their bodies attempt to divest themselves of patriarchy's normative performances, hang between the dystopia of their homophobic and transphobic environments, and invest in creating uplifting experiences, saturated with moments of freedom and boundlessness. To paraphrase Soyica Diggs Colbert's formulation, I situate Azor's representation of "the cultural conditions that hamper [queer bodies]' flight" and his subjects' recuperative modes of "resistance to black death-boundness."[11] I interpret Azor's process for imaging a queer Haitian body that aspires to derail national social codes yet feels weighed down by corrective behaviors on those who deviate from the norm. Examining how queer bodies teeter between past and present traditions, and their labor to ensure future empowering conditions for themselves, my chapter troubles dedouble's socially sanctioned commemoration of heteronormativity. I employ Azor's photographs to call attention to dedouble as a performance enacted by queer men and transwomen who self-present and self-double as *lougawou*. Using the figures herein, I contend that Azor's witnessing project reconfigures impassible knowledge production about *masisi* who feel lougawou and engenders specifically situated, dialogical albeit difficult relations, now or later.

The following sections locate the embodied, affective registers of Azor's models' emic identifications within contemporary antihomosexual unrest in Haiti and illuminate Azor's subjectivity as witness to the self-making potential of his lougawou counterparts. I draw insights from Édouard Glissant's theorizations of opacity to analyze how Azor's photographs chart queer Haitians' restructuring of nationalist identities. Azor's work communicates that interlocutors must resist viewing and grasping queer life-worlds superficially and reevaluate the interpretation that "masisi and madivin [women who desire women] are dragging Haiti backwards in time and that they are part of—if not key to—the nation's underdevelopment."[12]

Erin L. Durban-Albrecht's use of the word "drag" to summarize the ethos of antihomosexuality demonstrations arises from the popular protest refrain that same-sex-desiring persons "*trennen*" (lag, drag, dawdle, or linger).[13] They are asynchronous with Christian salvation that would "*mennen*," or lead, them toward collective "chrononormativity."[14] My analysis of figure 10.1 builds on Durban-Albrecht's deployment of "drag"—a temporal disjuncture between Haitian interlocutors and their disharmony over sexual politics—to operationalize it as a double-edged term that also indicates a time of terror, "a ground-level cultural terrorism that fiercely skewers both straight culture and reactionary components of gay culture."[15] The practice of cooptation, deconstruction, and recodification of derogatory nonnormative modalities to unsettle the foundations of gender, sexuality, ethnonationalism, and heteropatriarchy is an affinity that Azor's photodocumentation of drag performances shares with José Esteban Muñoz's affirmation about endeavors of drag superstar Vaginal Creme Davis. In my research, moral, religious, and state officials diagnose "drag" as one of the illicit time-lag performances that surely stall the development of Haiti and systematically derail its reproductive futurity. In a country where "pitit se byen malere" (children are the wealth of the poor), to display one's nonheterosexuality in public and private spaces and linger between gender and sexual dichotomies is to be a libertine non-Haitian who drastically decelerates if not upends the position of family and procreative values.[16]

Azor and his subjects respond to brutal contacts with homophobic and transphobic interlocutors or flash agents of communication by reconfiguring spaces, times, histories, and myths.[17] These modes of resistance are not only in the act of creation, but also in the act of viewing, especially for Haitians whose freedom of expression and association has been closely monitored. In *Create Dangerously: The Immigrant Artist at Work*, Edwidge Danticat states that creative practices by Haitians evolve into dangerous acts of witnessing. The author positions the Haitian artist as a witness who is both in and out of the story, much like Azor was as a target and visual chronicler of the boycotted engagement ceremony (figure 10.1). She writes, for example, of Haitian photojournalist Daniel Morel, who was present during the 1964 public execution of Louis Drouin and Marcel Numa, two opponents of the dictator Francois Duvalier's government. Morel's photographs of Haitian bodies, joyous or in pain, convey humility in retelling the stories gifted to him. "[His photographs] document acts that you'd expect people to take part in only when others are not around."[18] Thinking with Danticat, I analyze Azor's work to insist that memory is also the queer Haitian artist's preferred tool of activist resistance and a compass to chart liberatory spaces for contested bodies.

I also perform dedouble in this chapter via my critical and aesthetic strategies for reading the images featured here. I am especially attuned to the interactions among Azor, his subjects, and their spaces of liberation as well as the animosities they confront daily. My interpretive work about queerness in Haiti narrates conversations with my coconspirators—Azor included—to retell stories that remained unspoken yet palpable in our interviews, collaborations, and informal encounters.[19] I have also collaborated with the photographer in a number of artistic and research pursuits since 2015.[20] I am a gay Haitian American man who first heard and used the shorthand "lougawou" jokingly with gay Haitian friends at the turn of the twenty-first century. For us, lougawou expressed how our sexuality clashed seriously with nationalist and heteromasculine strictures. It reflected both the transformational act of dedouble and the stigma of gay identity. Recent conversations with friends and other kin reminded me that representations of the lougawou vary according to each person's imagination. The word "lougawou" derives from the French *loup-garou*, or werewolf. Haitian stories imagine the powerful being otherwise. She is at once a female werewolf, vampire, and bogeyman. A lougawou is able to live among men and spirits. She sheds her skin at midnight, sprouts wings, and steals children's breath. Her human side is hazily defined: she does not call attention to herself, inherits her supernatural gifts from her mother, or buys her skills from a Vodou practitioner. As popular tales disseminate, she is trapped in a sad existence, hence her need to fly the skies at night and/ or prey on children. My chapter, however, hones in on how queer Haitians dedouble in their performance of gender and sexually liberated lougawou to deflect psychic and physical violence.

Narrative accounts of my lived experiences, advocacy work, and witnessing of antihomosexuality demonstrations in Haiti are juxtaposed with formal interviews. This linkage enables me to respect anonymity produced out of a need for discretion (or by the presence of recording devices and undesirable listeners). I aim to protect issues that participants disclosed yet wanted to remain confidential and "show my hand and face" in loving support of Azor and his models' courageous efforts to enlarge their lives beyond their superficial depiction. Vigilant in my quest to create a horizontal connection with Azor and my Haitian counterparts, I am driven to indicate alternative spaces of self-possession and their temporalities that relate to Haitian performance, ones underexamined in the literature at home and elsewhere. Azor and I are twinned in reimagining what comprises a queer archive in Haiti and keeping the question above as our ethical compass as we mobilize our relative privilege to respond to criticisms and violence.

THE COCONSPIRATORS

Figure 10.1 is one of the early photographs of the "queer nightlife" subset of *Noctambules*. How life at night is vibrant and strategic is what motivated Azor to first explore the lives of street merchants, sex workers, and other night dwellers. Thirty years of blackouts have created an atmosphere of curfew at sunset, and generated fantasies of debauchery and illicit activities about those who eschew the safety of home. The "queer nightlife" series provided Azor the opportunity to show visions of joyful body doubles to queers Haitians might know, love, and/or despise. Documenting a gay engagement ceremony, Azor captured figure 10.1 as a piece of a larger tableau of other photographs that narrate a story of companionship among Haitians and their partners.

In chronological order, a dozen photographs show the decorated grounds, gender-queer guests dressed in orange and green (the official colors of the event), the ring exchange between a Haitian man and his white British fiancé, a crumpled invitation, and white guests in another damaged car whose faces show alarm. Azor also snapped photos of cars burning (figures 10.2 and 10.3).

Figure 10.1 zooms in on manmade fissures triggered by larger social ruptures postquake. American Baptist missionaries were first among Haiti's saviors. Their work implemented widespread evangelization of ruined Haitians, which contributed greatly to public and massive corrective violence toward people who engaged in same-sex relations.[21] The reconstruction of Haiti began with the mistreatment of gender and sexually nonconforming Haitians very similar to the persons in this essay's subject.[22]

In the private event preceding the altercation in figure 10.1, men and transwomen fully reveled in their femininity. Akin to their vision of a lougawou, they trade their everyday public attire for more provocative garb, dresses, and accessories. In doing so, queer and gender nonconforming Haitians also divest themselves of performances of respectability as social cover, an order of respectability demarcated by the rising and setting of the sun. Under the cover of night, the photographer explains: "There are the 'queens,' the extravagant ones, and the cross-dressers, and there are also the hyper 'macho' men. . . . I love to frequent this 'backstage' [space] where I encounter people who want to be totally themselves. I love to show the tenderness. That intimacy interests me and it remains a mystery for me. The person is his or her world. . . . A moment of diversion and of interaction."[23] Figure 10.1, however, not only reflects the discursive and physical violence toward Haitians who perform lougawou; it also invokes the hardships of Haitian women perceived to be lougawou.

On January 14, 1976, famed journalist Jean Dominique broadcast his encounter with a disoriented elderly woman accused of being a lougawou by Port-au-Prince residents. Accusers' brutality against the "lougawou" exposed "a crisis of collective anger, an equal amount of collective fear, a sense of folklore deeply Haitian, and belief in the marvelous."[24] Edwidge Danticat's lougawou in her story "nineteen thirty-seven" are women—witches and criminals—who "are seen at night rising from the ground like birds on fire."[25] The lougawou character is Manman, the member of a sisterhood that remembers the genocide of Haitians in 1937 Dominican Republic. They are women "who could go to the moon and back if that's what they wanted."[26] Impris-

FIGURE 10.2 *Noctambules* series, *Queer Nightlife*, 2013. COURTESY OF JOSUÉ AZOR.

FIGURE 10.3 *Noctambules* series, *Queer Nightlife*, 2013. COURTESY OF JOSUÉ AZOR.

oned with other gaunt women whose heads prison guards shave to resemble "crows, men," the character is carefully monitored by prison guards due to her loose skin that "barely clung to her bones, falling in layers, flaps, on her face and neck,[27] signs that she takes off her skin at night. As richly theorized by Colbert, "the story exemplifies the possibility of transmitting a liberating narrative from one generation to the next, even in the face of a purportedly shameful legacy."[28] Likewise, Haitian writer Patrick Sylvain's title character in his story "Odette" foresaw the coming of the 2010 earthquake and was blamed by neighbors for her granddaughter's demise during the natural disaster. A mob punished her severely before police officers rescued her.[29]

Cultural sediments that detractors endeavor to suppress might be the similarities that Haiti's women lougawou share with Yoruban women suspected of being Àjé: secret and covert witches who can fly to heaven and "turn themselves into nocturnal creatures such as bats, snakes, rats, and especially birds."[30] Yoruba societies acknowledge their cultural anxiety about the power of women by celebrating the Gelede, a festival to honor and appease the Great Mother. The entity epitomizes women's ability to give birth, which connects them more than men to spiritual (pro)creative powers. It also invokes the power of infertile and postmenopausal women who are akin to men in the influence they could wield in traditional societies.[31] These probable traces of Àjè duality in Haiti are met not with respect and celebration but with contempt, incarceration, and death, as narrated by Dominique, Danticat, and Sylvain.

By contrast to Haitian depictions of women lougawou, some gender and sexually nonconforming Haitian men and transwomen regard the night creature as symbols of fortitude: shedding one's skin signifies ridding oneself of the vagaries of Haitian life, perpetuated by patriarchal confines. I submit that, for queer Haitians, lougawou embodies feminist, shapeshifting, time-bending, and norm-breaking aptitude. They experience the fact that a lougawou who dedoubles undergoes a stormy journey, as figure 10.1 illuminates. To be queer and to perform lougawou enables them to rehearse the histories of patriarchy, sexism, homophobia, and transphobia in Haiti. Azor's subjects comprehend that lougawou cultivate the ability to bite or stumble, yet never fall when they land.[32] Reading the subject in figure 10.1 as a lougawou gestures to how he might channel Àjé strength as he stands in for other marginalized bodies—catapulted through circumstance, such as gender and sexual inequality on the island.

The self-doubling linkage I establish between Azor's collaborators and multiple manifestations of lougawou is a temporary transposition that in no way equates the experiences of male bodies (however womanly) to the practicalities of female-bodied women, especially those with the abilities to collapse and transform temporalities in Africa and its diasporas. Joseph Roach's caution, in *Cities of the Dead*, duly notes that the functions of a stand-in are temporary, however much the being or artifact participates in cultural continuity and sociocultural transgressions.[33]

Indeed, queer "surrogates" of lougawou eulogize nighttime as their moment of affirmation in the twenty-four-hour cycle when a future of their own imagination and creation is foreseeable. "Everynight life . . . delimit[s] a domain where minoritarian subjects enact theories and practices of resistance and social transformation," summarizes Shane Vogel in *The Scene of Harlem Cabaret*.[34] Extending the neologism coined by Celeste Fraser Delgado and José Esteban Muñoz, Vogel offers an astute examination of literary depictions and visual documentation of Harlem's nightlife that centers Harlem Renaissance luminaries' expressions and performances. The performers drew inspiration from nighttime's potential to transform and liberate Black subjects from superficially tolerant yet inherently oppressive edicts of African American personhoods and politics of respectability. Similarly, for queer Haitians, nighttime offers a chronological schism outside the daytime outcries of homophobes and transphobes. They would echo Muñoz's words that "there is indeed something about the transformative powers of nightlife that queers and people of color have always clung to."[35] Writes Azor,

> There is definitely a certain freedom that some people give to themselves, to be somebody else or to be themselves, to express themselves normally in a way that wouldn't be outside of these environments. There is ownership of their way of being in relation to those present at that moment. When you grow up with a lot of oppression, when you grow up with limited freedom of expression, there's a way you have to be, there's a way you have to behave. . . . So when those prescriptions are a strong part of your life, and then you discover those spaces, for me I entered a space of liberation. . . . The space is inherently alive for its duration. . . . What is also a source of knowledge is how at times people accept themselves and talk comfortably about gender fluidity when a person comes to the party dressed as "a man" and then, 10 minutes later, turns into "a woman." And that's alright. As soon as the party and its program are over, the person transforms into a man and that's just fine.[36]

Azor's subjects as lougawou stand-ins demonstrate agency in mobilizing nighttime to grow, bond, and reinvent gender and sexual politics, away from the judgmental gaze of day-walkers. Their surrogacy is a performance of resistance wherein they channel a body that jump-cuts through worlds of knowledge historically disregarded by Haitian and foreign interlocutors. In their fight against the brutalization of nonnormative Haitian bodies, they dedouble and bear characteristics of the lougawou, bolstered by the Haitian understanding that *all*—including the symbolic nature of the night creature—can be recycled and wielded for social, cultural, and political critique.

WITNESSING PRACTICE

Azor's exploration of queer Haitians who find the courage to develop joy and strength and devise forward-looking spaces is a practice that extends the temporality of the event and which Dwight Conquergood and D. Soyini Madison term "co-performative witnessing."[37] An ethical research behavior that Conquergood and Madison encourage ethnographers to adopt, the concept is also applicable to nonresearchers who inhabit the enclaves of their interlocutors as well as devote considerable time in pooling their resources, knowledge, and abilities with their collaborators. Because I believe Azor's queer body of work engages in a visual form of performative-witnessing, I value the practice as another dedouble function, a transformation that includes the bending of time. Thus far, the images we viewed map out how Azor uses performative-witnessing as a "communicative praxis of speaking and listening, conversation [that] demands co-presence even as it decenters the categories of knower and known."[38] His manifesto "Documenting Spaces of Liberation in Haiti" details his dialogic practices with his models. They share similar or converging temporalities. In considering Azor's activation of performative-witnessing, I doubly underscore how he subscribes to Danticat's "a witness but barely there" concept in *Create Dangerously*. Additionally, Madison's and Danticat's descriptions direct me to take stock of themes related to cultural memory and normative performances, which permeate exchanges between Azor and his subjects. I invoke these women's theorizations to underscore that for the Haitian photographer, witnessing is a practice that serves to understand how queer generations practice, reinvent, and transmit values to one another and their viewers while bridging their past to their future.

I led this chapter with figure 10.1 because the photograph centers on Azor's practice of witnessing. He is in the car with the party guest. In seeing, hearing, sensing, feeling, and living through his collaborator's terrors, the artist does dedouble by pivoting from a "me" to "not me" stance in his photographic testimonials. Azor partakes in dedouble by insisting on "showing his hand and face." This is to push back against the Haitian sociocultural prejudices that compel queer subjects to deny or keep silent about their disposition for same-sex intimacies. Being candid might have dire repercussions on their lives and livelihoods, the photograph indicates. To testify that his collaborators are fighting for full human rights and affirming futures, Azor *stands behind* his photographs to humbly *stand with* and *alongside* his acolytes, in a relational formation, to use Glissant's words, that "does not devise any legitimacy as its guarantee of entitlement, but circulates, newly extended."[39] In other words, Azor values the struggle, discomfort, and benefits that emerge from reimagining national identity, creates photographs that show Haitians performing multiple identities, and applauds his collaborators for stretching themselves beyond social, cultural, and political barriers.

Beyond my critical appreciation of Azor's artistry, which derails contemporary content about nonconforming Haitians, this chapter builds on the photographer's drive to safeguard his subjects' anonymity. Azor obtains their consent before taking photographs and explains the purposes of his documentation. His models participate in his projects, trusting that he will offer insights into their lives that are not exploitative or uselessly spectacular.[40] This approach converges with what Glissant terms "giving on and with [*donner-avec*]" that allows the listener, viewer, or documentarian to respect the dialogic relationship he established with the subjects.[41] I assert that Azor deploys this ethical aesthetic for two complementary reasons. He intends to upend sensational and facile portrayals of queer Haitians and their worlds as inconsequential, trivial, and decontextualized. Additionally, he instructs viewers to respect and value the unknown. Azor focuses attention on formations of relation in the creation and dissemination of a queer archive that cannot be easily understood and accessed without guidance from and kinship with its contributors. They choose how, when, and with whom to maintain or discard their brand of opacity. Azor's creative strategy demonstrates that he and his photographic subjects are undoubtedly complicit collaborators in the creation and documentation of their worlds.

The gift/burden of participating is at artists' disposal, as Azor implies in the epigraph. For Danticat and Azor, artistic testimonials are affective and regenerative only if their makers are humbly yet dynamically copresent, and journey with their interlocutors through sociopolitically charged endeavors. Danticat's limpid and provocative nonfiction commemorates creative responses by gender and sexually conforming oppressed Haitians during a prequake era in which, according to Durban-Albrecht, same-sex desires were largely ignored if LGBTI persons were sexually discreet.[42] Her theory also applies to gender nonconforming Haitians following the earthquake, in that I consider Azor's photodocumentary project a dangerous act of telling about the lives of men and transwomen who perform lougawou and self-possession. He is also their proxy. The privilege he holds as an educated, cosmopolitan middle-class man who affirms his gayness and might feel lougawou shields his less privileged brothers and sisters from backlash that may arise from their stance against Haitian politics of respectability. By accepting to be his subject's body double in public appearances, Azor partakes in a dedouble performance that mobilizes and extends "photography as a technology of the live in an inter(in)animate or syncopated relationship with other times and other places, so that it not only records but hails" a future free of the violence of national identity politics.[43] Rotating the scene in figure 10.1, the following section examines three photographs depicting not only that Azor's subjects dedouble or perform multiple lougawou facets but also that Azor performs dedouble as he offers glimpses into his subjects' inner sanctums. I submit that Azor celebrates life in the margins, what the general population considers underground debaucheries. The photographs defy easy generalizations of LGBTQI environments. Azor documents nonconforming Haitians' creation of personal and collective cultural memories, which instigates altercations, much like the one portrayed in figure 10.1.

HOW PHOTOGRAPHS PORTRAY DEDOUBLE

In Port-au-Prince on July 19, 2017, during the Haitian Coalition of Religious and Moral Organizations (CHO) antihomosexuality protests, the words "*nou pa dako*" became a festive mantra the clergy and their followers chanted, which meant: "we disagree" with homosexuality and homosexual marriage because they would destroy the sanctity of the Haitian family and the integrity of Haitian society.[44] On July 28, in Jacmel, hundreds of protesters shouted "*aba masisi*" ("down with masisi"). They rejected as surreptitious, bestial, and fruitless copulation between men, whose life-world was scapegoated for the woes of the nation and its moral and upstanding Haitians.

Observing dissenting men from the sidelines, I surmised that the poetics of desire and deep intimacy Azor captured in figure 10.4 were not qualities attributed to bodies that some Haitians perceive to lead confining and furtive

FIGURE 10.4 *Gason Solid* series, 2016. COURTESY OF JOSUÉ AZOR.

lives. Within the narrow frame, the space of these lougawous' interaction is sedate, vast, and inviting. Bright light bathes high white walls with red, pink, and orange tones, and it emits white streaks and shadows on the floor. For the two nude, brown men or male-women and the white cat that populate the portrait, time flows languidly. The subject in the left foreground stands against a doorjamb and shifts our attention to their partner seated on a stool and facing away. Coming together or drawing apart, these "strong men" (as the series title indicates) occupy a space that shelters them from the collective fury beyond the site of the image. Figure 10.4's subjects err toward boundless sexual identities that might disable institutions' preservation of homegrown values, evolving from the cultivation of indigenist forms of Blackness and heterosexist ideals,[45] inspired by the Bizango rebels I noted earlier. I posit this is perhaps where Azor's series struggle with the "unity-diversity" or recognition of the multiplicity of difference, which joins creolized spaces that Glissant theorizes.[46] Relation accounts for a cross-cultural alliance that circumvents oppression tied to racial segregation and the ravages of slavery. Yet, unexplored is the tension between the collective need and its internal marginalized communities that cannot and/or choose not to perform one or several norms of the dominant groups. The strong lougawou in figure 10.4 isolate themselves from deadly responses to the immediacy of internal contacts between conforming and liberated Haitians, exacerbated by the cruelty of religious zealots and their followers as "flash agents of communication."[47] The latter are the self-appointed regulators of institutional discourse and sharing of ideas, who vehemently discourage alternative forms of nationality performed by Haitians similar to Azor's subjects. Men like the ones in figure 10.4 evade nationalist ideals. As a result, religious and moral gatekeepers deny them access to systems of economy, education, and social structures.[48] With this photograph, Azor demystifies what might be perceived as queer Haitians' dismal marginal life. Yet "this is a personal, secret garden," writes Azor of such intimate queer moments. "I am very attentive to what happens before and after I take the photograph."[49]

Three tense years after the incident at the gay engagement ceremony, protests and violence resumed in September 2016 due to the national premiere of Festival Massimadi. It canceled its four-day celebration of performing and visuals arts by Haitian LGBTIs set to begin on September 27. Organizer Charlot Jeudy and members of his LGBTI rights organization Kouraj received death threats. Groups announced openly that they would destroy FOKAL (Fondasyon Konesans ak Libete or Foundation for Knowledge and Freedom), the host venue. Flash agents denounced the festival cosponsors, the French and Canadian embassies, for offenses against public order, mores, and decency. Aggressions to vulnerable LGBTIs ensued. Queer Haitians retreated underground once more.[50]

In figure 10.5, a person's profile emerges from a blurry crowd. Warm lights frame their high forehead. Viewers discern an eye that contains a spark or a soft fire that pierces the space. Their angular jaw is relaxed. It juts out almost stubbornly. Their lips are slightly parted and adorned with a touch of violet lipstick. A touch of powder graces the brown face, and a lone piece of glitter seems stranded on their left cheek, near a wide nose. Their shoulders are bare, with a protruding clavicle. A white necklace hangs around the neck. The person is looking up at a slight angle, which suggests that their body is stretching upward from a seated and grounded position. In that moment, the person

FIGURE 10.5 *Noctambules* series, *Queer Nightlife*, 2013. COURTESY OF JOSUÉ AZOR.

radiates poise, control, and focus. A hand with a white bracelet that reaches upward hides the left side of their face. Other people's body parts are in soft focus. A figure in very soft focus is in the background on the left. Their face is long and angular, framed by long hair, coiffed with a tiara. When antihomosexuality demonstrations resumed in September 2016, Azor hashtagged this photograph: "Kouraj." Courage.

"Homosexuality doesn't exist in Haiti. No one is gay," said Azor ironically.[51] He threw shade at elite, upwardly mobile, and/or intellectual queer Haitians who dissociate themselves from the scripts that might envelop the male-women and men he portrays. Affluent nonconforming Haitians resist tapping into their network to help less fortunate and more vulnerable LGBTI people, for fear they too would be targeted. Because "no one was gay" in the postquake era, figure 10.5 and the other photographs in Azor's *Noctambules* series converged with the motivation of LGBTIs and their allies to memorialize methodically the complex worlds of masisi, and their right to live as lougawou. The first of Azor's queer series, *Noctambules* elucidates how dwellers of underground and nocturnal environments are people with pasts and stories, who fight for their right to free, boundless, and cultural multiplicity, and invest in their future.

Azor's documentation, as shown in figure 10.5, overlaps with his work as an officer of Haiti's LGBTI organization Fondation SEROvie. He participated in government meetings, in large office rooms, in which Fondation SEROvie's executive director Réginald Dupont enumerated hurdles with which nonconforming Haitians must contend. Haiti does not have antisodomy laws, unlike numerous Caribbean islands. Yet there are no specific laws that protect sexual minorities. Social prejudice, intolerance, and physical and psychological violence against sexual minorities as well as HIV-positive people and their allies are rampant. Ignorance and taboos about nonheterosexuality prevail. Like elsewhere, many sexual minorities reject their sexuality due to the pressure for LGBTI people to subscribe to heteronormative practices and behaviors. Economic precariousness has engendered diminished access to education and professional training for Haitians, especially those who are read as gender and sexually fluid. As a result, these Haitians are also affected by high unemployment throughout the country. The neglect of issues related to nonheteromasculinity within Haitian and international aid agendas exacerbated the unhealthy conditions in which SEROvie beneficiaries live.

Figure 10.5 dedoubles or shows the flip side of this rhetoric. Azor encourages viewers to enter the world in figure 10.5, and imagine a small anteroom in which men and male-women are readying themselves for a special event. As Azor and I experience during our respective work as MSM (men who have sex with men) health managers for the same organization, the close-knit flurry of bodies signals that a show with dances, songs, theater skits, runway shows, and drag performances is underway. The subjects of figure 10.5 continue to reconfigure corporate conference rooms in urban spaces to small stuffy rooms on the outskirts of a village in order to rescript dominant discourses from their own standpoint. They wear bright-colored clothes. Some wear wigs. Others do not, such as the subject of this image. They enhance their face with makeup, accentuate the ears and neck with flashy jewelry, all to exteriorize their joy at being a diverse yet unified group. For about two hours, they put aside internal stratifications as well as external catcalls, jeers, and other forms of brutalization, to unwind and reach for joy.

This and similar fully sponsored special events are the bonuses accorded to participants of the health sessions Azor and I supervised and observed separately between 2011 and 2016. The event's format, lineup, and choice of music remain the same. During a freestyle dance session, one person's movements are always remarkable. They are quite unrestrained and add flourishes to tunes by Haitian divas Emeline Michel and Tifane and international sensations Beyoncé and Rihanna. At the end of an evening of mincing, prancing, strutting, and twerking, a lone participant (perhaps our friend in figure 10.5) will launch into a *laviwonndede* (whirling) when others seemed to have depleted their energy. Their dance is so unbridled and unapologetic that it energizes others to reenter the performance space. They dance as percussionists pound goat-skin drums or a DJ mixes Haitian with foreign musical hits seamlessly. Observers sway on the sidelines. The walls reverberate with all of these pulsations. The coalescence of these elements generates a euphoric high that will transport these beings through antipathies once they leave the event, until the next gathering. Flight, in figure 10.3, relates to lougawou's efforts to disrobe themselves of the disciplining effects of accepted identity performances. Moments of morphing and/in flight enact lougawou's right to difference, fluid identities, and multiplicity of practices. They constitute acts of resistance, which are at the core of Glissant's term "relationships of subversion."[52] Applied to performances of lougawou in Azor's photograph, the men and male-women in the anteroom participate in activating a network, founded on free speech, dissent, and nonconformity. The rapturous celebration of their identities is an exercise of liberation from nationalist filiation based on heteronormative practices and behaviors. This and similar images aid Azor in creating queer beacons that invite viewers to acknowledge ways that Haitians express their nonconformity, to remember or forget gender binary structures, and to build on or eschew those structures in the present in order to ensure a future in which they devise the parameters of their self-possession. For Azor, lougawou-ness is emerging, unfinished, in progress. The first figure suggests that Azor zooms in on the model bracing themself to move onward. To come out at parties, at night, they set aside the persona they don in unfriendly spaces, much like a lougawou would.

In figure 10.6, the lower halves of two male bodies in the missionary sex position are transposed over a Haitian landscape of rolling hills, lush green trees, and a few stately homes in the foreground. Gray brick houses perch on top of a hill in the upper left corner. On the horizon, in the upper section of the image, the cloudy sky merges with the Caribbean Sea. The bodies are seemingly nude, except for the man on the bottom who wears a boot. His leg is lifted and forms a right angle that fills up the frame of the photograph. The top body has round buttocks and legs. The image of the two men is overblown and so transparent that it seems to fuse with or fade out from the image of a landscape. The image of the copulating bodies is disproportionally larger than the one of the Haitian scenery. Azor has reworked the image during the resurgence of

FIGURE 10.6 *Erotes* series, 2016. COURTESY OF JOSUÉ AZOR.

homophobic violence in 2016, and posted it online with the caption "We are Love, Sex and Magic . . ."

The original image of the couple is from Azor's series *Erotes*, which exhibits two muscular men having sex. Shot in black and white, the men wrestle, lick, grope, and straddle one another and lead each other to ejaculation. Most of the images are shot closely and never reveal the models' faces. One has tattoos of large wings on his back. Emphasis is placed on a man's tongue licking the other's Adam's apple, one fondling the other's buttocks, and one man holding the other's erect penis. As an ensemble, the *Erotes* photographs show two men who exalt in an embodied freedom that only pleasurable consensual sex affords. It thrusts them over verbal and physical abuses that discipline them for being dual vectors of "'the Four-H Club,' a shorthand reference to homosexuals, Haitians, hemophiliacs, and heroin-users" at the onset of the HIV/AIDS epidemic.[53] *Erotes* retrieves voracious moments of ecstasy between men, in their flights toward self-empowerment. Figure 10.6 pays homage to ecstatic flights by Haitians who discard the strictures of institutionally sanctioned gender and sexual roles. They are proud lougawou who shed the skin despised by homophobes and transphobes and who feed on sex to live between world-views and space-times. They channel lougawou's flight.

With figure 10.6, Azor sees the potential for lougawou freedom that recuperates taboo yet enlightening registers of being related to Black ethnicities, class, gender, sexuality, and social efficacy. The photograph hails a future time beyond the era of massive incivility and violence toward LGBTI Haitians, in which those male-bodied lougawou not only subvert the machismo that anchors Haitian culture but also engulf the territory to make it a liberated space for all lougawou at home and in diasporic spaces.

The magic to which Azor aspires might be rooted in Vodou practices, which he documents. "It's a religion that allows you to be more. It's more permissive. . . . When you are in an environment when Vodou is very present, it's probably easier to see two men kissing. Even if it's within the Vodou ceremony proceedings. . . . Even if it's two spirits who are kissing. What remains is the image of the two men."[54] Azor and various scholars do not deny that heteropatriarchal structures prevail in Vodou's temples and compounds.[55] He is acknowledging that Vodou carves a space for the gender and sexually fluid people I have described in this chapter; they serve as priests and congregants who animate ceremonies. They are revered as enlightened gender-shifting messengers who facilitate communication between human and spiritual realms, maintain kinship bonds, and channel intergenerational transmission of knowledge among Haitians and their allies through space-time. As no one and nothing is lost to Vodou, the magic Azor invokes in figure 10.6 is one in which a fleeting image of sensual and sexual bonds between same-sex persons possesses the transformative potential to circumvent gender and sexual oppression on the island. Kissing and fucking have the power to divest Haitians and their detractors of their misconceptions about cowardice and courage, weakness and strength, and femininities and masculinities.

Erotes is Azor's visual medium to reanimate and cultivate love, sex, *and* love of sex in Haitians' lives, especially given that LGBTI persons (in Haiti and abroad) steadily receive the subliminal message that their ways of exercising love and desire lead to death—theirs and that of their kin—and are destructive to what has been popularly sanctioned as responsible personhood. Performing lougawou, LGBTI persons intercede in their descriptions as deathbound or socially dead by remembering, reflecting on, and reimagining legacies that have animated Haitians amid long-standing systems of oppression. Leaving the Haitian earth behind, these lougawou are escaping their labels as members of the most diseased and most at-risk group on the island. They teleport themselves to the Vodou continuum that collapses realms and temporalities, and in which partakers revel in the exhilarating pleasures that can be found through body-to-body and soulful contacts. They are reaching for modes of affection and play that have been denied to LGBTIS, ones they know they deserve.

CONCLUSION: VIEWING IMAGES AS WITNESSES

Recounting his experience during the engagement ceremony on August 10, 2013, Azor details his reticence about how viewers—at home and elsewhere—might understand the violence he documented in figures 10.1 and 10.3 without questioning their contexts: that is the assumption that Haitians are fundamentally violent, homophobic, and perhaps xenophobic, given the destruction that erupted around the interracial engagement ceremony.[56] Deeper still, antihomosexuality leaders' maneuvers are performances that outsiders might package as Black homophobia and violence, argues Durban Albrecht. A decontextualized focus on these performances in Black postcolonial places, such as Haiti, Jamaica, and Ghana, is an undercurrent of what Durban-Albrecht calls "postcolonial homophobia": long-standing American interests in Haiti, especially during and since its occupation of the nation (1915–34) have invested in representations of Haiti and its people as queerly subhuman and in need of salvation.[57] Many "Voodoo" qualifiers stem from that period. They continue to generate nightmarish and racist depictions of Haiti, based on the cultivation of black magic connected with all manner of perversions—human sacrifice, zombie creation, corrupt heterosexuality, and insatiable homosexuality. These attract "progressive" Americans and evangelist counterparts. For enlightened Americans and other white foreign bodies, Haitians' narrow-minded and brute resistance against allowing full human rights to LGBTI islanders further establishes anti-LGBTI protesters as backward and premodern. On the other hand, the antihomosexuality climate energizes American evangelists tasked by God to purge Haitians of their "Voodoo" sins. Responding to this history, Azor's photodocumentation confronts spectators with their (mis)conceptions of LGBTQI life, reclaims the misunderstood lifeworlds of masisi, and depicts multiple manners in which they embrace their lougawou existence. This is a performance modality termed a disidentification.[58] Azor directs attention to the position of queer sexuality as a site of toxic memory of identity-driven antipathy in Haiti to invite viewers to evaluate their relation to the images.

Azor, with multimedia artist Maksaens Denis, first previewed *Erotes*, on June 10, 2016, at Villa Kalewès, in Pétion-Ville, Haiti. The contemporary art event titled *Liber8tion*, produced by Kolektif 509, also included six other Haitian and expatriate visual artists whose works drew inspiration from the Haitian quotidian. A white room that a light bulb bathed in red was dedicated to a dozen of Azor's photographs and Denis's video installation. The latter included a flat screen television, within a tall and flat wrought-iron cage on a stand. The structure was about six feet tall. The projection of nude male bodies alone or copulating could not be easily viewed, as the cage was sealed with an iron grid, from which a silver car bumper and lead pipes stuck out. Intrigued viewers had to dance with, against, and around the installation to capture the information it relayed. However tempting, rehearsing an interpretation of Denis's arresting work would be a consuming and focus-stealing endeavor best reserved for another project.

Black, brown, beige, and white bodies streamed through the *Erotes* room, on the hot June night. Nearly three years after the highly publicized boycotted gay engagement ceremony, the pronounced victimization of lougawou seemed to have ceased. At Villa Kalewes, bodies that seemed relaxed or passive as they entered the second floor installation became attentive to or dismissive of the seedy, dangerous, and enticing mood conveyed by the exhibition. Some viewers sped through the room for reasons to which I am not privy. Others spent time closely inspecting the exhibited items. Selfies with Azor and Denis near their work were an added bonus. Gasps, laughter, and giggles permeated the room. Along with these sound bites, a number of ephemeral paralanguage and nonverbal forms of communication amounted to moments of emotional belonging or malaise that might, to quote Jill Dolan, "represent the apotheosis of fandom and fetishization, admiration or attraction (or actually, revulsion and repulsion), [which] allows the audience to see each other feeling, see each other reacting."[59] *Erotes* rehearsed a time-bending and norm-breaking utopic environment that evening.

Erotes, Gason Solid, and *Noctambules* engender resistance both in the act of creation and in the act of viewing, especially for his collaborators whose freedom of expression and association has been closely monitored. The series generate shifts in physicality, movement, and mood for viewers. In offering glimpses into their emotional state, viewers also betray that they register and reevaluate differences in taboo and sanctioned modes of kinship as well as perhaps their weak foundations. Additionally, through his online presence on Facebook and Instagram, Azor's numerous followers use these and other images to explicitly share and exchange ideas related to Haitian ethnicity, class, gender, and sexual politics, both through and across social and class delineations. In this virtual space, partakers are quicker to applaud the ways in which Azor is transporting lougawou lives and knowledge to a space-time in which identity is constructed, or imagined, through formations and relations other than those available in the present.

Azor's images presented here show male-bodied lougawou in symbolic instances of dedoubling through the contemporary history of violence against themselves. As visualized by the photographer, to dedouble is to blur binarisms in order to carve a space for affirming intricate performances and to channel a body that harbors, braids, and unbraids worlds of knowledge historically disregarded by Haitians and their foreign interlocutors. The bodies Azor documents writhe and stumble under societal pressures yet devise tactics to recover from dire conditions such as violence brought on by prejudices and stigmatization. Coperformances of witnessing, Azor's photographs of lougawou lives focus attention on remembering practices and traumatic historical events that affect and engage one's interlocutors in a dialogue that is transitive and transformative, and instills moral responsibility in the present. Last, viewing Azor's photographs and understanding the fraught contexts from which they emerge also creates openness and reflexivity between testifier Azor and us, the viewer-witnesses. Between Azor, his models, their allies, and— now—*us*, there exists acknowledgment, remembrance, and response-ability.

NOTES

1 In Haiti, "li" is the only third-person pronoun and does not specify gender. Here I use the neutral gender pronouns "they, them, their" for people and interlocutors who prefer this pronoun or who did not disclose their preference to me.

2 Brooks, *Bodies in Dissent*.

3 Glissant, *Poetics of Relation*, 111–20, 190–94.

4 Azor, "Documenting Spaces of Liberation in Haiti," 150.

5 Glissant, *Poetics of Relation*, 138–39.

6 LaMothe, "Dedouble and Jeanguy Saintus' Corporeal Gifts."

7 Louis-Jean, interview with author.

8 LaMothe, "Dedouble and Jeanguy Saintus' Corporeal Gifts."

9 Lane, "Hemispheric America in Deep Time," 114–17. Lane proposes performance as a means to reevaluate temporal systems and power dynamics in the Americas, which privilege demarcation of bodies in spaces such as the United States versus southern places in the hemisphere. As a result, Hemispheric American imperial legacies systematically persist in placing the minoritarian body in a time that precedes or is asynchronous with the timeline of colonizers' histories. "Deep time"—" a temporal measure that far exceeds the clocks of human history"— visualizes multidirectional and heterogeneous conceptions of time that contest sociohistorical demarcations and connect racialized and culturally distanced groups, via "the different tropes, genealogies and cultural forms that shape or are shaped by performance in the different cultures of imperialism in the Americas and in their contemporary legacies."

10 Lane, "Hemispheric America in Deep Time," 114–17.

11 Colbert, *Black Movements*, 34–41.

12 Durban-Albrecht, "Performing Postcolonial Homophobia," 162–63.

13 "More than 1,000 People March in Rare Anti-Gay Demonstration in Haiti."

14 Durban-Albrecht, "Performing Postcolonial Homophobia," 162.

15 Muñoz, *Cruising Utopia*, 102.

16 Andrésol, "Mise au point de Mario Andrésol."

17 Glissant, *Poetics of Relation*, 141.

18 Danticat, *Create Dangerously*, 140.

19 LaMothe, "Our Love on Fire."

20 At Duke University, I cocurated Azor's photographic series *Noctambules: Queer Nightlife in Haiti* with Dasha A. Chapman from November 2015 to January 2016. Azor's essay "Documenting Spaces of Liberation in Haiti" is in the Queer Haiti issue of *Women and Performance* that I coedited with Dasha A. Chapman and Erin L. Durban-Albrecht. We are collaborating on a series that reimagines the life and work of Haitian American playwright, poet, and activist Assotto Saint (1947–1994).

21 Durban-Albrecht, "Performing Postcolonial Homophobia," 143–58.

22 For a succinct analysis of the status of LGBTQI Haitians postquake, see IGLHRC (International Gay and Lesbian Human Rights Commission) and Fondation SE-ROvie's report: "The Impact of the Earthquake and Relief and Recovery Program on Haitian LGBT People."

23 Azor, "Noctambules," 118. Translation from the French by the author. "Il y a 'les folles,' l'extravagance, le travestissement, mais il y a aussi des hommes très 'virils.' . . . J'aime me render dans l'arrière scène, c'est là que je rencontre les gens alors qu'ils sont eux-mêmes. J'aime montrer la tendresse. L'intimité m'interesse. Cette dernière reste pour moi un mystère. C'est une personne dans son monde, un moment d'égarement, d'interaction."

24 Jean L. Dominique, "Lougawou ou pas lougawou?" Dominique, who was also a political dissident, is the subject of Demme's documentary *The Agronomist*.

25 Danticat, *Krik? Krak!*, 38–39.

26 Danticat, *Krik? Krak!*, 37.

27 Danticat, *Krik? Krak!*, 34.

28 Colbert, *Black Movements*, 34–35.

29 Sylvain, "Odette," 26.

30 Drewal and Drewal, *Gẹlẹdẹ*, 74.

31 Drewal and Drewal, *Gẹlẹdẹ*, 73–74.

32 LaMothe, *Jeanguy Saintus*. Preface for forthcoming Léna Blou book. October 12.

33 Roach, *Cities of the Dead*, 2. Roach's broad-scoped and interdisciplinary volume examines call and response performances (specifically those with funerary dimensions and layers) in the Atlantic basin, between New Orleans and London. The region is the locus of exchange among numerous cultures that have intermingled through inequities, and whose social memories often live on or have been reinvented by one another. His theorization of invention and reinvention through enactments of "surrogation" is germane to how I interpret some Haitians' self-identification with the mythical being as a substitute for their covert nocturnal habits. "Into the cavities created by loss and other forms of departure, survivors attempt to fit satisfactory alternates," Roach advances. Yet for queer Haitians who project themselves as otherworldly, "the fit cannot be exact."

34 Vogel, *Scene of Harlem Cabaret*, 17.

35 Muñoz, *Cruising Utopia*, 9.

36 Azor, "Documenting Spaces of Liberation in Haiti," 248–50.

37 Conquergood, *Cultural Struggles*, 75–78, 93; Madison, *Acts of Activism*, 24–25. Madison elaborates concepts of "dialogic performance" and "co-performance" advanced by Conquergood, which entreat qualitative researchers to share time, space, environments, and stories with their interlocutors as a means to diminish the othering ethnographic interactions might instigate. "The power dynamic of the research situation changes when the ethnographer moves from the gaze of the distanced and detached observer to the intimate involvement and engagement of 'coactivity' or co-performance with historically situated, named, 'unique individuals'" (Conquergood, *Cultural Struggles*, 93).

38 Madison, *Acts of Activism*, 87.

39 Glissant, *Poetics of Relation*, 144.

40 Azor, "Documenting Spaces of Liberation in Haiti," 248.

41 Glissant, *Poetics of Relation*, 144.

42 Durban-Albrecht, "Performing Postcolonial Homophobia," 143–58.

43 Schneider, *Performing Remains*, 141.

44 Durban-Albrecht, "Performing Postcolonial Homophobia," 143–58.

45 For a charged example of these discussions in Haiti, see Andrésol, "Mise au point de Mario Andrésol."

46　Glissant, *Poetics of Relation*, 79.

47　Glissant, *Poetics of Relation*, 141.

48　IGLHRC and Fondation SEROvie, "The Impact of the Earthquake, and Relief and Recovery Programs."

49　Azor, "Noctambules," 118.

50　LaMothe, "Our Love on Fire."

51　Azor, "Interview."

52　Glissant, *Poetics of Relation*, 105.

53　Farmer, *AIDS and Accusation*, 211.

54　Azor, "Documenting Spaces of Liberation in Haiti," 257.

55　See Brown, ""Afro-Caribbean Spirituality"; Strongman, "Syncretic Religion and Dissident Sexualities"; Strongman, "Transcorporeality in Vodou."

56　Azor, "Interview."

57　Durban-Albrecht, "Performing Postcolonial Homophobia," 143–58.

58　Muñoz, *Cruising Utopia*, 31, 169.

59　Dolan, *Utopia in Performance*, 31–32.

The Body Is Never Given,
nor Do We Actually See It

Black woman lying on a Chicago sidewalk. State Street. The Loop. Slack. No tension in her muscles. The calves and legs rest. Top of her feet touching the ground at the bridge where the toes emerge from her foot. Her face facing right, left cheek pressed into the concrete sustaining the weight of her head. Arms stretched at her side, top of the hands pressed to the ground, the skin from wrist to shoulder touching the ground. Body exposed to the November chill. A tension. Between a light, white dress and the cold. Between an artist's body lying slack, not seen, and the people in jackets and coats passing by not seeing. Between blackness and being, being seen and *being not seen*.

A black woman in a tan overcoat walks from south to north. It's possible that at first she doesn't see the body of the woman on the ground. But then she glances. A few steps forward, before being pushed off course by a cluster of bodies moving south, she resumes her walk then stalls, pausing, and looking back at the body on the ground. She hesitates for a moment, then she walks back to the woman on the ground and leans forward to say something to her. Perhaps: "Are you ok? What's happened to you? What do you need? What can I do for you now?" And though we cannot hear what they say to each other, whatever the woman on the ground says, it must have been enough, because the woman in the tan coat seems satisfied. She continues on her way.

In the piece *11/10/10* Alexandria Eregbu placed her body in different public places around Chicago: beneath benches, in parks, and on a busy sidewalk on State Street in the city's downtown Loop. The performance was photographed and the State Street segment was documented with a digital camera mounted on a tripod and tended by Eregbu's associate and fellow artist, Han Service-Rodriguez. In a thirteen-minute video hosted on the artist's website until the summer of 2017, the footage was edited at seemingly random intervals to feature a series of scenarios, including the exchange between the woman in the tan coat and the woman on the ground. In this footage, there are other people who stop and offer some measure of care for, to, or toward Eregbu. But the spectator mostly witnesses a stream of people who walk past and over Eregbu's body, only sometimes offering a passing glance at a black woman lying slack on the sidewalk. During the performance, Eregbu's body is simultaneously and dangerously hypervisible and invisible. We watch her, watch her body, which is also to watch and see her not being seen by the large number of the people moving past her, which could also be a way of describing the way that blackness is produced, and a blackened body may be held in the tension between blackness and being, being seen and *being not seen*.

Chicago is one of the most segregated cities in the United States and the footage captures a segregated response to Eregbu's punctuating (non)being and (non)presence. The white people walk on by. It is only apparently black people who break, pause, stop, turn, and *speak* with the woman on the ground, speech being emphasized because, although she is lying on the ground, her eyes are open and she will willingly speak to anyone willing to speak with her. But with the exception of a police officer, none of the people who express active attention toward Eregbu's presence, let alone speak with her, appear to be white, brown, or otherwise marked by race. There are plenty of white people who glance at the body for a moment, even hesitate. A small number of white women pause, but with the slightest assurance that Eregbu is okay (eye contact with Service-Rodriguez, a nervous glance at a black man handing out unrelated pamphlets to the side of the artist's body), or at least that someone else is handling the problem, these women move on. Surely the great number of people of color do just the same. But there is a relatively steady host of black people (at least the edited footage gives us this impression) who pause and hesitate to express concern or care for the woman on the ground.

A break, pause, stop, turn, speak: actions that interrupt the unspoken collective agreement dominating the surround to force a temporal and spatial rupture in which a visibly invisible body becomes acutely visible. Here, the passerby's interaction with (or in response to) Eregbu undoes the repertoire of actions through which the people of the city have silently agreed to not see or recognize the presence of her punctuating presence.[1] But this is also to say that the black people who break, pause, stop, turn and *speak* with Eregbu do what the rest of the people in the camera's frame do not or will not: they recognize her presence *within* the present. Speech again is emphasized because when these people stop to attend to and care for Eregbu, something else happens. They begin to talk to each other, to the man with the pamphlets, to Service-Rodriguez, to Eregbu herself. This is a practice of relation (of being with and in relation to each other) that can only happen within the time and space of a given present.

It is not that the break in the temporal and social routine of the surround pulls Eregbu's body back into a (white) present from which it has been banished. Instead, those who break, pause, stop, turn, or speak enter into the blackened time and space of (non)being and (non)presence emanating from Eregbu's body. This present, though forged through and against myriad histories of black life's negation, is still rich with the possibility for intraracial sociality, care, and self-recognition among and between black people. In other words, the present emanating from Eregbu's seemingly abject presence is itself a blackened time and space that fosters and facilitates performances of black care and as black power.

This chapter tells a story about blackness and being, black durational performance, black power and the powers that cohere in a blackened Now. Eregbu's performance, which grounds my analysis, embodies and articulates a body as that which is held and produced in the tense space between blackness and being, being seen and *being not seen*. In what follows, I ask how performance might be used to navigate the fraught and potentially foreclosed corporeal, spatial, visual, and above all temporal terrain through which blackness as (non)being and (non)presence emerges within the social by being banished from the presence of the present. Thus, to reiterate C. Riley Snorton's restatement of a famous statement by Fanon, "The problem considered here is one of time."[2]

In Eregbu's performance, the quite visibly present presence of a black woman is largely apprehended as if she were not there at all: she is in place by being no-place. The performance illustrates the way blackness and a black woman's body are always "out of place." Katherine McKittrick describes the out-of-place-ness of blackness as the result of sociogenic process through which the management of black female presence, itself overdetermined by a history of spatial displacement and bodily dispossession, "effectively, but not completely, displaces black geographic knowledge by assuming that black femininity is altogether knowable, unknowing, and expendable: she is seemingly in place by being out of place."[3] What Eregbu's performance reveals is that this despatialization of blackness and of the racialized body requires a concurrent process of differential temporalization. That is, the blackened may be out of space but it is also out of time.

When a body—spectacularly present in any range of corporeal forms, including race, gender, sex, sexuality, or ability—is both seen and not seen, it is phenomenally banished from both the space *and* time of the present. It is banished *from* the present. So while it has been often remarked that one of the major operations of racism, in the wake of slavery and colonization, has been to erase black pasts and continually foreclose black futures (and then legitimize both erasure and foreclosure), we are also facing the devastating effects of a social sphere in which black people (and blackness) are routinely denied access to the present. The denial of the present may be the most vicious of all temporal crimes against blackness. To live with a past that is under stubborn and willful erasure is to lose where you came from. To be denied the future through routine and systematic foreclosure is to lose the horizon of possibility. But to be denied the present is to be denied the grounds from which the future can be altered and the past reconstituted for better use. It is to lose all three as they collapse in upon a negated Now.

The project I describe here is not about recovering or recuperating blackness or the racialized body for a dominant, normative, or universal sense of time and space. Instead, I'm interested in how black performance generates its own spatial, temporal, and social material from the blackened grounds of (non)being and (non)presence. Eregbu's performance stages a practice of living in, lying in, yet somehow still *being* in a present that is denied and under erasure. With every person who passes her by, the overall effect of the performance is not the recovery of her presence, but more nearly a participation and confirmation of her body's tenuous (non)being and (non)presence as it lingers in the tension between blackness and being, being seen and *being not seen*. But this practice of living, lying, and being in the presence of (non)presence also generates a spatial and temporal field into which the other black people who break, pause, stop, turn, and speak can emerge and enter, giving way to new black powers that emerge from the type of blackened Now generated by Eregbu's performing presence.

I do not mean to suggest that the black powers I'm describing occur between and among black people in a fashion that is exclusive of relations with other minoritarian subjects who may be browned, racialized, (de)colonized, queer, and/or trans in their own stead. Service-Rodriguez's very presence in this performance suggests that the black powers referred to here are often relational to any range of minoritarian subjects living-in-difference. This essay's emphasis on intraracial acts of care between black people, underscored by Eregbu's edit of the filmic documentation of the performance, is simply meant to highlight an oft-elided truth: that black people have always been caring for each other from within the site of negation and that such acts of care (by, for, and between black people) consistently refuse the foreclosure of black life by performing black sociality as the negation of the negation.

The type of black power I'm describing thus owes a debt to Darieck Scott's theorization of a power counterintuitively emerging in and as a response to prevailing social conditions that produce blackness in and as abjection. In this form of black power, it is "the willed enactment of powerlessness that encodes a power of its own, in which pain or discomfort are put to multifarious uses."[4] Confronting oncoming foot traffic with the abject sight of a black woman's body lying slack on the sidewalk, Eregbu engages the sociogenic process through which a body is blackened, becoming a site of (non)being and (non) presence within a given social scenario. For Scott, following Fanon, sociogeny describes "the cultural construction of blackness": the social, cultural, and historical processes and practices through which blackness is made and, in the aftermath of colonization and slavery, is made as abject and powerless. To be blackened, in the Fanonian scheme, is to exist in the time after defeat, whether we are referring to the defeat wrought by colonization, slavery, and/or white supremacy's ongoing domination of, claim to, and hold over blackness and the blackened body in any range of local and global contexts.[5] In theorizing a mode of black power in and as abjection, Scott queries "whether it is also possible that even within Fanon's own account of a blackness-as-subjugation that must be abjured or surpassed, even within the lived experience of subjugation perceived to be at its worst, there are potential powers in blackness, uses that undermine or act against racist domination."[6]

Though performance studies has not always called upon the Fanonian vocabulary of "sociogeny" the field has produced a great deal of knowledge about the sociogenic process (i.e., the process through which subjects are made by, in, and for the social) and the powers inherent within it. Theorists of minoritarian performance and black performance (for example, Saidiya Hartman, José Muñoz, Karen Shimakawa, Daphne Brooks, or Tavia Nyong'o) have developed nuanced accounts of racial, sexual, and gender subject formation within and beyond the US context.[7] Such thinkers have produced a theoretical apparatus with a genealogy that may more accurately be traced to the work of black, feminist, and queer figures like Fanon, Du Bois, Judith Butler, Eve Sedgwick, or Hortense Spillers, than it is to the traditions of the mythical white fathers of the field (Schechner, Turner, Bacon, or Conquergood). This is a way of saying that the minoritarian branch of performance studies, genealogically rooted in the likes of Fanon, Du Bois, Spillers, Sedgwick, or Butler, has always already been producing a theory of the sociogenic process.

The theories of subject formation that commonly emerge within performance studies scholarship routinely emphasize the entanglements between embodiment, performance, and performativity, which has in turn generated a significant amount of thought about repetition, reproduction, and temporality. This emphasis produced a body of performance theory concerned with the iterative practices, embodied rituals, and "twice-behaved behaviors" that contribute to and reproduce the constitution of social reality along corporeal and social axes that include, but are not limited to, race, class, gender, sexuality, and ability. It has concurrently provided a conceptual toolbox with which intellectuals and artists of color have theorized the myriad ways minoritarian subjects navigate and remake reality by fostering and forging conditions of possibility where they are otherwise absent, while generating power from within spaces seemingly characterized by powerlessness.

In the work of thinkers like Shimakawa and Muñoz, who follow Butler and Shoshana Felman (and also Jacques Derrida and J. L. Austin), performativity and the iterative are theorized as embodied practices that produce social reality by drawing upon an accumulating and legitimating archive of repeated acts and utterances—iterations that are temporally marked by having recurred repeatedly in the past.[8] At the same time, and following Butler and Derrida's assertion that a performative utterance will necessarily issue a break with the context from which it draws its authority (or, per Felman and Austin, that every performative is predicated on its potential failure), performance theorists have shown performance to be a fecund site for minoritarian subjects to engage in the art of sociogeny by using performance to make and remake the self and others within a threatening and unsteady landscape that is overwhelmingly constrained by the limits of the here and now. This strand of thinking has often been conceived of as a discourse on futurity, in which the present is largely condemned for being a prime progenitor of minoritarian negation. But there are multiple valences to the present in minoritarian performance theory. It may be true that the pleasures of the moment are not all we have, but in the final instance, whether it is pleasurable or otherwise, the here and now are still the primary grounds of (and the most readily available grounds for) praxis and action.

Muñoz's work, and its reception, epitomize this fact. For Muñoz, the past (which plays a determinative role in constructing the limits defining and diminishing the minoritarian subject's present and presently available life chances) is both negotiated and disidentified with in the effort to survive a present that is both precarious and under erasure. At the same time, Muñoz insists that in performance (which has a unique relationship to the present and to presence) the minoritarian subject can work with the reconstructed material of the past in an attempt to construct a different and more livable future. The future-oriented horizon of utopia was, for Muñoz, less a destination than a temporal matter. That is, Muñozian utopia is not a place that one gets to, but a critical imaginary through which one critiques and survives the *damaging sociogenic forces of the past* and *the seemingly insurmountable insufficiencies of the present.* But this is only possible when utopia activates the powerful and creative sociogenic powers of the Now.

It is here that Muñoz's conception of "utopia" reveals its unavowed debt to Fanon, insofar as Fanon's project also describes a queer and nonlinear, even "counterlinear" temporality, characterized thus by Scott: "For Fanon, the present is *like* the past in its capacity to determine the future. In this sense, there is not only one past, forever lost to us but nevertheless enslaving present and future, but also the past being made (and ever receding) in the now, which, as future anterior, has the capacity retroactively to refigure even the more remote, traumatic past that we have no access to."[9] For Scott's Fanon, as for Muñoz, the present is the grounds on which the work of black and minoritarian survival and social transformation is carried out. For both, the body is a primary locus through which these acts can be achieved. It is curious, then, that much of the response to Muñoz's work has emphasized the futurity of "utopia" while dropping "cruising" from the equation altogether.

Cruising is, of course, a form of queer sexual performance that makes use of a corporeally charged Now to generate sexual futures from within an intensely fleshy present. As such, a consideration of the future-bound (utopia) without its anchor in present praxis (cruising) runs the risk of unmooring Muñoz's framing of utopia from his material concerns with the urgencies effecting, dulling, and diminishing queer of color lifeworlds in the here and now. That is, it steals from Muñoz's theory its politics and its critical goal of reconfiguring the past and mobilizing the future to survive, persist within, and transform the present.

To know that it is from the radical site of the Now that the alteration, determination, and remaking of possibility for both the past and future occur is to get a sense of the absolute dangers that inhere in the persistent and ongoing denial of the present for and to blackness, black people, black life, and the black body. It is also to gain a sense of the radical potentials (and responsibilities) for a performance theory that concerns itself with the temporality of the active and creative Now. By engaging performance's unique claim upon the present (a claim that I assert without affirming nor denying the Phelanian aphorism that performance's *only* life is in the present), Eregbu's durational performance documents the sociogenic process through which blackness coheres in the tension between blackness and being, being seen and *being not seen*.[10] It also affirms the sociogenic powers of black performance to generate conditions of possibility for and in the blackened present and from the grounds of a corporeal (non)presence and (non)being.

The sphere of performative behavior that reproduces the world anew each day coheres through routines and rituals that accumulate into performative reality, whereby a social fiction (that a body lying right in front of you is not, in fact, there) becomes a material fact. Eregbu's performance isn't merely critical of this process; it *participates* in it. The aesthetically heightened presence of her body on the sidewalk casts light on a disavowed but daily social ritual in most major US cities, whereby the routine act of walking by human beings (often racialized, poor, homeless, mentally ill, and/or impaired) in varying states of distress on the way to and from work and home is a part of the fabric of daily life that conditions people *to not see* that which is around them everywhere and every day. Indeed, these rituals train us to know what forms of life (often nonwhite and poor) are to be apprehended as disposable (non)presence, rather than beings worthy of care, which is to say, worthy of their presence within the present. But if Eregbu's performance participates in this process, she also interrupts it, staging temporal and social hiccups that open up altogether different and blackened possibilities for the time and space as they emanate from the (non)being and (non)presence of her performing body.

I borrow the language of the "hiccup" from Misty De Berry, whose thinking introduced me to Eregbu's work. De Berry argues that Eregbu's performance is predicated on a manipulation of the performative or sociogenic sphere of habituated, reiterated behaviors and affects that produce racialized and gendered realities. Eregbu's performance is thus conceived as a critical intervention in time: on the one hand, there is the work's repetitive staging of the routines and bodily rituals through which racism is reproduced as social reality and by which people do "not pause to make contact with a body, specifically a Black woman's body, lying in the middle of the sidewalk."[11] De Berry argues that in the temporal loop of the repetitive, embodied acts of passing by and over Eregbu, a social reality is affirmed and constituted in which "black women's bodies do not signal an ability to be grieved or recognized as worthy life in the general public imaginary."[12] But it is also by way of her punctuating presence, De Berry argues, that Eregbu also provokes a disruption in the temporal routines of daily life (minor hiccups in the social where, as is the case with the woman in the tan coat, hesitation and a glance give way to locution and communication between two black women). These temporal hiccups open up other possibilities of care and collectivity, giving way to new ways of being black and being together.

If Eregbu confronts the spectator with her body as (non)being and (non) presence with the potential to generate other times and spaces, the cumulative effect of watching people routinely and repeatedly refusing to see her illustrates Hortense Spillers's contention that (in "Western Culture")

> the "body" is neither *given* as an uncomplicated empirical rupture on the landscape of the human, nor do we ever actually "see" it. In a very real sense, the "body," insofar as it is an analytical construct, does not exist in person at all. When we invoke it, then, we are often confusing and conflating our own momentousness as address to the world, in its layered build-up of mortal complexities, with an idea on paper, only made vivid because we invest it with living dimensionality, mimicked, in turn, across the play of significations.[13]

Eregbu's performance does not so much confirm the presence of the body by placing it before the spectator, so much as we are given to witness the way that a particular type of body is apprehended *as if it were not* there. Presenting the body thus, the performance seems to confirm the theoretical paradox described by Spillers in which the blackened body (as a *being not seen*) can neither be "given" nor "seen" in its apparent presence, shuttling as it does between visibility and invisibility, subjecthood and objecthood, fixity and fugitivity, but somehow always just outside the time and space of the Now.

Eregbu's performance recalls Audre Lorde's description of the tense space black women in the United States occupy between hypervisiblity and invisibility: "Within this country where racial difference creates a constant, if unspoken, distortion of vision, black women have on the one hand always been highly visible, and so, on the other hand, have been rendered invisible through the depersonalization of racism."[14] This depersonalization occurs through forms of detemporalization and despatialization that structure the (in)visibility of Eregbu's blackened body. Now, the realm of visibility is something that black people (and other racial, social, and sexual minorities) cannot not want insofar as representation is commonly the grounds of political subjectivity, social recognition, and enfranchisement within the liberal order of the United States. Representation can be a prime means for making a claim to being in the present, which can be of vital necessity when this claim is under violent erasure. In very material ways, to be visible is to be a subject worthy of sustained attention and care—an assumption that undergirds the many and fraught debates over the stakes, necessity, power, and effects of political and aesthetic representation for/of raced, sexed, and gendered subjects. The assertion of visibility and the demand to be seen may be tied to the minoritarian subject's desire or need for sustained attention that confirms the presence of the seen as *more than* an object for apprehension rather than for flashing recognition, a quest to be confirmed as a subject with interiority, difference, and relational standing.

Durational performance often calls upon a spectator to sustain attention to the presence of the artist's body as it shares space and time with the spectator. Performance involves sharing a temporal and spatial present, so this presencing of the body through performance can be indicative of a certain desire to be beheld as a subject that is nonetheless rich with interior difference. In other words, to being a being of, for, and in the present. Following Fred Moten, "What one is after, by way of a certain sustenance of attention, is the presentness of the object in all of its internal difference, in all of its interiority and internal space."[15] As such a being claims time and place within a present generated by a performance, both spectator and artist may experience the forms of interiority and interior difference that characterize any being's experience of the present. As Kevin Quashie teaches us, this interior domain, defined as "quiet," has radical implications for black life insofar as quiet describes "a metaphor for the full range of one's inner life—one's desires, ambitions, hungers, vulnerabilities, fears"—a range that is often foreclosed and denied through the denial of black presence within and for the present.[16] But, importantly, the sustenance of attention, which might lead to the recognition of the subject's complex internal difference, or "quiet," is not necessarily the same thing as visibility, which can also lead to the subject's entrapment and foreclosure.

For the minoritarian subject, visibility is often achieved through what Rey Chow describes as coercive mimeticism, or what Hartman, Butler, and Louis Althusser separately theorize as the process of subjection.[17] By taking on and performing a recognizable subject position—by becoming subjects *for* the dominant ideology—the racialized subject may gain recognition within the realm of legal and social visibility. However, this often occurs by taking on a scripted or performatively produced role or identity that overwrites, displaces, flattens, or erases the complexity, richness, or quiet of the racialized subject's interior *and* exterior (social/relational) existence. Obscured behind the sign of socially recognizable identity she may be "rendered invisible through the depersonalization of racism," and cast outside of the ineffable space and time of her actually existing corporeal present.

The spaces between hypervisibility and invisibility, being and nonbeing, *being not seen* and presence without a present are the treacherous straits that black people have to navigate in order to survive, evade, go beyond, and make fugitive from the conditions assured by white supremacy in the United States. "For to survive in the mouth of this dragon we call America," wrote Lorde, "we have had to learn this first and most vital lesson—that we were never meant to survive. Not as human beings."[18] Lying on the ground, unworthy of sustained attention, Eregbu's body becomes a stage on which the people passing by may play out the sociogenic dynamics through which a visible subject becomes an invisible object with claim to neither the space nor time of the Now. When the body becomes visible as an object, the piece suggests, it may be seen, but not necessarily seen as a subject in space, of time, and *for* care. Indeed, the stillness and unmoving nature of Eregbu's pose suggest that if her body is seen, in this instance, it is often apprehended less as a subject than as object. Lying on the street, *she* becomes a *thing*.

Under these circumstances, the body may paradoxically become visible by occupying the recognizable (non)beingness of the thing, object, or commodity. Her visibility may thus be the grounds on which she is "rendered invisible through the depersonalization of racism," which is why, for Lorde, "Even within the women's movement, [black women] have had to fight, and still do, for that very visibility which also renders us most vulnerable, our Blackness."[19] Working through this contradiction, Lorde insists that "that visibility which makes us most vulnerable is that which also is the source of our greatest strength."[20] It is as the subject navigates this paradox from the place and time of the present that this strength can become a kind of black power.

Eregbu's presence on the sidewalk, her generation of the present from the site of (non)being and (non)presence, unmasks the "distortion of vision" that continues to render the abject black femme body spectacularly visible (recognizable, even, as an object or *thing* to be had) and simultaneously invisible (unrecognizable as a subject for or worthy of care). The radicality of Eregbu's performance lies not merely in the success of its documentation of the sociogenic process through which blackness is produced in and as abjection with a claim to neither the space nor time of the present. The work's power also lies in both its confirmation of the "interiority and internal space" of the artist and its staging of a conversation with the other people who enter into the Now the performance is generating.

If Eregbu looks inanimate, or looks dead, she is very much an alive, thinking, agential being: indeed, she is the subject who has arranged this entire scenario. At one point during the performance a young black man in a white T-shirt approaches Eregbu's accomplice, Service-Rodriguez, to ask about the performance. "She's acting like she's dead," the man notes, before Service-Rodriguez responds, "She's not acting like she's dead. If people ask her what's going on, she answers them." Though, as the artist lies on the ground, she may *seem* unconscious or living in living-death, she is in fact quite conscious, quite present, and able to speak with anyone (the woman in the tan coat, for example) who approaches to speak with her. Within the presence of Eregbu's blackened present, there can be no real question about the fact of her interiority or interior difference.

This opening to ethical relationality comes by way of Eregbu's paradoxical performance of objecthood, and my argument thus far owes a significant debt to Uri McMillan's theorization of the performance of objecthood in his genealogy of black feminist performance. For McMillan, performing objecthood becomes a condition for articulating and proliferating a range of possibilities for black life.[21] Indeed, we might locate Eregbu's performance in a genealogical relation with conceptual artist Adrian Piper, who also occupies a central place in McMillan's study.

In Piper's written accounts of her experience of the *Catalysis* works, she offers a direct means of speculating further on the contention that the radicality of a performance such as Eregbu's rests, in part, on the presentation of the black body both as an object in relation to other objects and as simultaneously a site of "interiority and internal space" that is not anathema to, but generated from within a blackened Now of (non)presence and (non)being. By drawing Piper into my discussion of Eregbu, I mean to gesture to a formal resemblance between their practice, which engages (in different ways) with the question of black (non)being as it surfaces within the time and space of a blackened present through performance. In the 1970s Piper undertook a transition from making discrete art objects to performances in which she became an art object. She undertook this transition in an attempt to amplify what she described as the catalytic powers of the art object, its ability to, as she wrote in 1970 "induce a reaction or change in the viewer. . . . The work is a catalytic agent, in that it promotes a change in another entity (the viewer) without undergoing any permanent change itself."[22] Throughout the 1960s, Piper became increasingly dissatisfied with the distance produced between the viewer's reaction and the discrete art object's catalytic potency. "The characteristics of any discrete form that occupies its own time and/or space apart from the artist limit the viewer's reaction to the work," she concluded, before turning to performance to close this gap: "The strongest, most complex, and most aesthetically interesting catalysis is the one that occurs in uncategorized, nonpragmatic human confrontation."[23] Her body thus became her medium and since, for Piper, museums and galleries further removed the art object from the world, containing and diminishing its catalytic affect, her actions could not occur within institutional art settings. They had to move out into the streets, which is to say that the works required the coterminous encounter between artist and spectator within the simultaneous space and time of the present.

Moten opens a reading of Piper's work by describing her as confronting the spectator's *unwillingness* to pay attention, as characterized in the act of the fleeting "glance." As with Eregbu, Piper's performance draws us to a critical set of questions: "What if the beholder glances," Moten writes, "glances away, driven by aversion as much as desire? This is to ask not only, what if beholding were glancing; it is also—or maybe even rather—to ask, what if glancing is the aversion of the gaze, a physical act of repression, the active forgetting of an object whose resistance is now not the avoidance but the extortion of the gaze?"[24] The glance, in this sense, is not *to see*, but the result of a labored effort *not* to see. The glance is to *avoid* seeing, to quickly forget how to see *what or who is right in front of you demanding to be seen.* Like Piper, Eregbu places her body in your path knowing, or maybe sensing, or perhaps worrying that you will pass by with little more than a glance. But unlike Eregbu, Piper gives us a window into the interior process undertaken by the artist in her navigation of Now.

In *Catalysis III* Piper walked through public space with a "Wet Paint" sign hung around her neck, and in *Catalysis IV*: "I dressed very conservatively but stuffed a large white bath towel into the sides of my mouth."[25] In these and other works, "my own aesthetic concerns remain unspoken: they are totally superseded by the audience's interpretation of my presence."[26] In other words, the work became itself as Piper became an object *for* the viewer, but also a *presence* within a shared present. As McMillan writes, for Piper and others: "Becoming objects [and] performing objecthood becomes an adroit method of circumventing prescribed limitations on black women in the public sphere while staging art and alterity in unforeseen places."[27] But as McMillan would likely agree, and as the unfolding scenario of *11/10/10* suggests, given the history of black objectification, the process of black performers becoming objects is not without its risks. Nor is it only a problem of place. It is also a problem of and for time.

The afterlife of slavery and colonization is such that the assumption of black objecthood, though a potential path beyond the "prescribed limitations on black women in the public sphere," may also reproduce and reinscribe social logics that characterize the racialized body as an object to be *held* by (white) power. As Christina Sharpe describes it, "Living in/the wake of slavery is living 'the afterlife of property' and living the afterlife of *partus sequitur ventrem* (that which is brought forth follows the womb), in which the Black child inherits the non-status, the non-being of the mother. That inheritance of a non-status is everywhere apparent *now* in the ongoing criminalization of Black women and children."[28] And, indeed, this "ongoing criminalization" surfaces throughout *11/10/10* as the threat of police interference encroaches upon the body of the woman on the sidewalk.

For De Berry, the glances and various points of hesitation embodied by different spectators who encounter Eregbu might suggest "breaks in the habitual body—a possible opening for alternative ways of being with one another, if only within the durational encounter of a hiccup" or of the performance.[29] But the performance also frames the limited range of options one may have at one's disposal by asking, quite plainly: What would *you* do if you encountered the unconscious body of a black woman lying on a public street? As the woman in the tan coat's conversation makes clear, there is a range of possible responses. One of these includes what is perhaps the most common choice: to alert the "proper" authorities.

At one point a black couple in black leather coats walk past Eregbu's body, pause, turn, and speak, stopping just past her body to make a telephone call. The man is looking around, as if he is trying to identify his location for the person on the other end of the line, before he approaches and disappears behind the stationary camera to speak with Service-Rodriguez:

MAN WITH CELLPHONE: You all filming this or something?

SERVICE-RODRIGUEZ: Yeah.

MAN WITH CELLPHONE: [*into phone*] Ok. Nevermind, police. Nevermind. Yeah, it's a film. I thought something was wrong. Ok. Alright. Bye-bye. [*to Service-Rodriguez*] What are you all doing? Tell me?

SERVICE-RODRIGUEZ: It's art.

MAN WITH CELLPHONE: It's art? Ok. 'Cause I looked and like, what's the matter now, it's shame [*inaudible*] let her lay in the streets and we'll call the police and get her some help.

SERVICE-RODRIGUEZ: Yeah, There's actually been a few people who tried to call the police. So there is some citizenry here.

Among other things, this exchange reveals the ease with which black life is placed on a trajectory toward the body being held in the hold of police power.

As De Berry notes, Service-Rodriguez's presence near the camera might relieve the potential discomfort caused by the disruptive punctum of Eregbu's body, contributing to the majority of people's choice to walk right past her. That is, Service-Rodriguez's presence might allow the spectator passing by to assume that there is some degree of "authority over a controlled environment."[30] At the level of speech, the man with the cellphone slightly displaces this assumption, ascribing collective authority to the work in a fashion that seems to encompass Eregbu ("*you all* filming this or something"). And though the work's status as "art" seemingly relieves the man of the ethical responsibility to intervene in the circumstances that have placed Eregbu's body in front of him, he implies that were it not "art," the readiest response was to "call the police and get her some help." Service-Rodriguez confirms this assumption, by describing the will to call the police as a performance of "citizenry," a chilling conception of citizenship given the violent history of police interaction with the black body in a place like Chicago.

In a 2016 US Department of Justice investigation of the Chicago Police Department, investigators described the routine means through which the Chicago police apprehend and engage with black and brown people as suffused with a "pattern or practice of misconduct and systemic deficiencies [that] has indeed resulted in routinely abusive behavior within CPD, especially towards black and Latino residents of Chicago's most challenged neighborhoods. Black youth told us that they are routinely called 'nigger,' 'animal,' or 'pieces of shit' by CPD officers. . . . One officer we interviewed told us that he personally has heard co-workers and supervisors refer to black individuals as monkeys, animals, savages, and 'pieces of shit.'"[31] Imagine, for a moment, that the body on the ground was not the body of an artist or that no cameras were present. Imagine she was passed out due to incapacitation, that she was unwell or nonresponsive. What could have happened to her? The CPD's record should give one pause regarding the wisdom of calling the police. Again, the Justice Department report is telling: "Consequently, all we know are the broad contours of terribly sad events—that officers used force against people in crisis who needed help."[32] This is one of the fundamental risks of Eregbu's performance of objecthood, (non)presence and (non)being, insofar as the performance might contribute to the desubjectification of her body and to her dehumanization to a status beneath "savage" or animal: not a living being to sense and to see, but a thing to have or hold in police custody.

At the conclusion of the thirteen-minute film documenting Eregbu's performance, Service-Rodriguez and the young man who asked if Eregbu was "acting like she's dead" are interrupted by the arrival of the police:

MAN IN WHITE SHIRT: She's acting like she's dead?

SERVICE-RODRIGUEZ: She's not acting like she's dead. If people ask her what's going on, she answers them. . . . [*seeing the police*] We're about to get busted up.

MAN IN WHITE SHIRT: Aw, get your ass up.

The gentleman's admonitions are detached and playful enough, but one can locate in this warning ("Aw, get your ass up") an expression of the kind of temporally reflective blackened consciousness that comes from the collective knowledge that "we were never meant to survive. Not as human beings." Indeed, black survival has long depended upon powers of anticipatory reflexivity, preparing for the imminent dangers posed by the future by way of a consciousness which is firmly rooted in the accumulation of the traumatic experiences of any host of antiblack pasts. As Scott emphasizes, Fanon describes this process by way of attention to the muscular spasms and tensions betrayed by the colonized subject. Where Fanon understands this muscular tension as the sedimented result of histories of abuse, it is also a means through which the colonized subject resists and thwarts that violence which is yet to come. Following Scott: "Muscle tension in Fanon is a state of death-in-life and life-in-death; it describes the paradox of a being who experiences utter defeat but who is nonetheless not fully defeated."[33] If calling the CPD may inadvertently become the means through which a body (still alive, though "acting like she's dead") accelerates a trajectory toward actual death, the call to stand in the present (to literally "get your ass up") might thus be reflective of a form of black power rooted in the recognition that defeat may be imminent, but that it may also be resisted from the radical space and time of a collective blackened present. His (perhaps hardened) expression of care for Eregbu's well-being is itself indicative of the forms of black power that surface as black people stand in the presence of the present to take care of each other and keep each other alive. But I am just as interested in the powers that we can locate in Eregbu's act of lying prone within, and generative of, this blackened Now.

Remember that even if the performer *seems* to be an object, or to be dead, "She's not acting like she's dead. If people ask her what's going on, she answers them." Eregbu is doubled many times over throughout the performance: she is both a performer acting as if she were immobile and a woman who is very much alive; she is in and out of space and time, a body suspended between object and subject, hypervisibility and invisibility, presence and absence, life-in-death and death-in-life. This doubling, and self-awareness of it, can be constitutive of a form of the uniquely black (double) consciousness described by Du Bois, Fanon, Spillers, and many others besides. For Fanon, such consciousness (the ego-splitting experience of seeing oneself as the white world sees you) is an experience of negation. "And then the occasion arose when I had to meet the white man's eyes," he writes. "Consciousness of the body is solely a negating activity" in part, because in meeting "the white man's eyes" the black subject may experience the negation of self by apprehending oneself (through the external subject's white eyes) as an object that is denied presence within the space and time of the white Other's present.[34] Performance, as Piper and Eregbu both demonstrate, can be a fruitful means for working through, with, and against negation, while generating forms of self- and collective consciousness that surface as the expression of the black powers inherent to a blackened present.

Reflecting on her catalytic performances, Piper, like Fanon, comes to experience a form of double consciousness. But unlike Fanon's it is a mode of consciousness that reveals the complex interaction between her interior world and apprehension by the exterior world, rather than the obliteration of the former by the latter. In other words, and through performance, Piper enters into a complex ("indexical") present in which her interior world enters into a congress with the time and space of her present surroundings, undoing the oppositions between self and other, object and subject, or even interior and exterior to open out onto a new plane of relational existence. This is the domain of being together and being with.

In one work, she performed a monologue on the street while attending to and indexing others' observations of her eccentric behavior. In another, she attempted to elicit as much information from her interlocutors on the street as possible, while giving away very little about herself. As the artist described these works, "I became aware of the extreme disparity between my inner self-image and the one they had of me. In [the first] it seems that I have pushed this disparity further; in [the latter] . . . I have done the opposite, attempting to assimilate as much of the consciousness of another into my own as possible."[35] This assimilation of the other does not negate Piper's experience of her internal life; however, it amplifies it, as occurred in another performance through which she introjected another's perception of her: "By assimilating an 'other' in my sense of self to the extent I did, I became increasingly reflective or self-conscious about my actions as object by myself."[36] In other words, Piper entered into a relationship with herself (and others) within the time and space of the present generated through her performance.

Here, Piper seems to be working through a problem that is at the heart of Spillers's inquiry regarding the relationship between "psychoanalysis" and "race." Spillers asks what might be learned by thinking "psychoanalysis" and "race" beside each other, a question that continues to remain a point of critical friction.[37] If black life is routinely apprehended through the body's reduction to a state of objecthood that lacks interiority and subjectivity, psychoanalytic theory (occupied as it is with the subject's shuttling between the interior and exterior worlds) poses unique possibilities and challenges for working through the social realities of race and racism. In Spillers's hands, psychoanalytic theory provides a vocabulary to describe self-interrogation and self-thought. This helps us to approach the critical question of how to open up the complex inner lives of black people to the realm of self-signification, language, and common relationality as they occur within the present. This is, as Spillers describes it, a "strategy for gaining agency": "I have chosen to call this strategy the *interior intersubjectivity*, which I would, in turn, designate as the locus at which *self-interrogation* takes place."[38] Black self-interrogation and intramural didacticism, as she notes, are the powerfully insurgent grounds of self-making. However, she insists that this practice of self-making need not be realized in the scene of (psycho)analytic encounter: "My interest in this ethical self-knowing wants to unhook the psychoanalytic hermeneutic from its rigorous curative framework and try to recover it in a free-floating realm of self-didactic possibility that might decentralize and disperse the knowing one."[39] Spillers concludes by reminding us that such powers and practices are already everywhere present in the commons of black language play and sociality. They are present, as well, in the blackened presents generated in and by Eregbu's and Piper's performances of objecthood, blackness, and (non)being.

Psychoanalysis's will to disclosure and its centralizing of a source of authority ("the knowing one," in which the analyst mirrors the overseer) may threaten the black subject with epistemological capture or, worse, a curative protocol that approaches blackness as pathology. But performance (as it was for Piper and as it is in *11/10/10*) offers a terrain on which we can produce and proliferate moments within the present where the enactment of black *interior intersubjectivity* can occur. Performance, in other words, allows for an experience of interior intersubjectivity that doesn't subject a black being to collection (or possession) by "the knowing one." Through Piper or Eregbu's performance, once more drawing upon Spillers, the artists "substitute an *agent* for a spoken-for, [becoming] a 'see-er,' as well as a 'seen.'"[40]

Performance can be the grounds for an ethical congress *between* black people and the world, constituted within the blackened present we see flickering into being throughout Eregbu's and Piper's performances. In Piper's account of her work, the present generated in and by performance is the grounds for an encounter with the self. That is, Piper came *to see herself* as if she were outside herself: "When I do a work in private, I perceive myself . . . through the eyes of the general audience, that is, the world in general, for whom an art object—myself—exists."[41] What's critical is not just the confirmation of Piper's existence, but also the recognition that this existence is bound up in the sphere of social relations *with other people*. By becoming an object for others' appraisal, she appraises herself as an object within a world of other objects.

Fanon describes this as the experience of "crushing objecthood" in which "I found that I was an object in the midst of other objects."[42] But for both Spillers and Piper, this realization can be the foundation for ethical relationality, even insurrectionary and emancipatory black collective consciousness. "At the very least," writes Spillers, "I am suggesting that an aspect of the emancipatory project hinges on what would appear to be simple-self-attention, except that reaching the articulation requires a process, that of making one's subjectness the object of a disciplined and potentially displaceable attentiveness."[43] Through the generation and proliferation of a blackened present, black performance creates a time and space on which the staging of a "disciplined and potentially displaceable attentiveness" to the self (and to others) becomes possible, opening up the possibility for the care of self and other from within its zone of instantiation. As Piper wrote, "The more I assimilate [the external world into myself], the more easily I am able to see myself as 'an object in the world among others.'"[44]

In the wake of what Moten describes as "the historical reality of commodities who spoke," for a black person to experience oneself as an "object in the midst of other objects" can certainly function as the experience of shattering negation (as it does for Fanon). But it might also be the most immediate grounds available on which one can stand and perform the work of affirming the intellectual and interior life of both self and other. It can be a means for opening up a present that is rich with the possibility for both self-interrogation *and* the generation of shared (blackened) consciousness on which the emancipatory project hinges.[45] This is less because Eregbu's and Piper's actions pursue a mythical future of recognition and restitution by grabbing for the attention of those who refuse, time and again, to see that which is right in front of them. Rather, such performances create sites for blackness to be and be within the Now, offering blackened objects in the midst of other objects the ability to interrogate both self and other.

This blackened Now is the grounds on which the subject can recognize in the interplay between self and other a vibrant, creative intersubjectivity rich with the powers of blackness. From within the Now generated within such performances, one "object" can and does indeed turn and speak to the other. Such a gesture marks the collective transition from, and refusal of, the silence of (non)being and (non)presence, giving way to common, uncontainable, and insurgent black speech, always at difference with itself from the inside out. It's a bodily thing, a collective thing, a kind of gesture that black people have always known how to perform as they (we) lay collective claim to and activate the long deferred Now from which all time and space is made, unmade, and remade *for* black life.

NOTES

This chapter began as a talk delivered at Brown University for the "Provoking Attention" conference (April 7–8, 2017) organized by Amanda Brown and David Russell. I am grateful to the organizers, participants, and attendees for their generative engagement with this material, as I am to participants in a workshop organized by the editors of this volume at Indiana University Bloomington on May 27, 2017, as well as the anonymous readers for this volume. Thanks also to Alexandria Eregbu, for her generosity of work and time, Misty De Berry for sharing her brilliant early work on Eregbu, and Ali Faraj for providing ace editorial support as I prepared the final manuscript.

1   As I discuss later, this approach to Eregbu's work is inspired by and in conversation with Misty De Berry, "Break, Flatten, Surge," 3.
2   Snorton, *Black on Both Sides*; Fanon, *Black Skin, White Masks*.
3   McKittrick, *Demonic Grounds*, xv.
4   Scott, *Extravagant Abjection*, 164.
5   Scott, *Extravagant Abjection*, 38.
6   Scott, *Extravagant Abjection*, 39.
7   Hartman, *Scenes of Subjection*; Muñoz, *Disidentifications*; Shimakawa, *National Abjection*; Brooks, *Bodies in Dissent*; Nyong'o, *Amalgamation Waltz*.
8   Felman, *Scandal of the Speaking Body*; Derrida, *Limited Inc.*; Butler, *Bodies That Matter*.
9   Scott, *Extravagant Abjection*, 52.
10 Phelan, *Unmarked*.
11 De Berry, "Break, Flatten, Surge," 3.
12 De Berry, "Break, Flatten, Surge," 3.
13 Spillers, "Peter's Pans," 21
14 Lorde, *Sister Outsider*, 42.
15 Moten, *In the Break*, 239.
16 Quashie, *Sovereignty of Quiet*, 6.
17 Hartman, *Scenes of Subjection*; Butler, *Psychic Life of Power*; Althusser, *On the Reproduction of Capitalism*; Chow, *Protestant Ethnic*, 95–127.
18 Lorde, *Sister Outsider*, 42.
19 Lorde, *Sister Outsider*, 42.
20 Lorde, *Sister Outsider*, 42.
21 McMillan, *Embodied Avatars*.

22 Piper, "Talking to Myself," 32.

23 Piper, "Talking to Myself," 42.

24 Moten, *In the Break*, 233.

25 Piper, "Talking to Myself," 42, 43.

26 Piper, "Talking to Myself," 47.

27 McMillan, *Embodied Avatars*, 7.

28 Sharpe, *In the Wake*, 15.

29 De Berry, "Break, Flatten, Surge," 5.

30 De Berry, "Break, Flatten, Surge," 3.

31 US Department of Justice, *Investigation*, 146.

32 US Department of Justice, *Investigation*, 37.

33 Scott, *Extravagant Abjection*, 72.

34 Fanon, *Black Skin, White Masks*, 110.

35 Piper, "Talking to Myself," 47.

36 Piper, "Talking to Myself," 50.

37 "How might psychoanalytic theories speak about 'race' as a self-consciously asser-
    tive reflexivity, and how might 'race' expose the gaps that psychoanalytic theories
    awaken?" Spillers, "'All the Things You Could Be by Now,'" 376.

38 Spillers, "'All the Things You Could Be by Now,'" 383.

39 Spillers, "'All the Things You Could Be by Now,'" 427.

40 Spillers, "'All the Things You Could Be by Now,'" 397.

41 Piper, "Talking to Myself," 52.

42 Fanon, *Black Skin/White Masks*, 109.

43 Spillers, "'All the Things You Could Be by Now,'" 400.

44 Piper, "Talking to Myself," 51. Here, it's worth noting that she not only echoes
    Fanon, but also Marx, when he writes that the "emancipation of the senses"
    through the abolition of private property would result in a social situation in
    which "the senses and minds of other men have become my *own* appropria-
    tion. . . . Thus, for instance, activity in direct association with others, etc., has
    become an organ for *expressing* my own *life*, and a mode of appropriating *human*
    life." Marx, *Economic and Philosophic Manuscripts*, 140.

45 Moten, *In the Break*, 6.

BIBLIOGRAPHY

Abraham, Nicolas, and Maria Torok. *The Shell and the Kernel.* Vol. 1. Chicago: University of Chicago Press, 1994.

Adam, Barbara. *Timewatch: The Social Analysis of Time.* Cambridge, UK: Polity, 1995.

Adams, Bluford. *E Pluribus Barnum: The Great Showman and the Making of U.S. Popular Culture.* Minneapolis: University of Minnesota Press, 1997.

Alexander, Leslie L. "Susan Smith McKinney, M.D., 1847–1918: First Afro-American Woman Physician in New York State." *Journal of the National Medical Association* 67, no. 2 (1975): 173–75.

Alexander, Michelle. *The New Jim Crow: Mass Incarceration in the Age of Colorblindness.* New York: New Press, 2010.

Alkebulan, Paul. *Survival Pending Revolution: The History of the Black Panther Party.* Tuscaloosa: University of Alabama Press, 2007.

Althusser, Louis. *On the Reproduction of Capitalism: Ideology and Ideological State Apparatuses.* Translated by G. M. Goshgarian. London: Verso, 2014.

Amato, Sarah. "The White Elephant in London: An Episode of Trickery, Racism and Advertising." *Journal of Social History* 43, no. 1 (2009): 31–66.

Andrésol, Mario. "Mise au point de Mario Andrésol." *Le Nouvelliste,* August 12, 2013.

Archer-Straw, Petrine. *Negrophilia: Avant-Garde Paris and Black Culture in the 1920s.* London: Thames and Hudson, 2000.

Arendt, Hannah. *The Human Condition.* 2nd ed. Chicago: University of Chicago Press, 1998.

The Armory Show. Accessed February 11, 2018. https://www.thearmoryshow.com /info/about-us.

"Attucks." Every Chicago Public School Is My School, May 5, 2013. https:// everyschoolismyschool.org/2013/05/05/attucks/.

"Attucks." School Cuts. http://www.schoolcuts.org/schools/5.

"Audra McDonald and George C. Wolfe Interview, TimesTalks." YouTube. Posted by Times Talk, February 26, 2016. https://www.youtube.com/watch?v=oJDbKo306d8.

Austin, Curtis J. *Up Against the Wall: Violence in the Making and Unmaking of the Black Panther Party.* Fayetteville: University of Arkansas Press, 2008.

Azor, Josué. "Documenting Spaces of Liberation in Haiti." In "Nou Mache Ansanm (We Walk Together): Queer Haitian Performance and Affiliation." Special issue, *Women and Performance: A Journal of Feminist Theory* 27, no. 2 (2017): 247–58.

Azor, Josué. Interview with Mario LaMothe. Port-au-Prince, Haiti. 2015.

Azor, Josué. "Noctambules." *Revue Trois/Cent/Soixante*, no. 2 (2017): 108–18.

Badhwar, Natasha. "Can't Compare Brutal Gang-Rape with Forced Oral Sex." *Outlook Magazine*, September 2016. https://www.outlookindia.com/magazine/story/cant -compare-brutal-gang-rape-with-forced-oral-sex/297766.

Baik, Crystal Mun-Hye. "MAGO and Communal Ritual as Decolonial Praxis: An Exchange with Dohee Lee." *Verge: Studies in Global Asias* 2, no. 2 (Fall 2016): 1–16.

Bailkin, Jordanna. *The Afterlife of Empire*. Berkeley: University of California Press, 2015.

Baker, Jean-Claude, and Chris Chase. *Josephine: The Hungry Heart*. New York: Cooper Square, 2001.

Baldwin, James. "My Dungeon Shook." In *Vintage Baldwin*, 3–9. New York: Vintage, 2004.

Baptist, Edward E. *The Half Has Never Been Told: Slavery and the Making of American Capitalism*. New York: Basic Books, 2014.

Baraka, Amiri (LeRoi Jones). "The Changing Same (R&B and New Black Music)." In *The Black Aesthetic*, edited by Addison Gayle, 118–31. Garden City, NY: Doubleday, 1971.

Baraka, Amiri (LeRoi Jones). *Home: Social Essays*. 1968. New York: Akashic, 2009.

Baraka, Amiri. (LeRoi Jones). *Slave Ship: A Historical Pageant*. [1967]. In *Crosswinds: An Anthology of Black Dramatists in the Diaspora*, edited by William B. Branch, 250–59. Bloomington: Indiana University Press, 1993.

Barr, William P. Introductory letter. *The Case for More Incarceration*. Washington, DC: US Department of Justice, 1992. National Criminal Justice Reference Service, NCJ-139583. https://www.ncjrs.gov/pdffiles1/Digitization/139583NCJRS.pdf.

Batiste, Stephanie Leigh. *Darkening Mirrors: Imperial Representation in Depression-Era African American Performance*. Durham, NC: Duke University Press, 2011.

Batson, Charles R. "Les 7 doigts de la main and Their Cirque: Origins, Resistances, Intimacies." In Leroux and Batson, *Cirque Global*, 99–121.

Baxi, Pratiksha. "'Carceral Feminism' as Judicial Bias: The Discontents around *State v. Mahmood Farooqui*." *Interdisciplinary Law*, no. 3 (October 2016): 1–34.

Bay-Cheng, Sarah. "Theater Is Media: Some Principles for a Digital Historiography of Performance." *Theater*, May 2012, 27–41.

Benjamin, Walter. "Theses on the Philosophy of History." In *Illuminations*, by Walter Benjamin, edited by Hannah Arendt, translated by Harry Zohn, 245–55. New York: Schocken, 1968.

Berger, Dan, Mariame Kaba, and David Stein. "What Abolitionists Do." *Jacobin*, August 24, 2017. https://www.jacobinmag.com/2017/08/prison-abolition-reform -mass-incarceration.

Bhabha, Homi K. "Of Mimicry and Man: The Ambivalence of Colonial Discourse." In *The Location of Culture*, 85–92. New York: Routledge, 1994.

Bhalla, Angad Singh, dir. *Herman's House*. PBS, 2012.

"Black Panther Rally at Bobby Hutton Memorial Park." KPFA Berkeley: Pacifica Radio Archives, November 14, 1969.

Blank Noise website. http://blog.blanknoise.org. Accessed January 28, 2020.

Blaylock, Reed, Nimisha Patil, Timothy Greer, and Shrikanth Narayanan. "Sounds of the Human Vocal Tract." Paper presented at Interspeech 2017, August 20–24, 2017, Stockholm, Sweden, 2287–91.

Bloom, Joshua, and Waldo E. Martin Jr. *Black against Empire: The History and Politics of the Black Panther Party*. Berkeley: University of California Press, 2013.

Boddy, Kasia. *Boxing: A Cultural History*. London: Reaktion, 2008.

Bogdan, Robert. *Freak Show: Presenting Human Oddities for Amusement and Profit*. Chicago: University of Chicago Press, 1988.

Boudreault, Françoise. "Le cirque parlant des 7 doigts de la main." *Jeu* 145, no. 4 (2012): 125–33.

Bradley, Rizvana. "Going Underground: An Interview with Simone Leigh." *Art in America*, August 20, 2015. http://www.artinamericamagazine.com/news-features /interviews/going-underground-an-interview-with-simone-leigh/.

"Bring in 'da Noise, Bring in 'da Funk." Internet Broadway Database. Accessed December 10, 2018. https://www.ibdb.com/broadway-production/bring-in-da -noise-bring-in-da-funk-4789.

Broadway Advocacy Coalition. December 10, 2018. http://www .bwayadvocacycoalition.org/.

Brooks, Andrew. "Glitch/Failure: Constructing a Queer Politics of Listening." *Leonardo Music Journal*, no. 25 (December 2015): 37–40.

Brooks, Daphne. *Bodies in Dissent: Spectacular Performances of Race and Freedom, 1850–1910*. Durham, NC: Duke University Press, 2006.

Brooks, Daphne, and Roshanak Kheshti. "The Social Space of Sound." *Theatre Survey* 52 no. 2 (November 2011): 329–35.

Brooks, Peter. "Melodrama, Body, Revolution." In *Melodrama: Stage Picture Screen*, edited by Jacky Bratton, Jim Cook, and Christine Gledhill, 11–24. London: British Film Institute, 1994.

Brown, DeNeen L. "Olivia Hooker, One of the Last Survivors of the 1921 Tulsa Race Massacre, Dies at 103." *Washington Post*, November 22, 2018.

Brown, DeNeen L. "They Was Killing Black People." *Washington Post*, September 28, 2018.

Brown, Elaine. *Seize the Time*. Vault Records, 1969.

Brown, Jayna. *Babylon Girls: Black Women Performers and the Shaping of the Modern*. Durham, NC: Duke University Press, 2008.

Brown, Karen McCarthy. "Afro-Caribbean Spirituality: A Haitian Case Study." In *Vodou in Haitian Life and Culture: Invisible Powers*, edited by Claudine Michel and Patrick Bellegarde-Smith, 1–26. New York: Palgrave, 2006.

Brown, Ross. *Sound: A Reader in Theatre Practice*. New York: Palgrave, 2009.

Brown, Wendy, and Janet Halley. *Left Legalism/Left Critique*. Durham, NC: Duke University Press, 2003.

Buckley, Cara. "A Life Celebrated, and a City Criticized." *New York Times*, July 7, 2008.

Butler, Judith. *Bodies That Matter: On the Discursive Limits of "Sex."* New York: Routledge, 1993.

Butler, Judith. *Gender Trouble: Feminism and the Subversion of Identity*. New York: Routledge, 2006.

Butler, Judith. *The Psychic Life of Power: Theories in Subjection*. Stanford, CA: Stanford University Press, 1997.

Campt, Tina. *Listening to Images*. Durham, NC: Duke University Press, 2017.

Canadian Multiculturalism Act. R.S.C. 1985, c. 24. https://laws-lois.justice.gc.ca/eng /acts/C-18.7/page-1.html#h-1.

Carleton, Mark T. *Politics and Punishment: The History of the Louisiana State Penal System*. Baton Rouge: Louisiana State University Press, 1971.

Carlson, Marvin A. *The Haunted Stage: The Theatre as Memory Machine*. Ann Arbor: University of Michigan Press, 2002.

"Carol Becker in Conversation with Theaster Gates." In *Theaster Gates*, edited by Achim Borchardt-Hume, Carol Becker, and Lisa Yun Lee, 7–38. New York: Phaidon, 2015.

Carroll, Shana, and Sébastien Soldevila, dirs. *Sept doigts de la main, Cuisine et confessions*. 2014. http://medias.7doigts.ca:8080/pages/view.php?ref=7568&k =89a07ed5e2.

Caruth, Cathy. *Unclaimed Experience: Trauma, Narrative, and History*. Baltimore, MD: Johns Hopkins University Press, 1996.

Casillas, Inés. *¡Sounds of Belonging: U.S. Spanish-Language Radio and Public Advocacy!* New York: New York University Press, 2014.

Chambers-Letson, Joshua. "Reparative Feminisms, Repairing Feminism—Reparation, Postcolonial Violence, and Feminism." *Women and Performance: A Journal of Feminist Theory* 16, no. 2 (2006): 169–89.

Chang, Jeff. *Can't Stop Won't Stop: A History of the Hip-Hop Generation*. New York: Macmillan, Picador, 2005.

Chang, Jeff. *Total Chaos: The Art and Aesthetics of Hip-Hop*. New York: Civitas, 2007.

Cheng, Anne Anlin. *Second Skin: Josephine Baker and the Modern Surface*. New York: Oxford University Press, 2011.

Cho, Oh-Kon. *Traditional Korean Theatre*. Fremont, CA: Asian Humanities Press/ Jain, 1988.

Choi, N. *Josen Sang-sik Mun-dab* [Questions and Answers on the Joseon Dynasty]. Seoul: Dongmyungsa, 1946.

Chon, Kyong-uk. *Korean Mask Dance Dramas: Their History and Structural Principles*. Translated by Do-seon Ur. Paju-si: Youlhwadang, 2005.

Chow, Rey. *The Protestant Ethnic and the Spirit of Capitalism*. New York: Columbia University Press, 2002.

Christian, Nichole M. "Hidden in Brooklyn, a Bit of Black History; Freedmen's Homes Seen as Attraction." *New York Times*, October 29, 2001.

Christie, Nils. *Crime Control as Industry*. New York: Routledge, 2000.

Christol, Hélène. "Writing History: Time and Event in Bobby Seale's *Seize the Time*." In *Incidences de l'événement: Enjeux et résonances du mouvement des droits civiques*, edited by Hélène Le Dantec-Lowry and Claudine Raynaud. Tours: Presses universitaires François-Rabelais, 2007. http://books.openedition.org/pufr/5516.

Chude-Sokei, Louis Onuorah. *The Sound of Culture: Diaspora and Black Technopoetics*. Middletown, CT: Wesleyan University Press, 2016.

Clark, Emily. Email correspondence with Catherine M. Young, October 13, 2018.

Clemons, Michael L., and Charles E. Jones. "Global Solidarity." In *Liberation, Imagination, and the Black Panther Party: A New Look at the Panthers and Their Legacy*, edited by Kathleen Cleaver and George Katsiaficas, 20–39. New York: Routledge, 2001.

Colbert, Soyica Diggs. *Black Movements: Performance and Cultural Politics*. New Brunswick, NJ: Rutgers University Press, 2017.

Coleman, Kevin. "Practices of Refusal in Images: An Interview with Tina M. Campt." *Radical History*, no. 132 (2018): 209–19.

Conquergood, Dwight. *Cultural Struggles: Performance, Ethnography, Praxis*. Ann Arbor: University of Michigan Press, 2016.

Conquergood, Dwight. "Of Caravans and Carnivals: Performance Studies in Motion." *TDR: The Drama Review* 39, no. 4 (Winter 1995): 26–31.

Cooke, Alistair. *Letter from America, 1946–2004*. New York: Knopf, 2004.

Cooper, Brittney. "The Racial Politics of Time." October 2016. *TEDWomen*. https://www.ted.com/talks/brittney_cooper_the_racial_politics_of_time?language=en.

Cruz, Carlos Alexis. "Contemporary Circus Dramaturgy: An Interview with Louis Patrick Leroux." *Theatre Topics* 24, no. 3 (2014): 269–73.

Cummings, Jack, dir. *Crazy House*. Metro-Goldwyn-Mayer Studios, 1930.

Danticat, Edwidge. *Create Dangerously: The Immigrant Artist at Work*. Princeton, NJ: Princeton University Press, 2010.

Danticat, Edwidge. *Krik? Krak!* 20th ed. New York: Soho Press, 2015.

Davis, Angela Y. *Are Prisons Obsolete? An Open Media Book*. New York: Seven Stories, 2003.

Davis, Janet M. *The Circus Age: Culture and Society under the American Big Top*. Chapel Hill: University of North Carolina Press, 2002.

Davis, Samara. "Room for Care: Simone Leigh's *Free People's Medical Clinic*." *TDR: The Drama Review* 59, no. 4 (Winter 2015): 169–76.

Dayan, Colin [Joan]. *The Law Is a White Dog: How Legal Rituals Make and Unmake Persons*. Princeton, NJ: Princeton University Press, 2011.

De Berry, Misty. "Break, Flatten, Surge: Durational Performance and the Unlearning of Habitual Affect." Unpublished manuscript 2017.

Debord, Guy. *Society of the Spectacle*. London: Black and Red, 2002.

DeFrantz, Thomas F. "The Black Beat Made Visible: Hip Hop Dance and Body Power." In *Of the Presence of the Body: Essays on Dance and Performance Theory*, edited by André Lepecki, 64–81. Middletown, CT: Wesleyan University Press, 2004.

DeFrantz, Thomas F. "Black Bodies Dancing Black Culture—Black Atlantic Transformations." Foreword to *EmBODYing Liberation: The Black Body in American Dance*, edited by Dorothea Fischer-Hornung and Alison D. Goeller, 11–16. Munich: Lit, 2001.

Deleuze, Gilles. *Difference and Repetition*. New York: Columbia University Press, 1994.

Deleuze, Gilles, and Felix Guattari. *A Thousand Plateaus: Capitalism and Schizophrenia*. Minneapolis: University of Minnesota Press, 1987.

Demme, Jonathan, dir. and writer. *The Agronomist*. Produced by Jonathan Demme, Edwidge Danticat, Bevin McNamara, and Peter Saraf. New York: THINKFilm, 2003.

"The Demographics of the Broadway Audience, 2015–2016 Season." Broadway League, 2017. https://www.broadwayleague.com/research/research-reports/.

Derrida, Jacques. *Limited Inc*. Evanston, IL: Northwestern University Press, 1988.

Diamond, Elin. Introduction to *Performance and Cultural Politics*, 1–14. London: Routledge, 1996.

Dinerstein, Joel. *Swinging the Machine: Modernity, Technology, and African American Culture between the World Wars*. Amherst: University of Massachusetts Press, 2003.

Dolan, Jill. *Utopia in Performance: Finding Hope at the Theater*. Ann Arbor: University of Michigan Press, 2005.

Dominique, Jean L. "Lougawou ou pas lougawou?" Soundcloud, January 14, 1976. Posted by RadioHaitiArchives. https://soundcloud.com/radiohaitiarchives/lougawou-ou-pas-lougawou-jean-l-dominique-14-janvier-1976.

Drewal, Henry John, and Margaret Thompson Drewal. *Gelede: Art and Female Power among the Yoruba*. Indianapolis: Indiana University Press, 1983.

Du Bois, W. E. B. *The Souls of Black Folk*. 1903. New York: Penguin, 1989.

Ducker, Eric. "Behind the Scenes of Flying Lotus' 'Never Catch Me' Video with Director Hiro Murai." *Fader*, October 9, 2014. http://www.thefader.com/2014/10/09/flying-lotus-never-catch-me-behind-the-scenes-hiro-murai.

Dunkley, Charles. "Joe Louis Stops Levinsky in First Round." *Twin Falls Daily News*, August 8, 1935. http://access.newspaperarchive.com/Viewer/fullpagepdfviewer?img=170005118.

Durban-Albrecht, Erin L. "Performing Postcolonial Homophobia: A Decolonial Analysis of the 2013 Public Demonstrations against Same-Sex Marriage in Haiti." In "Nou Mache Ansanm (We Walk Together): Queer Haitian Performance and Affiliation." Special issue, *Women and Performance: A Journal of Feminist Theory* 27, no. 2 (2017): 160–75.

Dutt, Bishnupriya. "Performing Resistance with Maya Rao: Trauma and Protest in India." *Contemporary Theatre Review* 25, no. 3 (July 2015): 371–85.

Edelman, Lee. *No Future: Queer Theory and the Death Drive*. Durham, NC: Duke University Press, 2004.

Eidsheim, Nina Sun. *The Race of Sound: Listening, Timbre, and Vocality in African American Music*. Durham, NC: Duke University Press, 2019.

Elam, Harry J., Jr. *Taking It to the Streets: The Social Protest Theater of Luis Valdez and Amiri Baraka*. Ann Arbor: University of Michigan Press, 1997.

Emery, Lynn Fauley. *Black Dance: From 1619 to Today*. Hightstown, NJ: Princeton Book, 1998.

Enck-Wanzer, Darrel, ed. *The Young Lords: A Reader*. New York: New York University Press, 2010.

Encyclopedia of Korean Folk Literature. Seoul: National Folk Museum of Korea, 2014.

Eng, David L. "Colonial Object Relations." *Social Text* 34, no. 1 (March 1, 2016): 1–19.

Evans, Orrin C. "Joe Louis Revenge: Harlem Hits the Top and 'Blows Lid Off' after Louis Victory." *Philadelphia Tribune*, June 23, 1938.

Facio, Elisa, and Irene Lara, eds. *Fleshing the Spirit: Spirituality and Activism*. Kindle Edition. Tucson: University of Arizona Press, 2014.

Fanon, Frantz. *Black Skin, White Masks*. Translated by Richard Philcox. New York: Grove, 1952.

Farmer, Paul. *AIDS and Accusation: Haiti and the Geography of Blame*. Updated ed. with a new preface. Berkeley: University of California Press, 1992.

Federal Bureau of Investigation. Memo. FBI Director to All Offices, on Counter-Intelligence Program, Black Nationalist Hate Groups, Internal Security, August 25, 1967. *The Counter-Intelligence Program of the FBI*. Microfilm, 30 reels. Wilmington, DE: Scholarly Resources, 1978.

Federal Bureau of Investigation. Memo. G. C. Moore to W. C. Sullivan, on Counter-Intelligence Program, Black Nationalist Hate Groups, Racial Intelligence, May 14, 1970. *The Counter-Intelligence Program of the FBI*. Microfilm, 30 reels. Wilmington, DE: Scholarly Resources, 1978.

Felman, Shoshana. *The Scandal of the Speaking Body: Don Juan with J. L. Austin, or Seduction in Two Languages*. Stanford, CA: Stanford University Press, 2003.

Ferguson, Roderick. *Aberrations in Black: Toward a Queer of Color Critique*. Minneapolis: University of Minnesota Press, 2004.

Ferguson, Roderick. *The Reorder of Things: The University and Its Pedagogies of Minority Difference*. Minneapolis: University of Minnesota Press, 2012.

Fernandez, Johanna. "Between Social Service Reform and Revolutionary Politics: The Young Lords, Late Sixties Radicalism, and Community Organizing in New York City." In *Freedom North: Black Freedom Struggles outside the South, 1940–1980*, edited by Jeanne Theoharis and Komozi Woodard, 255–85. New York: Palgrave Macmillan, 2003.

Fernandez, Johanna. "The Young Lords: Its Origins and Convergences with the Black Panther Party." Sonja Hayes Stone Center for Black Culture and History. Accessed June 5, 2017. http://www.ibiblio.org/shscbch/ribb/lords.

Fernandez, Johanna. "The Young Lords and the Social and Structural Roots of Late Sixties Urban Radicalism." In *Civil Rights in New York City: From World War II to the Giuliani Era*, edited by Clarence Taylor, 141–60. New York: Fordham University Press, 2011.

Fischer-Lichte, Erika. *The Transformative Power of Performance: A New Aesthetics.* New York: Routledge, 2008.

Flatley, Jonathan. *Affective Mapping: Melancholia and the Politics of Modernism.* Cambridge, MA: Harvard University Press, 2008.

Flying Lotus, featuring Kendrick Lamar. "Never Catch Me." *You're Dead.* Warp Records, 2014.

Fong, Adam. "Dohee Lee: Chapter One." Herb Alpert Award in the Arts, March 9, 2016. http://herbalpertawards.org/artist/chapter-one-5.

Fong, Adam. "Dohee Lee: Chapter Two." Herb Alpert Award in the Arts, March 9, 2016. http://herbalpertawards.org/artist/chapter-two-5.

Foster, Susan Leigh. *Choreographing Empathy: Kinesthesia in Performance.* New York: Routledge, 2011.

Freccero, Carla. "Queer Times." *South Atlantic Quarterly* 106, no. 3 (July 1, 2007): 485–94.

"Free People's Medical Clinic." Vimeo. Posted by Simone Leigh, 2015. https://vimeo .com/117195615.

French, Howard W. "South Koreans Seek Truth about '48 Massacre." *New York Times,* October 24, 2001.

Freud, Sigmund. *Beyond the Pleasure Principle.* Translated by James Strachey. New York: Norton, 1961.

Freud, Sigmund. *Wild Analysis.* London: Penguin, 2003.

Fricker, Karen. "Cuisine and Confessions a Little Undercooked: Review." *Toronto Star,* November 3, 2016.

Fricker, Karen. "'Somewhere between Science and Legend': Images of Indigeneity in Robert Lepage and Cirque du Soleil's *Totem.*" In Leroux and Batson, *Cirque Global,* 140–60.

Garner, Stanton B., Jr. "Sensing Realism: Illusionism, Actuality, and the Theatrical Sensorium." In *The Senses in Performance,* edited by Sally Banes and André Lepecki, 115–22. London: Routledge, 2009.

Gaur, K. D. *Textbook on Indian Penal Code.* 4th ed. New Delhi: Universal Law, 2011.

George-Graves, Nadine. "'Just Like Being at the Zoo': Primitivity and Ragtime Dance." In *Ballroom, Boogie, Shimmy Sham, Shake: A Social and Popular Dance Reader,* edited by Julie Malnig, 55–71. Urbana: University of Illinois Press, 2009.

Ghosh, Bishnupriya. "Performing Resistance with Maya Rao: Trauma and Protest in India." *Contemporary Theatre Review* 25, no. 3 (2015): 371–85.

Gibson, Bill. "Louis, Uncrowned Champ by Victory over Max Baer." *Baltimore Sun*, September 28, 1935.

Gilmore, Ruth Wilson. *Golden Gulag: Prisons, Surplus, Crisis, and Opposition in Globalizing California*. Berkeley: University of California Press, 2007.

Gilroy, Paul. *The Black Atlantic: Modernity and Double-Consciousness*. Cambridge, MA: Harvard University Press, 1993.

Gioia, Michael. "Why Black Lives Matter, Especially to Broadway." *Playbill*, August 2, 2016. http://www.playbill.com/article/why-black-lives-matter-especially-to-broadway.

Glissant, Édouard. *Poetics of Relation*. Translated by Betsy Wing. Ann Arbor: University of Michigan Press, 1996.

Gómez-Cruz, Roy. Correspondence with Katherine Zien, May 7, 2017.

Gordon, Avery. *Ghostly Matters: Haunting and the Sociological Imagination*. Minneapolis: University of Minnesota Press, 2008.

Gosa, Travis L., and Erik Nielson, eds. *The Hip Hop and Obama Reader*. New York: Oxford University Press, 2015.

Gottschild, Brenda Dixon. *Digging the Africanist Presence in American Performance: Dance and Other Contexts*. New York: Praeger, 1998.

Graver, David. "The Actor's Bodies." *Text and Performance Quarterly* 17, no. 3 (1997): 221–35.

Green, Jesse. "The Anxiety and the Ecstasy." *New York Magazine*, March 7–20, 2016.

Grossman, Wendy A. *Man Ray, African Art, and the Modernist Lens*. Washington, DC: International Art and Artists, 2009.

Gupta, Hemangini. "One Night Stand on the Streets." *The Hindu* (Bangalore), July 12, 2005. http://www.thehindu.com/thehindu/mp/2005/07/12/stories/2005071200450400.htm.

Gupta, Hemangini. "Taking Action: The Desiring Subjects of Neoliberal Feminism in India." *Journal of International Women's Studies* 17, no. 1 (January 2016): 152–68.

Guterl, Matthew Pratt. *Josephine Baker and the Rainbow Tribe*. Cambridge, MA: Belknap Press of Harvard University Press, 2014.

Haas, Jeffrey. *The Assassination of Fred Hampton: How the FBI and the Chicago Police Murdered a Black Panther*. Chicago: Chicago Review Press, 2011.

Haksar, Nandita. "Human Rights Lawyering: A Feminist Perspective." In *Writing the Women's Movement: A Reader*, edited by Mala Khullar, 131–51. New Delhi: Zubaan, 2005.

Hall, Stuart. "Cultural Identity and Diaspora." In *Colonial Discourse and Post-Colonial Theory: A Reader*, edited by Patrick Williams and Laura Chrisman, 392–403. New York: Columbia University Press, 1994.

Halley, Janet E. *Split Decisions: How and Why to Take a Break from Feminism*. Princeton, NJ: Princeton University Press, 2006.

Hanchard, Michael. "Afro-Modernity: Temporality, Politics, and the African Diaspora." *Public Culture* 11, no. 1 (1999): 245–68.

Hanson, Ellis. "The Future's Eve: Reparative Reading after Sedgwick." *South Atlantic Quarterly* 110, no. 1 (2011): 101–19.

Harker, Brian. "Louis Armstrong, Eccentric Dance, and the Evolution of Jazz on the Eve of Swing." *Journal of the American Musicology Society* 61, no. 1 (Spring 2008): 67–121.

"Harlem Celebrants Toss Varied Missiles." *New York Times*, June 23, 1938.

Harney, Stefano, and Fred Moten. *The Undercommons: Fugitive Planning and Black Study*. Brooklyn, NY: Minor Compositions, 2013.

Hartman, Saidiya V. *Lose Your Mother: A Journey along the Atlantic Slave Route*. New York: Farrar, Straus and Giroux, 2008.

Hartman, Saidiya V. *Scenes of Subjection: Terror, Slavery, and Self-Making in Nineteenth-Century America*. New York: Oxford University Press, 1997.

Hartman, Saidiya V. "Venus in Two Acts." *Small Axe* 12, no. 2 (2008): 1–14.

Harvie, Jen, and Erin Hurley. "States of Play: Locating Québec in the Performances of Robert Lepage, Ex Machina, and the Cirque Du Solei." *Theatre Journal* 51, no. 3 (October 1999): 299–315.

Hazzard-Gordon, Katrina. *Jookin': The Rise of Social Dance Formations in African-American Culture*. Philadelphia: Temple University Press, 1990.

Herrera, Brian Eugenio. "I Was a Teenaged Fabulist: The Dark Play of Adolescent Sexuality in U.S. Drama." *Modern Drama* 53, no. 3 (2010): 332–49.

Herrera, Patricia, and Marci McMahon. "¡Oye, Oye!: A Manifesto for Listening to Latinx Theater." *Aztlán: A Journal of Chicano Studies* 44, no. 1 (Spring 2019): 239–48.

Hershberg, Marc. "Audra McDonald Stars in New Lawsuit." *Forbes*, November 14, 2016.

Hershberg, Marc. "New Claims in Audra McDonald Case." *Forbes*, December 24, 2016.

Hill, Constance Valis. *Tap Dancing America: A Cultural History*. Oxford: Oxford University Press, 2014.

History.com Editors. "Police Kill Two Members of the Black Panther Party." History (A&E Television Networks). November 13, 2009. https://www.history .com/this-day-in-history/police-kill-two-members-of-the-black-panther -party.

Hoby, Hermione. "Storyboard P: 'I'm Pretty Animated, Y'Know?'" *Guardian* (London), April 12, 2014.

Holland, Sharon Patricia. *Raising the Dead: Readings of Death and (Black) Subjectivity*. Durham, NC: Duke University Press, 2000.

"Homeless Children Are 8% of 31,438 Students Impacted by Chicago Public Schools' Closing/Merger Plans." Chicago Coalition for the Homeless, May 22, 2013. https://www.chicagohomeless.org/cpsclosures/.

Honig, Bonnie. "Antigone's Two Laws: Greek Tragedy and the Politics of Humanism." *New Literary History* 41, no. 1 (Winter 2010): 1–33.

"How Amber Iman Created Broadway for Black Lives Matter and Broadway Advocacy Coalition." YouTube. Posted by NewYorkTheater, January 29, 2017. https://www.youtube.com/watch?v=MdA_B_95sMA&feature=youtu.be.

Howard, Rachel. "'ARA Gut': South Korea Roots Move Dancer Dohee Lee." *SFGate*, January 15, 2014. http://www.sfgate.com/performance/article/ARA-Gut-South-Korea-roots-move-dancer-Dohee-Lee-5146167.php#photo-5706524.

Hughes, Amy E.. *Spectacles of Reform: Theater and Activism in Nineteenth-Century America*. Ann Arbor: University of Michigan Press, 2012.

Hughes, Langston. *The Big Sea: An Autobiography*. New York: Hill and Wang, 1940.

Hurley, Erin. "The Multiple Bodies of Cirque du Soleil." In Leroux and Batson, *Cirque Global*, 71–78.

Hurston, Zora Neale. "How It Feels to Be Colored Me." In *Folklore, Memoirs, and Other Writings*, edited by Cheryl A. Wall, 826–29. New York: Library of America, 1995.

IGLHRC (International Gay and Lesbian Human Rights Commission) and Fondation SEROvie. *The Impact of the Earthquake and Relief and Recovery Program on Haitian LGBT People*. New York: OutRight Action International, 2011.

Iman, Amber. Interview with Catherine M. Young. April 2017.

Jacobs-Jenkins, Branden. *An Octoroon*. New York: Dramatists Play Service, 2015.

Jeffries, Judson L., ed. *The Black Panther Party in a City near You*. Athens: University of Georgia Press, 2018.

Jeffries, Judson. *Huey P. Newton: The Radical Theorist*. Jackson: University Press of Mississippi, 2002.

Jeffries, Judson L., ed. *On the Ground: The Black Panther Party in Communities across America*. Jackson: University Press of Mississippi, 2010.

Jones, Charles E., ed. *The Black Panther Party Reconsidered*. Baltimore, MD: Black Classic Press, 1998.

Judge, Monique. "Fred Hampton's Death Is Just One Example of the Government's Covert Disruption of Black Lives." *The Root*. December 4, 2018. https://www.theroot.com/fred-hampton-is-just-one-example-of-the-states-history-1830865895.

Jules-Rosette, Bennetta. *Josephine Baker in Art and Life: The Icon and the Image*. Urbana: University of Illinois Press, 2007.

Kapur, Ajay, Manj Benning, and George Tzanetakis. "Query-by-Beatboxing: Music Retrieval for the DJ." In *Proceedings of the Fifth International Conference on Music Information Retrieval*. Barcelona, Spain, October 2004, 170–77.

Karikis, Mikhail. "Artist's Statement: The Vanishing Community of Haenyeo All-Women Seaworkers on a Pacific Island." Culture24, November 6, 2015. http://www.culture24.org.uk/art/photography-and-film/art540967-mikhail-seawomen-pacific-earsthetic-brighton-dome.

Keeling, Kara, and Josh Kun. "Introduction: Listening to American Studies." In "Sound Clash: Listening to American Studies." Special issue of *American Quarterly* 63, no. 3 (2011): 445–59.

Kelley, Robin D. G. "Stormy Weather: Reconstructing Black (Inter)Nationalism in the Cold War Era." In *Is It Nation Time? Contemporary Essays on Black Power and Black Nationalism,* edited by Eddie S. Glaude Jr., 67–90. Chicago: University of Chicago Press, 2001.

Kelly, Caleb. *Cracked Media: The Sound of Malfunction.* Cambridge, MA: MIT Press, 2009.

Kheshti, Roshanak. "Touching Listening: The Aural Imaginary in the World Music Culture Industry." *American Quarterly* 63 (2011): 711–31.

Kierkegaard, Søren. *Repetition* and *Philosophical Crumbs.* Translated by M. G. Piety. Oxford: Oxford University Press, 2009.

Kim, Hun Joon. *The Massacres at Mt. Halla: Sixty Years of Truth Seeking in South Korea.* Ithaca, NY: Cornell University Press, 2014.

Kim, Jodi. *Ends of Empire: Asian American Critique and the Cold War.* Minneapolis: University of Minnesota Press, 2010.

King, Martin Luther, Jr. *A Testament of Hope: The Essential Writings of Martin Luther King, Jr.* San Francisco: Harper and Row, 1986.

Kirshenblatt-Gimblatt, Barbara. "Making Sense of Food in Performance: The Table and the Stage." In *The Senses in Performance,* edited by Sally Banes and André Lepecki, 71–89. London: Routledge, 2012.

Kourlas, Gia. "Lil Buck and Jon Boogz, Wearing Paint as They Tell a Tale." *New York Times,* September 18, 2016.

Kracauer, Siegfried. "The Mass Ornament." In *The Mass Ornament: Weimar Essays,* edited and translated by Thomas Y. Levin, 75–86. Cambridge, MA: Harvard University Press, 1995.

Krasner, David. *A Beautiful Pageant: African American Theatre, Drama, and Performance in the Harlem Renaissance, 1910–1927.* New York: Palgrave Macmillan, 2002.

Krasner, David. *Resistance, Parody, and Double Consciousness in African American Theatre, 1895–1910.* New York: St. Martin's, 1997.

Kraut, Anthea. "Between Primitivism and Diaspora: The Dance Performances of Josephine Baker, Zora Neale Hurston, and Katherine Dunham." *Theatre Journal* 55, no. 3 (October 2003): 433–50.

Krishnan, Kavita. "Rape and Rakhi—Patriarchal-Communal Narratives: Kavita Krishnan." Kafila, November 8, 2014. https://kafila.online/2014/08/11/rape-and-rakhi-patriarchal-communal-narratives-kavita-krishnan/.

Kulmatitskiy, Nikolay, Lan Ma Nygren, Kjell Nygren, Jeffrey S. Simonoff, and Jing Cao. "Survival of Broadway Shows: An Empirical Investigation of Recent Trends." *Communications in Statistics: Case Studies, Data Analysis and Applications* 1, no. 2 (2015): 114–24.

Lacan, Jacques. *The Seminar of Jacques Lacan.* Translated by Alan Sheridan. Vol. 11. New York: Norton, 1988.

LaMothe, Mario. "Dedouble and Jeanguy Saintus' Corporeal Gifts." *Caribbean Rasanblaj, emisférica* 12, no. 1 (2015). https://hemisphericinstitute.org/en/emisferica

-121-caribbean-rasanblaj/12-1-dossier/e-121-dossier-lamothe-dedouble-and
-jeanguy.html.

LaMothe, Mario. "Jeanguy Saintus et Léna Blou: Entre le 'Bite' et le Bigidi."
In *Techni'ka, Bigidi'Art: Méthode d'enseignement pour l'étude la danse
gwoka*, by Léna Blou. Pointe-à-Pitre, Guadeloupe: Jasor, forthcoming.

LaMothe, Mario. "Our Love on Fire: Gay Men's Stories of Violence in Haiti." In "Nou
Mache Ansanm (We Walk Together): Queer Haitian Performance and Affiliation." Special issue, *Women and Performance: A Journal of Feminist Theory* 27,
no. 2 (2017): 259–70.

Lane, Jill. "Hemispheric America in Deep Time." *Theatre Research International* 35,
no. 2 (May 2010): 111–25.

Larson, Doran, ed. *Fourth City: Essays from the Prison in America*. East Lansing:
Michigan State University Press, 2013.

Law, Victoria. "Against Carceral Feminism." *Jacobin Magazine*, October 2014. https://
www.jacobinmag.com/2014/10/against-carceral-feminism.

Lazú, Jacqueline. "El Bloque, a Young Lords Story." Unpublished script, 2007.

Lazú, Jacqueline. "The Chicago Young Lords: Constructing Knowledge and Revolution." *Centro: Journal of the Center for Puerto Rican Studies* 25, no. 2 (2013):
28–59.

Lee, Dohee. "ARA Project, 2014–2018." Dohee Lee website. Accessed October 29, 2019.
https://www.doheelee.com/ara.

Lee, Dohee. Interview with Elizabeth W. Son. Oakland, CA. January 20, 2017.

Lee, Dohee. "MAGO Project, 2011–14." Dohee Lee website. Accessed October 29, 2019.
https://www.doheelee.com/mago.

Lee, Dohee. "SPEAK: Inner Travel with Myth and Past Lives, History and Stories,
Dreams and Future." Dancers' Group, July 1, 2014. http://dancersgroup.org/2014
/07/speak-dohee-lee/.

Lee, Nami. "Reflections on Mago, a Goddess in Korea." In *Facing Multiplicity: Psyche,
Nature, Culture*, edited by Pramila Bennett, 765–77. Einsiedeln: Daimon, 2012.

Leroux, Louis Patrick. "Reinventing Tradition, Building a Field: Quebec Circus and
Its Scholarship." In Leroux and Batson, *Cirque Global*, 3–22.

Leroux, Louis Patrick, and Charles R. Batson, eds. *Cirque Global: Quebec's Expanding
Circus Boundaries*. Montreal: McGill–Queen's University Press, 2016.

Lieder, K. Frances. "Performing Loitering: Feminist Protest in the Indian City." *TDR:
The Drama Review* 62, no. 3 (Fall 2018): 145–61.

Lipsitz, George. *How Racism Takes Place*. Philadelphia: Temple University Press, 2011.

Lorde, Audre. *Sister Outsider: Essays and Speeches*. Berkeley, CA: Crossing, 2007.

Louis-Jean, Jean Wesler. Interview by Mario LaMothe. Gonaives, Haiti. 2014.

Macaulay, Alastair. "On Point, in Their Jeans and Sneakers." *New York Times*, November 2, 2012.

Madison, D. Soyini. *Acts of Activism: Human Rights as Radical Performance*. Cambridge, UK: Cambridge University Press, 2010.

Malloy, Sean L. *Out of Oakland: Black Panther Party Internationalism during the Cold War*. Ithaca, NY: Cornell University Press, 2017.

Malone, Jacqui. *Steppin' on the Blues: The Visible Rhythms of African American Dance*. Urbana: University of Illinois Press, 1996.

Manning, Susan. *Modern Dance, Negro Dance: Race in Motion*. Minneapolis: University of Minnesota Press, 2004.

Martin, John Joseph. *The Dance in Theory*. Princeton, NJ: Princeton Book, 1990.

Martin, Joshua, dir. *The Champ*. Burbank, CA: Warner Home Video, 2006.

Marx, Karl. *Economic and Philosophic Manuscripts of 1844*. Edited by Dirk J. Struik. Translated by Martin Milligan. New York: International, 2014.

Mbembe, Achille. "Necropolitics." *Public Culture* 15, no. 1 (2003): 11–40.

McClintock, Anne. *Imperial Leather: Race, Gender and Sexuality in the Colonial Contest*. New York: Routledge, 1995.

McCormick, Bill. "Joe Louis Perfects Two-Fisted Body Attack for Carnera Bout." *Washington Post*, June 5, 1935.

McDonald, Audra. Twitter post, May 10, 2016, 12:54 pm, https://twitter.com /AudraEqualityMc/status/730078509926854656.

McDonough, Tom. "Theaster Gates." *Bomb*, Winter 2013. https://bombmagazine.org /articles/theaster-gates.

McKittrick, Katherine. *Demonic Grounds: Black Women and the Cartographies of Struggle*. Minneapolis: University of Minnesota Press, 2006.

McMillan, Uri. *Embodied Avatars: Genealogies of Black Feminist Art and Performance*. New York: New York University Press, 2016.

McMullen, Ken, dir. *Ghost Dance*. Channel Four Films, 1983. DVD.

Menon, Nivedita, and J. Devika. "The Mahmood Farooqui Rape Conviction—A Landmark Verdict." Kafila, August 14, 2016. https://kafila.online/2016/08/14/the -mahmood-farooqui-rape-conviction-a-landmark-verdict-j-devika-nivedita -menon/.

Merleau-Ponty, Maurice. *Phenomenology of Perception*. Translated by Donald A. Landes. London: Routledge, 1945.

Merrill, John. "The Cheju-do Rebellion." *Journal of Korean Studies* 2 (1980): 139–97.

Miller, Flournoy, Aubrey Lyles, Eubie Blake, and Noble Sissle. *Shuffle Along*, libretto. 1921. New York Public Library. http://static.nypl.org/MOTM/ShuffleAlong /ShuffleAlong.pdf.

Mills, Charles. *The Racial Contract*. Ithaca, NY: Cornell University Press, 1997.

"More Than 1,000 People March in Rare Anti-Gay Demonstration in Haiti." YouTube. Posted by WesterNNews, July 20, 2013. https://www.youtube.com/watch?v =OhoXIUy2XZQ.

Morgan, Fiona. "Bush's Public Enemy No. 1." *Salon*, March 28, 2001. http://www.salon .com/2001/03/28/bush_99/.

Morrison, Toni. *Beloved*. London: Penguin, 1987.

Moten, Fred. "Black Mo'nin.'" In *Loss: The Politics of Mourning*, edited by David L. Eng and David Kazanjian, 59–67. Berkeley: University of California Press, 2003.

Moten, Fred. "The Case of Blackness." *Criticism* 50, no. 2 (2008): 177–218.

Moten, Fred. *In the Break: The Aesthetics of the Black Radical Tradition*. Minneapolis: University of Minnesota Press, 2003.

Muñoz, José Esteban. *Cruising Utopia: The Then and There of Queer Futurity*. New York: New York University Press, 2009.

Muñoz, José Esteban. *Disidentifications: Queers of Color and the Performance of Politics*. Minneapolis: University of Minnesota Press, 1999.

Muñoz, José Esteban. "Feeling Brown: Ethnicity and Affect in Ricardo Bracho's 'The Sweetest Hangover (and Other STDs)." *Theatre Journal* 52, no. 1 (March 2000): 67–79.

Muñoz, José Esteban. "Feeling Brown, Feeling Down: Latina Affect, the Performativity of Race, and the Depressive Position." *Signs* 31, no. 3 (2006): 675–88.

Muñoz, José Esteban. "Race, Sex, and the Incommensurate: Gary Fisher with Eve Kosofsky Sedgwick." In *Queer Futures: Reconsidering Ethics, Activism, and the Political*, edited by Elahe Haschemi Yekani, Eveline Kilian, and Beatrice Michaelis, 103–15. Surrey, UK: Ashgate, 2013.

Muñoz, José Esteban. "Teaching, Minoritarian Knowledge, and Love." *Women and Performance: A Journal of Feminist Theory* 14, no. 2 (2005): 117–21.

Murch, Donna Jean. *Living for the City: Migration, Education, and the Rise of the Black Panther Party in Oakland, California*. Chapel Hill: University of North Carolina Press, 2010.

Nancy, Jean-Luc. *Being Singular Plural*. Stanford, CA: Stanford University Press, 2000.

Nataraj, Nirmala. "The MAGO Project." Dancers' Group, November 1, 2014. http://dancersgroup.org/2014/11/mago-project/.

National Lawyers Guild Counterintelligence Documentation Center. *Counter-Intelligence: A Documentary Look at America's Secret Police*. 4th ed. Chicago: Citizens in Defense of Civil Liberties, 1982.

Neal, Mark Anthony. *Soul Babies: Black Popular Culture and the Post-Soul Aesthetic*. New York: Routledge, 2004.

Negrón-Muntaner, Frances. "The Look of Sovereignty: Style and Politics in the Young Lords." *Centro Journal* 25, no. 1 (Spring 2015): 4–33.

Nelson, Alondra. *Body and Soul: The Black Panther Party and the Fight against Medical Discrimination*. Minneapolis: University of Minnesota Press, 2013.

Newton, Michael. *The FBI Encyclopedia*. Jefferson, NC: McFarland, 2015.

Norfleet, Dawn M. "Hip Hop and Rap." In *African American Music: An Introduction*, edited by Mellonee V. Burnim and Portia K. Maultsby, 354–90. New York: Routledge, 2006.

Nunn, William G. "Bill Nunn Writes His Story 10,000 Feet in the Air." *Pittsburgh Courier*, June 29, 1935.

Nunn, William G. "*Courier* Scoops Field Again!" *Pittsburgh Courier*, September 14, 1935.

Nunn, William G. "We Looked at the Next Heavyweight Champ of the World Friday Night." *Pittsburgh Courier*, April 6, 1935.

Nyong'o, Tavia. *The Amalgamation Waltz: Race, Performance, and the Ruses of Memory*. Minneapolis: University of Minnesota Press, 2009.

O'Connell, Grattan. "Many Like Baer (Calling 'em Right)." *Hartford Courant*, August 11, 1935.

Ogbar, Jeffrey O. G. *Black Power: Radical Politics and African American Identity*. Baltimore, MD: Johns Hopkins University Press, 2004.

O'Halligan, Jimmy, dir. *The Angola 3: Black Panthers and the Last Slave Plantation*. Perf. Robert King, Albert Woodfox, and Herman Wallace. Obstacle Illusions, 2008.

Olmstead, Alan L., and Paul W. Rhode. "Wait a Cotton Pickin' Minute: A New View of Slave Productivity." Abstract. *Journal of Economic History* 67, no. 2 (2007): 525.

Ongiri, Amy Abugo. *Spectacular Blackness: The Cultural Politics of the Black Power Movement and the Search for a Black Aesthetics*. Charlottesville: University of Virginia Press, 2009.

Oshinsky, David. "The View from Inside." *New York Times*, June 11, 2010.

Ovadija, Mladen. *Dramaturgy of Sound in the Avant-Garde and Postdramatic Theatre*. Montreal: McGill–Queen's University Press, 2013.

Owen, Frank. "Fab 5 Freddy and Max Roach: Hip Hop Bebop." *Spin*, October 1988. https://fxowen.wordpress.com/golden-oldies/fab-5-freddy-max-roach-hip-hop-bebop-spin-october-1988/.

Pager, Devah. *Marked: Race, Crime, and Finding Work in an Era of Mass Incarceration*. Chicago: University of Chicago Press, 2007.

Pal, Sanchari. "Reclaiming the Streets: Bengaluru's Blank Noise Project Is Encouraging Women to Fight Fear." *The Better India*, September 6, 2016. http://www.thebetterindia.com/67337/blank-noise-jasmeen-patheja-bengaluru-women-india/.

Park, C. S. *Budoji*. Translated by E. Kim. Seoul: Hanmunwha, 1986.

Parks, Suzan-Lori. *Venus*. New York: Theatre Communications Group. 1997.

Patheja, Jasmeen. "Challenge Is in Developing Empathy among People." *Economic Times* (Mumbai), January 5, 2017. https://economictimes.indiatimes.com/news/politics-and-nation/challenge-is-in-developing-empathy-among-people/articleshow/56348883.cms.

Pellegrini, Ann. *Performance Anxieties: Staging Psychoanalysis, Staging Race*. London: Routledge, 1997.

Perlongher, Néstor, and Cristel M. Jusino Díaz. "Minoritarian Becomings." *E-misférica* 10, no. 2 (2013). https://hemisphericinstitute.org/en/emisferica-102/10-2-essays/minoritarian-becomings.html.

Phelan, Peggy. *Unmarked: The Politics of Performance*. London: Routledge, 1993.

Picariello, Jil. "Review: *Party People* at the Public Preaches without Pleasing." *Zeal NYC*. Accessed November 28, 2016. https://zealnyc.com/review-party-people-at-the-public-preaches-without-pleasing/.

Piper, Adrian. "Talking to Myself: The Ongoing Autobiography of an Art Object." *Out of Order, Out of Sight.* Vol. 1, *Selected Writings in Meta-Art, 1968–1992.* Cambridge, MA: MIT Press, 1996.

"The Project That Inspired the Film." Herman's House website. Accessed April 24, 2016. http://hermanshouse.org.

"Public Art (Now): Claire Doherty Talks to Theaster Gates." Vimeo. Posted by SituationsUK, 2015. https://vimeo.com/143651490.

Quashie, Kevin. *The Sovereignty of Quiet: Beyond Resistance in Black Culture.* New Brunswick, NJ: Rutgers University Press, 2012.

Ramirez, Anthony. "Haven for Blacks in Civil War Riots Now Safeguards History." *New York Times,* June 5, 2005.

Randall, Alice. *The Wind Done Gone.* New York: Houghton Mifflin, 2001.

Rankine, Claudia. "The Condition of Black Life Is One of Mourning." *New York Times,* June 22, 2015.

Ravine, Jai Arun. "Resonance and Resistance: A Preview of Dohee Lee's MAGO." *Jai Arun Ravine Blog,* October 31, 2014. http://web.archive.org/web/20141114102048 /http://jaiarunravine.com/preview-resonance-and-resistance-in-dohee-lees -mago/.

Rayner, Alice. *Ghosts: Death's Double and the Phenomena of Theatre.* Minneapolis: University of Minnesota Press, 2006.

Rayner, Alice. "Keeping Time." *Performance Research* 19, no. 3 (August 2014): 32–36.

Reitan, Ruth. "Cuba, the Black Panther Party, and the U.S. Black Movement in the 1960s: Issues of Security." In *Liberation, Imagination, and the Black Panther Party: A New Look at the Panthers and Their Legacy,* edited by Kathleen Cleaver and George Katsiaficas, 164–74. New York: Routledge, 2001.

"Remixing *Shuffle Along.*" PBS *NewsHour,* April 29, 2016. http://www.pbs.org /newshour/bb/remixing-shuffle-along-a-musical-that-brought-new-sounds-and -moves-to-broadway.

Reynolds, Diamond. Facebook Live Video, July 6, 2016. YouTube, posted June 20, 2017. https://www.youtube.com/watch?v=6DUfa4LTgOs.

Rice, Grantland. "Another Nickname (The Sportlight)." *Hartford Courant,* May 21, 1935.

Richardson, Brian. "'Time Is Out of Joint': Narrative Models and the Temporality of the Drama," *Poetics Today* 8, no. 2 (1987): 299–309.

Rivera-Servera, Ramón H. "Moving from Realism to the Hip-Hop Real: Transnational Aesthetics in Canadian Latina/o Performance." In *Latina/o Canadian Theatre and Performance,* edited by Natalie Alvarez, 133–50. Toronto: Playwrights Canada Press, 2013.

Roach, Joseph. *Cities of the Dead: Circum-Atlantic Performance.* New York: Columbia University Press, 1996.

Roberts, Randy. *Joe Louis: Hard Times Man.* New Haven, CT: Yale University Press, 2010.

Rose, Tricia. *Black Noise: Rap Music and Black Culture in Contemporary America.* Hanover, NH: Wesleyan University Press, 1994.

Ross, Daniel. "Active History on Stage: *Party People* at the Oregon Shakespeare Festival." Active History: History Matters, September 19, 2012. http://activehistory .ca/2012/09/active-history-on-stage-party-people-at-the-oregon-shakespeare -festival/.

Roychowdhury, Poulami. "'The Delhi Gang Rape': The Making of International Causes." *Feminist Studies* 39, no. 1 (2013): 282–92.

Rubin, William, ed. *"Primitivism" in the 20th Century Art: Affinity of the Tribal and the Modern.* 2 vols. New York: Museum of Modern Art, 1984.

Sacks, Ethan. "Indian Director Mahmood Farooqui Convicted of Raping American Graduate Student." *New York Daily News,* August 1, 2016.

Salamon, Gayle. *Assuming a Body: Transgender and Rhetorics of Materiality.* New York: Columbia University Press, 2010.

Samuels, Ellen. "Six Ways of Looking at Crip Time." *Disability Studies Quarterly* 37 no. 3 (2017). DOI: 10.18061/dsq.v37i3.5824

Savran, David. "Toward a Historiography of the Popular." *Theatre Survey* 45, no. 2 (2004): 211–17.

Sayej, Nadja. "Simone Leigh's *The Waiting Room*: Art That Tries to Heal Black Women's Pain." *Guardian* (London), June 29, 2016.

Scarry, Elaine. *The Body in Pain: The Making and Unmaking of the World.* New York: Oxford University Press, 1985.

Schechner, Richard. *Between Theater and Anthropology.* Philadelphia: University of Pennsylvania Press, 1985.

Schechner, Richard. *The Future of Ritual: Writings on Culture and Performance.* London: Routledge, 1993.

Schloss, Joseph Glenn. *Making Beats: The Art of Sample-Based Hip-Hop.* Middletown, CT: Wesleyan University Press, 2004.

Schneider, Rebecca. *Performing Remains: Art and War in Times of Theatrical Reenactment.* New York: Routledge, 2011.

Scott, Darieck. *Extravagant Abjection: Blackness, Power, and Sexuality in the African American Literary Imagination.* New York: New York University Press, 2010.

Seale, Bobby. *Seize the Time: The Story of the Black Panther Party and Huey Newton.* Baltimore, MD: Black Classic Press, 1991.

Seibert, Brian. *What the Eye Hears: A History of Tap Dancing.* New York: Farrar, Straus and Giroux, 2015.

Seltzer, Mark. *Bodies and Machines.* New York: Routledge, 1992.

Seo, Bong-Ha. "White Hanbok as an Expression of Resistance in Modern Korea." *Journal of the Korean Society of Clothing and Textiles* 29, no. 1 (2015): 121–32.

Sethi, Manisha. "Why the Mahmood Farooqui Judgment Is Deeply Flawed." *Hard News,* August 23, 2016. http://www.hardnewsmedia.com/2016/08/why -mahmood-farooqui-judgment-deeply-flawed.

Sharpe, Christina. "Black Studies: In the Wake." *Black Scholar* 44, no. 2 (Summer 2014): 49–60.

Sharpe, Christina. *In the Wake: On Blackness and Being*. Durham, NC: Duke University Press, 2014.

Sharpe, Christina. *Monstrous Intimacies: Making Post-Slavery Subjects*. Durham, NC: Duke University Press, 2010.

Shimakawa, Karen. *National Abjection: The Asian American Body Onstage*. Durham, NC: Duke University Press, 2002.

"*Shuffle Along*." *Theater Talk*. May 28, 2016. http://www.cuny.tv/show/theatertalk /PR2005265.

Shuffle Along; or, The Making of the Musical Sensation of 1921 and All That Followed, performance. Libretto by George C. Wolfe, dir., choreography by Savion Glover. Music Box Theatre, July 19, 2016. New York Public Library of the Performing Arts Theatre on Film and Tape Archive.

"*Shuffle Along* Sets Sudden Broadway Closing after Audra McDonald Departs." BroadwayWorld, June 23, 2016. http://www.broadwayworld.com/article /SHUFFLE-ALONG-Sets-Sudden-Broadway-Closing-After-Audra-McDonald -Departs-20160623.

"Simone Leigh." Creative Time. http://creativetime.org/projects/black-radical -brooklyn/artists/simone-leigh/.

Sklar, Deidre. "Five Premises for a Culturally Sensitive Approach to Dance." In *Moving History/Dancing Cultures: A Dance History Reader*, edited by Ann Dils and Ann Cooper Albright, 30–32. Middletown, CT: Wesleyan University Press, 2001.

Smalls, Shanté Paradigm. "'Make the Music with Your Mouth': Sonic Subjectivity and Post-Modern Identity Formations in Beatboxing." *Lateral* 3 (Spring 2014). http:// csalateral.org/original/issue3/queer-the-noise/paradigm-smalls.

Smith, Mark M. "Listening to the Heard Worlds of Antebellum America." In *The Auditory Culture Reader*, edited by Michael Bull and Les Back, 137–64. Oxford: Berg, 2003.

Smith, Roger Guenveur. "A Huey P. Newton Story." Unpublished script, 1996.

Snead, James A. "On Repetition in Black Culture." *Black American Literature Forum* 15, no. 4 (Winter 1981): 146–54.

Snorton, C. Riley. *Black on Both Sides: A Racial History of Trans Identity*. Minneapolis: University of Minnesota Press, 2017.

Snorton, C. Riley. "What More Can I Say? (A Prose-Poem on Antiblackness)." *Feminist Wire*, September 3, 2014.

Solitary Gardens. Accessed May 12, 2017. http://www.solitarygardens.org/.

Sood, Mihira. "Why the Backlash against the Mahmood Farooqui Judgment Is Manipulative and Dangerous." *Huffington Post*, August 29, 2016. https://www .huffingtonpost.in/mihira-sood/why-the-backlash-against-the-mahmood -farooqui-judgment-is-manipu_a_21461459/.

Spencer, Robyn C. *The Revolution Has Come: Black Power, Gender, and the Black Panther in Oakland*. Durham, NC: Duke University Press, 2016.

Spillers, Hortense J. "'All the Things You Could Be by Now, If Sigmund Freud's Wife Was Your Mother': Psychoanalysis and Race." In *Black, White, and in Color: Essays on American Literature and Culture*, 376–427. Chicago: University of Chicago Press, 2003.

Spillers, Hortense J. "Peter's Pans: Eating in the Diaspora." In *Black, White, and in Color: Essays on American Literature and Culture*, 1–64. Chicago: University of Chicago Press, 2003.

Stadler, Gustavus. "On Whiteness and Sound Studies." *Sound Out!*, July 6, 2015. https://soundstudiesblog.com/2015/07/06/on-whiteness-and-sound-studies/.

Stallings, L. H. *Funk the Erotic: Transaesthetics and Black Sexual Cultures*. Urbana: University of Illinois Press, 2015.

States, Bert O. *Seeing in the Dark: Reflections on Dreams and Dreaming*. New Haven, CT: Yale University Press, 1997.

Stearns, Marshall, and Jean Stearns. *Jazz Dance: The Story of American Vernacular Dance*. New York: Macmillan, 1968.

Stevenson, Bryan. *Just Mercy: A Story of Justice and Redemption*. New York: Spiegel and Grau, 2014.

Stoever, Jennifer Lynn. *The Sonic Color Line: Race and the Cultural Politics of Listening*. New York: New York University Press, 2016.

Stowell, Dan, and Mark D. Plumbley. "Characteristics of the Beatboxing Vocal Style." Dept. of Electronic Engineering, Queen Mary, University of London, Technical Report. Centre for Digital Music CD4MTR-01. February 2008.

Strongman, Roberto. "Syncretic Religion and Dissident Sexualities." In *Queer Globalizations: Citizenship and the Afterlife of Colonialism*, edited by Arnaldo Cruz and Martin F. Manalansan IV, 176–92. New York: New York University Press, 2002.

Strongman, Roberto. "Transcorporeality in Vodou." *Journal of Haitian Studies* 14, no. 2 (2008): 4–29.

Sullivan, Megan. "African-American Music as Rebellion: From Slavesong to Hip-Hop." *Discoveries* 3 (2001): 21–39.

Sumell, Jackie, and Herman Wallace. *The House That Herman Built*. Stuttgart, Germany: Akademie Schloss Solitude, 2006.

Sylvain, Patrick. "Odette." In *Haiti Noir*, edited by Edwidge Danticat, 19–26. New York: Akashic Books, 2011.

Symons, Stéphane. "Benjamin's Philosophy of History: The Messianic Is Now." In *Walter Benjamin: Presence of Mind, Failure to Comprehend*, 13–49. Boston: Brill, 2013.

Taylor, Keeanga-Yamahtta. *From #BlackLivesMatter to Black Liberation*. Chicago: Haymarket, 2016.

Tembeck, Iro. *Danser à Montréal: germination d'une histoire chorégraphique*. Sillery: Presses de l'Université du Québec, 1991.

Terry-Morgan, Elmo. "*Noise/Funk*: Fo' Real Black Theatre on 'da Great White Way.'" *African American Review* 31, no. 4 (Winter 1997): 677–86.

"Theaster Gates AI Interview." YouTube. Posted by Blouin Artinfo, March 23, 2012. https://www.youtube.com/watch?v=4jz_4x8ViEc.

"Theaster Gates: *Holding Court* (2012), part 1." YouTube. Posted by the Studio Museum in Harlem, April 8, 2014. https://www.youtube.com/watch?v=bgv49RuzNWw.

Thorpe, Edward. *Black Dance*. Woodstock, NY: Overlook Press, 1990.

Tocci, Laurence. *The Proscenium Cage: Critical Case Studies in U.S. Prison Theatre Programs*. Amherst, NY: Cambria Press, 2007.

Torres, Andrés. "Introduction: Political Radicalism in the Diaspora—The Puerto Rican Experience." In *The Puerto Rican Movement: Voices from the Diaspora*, edited by Andrés Torres and José Emiliano Velázquez, 1–22. Philadelphia: Temple University Press, 1998.

Turner, Victor. *Dramas, Fields, and Metaphors: Symbolic Action in Human Society*. Ithaca, NY: Cornell University Press, 1974.

Turner, Victor. *From Ritual to Theatre: The Human Seriousness of Play*. New York: Performing Arts Journal Publications, 1982.

Turner, Victor. *The Ritual Process: Structure and Anti-Structure*. Chicago: Aldine Transaction, 1969.

TyTe and White Noise. "Part 2: Old Skool: Introduction." The Real History of Beatboxing: Part 2. Accessed September 29, 2009. http://www.humanbeatbox.com/forum/content.php?35-The-Real-History-of-Beatboxing-Part-2.

Universes. *Party People*. Kindle Direct Publishing, July 26, 2012.

US Department of Justice, Civil Rights Division, and US Attorney's Office, Northern District of Illinois. *Investigation of the Chicago Police Department*. Washington, DC: Department of Justice, 2017. http://purl.fdlp.gov/GPO/gpo83890

van der Kolk, Bessel A. *The Body Keeps the Score: Brain, Mind, and Body in the Healing of Trauma*. New York: Penguin Books, 2014.

Van Every, Edward. *Joe Louis: Man and Super-Fighter*. New York: Stokes, 1936.

Vargas, Deborah. *Dissonant Divas in Chicana Music*. Minneapolis: University of Minnesota Press, 2012

Vazquez, Alexandra T. *Listening in Detail: Performances of Cuban Music*. Durham, NC: Duke University Press, 2013.

Vogel, Shane. *The Scene of Harlem Cabaret: Race, Sexuality, Performance*. Chicago: University of Chicago Press, 2009.

Wade, Jacqueline. "Black Panther Women." Unpublished script, 2016.

Walsh, Brian. "Theatrical Temporality and Historical Consciousness in 'The Famous Victories of Henry V.'" *Theatre Journal* 59, no. 1 (March 2007): 57–73.

Watching Dance Project. "Watching Dance: Kinesthetic Empathy." Accessed July 7, 2017. http://www.watchingdance.org/research/.

Weeksville Heritage Center. Accessed October 29, 2019. http://www.weeksvillesociety .org.

Weiner, Jonah. "The Impossible Body: Storyboard P, the Basquiat of Street Dancing." *New Yorker*, January 6, 2014.

Wellman, Judith. *Brooklyn's Promised Land: The Free Black Community of Weeksville, New York*. New York: New York University Press, 2014.

West, Cornel. *Prophesy Deliverance! An Afro-American Revolutionary Christianity*. Anniversary ed. Louisville, KY: Westminster John Knox Press, 2002.

Wilderson, Frank B., III. *Red, White, and Black : Cinema and the Structure of U.S. Antagonisms*. Durham, NC: Duke University Press, 2010.

Williams, Jakobi. *From the Bullet to the Ballot: The Illinois Chapter of the Black Panther Party and Racial Coalition Politics in Chicago*. Chapel Hill: University of North Carolina Press, 2013.

Williams, Raymond. *Marxism and Literature*. Oxford: Oxford University Press, 2009.

Williams, Yohuru R. *Black Politics/White Power: Civil Rights, Black Power, and the Black Panthers in New Haven*. Malden, MA: Wiley-Blackwell, 2000.

Williams, Yohuru R., and Jama Lazerow, eds. *In Search of the Black Panther Party: New Perspectives on a Revolutionary Movement*. Durham, NC: Duke University Press, 2006.

Williams, Yohuru R., and Jama Lazerow, eds. *Liberated Territory: Untold Local Perspectives on the Black Panther Party*. Durham, NC: Duke University Press, 2008.

Wilson, Jamie Jaywann. *The Black Panther Party: A Guide to an American Subculture*. Santa Barbara, CA: Greenwood, 2018.

Witt, Andrew. *The Black Panthers in the Midwest: The Community Programs and Services of the Black Panther Party in Milwaukee, 1966–1977*. New York: Routledge, 2007.

Woll, Allen. *Black Musical Theatre: From "Coontown" to "Dreamgirls."* Baton Rouge: Louisiana State University Press, 1989.

Woodfox, Albert, and Jackie Sumell. "Prison Industrial Complexity." *TDR: The Drama Review* 55, no. 4 (Winter 2011): 2–3.

Workman, Galen. "*Party People*." Dangerous Common Sense (blog). August 22, 2012. http://ozdachs.livejournal.com/227728.html.

Worth, Libby, and Helen Poynor. *Anna Halprin*. London: Routledge, 2004.

Wright, Michelle M. *Physics of Blackness: Beyond the Middle Passage Epistemology*. Minneapolis: University of Minnesota Press, 2015.

Wright, Richard. "Joe Louis Uncovers Dynamite." *New Masses*, October 8, 1935, 18–19.

Yerba Buena Center for the Arts. *MAGO Playbill*. N.p., 2014.

Yong, Byron Au. "Artist to Artist: Byron Au Yong Interviews Dohee Lee." Creative Capital Blog, November 5, 2014. http://blog.creative-capital.org/2014/11/artist -artist-dohee-lee-byron-au-yong/.

Yoo, Chul-in. "Hardy Divers Gather Seafood from the Ocean Floor." *Koreana: Journal of the Korean Foundation* 28, no. 2 (Summer 2014): 12–17.

Young, Catherine M. "Don't Blame Pregnancy for *Shuffle Along* Closing." Howl-Round, July 18, 2016. http://howlround.com/don-t-blame-pregnancy-for-shuffle -along-closing.

Young, Harvey. *Embodying Black Experience: Stillness, Critical Memory, and the Black Body.* Ann Arbor: University of Michigan Press, 2010.

CONTRIBUTORS

JOSHUA CHAMBERS-LETSON is Associate Professor of performance studies at Northwestern University. He is the author of *After the Party: A Manifesto for Queer of Color Life* (2018) and *A Race So Different: Law and Performance in Asian America* (2013). With Tavia Nyong'o, he is the editor of José Esteban Muñoz's *The Sense of Brown*, forthcoming from Duke University Press (2020). His essays have circulated in both academic and art venues, and with Ann Pellegrini and Tavia Nyong'o, he is a coeditor of the Sexual Cultures series at NYU Press.

SOYICA DIGGS COLBERT is the Vice Dean of Faculty and Idol Family Professor of the College of Arts and Sciences at Georgetown University. She is the author of *The African American Theatrical Body: Reception, Performance and the Stage* (2011) and *Black Movements: Performance and Cultural Politics* (2017). Colbert coedited *The Psychic Hold of Slavery: Legacies in American Expressive Culture* (2016). She is currently working on a forthcoming book project, "Becoming Free: An Intellectual Biography of Lorraine Hansberry."

NICHOLAS FESETTE is an Assistant Professor of Theater at Oxford College of Emory University, where he also serves as Director of the Theater Program. His research interests include theater and performance practice, critical prison studies, trauma theory, and adaptation. His book project, "Cagecraft: Performance, Race, and Trauma in Carceral America," examines modern and contemporary performances in order to understand how the US prison system itself performs racist and classist violence. This writing draws in part on his experience working as a volunteer artist with the Phoenix Players Theatre Group inside Auburn Correctional Facility, a maximum-security prison in upstate New York. He earned his PhD at Cornell University.

PATRICIA HERRERA is Associate Professor of Theater affiliated with American Studies and Women, Gender, and Sexuality Studies programs at the University of Richmond. Her teaching and research focus on contemporary theater and performance, with an emphasis on social justice, Latinx cultural production, transnationalism, and identity politics. She is the author of *Nuyorican Feminist Performance: From the Café to Hip Hop* (2020). Since 2011 Dr. Herrera has engaged with the greater Richmond community on a public humanities project, "Civil Rights and Education in Richmond, Virginia: A Documentary Project," which has led to the production of a digital archive (*The Fight for Knowledge*) as well as three community exhibitions at the Valentine Museum (*Made in Church Hill* [2015], *Nuestras Historias: Latinos in Richmond* [2017], and *Voices from Richmond's Hidden Epidemic* [2020]) and a series of six documentary plays about gentrification, educational disparities, HIV/AIDS, segregation, and Latinos in Richmond. Her writing appears in *Aztlán: A Journal of Chicano Studies, Theatre Topics, Café Onda: The Journal of the Latinx Theatre Commons, Public: A Journal of Imagining America, Chicana/Latina Studies: The Journal of MALCS, African American Review,* and *Transformations: The Journal of Inclusive Scholarship and Pedagogy.*

JASMINE JOHNSON is Assistant Professor of Africana Studies at the University of Pennsylvania. Her interdisciplinary research and teaching are situated at the intersection of diaspora theory, dance and performance studies, ethnography, and black feminism. Her work has been published by *The Black Scholar, TDR/The Drama Review, ASAP Journal, Dance Research Journal, African and Black Diaspora: An International Journal, Theatre Survey,* and elsewhere. Johnson has been awarded fellowships from the Ford Foundation, the National Endowment for the Humanities, and the Schomburg Center for Research in Black Culture. She is a Founding Board Member for the Collegium for African Diaspora Dance and a Board Director for the Dance Studies Association.

DOUGLAS A. JONES JR. is Assistant Dean of Humanities at Rutgers University. He is the author of *The Captive Stage: Performance and the Proslavery Imagination of the Antebellum North* (2014). His essays on (African) American literature and performance cultures have appeared or are forthcoming in *American Literary History, Early American Literature, J19: The Journal of Nineteenth-Century Americanists, TDR/The Drama Review,* and elsewhere. Most recently, he edited the "Slavery's Reinventions" special issue of *Modern Drama* (Winter 2019).

MARIO LAMOTHE is Assistant Professor of Black Studies and Anthropology at the University of Illinois at Chicago, where he is also a Faculty Affiliate in Gender and Women's Studies and Museum and Exhibition Studies. He received a doctorate in Performance Studies from Northwestern University. Mario's research focuses on embodied pedagogies of Caribbean arts and expressive cultures and the intersections of queer lifeworlds and social justice in Haiti. A performance artist, his work has appeared in *e-misférica*, *Conversations across the Field of Dance Studies*, *Women and Performance*, *The Journal of Haitian Studies*, and *The Routledge Companion to African American Theatre and Performance*.

JISHA MENON is Associate Professor of Theatre and Performance Studies at Stanford University and director of the Stanford Center for South Asia. She also serves as the Denning Faculty Director of the Stanford Arts Institute and the Faculty Director of the Centre for South Asia. She is author of *The Performance of Nationalism: India, Pakistan, and the Memory of Partition* (2013) and coeditor, with Patrick Anderson, of *Violence Performed: Local Roots and Global Routes of Conflict* (2009) and with Milija Gluhovic of *Performing the Secular: Religion, Representation, and Politics* (2017.)

TAVIA NYONG'O is Professor of African American Studies, American Studies, and Theater and Performance Studies at Yale University. He is the author of two award-winning books, *The Amalgamation Waltz: Race, Performance, and the Ruses of Memory* (2009) and *Afro-Fabulations: The Queer Drama of Black Life* (2018). His new work concerns speculative genders and sexualities in the African diaspora. He coedits the Sexual Cultures book series at NYU Press and is a long-serving member of the *Social Text* collective.

TINA POST is Assistant Professor in the English Department at the University of Chicago, where she is also affiliated with Theater and Performance Studies and the Center for Race, Politics, and Culture. Her first book project, "Deadpan," examines expressionlessness and affective withholding in a range of black cultural and artistic sites. Her scholarly work has appeared in *Modern Drama*, TDR/*The Drama Review*, and the *International Review of African American Art* and is forthcoming in *ASAP Journal*. Her creative work can be found in *ImaginedTheatres.com*, *Stone Canoe*, and *The Appendix*.

ELIZABETH W. SON is Associate Professor in the Department of Theater at Northwestern University. Her research focuses on the interplay between histories of gender-based violence and transnational Asian

American performance-based art and activism. She is the author of the award-winning *Embodied Reckonings: "Comfort Women," Performance, and Transpacific Redress* (2018). As a Mellon/ACLS Scholars and Society fellow, she is working on her next book, "Possessing History," which examines the interrelationships between Korean diasporic women's experiences of social and political violence, place, and performance.

SHANE VOGEL is Ruth N. Halls Professor of English at Indiana University. He is the author of *Stolen Time: Black Fad Performance and the Calypso Craze* (2018) and *The Scene of Harlem Cabaret: Race, Sexuality, Performance* (2009). His research has been supported by fellowships from the National Endowment for the Humanities, the American Council of Learned Societies, and the Fox Center for Humanistic Inquiry at Emory University. He is coeditor of the Minoritarian Aesthetics series from New York University Press.

CATHERINE M. YOUNG studies the politics of representation in popular US entertainments, including vaudeville, circus, and musicals. She is particularly interested in how interspecies performances shaped modern racial categories and gender normativity in the early twentieth century. Her book on transatlantic animal performance during the vaudeville era is forthcoming. Catherine is a Lecturer in the Princeton Writing Program, Princeton University.

KATHERINE ZIEN is Associate Professor in the Department of English at McGill University. Her pedagogy and research focus on theater and performance in the Americas. Her book, *Sovereign Acts: Performing Race, Space, and Belonging in Panama and the Canal Zone* (2017), investigates performances of imperialism, race, and nation-state sovereignty in the Panama Canal Zone. She is currently working on a project to examine theater and militarization during Latin America's Cold War.

INDEX

Muñoz, José Esteban: feeling brown theory, 129, 137; on nightlife, 253; on the past, 276; performativity theory, 275; on potentiality, 177; queer futurity concept, 72, 155; reparative reading, 41–42; utopia concept, 104, 116, 276–77

music, 11, 15. *See also* hip-hop

natality, 221–22, 229, 231
Nataraj, Nirmala, 177, 190
Neal, Mark Anthony, 75
Negrón-Muntaner, Frances, 81
neoliberal feminism, 235
"Never Catch Me" music video: overview of, 127–28; children and death, 138–39; child's dance in, 128–29; eccentric dance in, 129, 135–36, 138–40; ending of, 139; and feeling brown, 137–38; Hiro Murai on, 138–39; and mourning, 137; and sorrow, 139
new circus, Quebecois: aesthetics of, 150–51; Cirque du Soleil, 150–53, 170n21; and the historical body problem, 150–51; historical contexts, 149–50; history of, 150; narrative in, 151; and the National Circus School, 151–52; and realism, 146, 151–55. *See also Cuisine et confessions;* Seven Fingers of the Hand circus
Newton, Huey, 213–14
nightlife, 253
Noise/Funk musical, 50, 60, 69n45

objecthood, performing, 280–83, 288–89
An Octoroon (Jacobs-Jenkins): overview of, 30; acting out–working through dyad, 30, 34; antiblackness, recurrence of, 33; audience, implication of, 38, 40, 42–43; as autobiographical, 29–30; BJJ character, 29–31, 34; Boucicault in, 35;

casting, cross-racial, 32, 35; closing song, 33, 43; dark reparation strategy, 35, 37–40, 42; Dido and Minnie, 36–38, 40, 42; melodrama of, 32, 34–35, 37–38; metamorphoses in, 30, 32, 43; and *The Octoroon,* 35, 38, 42, 44n11; and photography, 39–40, 42; the playwright in, 38–39, 43; production, aborted, 30–31, 33; and the racial contract, 31–35, 38; racial melodrama in, 30; and reparative reading, 40–43; slave status naturalization, 32; steamboat metaphors, 37; theatrically, shifts from, 32, 44n9; and therapy, 29–31, 34; title of, 34–35; and trauma, intergenerational, 34, 36, 38, 40, 42; urban black vernacular use, 36–37, 39; wild analyses of, 31–33, 40; Zoe, 38
The Octoroon (Boucicault), 30, 32, 35, 38, 42, 44n11
opacity theory, 247
Oregon Shakespeare Festival's United States History Cycle, 74, 95n12
Oshinsky, David, 205
Othering, 75–76, 113
Ovadija, Mladen, 79

paranarratives, 145–56, 149
Parks, Suzan-Lori, 207
Party People (Universes): overview of, 71, 85–86; beatboxing, 91–92, 94; and Black Lives Matter, 75; and BPP, 72–73, 86–87, 89–90, 93–94; disruption strategies, 92–93; end of, 90; gospel songs, 92; historical contexts, 75; intelligibility of, 76–77; interviews for writing, 85, 99n67; Jimmy, 85–86, 90–92, 94, 100n78; Malik, 85–86, 88–91, 94, 100n78; opening scene, 100n75; origins of, 74; "Party People" exhibit, 86; photographs of, 85; runs of, 96n14; sonic ruptures, 88; youth as

Shimakawa, Karen, 275

Shuffle Along: overview of, 51; Adrienne Warren on, 55; Amber Iman on, 55–56; Aubrey Lyles in, 51, 53, *54*; Audra McDonald on, 55; Billy Porter on, 55; blackface, use of, 53; book, 51; chorus, 52–53; dance in, 50–53, 68n12; first black kiss, 51, 57; Flournoy E. Miller in, 51, 53, *54*; historical accounts of, 53, 55; historical import of, 53; impact of, 53, 55, 66; Josephine Baker and, 132; Langston Hughes on, 46–47; Lottie Gee in, *52*, 53, 57; photographs of, *52*; progressive elements, 51; regressive elements, 51, 53, 55; Roger Matthews in, *52*; shame, as causing, 55; success of, 46–47; and Tulsa Race Massacre, 49; vaudevillian elements, 51; white audience of, 59–60

Shuffle Along . . . and All That Followed: overview of, 46–47, 56; advertisements, use of, 58; Amber Iman, 55–56, 61; audience of, 59–60; Audra McDonald in, 47–48, 57–58, 61–63; Billy Porter, 55; and Black Lives Matter, 49; Brandon Victor Dixon, 57–58; Brian Stokes Mitchell, 57, 62, 65–66; chorus, 59; closure of, 48, 60–62; educational aspects, 50–51, 55–56, 67; and history, 47; "I'm Just Wild about Harry," 56; "Love Will Find a Way," 56–57; and power structures, racial, 48–49; rehearsal scene, 58–59; run of, 56, 61; Sam Ashmanskas, 59–60; Santo Loquasto, 58; Savion Glover, 47–48, 50; scenic design, 58; Scott Rudin and, 48, 60–63; *Shuffle Along* incorporations, 56, 58; songs omitted, 56, 58; source material, cast familiarity with, 55; tap emphasis, 50; the Walton-Williams kiss in, 56–57

Shuffle Along . . . and All That Followed, and temporalities: and the actors, 47–48; audiences, 59; Black Lives Matter, 49, 63–67; changes in, 56; direct address, 56; external *versus* internal, 48–50; "Love Will Find A Way," 57; McDonald's pregnancy and leave, 61–63; racial, 48–49, 67–68; Tony Awards season, 48, 60–62; uses of, 47

Singh, Jyoti, rape and murder of: overview of, 220, 223–24; and culture clash narratives, 224; international legibility of, 224; legal amendments after, 224–25, 227–28; and Mahmood Farooqui case, 240n22; perpetrators of, 224; responses to, 220–21, 224, 227

Sklar, Deidre, 121–22

slavery: afterlife of, 283; naturalization of, 32; and prison, 204–5; sound and time, 77–78

Slave Ship: A Historical Pageant (Baraka), 10–11

Smith, Mark, 78, 97n31

Snead, James, 11–12

Snorton, C. Riley, 162

soap advertisements, 58

social dramas, 176

sociogeny, 274–75

Sood, Mihira, 228

sound, 77–79. *See also* Universes

sound studies, 78–79

the spectral, 206–7

speech act theory, 7

Spillers, Hortense, 275, 278, 286–89

sports commentary, 120, 122

Stearns, Marshall and Jean, 117, 125n48, 125n53, 130–31

Sterling, Alton, 64

Steward, Susan Smith McKinney, 5

Stoever, Jennifer, 75, 78

Storyboard P, 119

subject formation theories, 275

subjection theory, 280

Sumell, Jackie, 208–9, 216–17. *See also The House That Herman Built*

swing music, 110, 114
Symons, Stéphane, 116